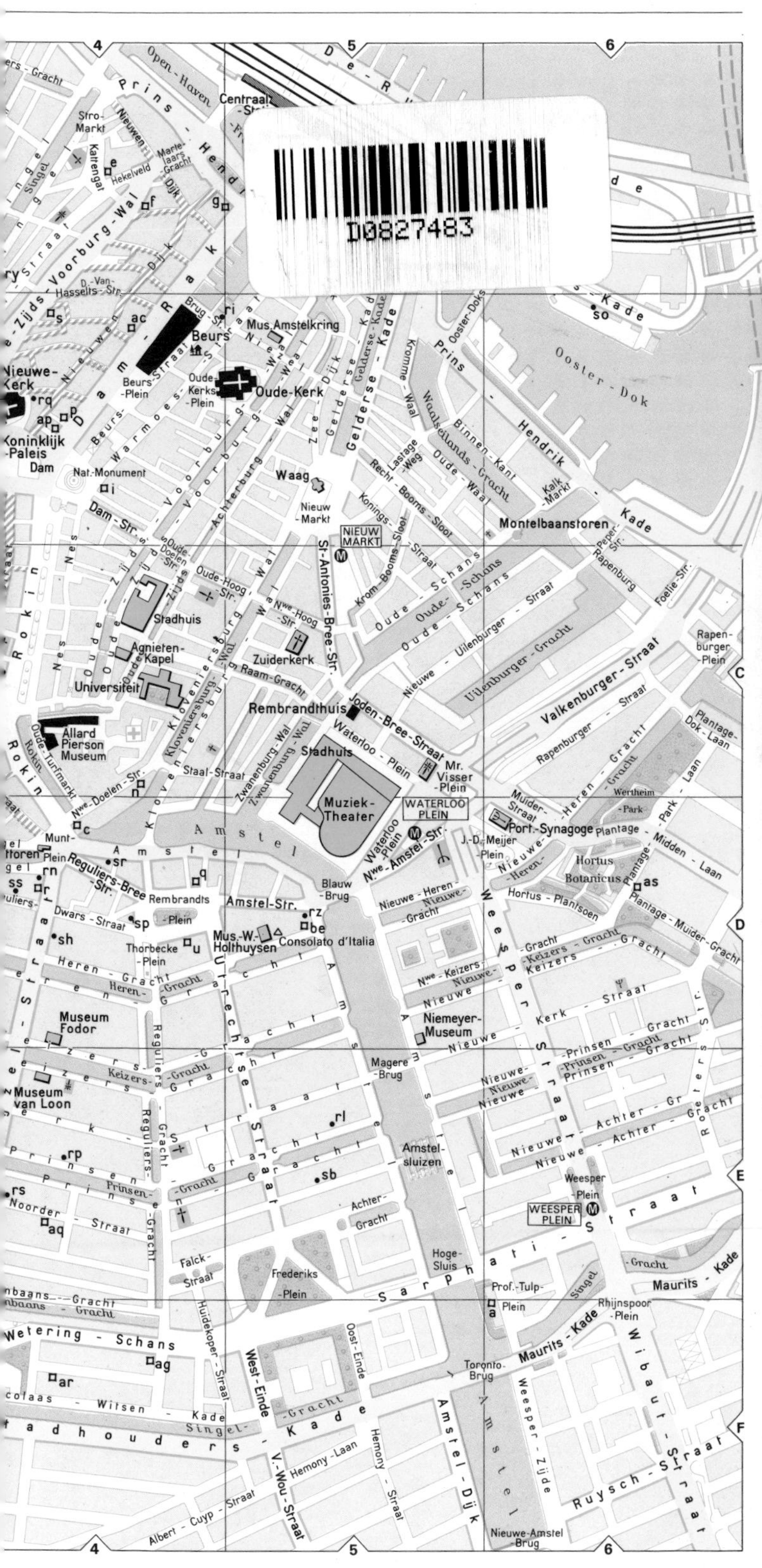
D0827483
Centraal Station
Beurs
Mus. Amstelkring
Oude-Kerk
Nieuwe-Kerk
Koninklijk Paleis
Dam
Nat.-Monument
Waag
Nieuw Markt
NIEUW MARKT
Montelbaanstoren
Ooster-Dok
Stadhuis
Agnieten-Kapel
Universiteit
Zuiderkerk
Rembrandthuis
Allard Pierson Museum
Stadhuis
Muziek-Theater
WATERLOO PLEIN
Mr. Visser-Plein
Port.-Synagoge
J.-D.-Meijer-Plein
Hortus Botanicus
Blauw Brug
Rembrandts-Plein
Mus.-W.-Holthuysen
Consolato d'Italia
Thorbecke-Plein
Museum Fodor
Niemeyer-Museum
Magere-Brug
Museum van Loon
Amstel-sluizen
Weesper-Plein
WEESPER PLEIN
Hoge-Sluis
Frederiks-Plein
Prof.-Tulp-Plein
Rhijnspoor-Plein
Toronto-Brug
Nieuwe-Amstel-Brug
Amstel
Prins Hendrik Kade
Damrak
Rokin
Sarphati-Straat
Weesper-Straat
Wetering-Schans
Stadhouders-Kade
Maurits-Kade
Wibaut-Straat
Utrechtse-Straat
Reguliers-Gracht
Keizers-Gracht
Heren-Gracht
Prinsen-Gracht
Nieuwe-Achter-Gracht
Plantage-Midden-Laan
Plantage-Park-Laan
Valkenburger-Straat
Rapenburger-Plein
Joden-Bree-Straat
St-Antonies-Bree-Str.
Kloveniersburg-Wal
Gelderse-Kade
Oude-Schans
Ruysch-Straat
Albert-Cuyp-Straat
Amstel-Dijk
Hemony-Laan
Huidekoper-Straat
West-Einde
Oost-Einde
4
5
6
C
D
E
F

1724
E KLEINE WINST. P.S.BARBER.
ANUFACTUREN & MODEARTIKELEN.

Boats stuck in the ice on the Waalseilandsgracht and, below, moored in the north of the western isles, in Houthaven (photographs by J. Olie and G. Breitner).

Bridge at the junction of the Lindengracht and the Lijnbaansgracht, in the Jordaan district (photograph by G. Breitner).

Warehouses near the port on Prinseneiland, one of the western isles (photograph G. Breitner).

The Damrak (below) and Rokin (right). Department stores and electric trams have replaced the street vendors and the horsedrawn carriages of the late 19th century (photographs by J. Olie and G. Breitner).

EVERYMAN GUIDES
PUBLISHED BY DAVID CAMPBELL PUBLISHERS LTD, LONDON

TITLE: ISBN 1 85 715 820 2

First published September 1993
Second printing June 1995

NUMEROUS SPECIALISTS AND ACADEMICS HAVE CONTRIBUTED TO THIS GUIDE.

AUTHORS AND EDITORS: Dedalo Carasso, Nico Haafkens, Willem Heinemeijer, Patrick Jusseaux, Dominique Marchal, Erik Mattie, Martin Melchers, Gerard Nijssen, Marc d'Orry, Henri Peretz, Danièle Pin, Laurent-Philippe Réguer, Geert Timmermans, Maïke van Stiphout, Ruud Vlek.

ILLUSTRATORS AND ICONOGRAPHERS: .Michel Aubois, Anne Bodin, Malou Camolli Beauchesne, Jean Chevallier, Denis Clavreul, François Desbordes, Claire Felloni, Valérie Gevers, Gilbert Houbre, Donald Grant, Guy Michel, Fabrice Moireau, François Place, Maurice Pommier, Pierre Poulain, Anabelle Rebière, Pascal Robin, Frédérique Schwebel, Michel Sinier, Gabor Szitia.

PHOTOGRAPHER: Paul van Dijk.

WE WOULD ALSO LIKE TO THANK:
René Meissel, Joka Haafkens, Anneke Kerkhof (Dutch Institute, Paris), Ghislaine Berthon (Dutch Tourist Office, Paris), Caroline Palmer, Lucinda Gane and Jan Michael.

WE WOULD LIKE TO GIVE SPECIAL THANKS TO:
Henri Peretz.

TRANSLATED BY ROS SCHWARTZ
EDITED AND TYPESET BY BOOK CREATION SERVICES, LONDON
PRINTED IN ITALY BY EDITORIALE LIBRARIA

EVERYMAN GUIDES
79 Berwick Street
London W1V 3PF

AMSTERDAM

EVERYMAN GUIDES

Contents

Natural history, *15*

The Amsterdam region, *16*
Canals, *18*
Waterland : an ancient polder, *20*
Dunes, *22*
Bulbs, *24*
Dutch cheeses, *26*

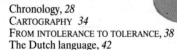

History and language, *27*

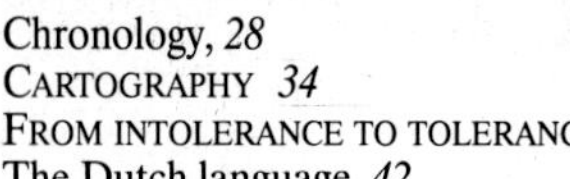

Chronology, *28*
Cartography *34*
From intolerance to tolerance, *38*
The Dutch language, *42*

Crafts and traditions, *45*

Festivals, *46*
Music, *48*
Cafés, *50*
Traditional shops, *52*
Old books, *54*
Furniture, *56*
Bicycles, *58*
Sport, *60*
Gastronomy, *62*
Specialties, *64*

Architecture, *65*

Bridges and locks, *66*
Windmills, *68*
House construction, *70*
Gabled houses, *72*
From classical mansion to eclectic house, *74*
Warehouses, *76*
Religious buildings, *78*
Monuments of the 19th century, *80*
Fin-de-siècle architecture, *82*
The Amsterdam School, *84*
Modern architecture, *86*

Amsterdam as seen by painters, *87*

The river IJ, *88*
The old city and the canals, *90*
The port, *92*
The canals, *94*

Amsterdam as seen by writers, *97*

A free and open city, *98*
Life on the water, *104*
Snapshots of the city, *108*

CITY CENTER WEST, *119*

Begijnhof, *122*
HISTORICAL MUSEUM, *124*
Dam Square, *128*
Oude Kerk, *134*
Amstelkring Museum, *137*

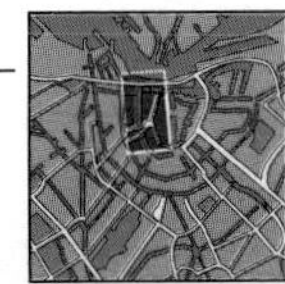
CITY CENTER WEST

CITY CENTER EAST, *139*

The three canals, *142*
DUTCH EAST INDIA COMPANY, *146*
Nieuwmarkt, *152*
Rembrandthuis, *156*
Waterlooplein, *160*

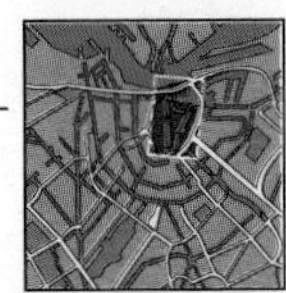
CITY CENTER EAST

NORTHERN CANALS, *161*

Singel, *164*
AMSTERDAM, «VENICE OF THE NORTH», *168*
Herengracht, *170*
Keizersgracht, *173*
Prinsengracht, *176*
ANNE FRANK, *180*

NORTHERN CANALS

SOUTHERN CANALS, *189*

Leidseplein, *190*
The Golden Bend, *198*
Rembrandtplein, *207*

SOUTHERN CANALS

AROUND THE MUSEUMS, *209*

Museumplein, *210*
Concertgebouw, *216*
AMSTERDAM COLLECTIONS, *218*

THE MUSEUMS

JORDAAN, *235*

Noordermarkt and Noorderkerk, *239*
The Provos, *243*

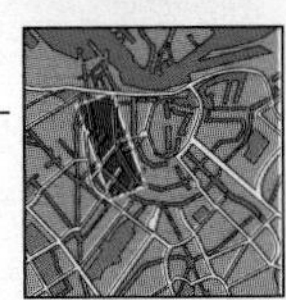
JOORDAN

OLD PORT WEST, *249*

Haarlemmerbuurt, *251*
The «Ship», *256*

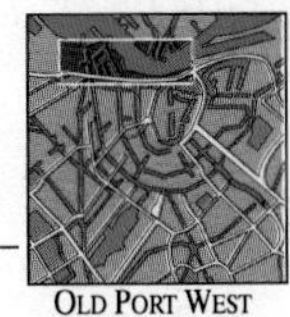
OLD PORT WEST

PLANTAGE, *263*

MARITIME MUSEUM, *269*

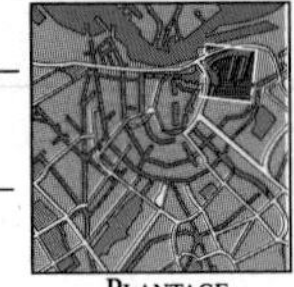
PLANTAGE

DE PIJP AND THE SOUTH, *275*

PRACTICAL INFORMATION, *280*

APPENDICES, *327*

Bibliography, *328*
List of illustrations, *330*
Index, *337*

Amsterdam

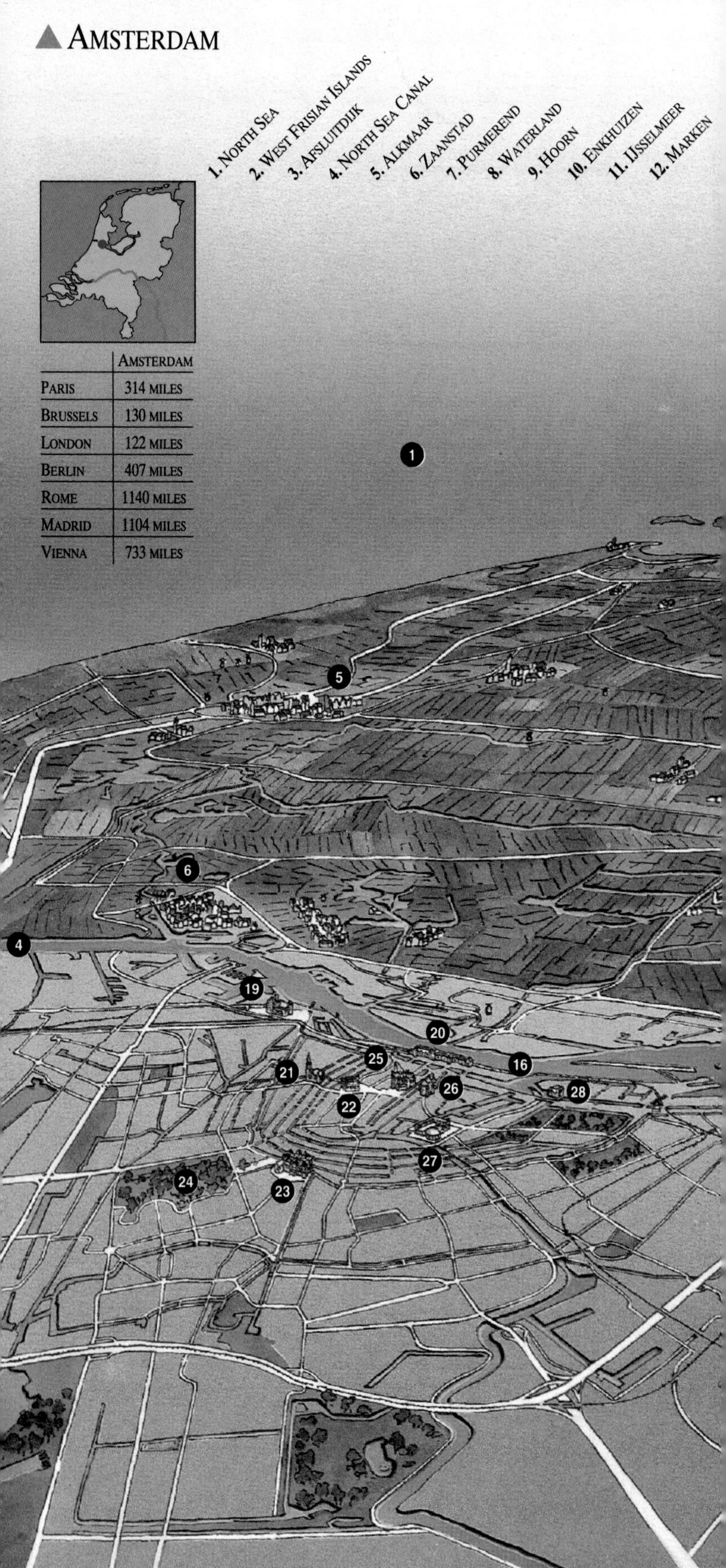

	Amsterdam
Paris	314 miles
Brussels	130 miles
London	122 miles
Berlin	407 miles
Rome	1140 miles
Madrid	1104 miles
Vienna	733 miles

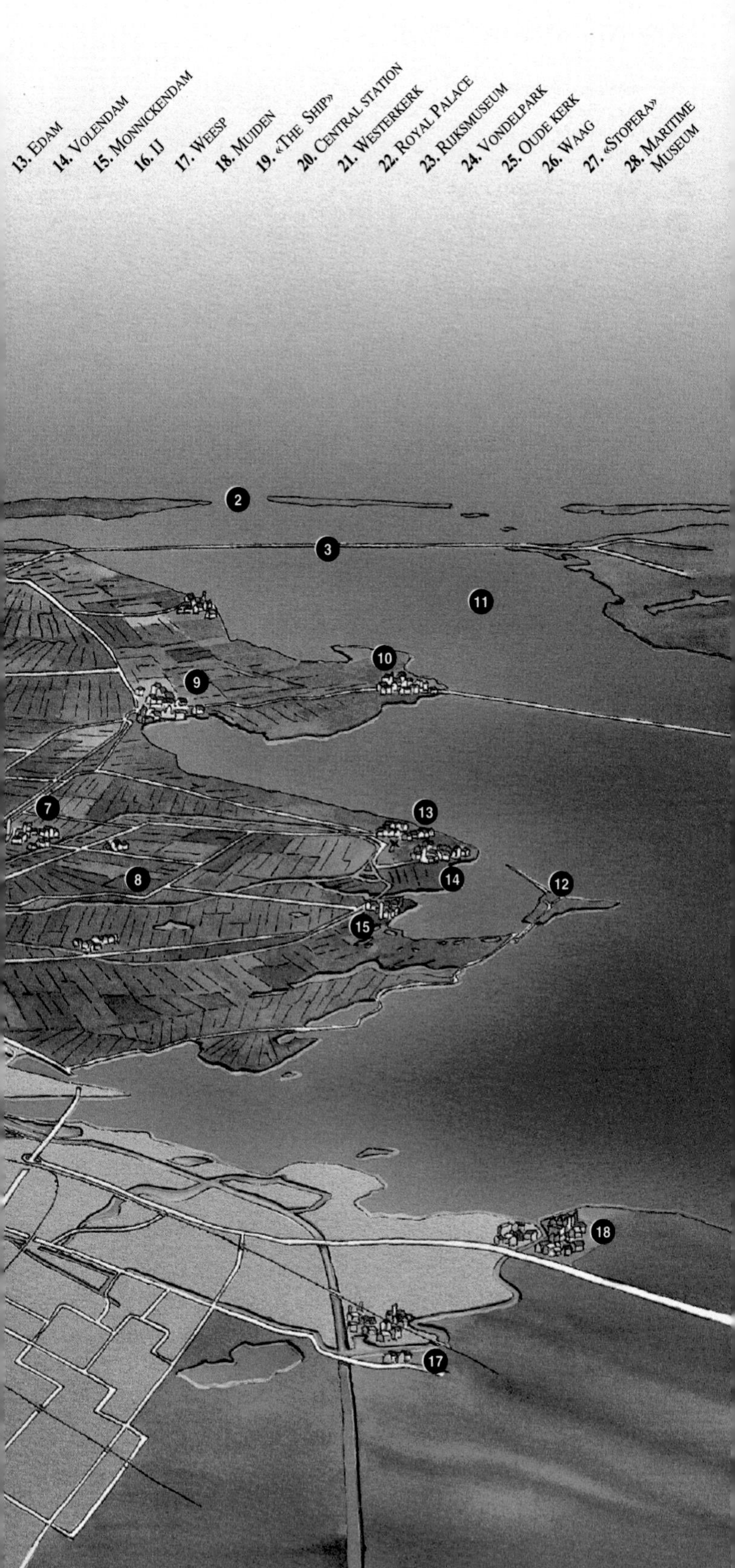
13. Edam
14. Volendam
15. Monnickendam
16. IJ
17. Weesp
18. Muiden
19. «The Ship»
20. Central station
21. Westerkerk
22. Royal Palace
23. Rijksmuseum
24. Vondelpark
25. Oude kerk
26. Waag
27. «Stopera»
28. Maritime Museum
2
3
11
10
9
7
13
8
14
12
15
18
17

How to Use this Guide

The symbols at the top of each page refer to the different parts of the guide.

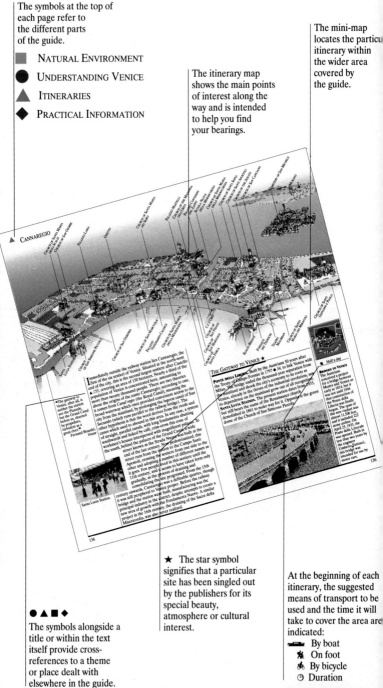

■ Natural Environment

● Understanding Venice

▲ Itineraries

◆ Practical Information

The itinerary map shows the main points of interest along the way and is intended to help you find your bearings.

The mini-map locates the particu itinerary within the wider area covered by the guide.

★ The star symbol signifies that a particular site has been singled out by the publishers for its special beauty, atmosphere or cultural interest.

●▲■◆
The symbols alongside a title or within the text itself provide cross-references to a theme or place dealt with elsewhere in the guide.

At the beginning of each itinerary, the suggested means of transport to be used and the time it will take to cover the area are indicated:

- By boat
- On foot
- By bicycle
- Duration

The Gateway to Venice ★

Ponte della Liberta. Built by the Austrians 50 years after the Treaty of Campo Formio in 1797 ● *34,* to link Venice with Milan. The bridge ended the thousand-year separation from the mainland and shook the city's economy to its roots as Venice, already in the throes of the industrial revolution, saw

Half a day

Bridges to Venice

NATURAL HISTORY

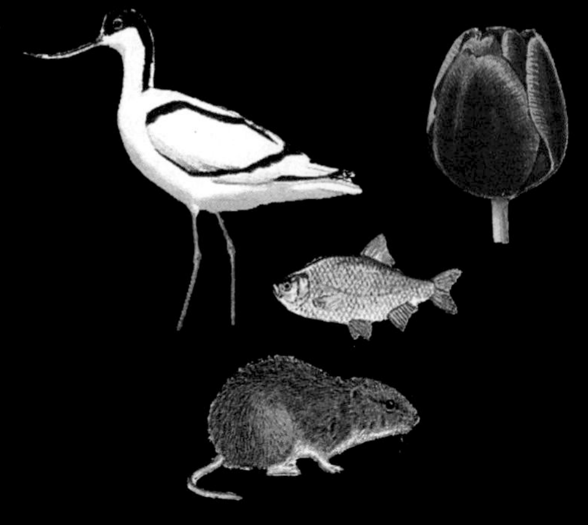

THE AMSTERDAM REGION, *16*
CANALS, *18*
WATERLAND:
AN ANCIENT POLDER, *20*
DUNES, *22*
BULBS, *24*
DUTCH CHEESES, *26*

THE AMSTERDAM REGION

Today there are around a thousand remaining windmills, two hundred of which are still working.

In the Netherlands, and particularly in Amsterdam, the struggle against the sea involves two primary objectives: to prevent the sea from flooding the land below sea level and to increase the available land surface. Over the centuries these tasks have been carried out in various stages. First protection against the sea was created through the construction of dunes, dykes, dams, canals, deep foundations and locks. Techniques for drying the marshlands and lakes were then developed, and eventually windmills and steam engines made it possible to develop and exploit the polders and the Amsterdam region.

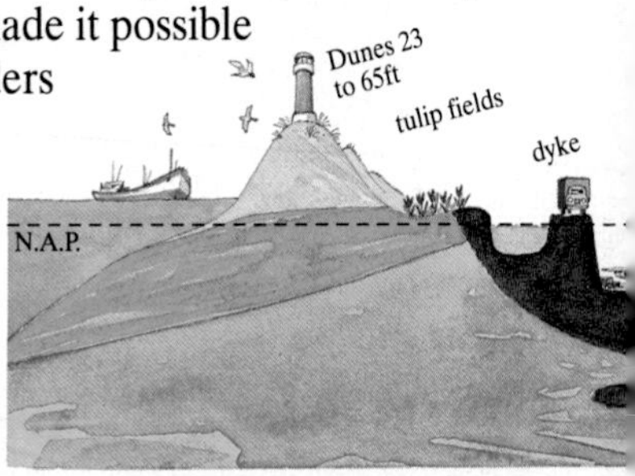

Dunes 23 to 65ft

tulip fields

dyke

N.A.P.

60 percent of the Dutch population lives below the N.A.P. (Normaal Amsterdams Peil), the Amsterdam benchmark for measuring the level of the polders.

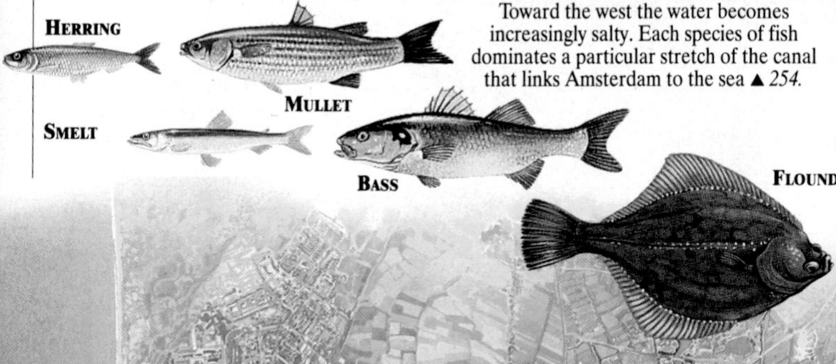

HERRING

MULLET

SMELT

BASS

FLOUNDI

Toward the west the water becomes increasingly salty. Each species of fish dominates a particular stretch of the canal that links Amsterdam to the sea ▲ *254*.

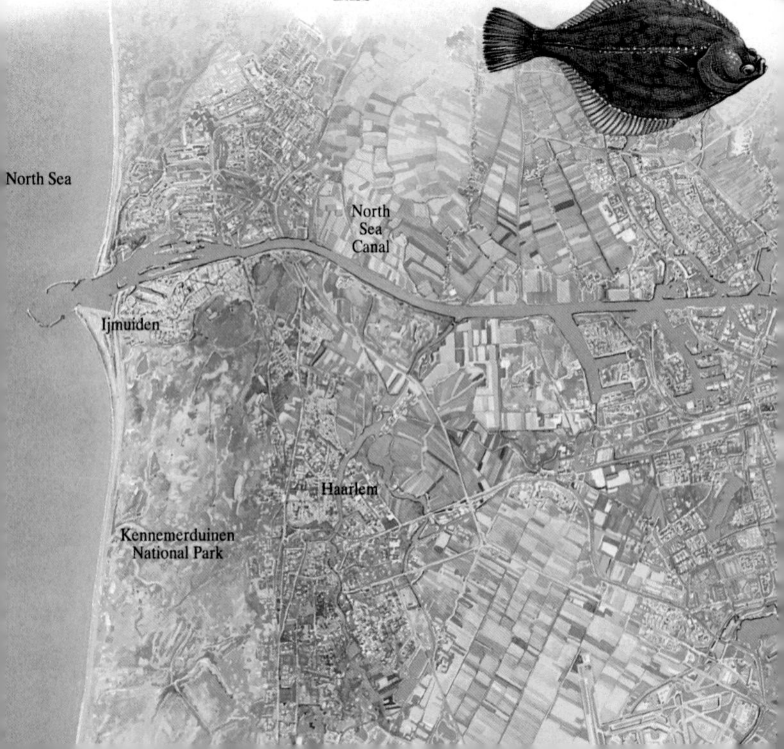

North Sea

North Sea Canal

Ijmuiden

Haarlem

Kennemerduinen National Park

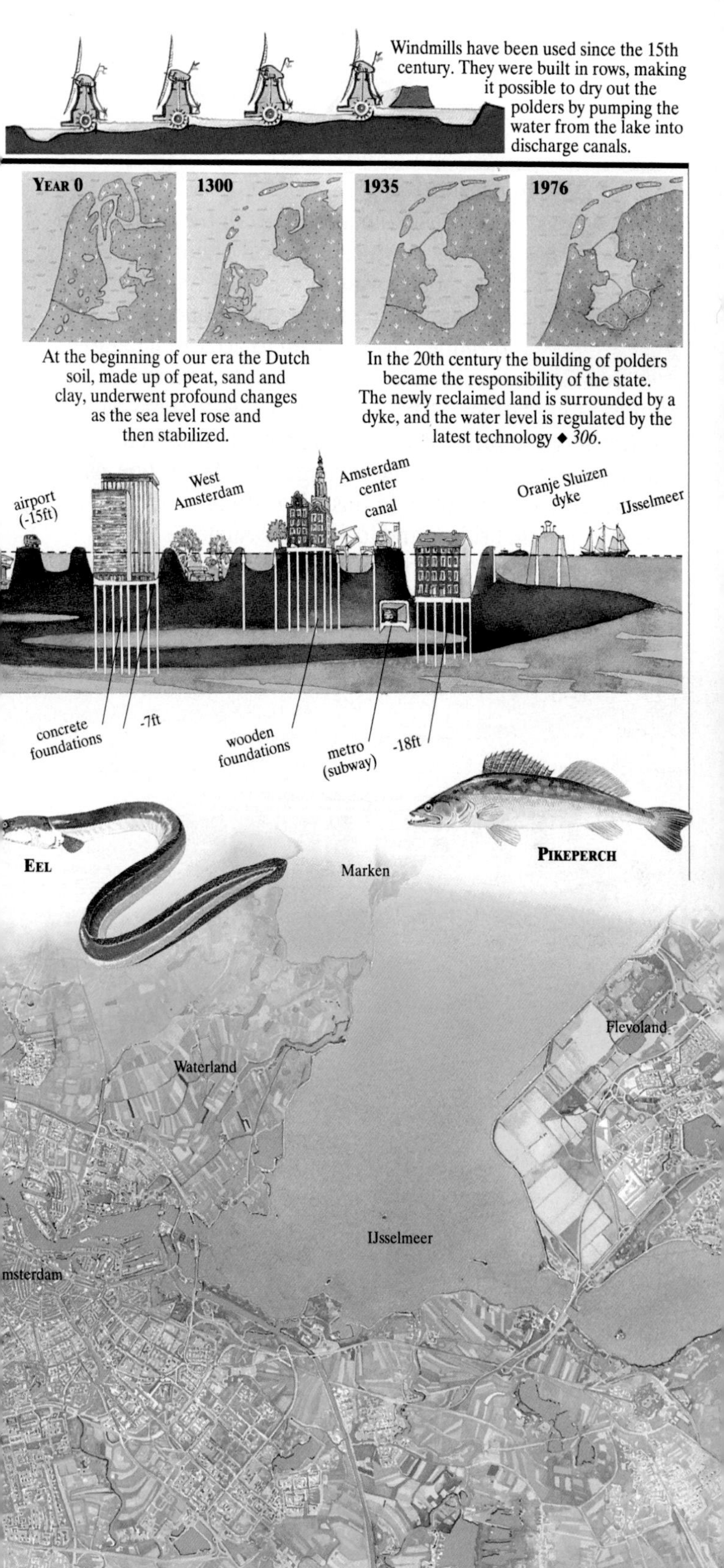
Windmills have been used since the 15th century. They were built in rows, making it possible to dry out the polders by pumping the water from the lake into discharge canals.
YEAR 0
1300
1935
1976
At the beginning of our era the Dutch soil, made up of peat, sand and clay, underwent profound changes as the sea level rose and then stabilized.
In the 20th century the building of polders became the responsibility of the state. The newly reclaimed land is surrounded by a dyke, and the water level is regulated by the latest technology ◆ 306.
airport (-15ft)
West Amsterdam
Amsterdam center
canal
Oranje Sluizen dyke
IJsselmeer
concrete foundations
-7ft
wooden foundations
metro (subway)
-18ft
EEL
PIKEPERCH
Marken
Flevoland
Waterland
IJsselmeer
msterdam

The lock system on the Amstel in the 16th century.

Amsterdam provides a remarkable example of the canal landscape which is typical of northern European towns. It was the product of an ingenious urban expansion policy ● *34*, prompted by the need to acquire habitable land. In the 17th century, five hundred years after the foundation of "Amstelledamme" ● *28* (dam on the Amstel), the future shape of the city was sketched out: a girdle of parallel canals arranged in a horseshoe around the historic center. In this labyrinth of waterways, amid bridges and locks, the casual stroller can observe the powers of adaptation of a generally rural wildlife that has succeeded in finding food and lodging in the urban environment.

SWIFT

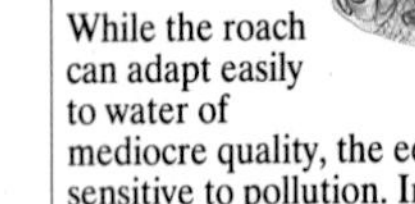

PERCH

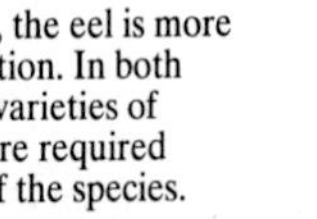

ROACH

EEL

While the roach can adapt easily to water of mediocre quality, the eel is more sensitive to pollution. In both cases, particular varieties of flora and fauna are required for the survival of the species.

In winter, until the canals are frozen over they are home to many wildlife species. These creatures have grown accustomed to people, who are in the habit of feeding them.

Pipistrelle
On spring and summer evenings these little bats can be seen darting to and fro under the eaves of the buildings.

Feral pigeon
This bird has lived among people for a long time. It can be a nuisance, ruining façades and statues with its droppings.

Grey mouse

Wharf rat

These two species of rodent are everywhere, though they are rarely seen (the rat generally lives underground).

The locks were built to prevent flooding in the areas situated below sea level.

In the spring small plants appear in cracks in the paving stones. They are quite resistant to being trodden underfoot.

Black-headed gull
All year gulls fly up and down the canals in their search for food.

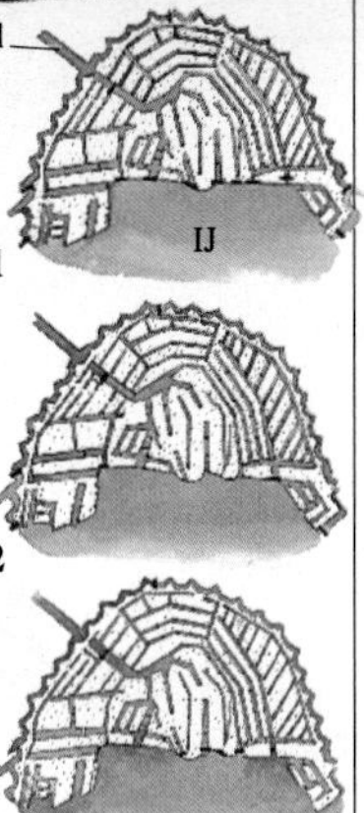

Mallard
Though wild, these ducks are quite likely to come and eat out of your hand.

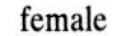

Grey heron
Amsterdam is one of the only European cities where you can find grey herons in the city center.

Great crested grebe
Every year a few pairs build their nests along the city's canal banks.

In the past the canals served as sewers. The contaminated water (1) was sluiced out once a day with salt water from the Zuidersee (2, 3). Today the water is replaced with that of the IJ (twice a week in winter and four times in summer).

Waterland: an ancient polder

It was around the year 1100 that the peat bogs were cleared and transformed into arable and pasture land.

The Waterland, a typical region of the Netherlands, is a vast area of marshland crisscrossed by a maze of channels and canals. These "porous" lands are constantly changing: in the Middle Ages the layer of peat was over 2 yards above sea level, whereas today it is about 1 or 2 yards below. This phenomenon can be explained by subsidence of the terrain and a rise in sea level. Little agriculture takes place in the region nowadays, but it has its own flora and fauna ◆ *306*.

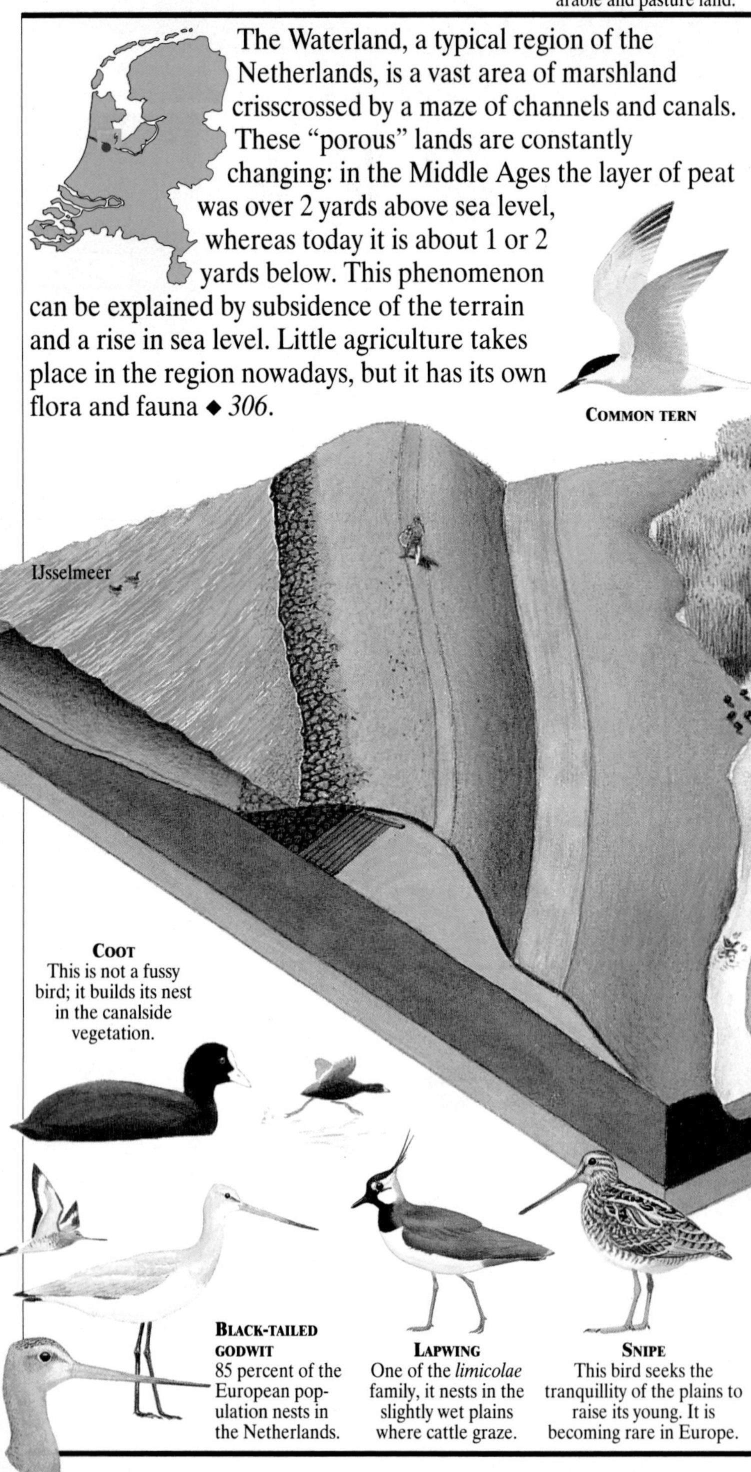

Common tern

Coot
This is not a fussy bird; it builds its nest in the canalside vegetation.

Black-tailed godwit
85 percent of the European population nests in the Netherlands.

Lapwing
One of the *limicolae* family, it nests in the slightly wet plains where cattle graze.

Snipe
This bird seeks the tranquillity of the plains to raise its young. It is becoming rare in Europe.

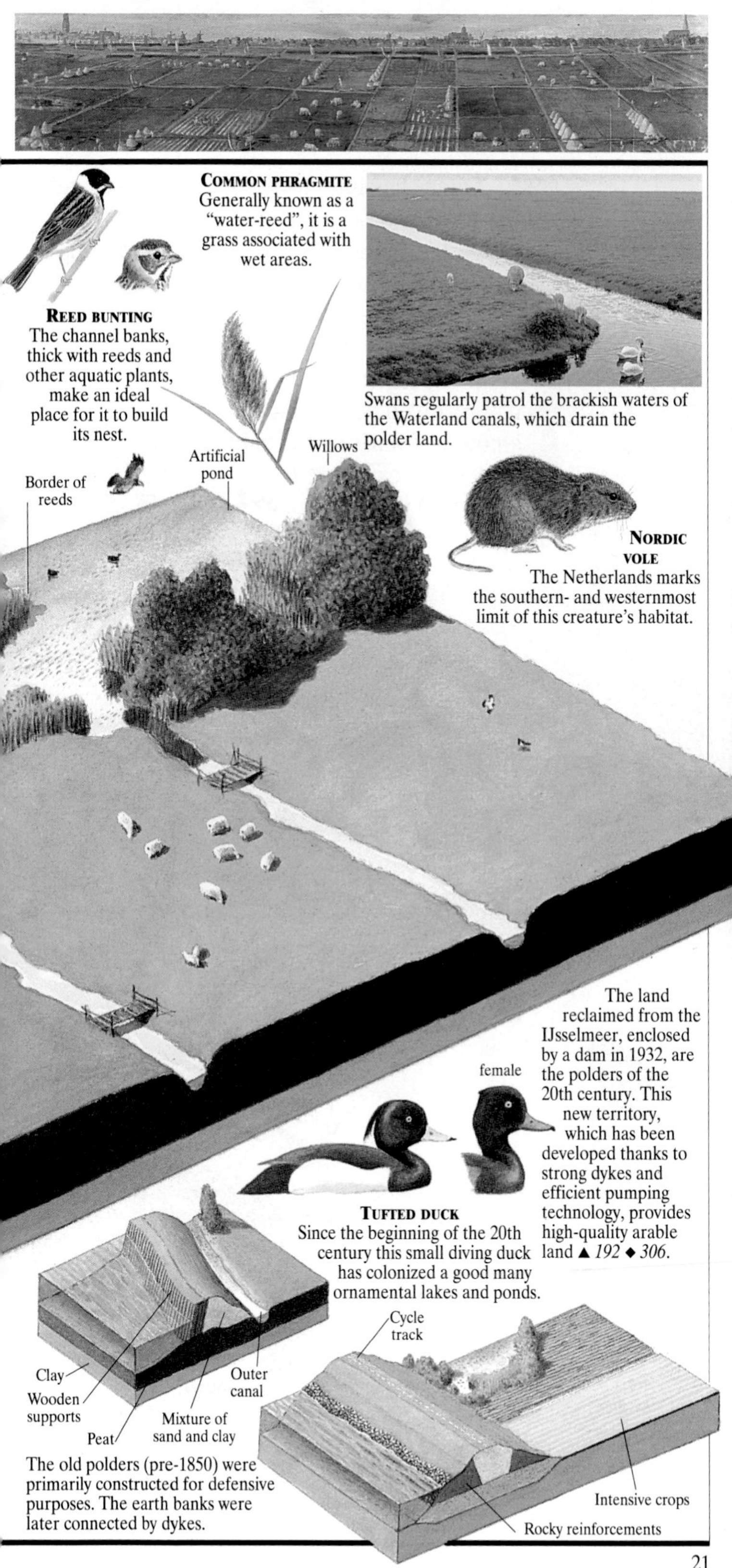

Common phragmite Generally known as a "water-reed", it is a grass associated with wet areas.

Reed bunting The channel banks, thick with reeds and other aquatic plants, make an ideal place for it to build its nest.

Swans regularly patrol the brackish waters of the Waterland canals, which drain the polder land.

Nordic vole The Netherlands marks the southern- and westernmost limit of this creature's habitat.

The land reclaimed from the IJsselmeer, enclosed by a dam in 1932, are the polders of the 20th century. This new territory, which has been developed thanks to strong dykes and efficient pumping technology, provides high-quality arable land ▲ *192* ◆ *306*.

Tufted duck Since the beginning of the 20th century this small diving duck has colonized a good many ornamental lakes and ponds.

The old polders (pre-1850) were primarily constructed for defensive purposes. The earth banks were later connected by dykes.

Dunes

Sea holly
Increasingly rare as a result of being trampled on and picked, and because of the destruction of the dunes.

Dunes began to form some five thousand years ago on the shores of the Netherlands. There are two generations of sand deposits: the "old" dunes, which were not very high, and the "young" dunes, which cover them. On this narrow cordon, varieties of flora and fauna have evolved depending on the amount of water in the habitat, the level of exposure to the wind and the chalky soil ◆ *304*.

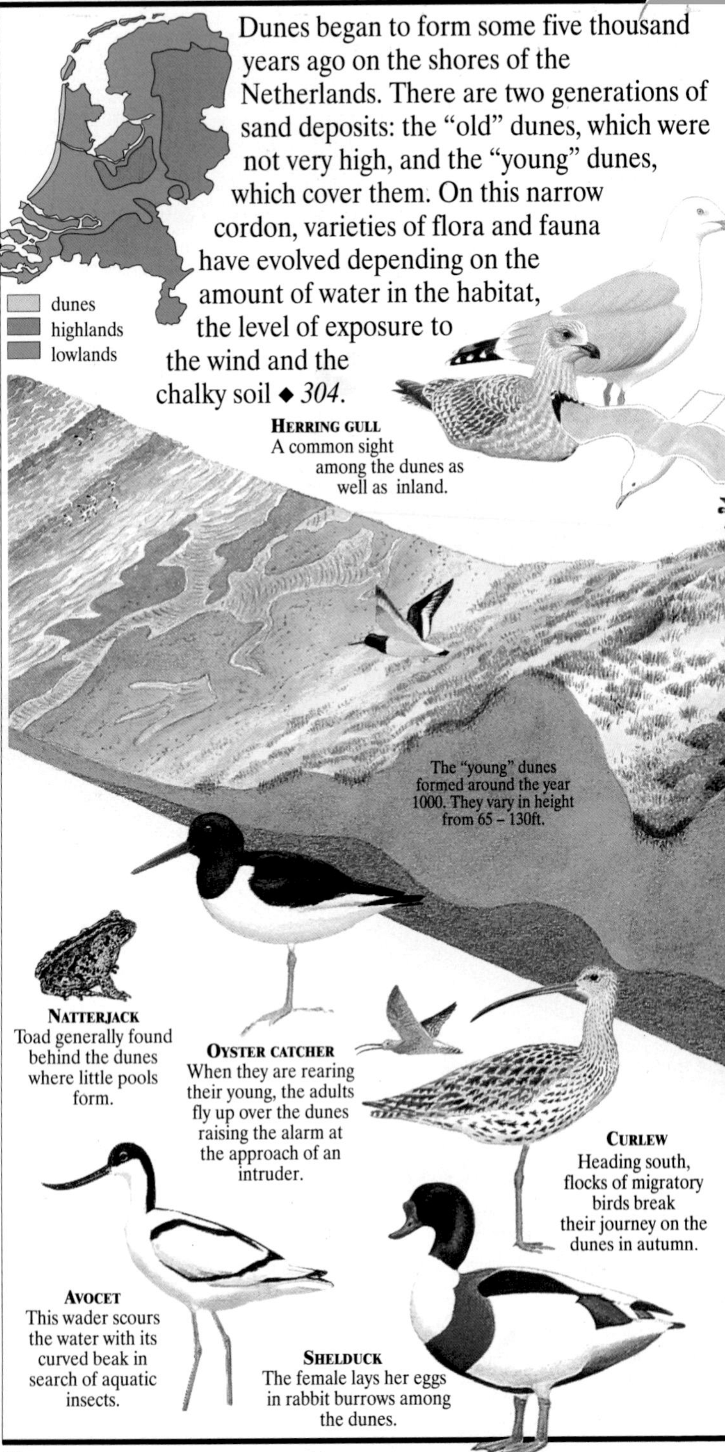
dunes
highlands
lowlands
The "young" dunes formed around the year 1000. They vary in height from 65 – 130ft.

Herring gull
A common sight among the dunes as well as inland.

Natterjack
Toad generally found behind the dunes where little pools form.

Oyster catcher
When they are rearing their young, the adults fly up over the dunes raising the alarm at the approach of an intruder.

Curlew
Heading south, flocks of migratory birds break their journey on the dunes in autumn.

Avocet
This wader scours the water with its curved beak in search of aquatic insects.

Shelduck
The female lays her eggs in rabbit burrows among the dunes.

Sea buckthorn grows in abundance in the area behind the dunes. Its orange berries are rich in vitamin C.

Skylark
Its melodious song can be heard from the close of winter. The male sings in flight.

Dune grasses help to stabilize the dunes.

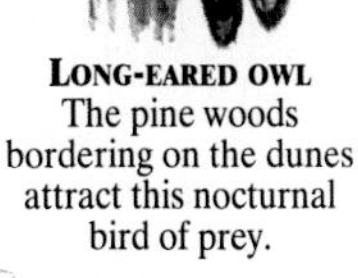

Long-eared owl
The pine woods bordering on the dunes attract this nocturnal bird of prey.

Sedge warbler
This aquatic warbler has an imitative cry. A fearful bird, it remains hidden in the vegetation.

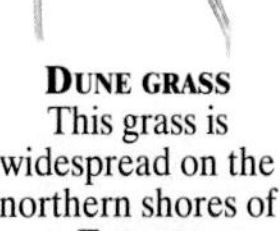

Dune grass
This grass is widespread on the northern shores of Europe.

Sea Bindweed
A plant with large pink flowers that grows in the sand.

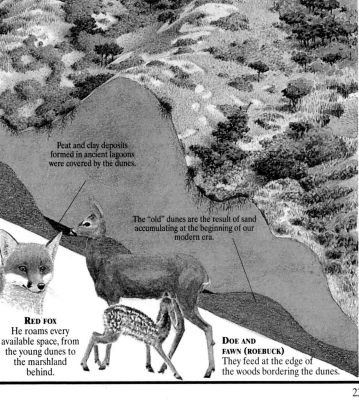

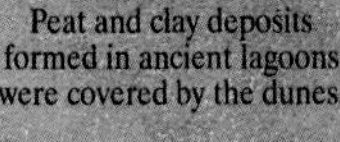

Peat and clay deposits formed in ancient lagoons were covered by the dunes.

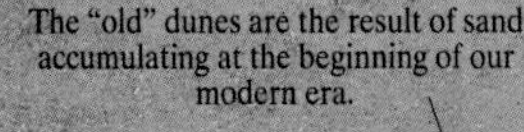

The "old" dunes are the result of sand accumulating at the beginning of our modern era.

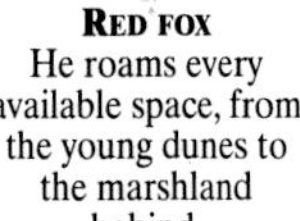

Red fox
He roams every available space, from the young dunes to the marshland behind.

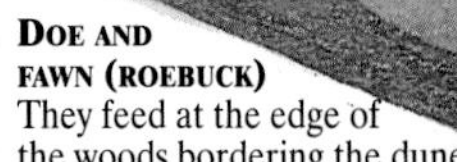

Doe and fawn (roebuck)
They feed at the edge of the woods bordering the dunes.

BULBS

Spring flowering bulbs

Bulb-growing developed from the 16th century in the area around the old dunes, where the chalky, sandy soil was particularly well suited to this type of culture. Most of the plants were imported and then selected and acclimatized. Today bulb-growing, which occupies around 40,000 acres, includes two types of plant: bulbs (tulips, hyacinths, for example) and rhizomes (dahlias and gladioli). Bulbs are grown either to be sold "dry", as plants for gardens, or are forced for the production of hothouse cut flowers.

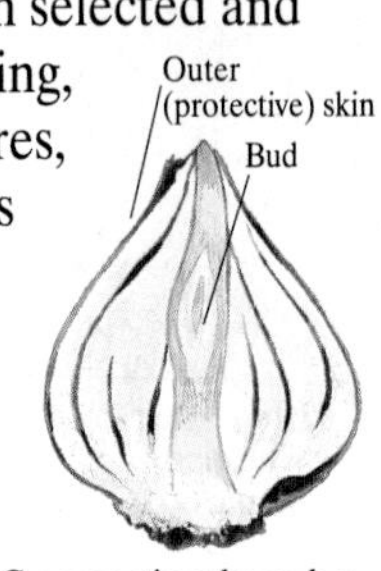

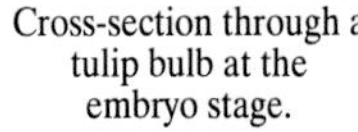

Cross-section through a tulip bulb at the embryo stage.

SPRING FLOWERING/ AUTUMN PLANTING

There are around three hundred varieties, or cultivars, of tulip. The tulip bulb is grown in an area of over 17,000 acres.

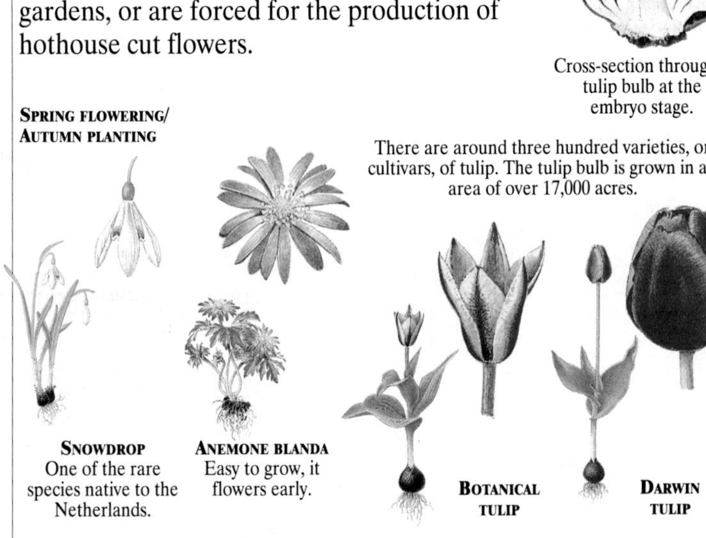

SNOWDROP One of the rare species native to the Netherlands.

ANEMONE BLANDA Easy to grow, it flowers early.

BOTANICAL TULIP

DARWIN TULIP

SUMMER FLOWERING/SPRING PLANTING

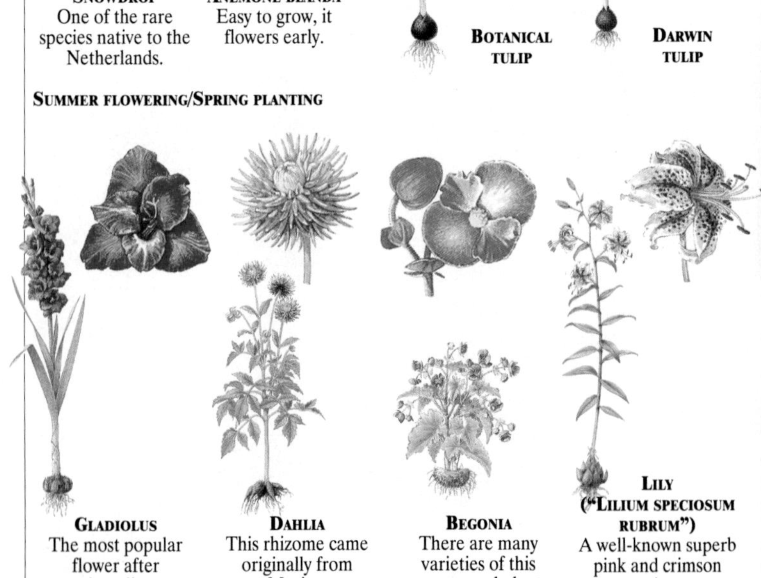

GLADIOLUS The most popular flower after the tulip.

DAHLIA This rhizome came originally from Mexico.

BEGONIA There are many varieties of this ornamental plant.

LILY ("LILIUM SPECIOSUM RUBRUM") A well-known superb pink and crimson variety.

At Aalsmeer you can attend the flower auctions. The tulip plantations at the Keukenhof Gardens near Lisse ◆ *304* are also well worth a visit.

Bulb-growing is essentially a seasonal occupation. During the winter months the growers turn to producing hothouse plants. This horticultural activity occupies more than seventy thousand people. It is said that the Netherlands are the florists of Europe. They supply 70 percent of the world market.

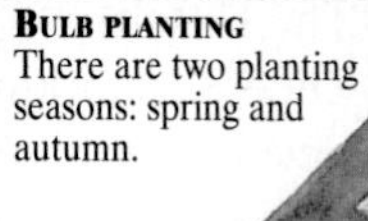

Bulb planting
There are two planting seasons: spring and autumn.

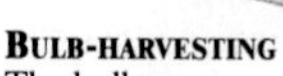

Flower-harvesting
The flowers are cut immediately after blooming. That way the bulb, which remains in the earth, benefits from the nutrients intended for the flower.

Bulb-harvesting
The bulbs are harvested two or three months after the flowers have been cut.

Hyacinth
Hyacinths are produced commercially only in the Netherlands.

Daffodil
This early flower also grows wild.

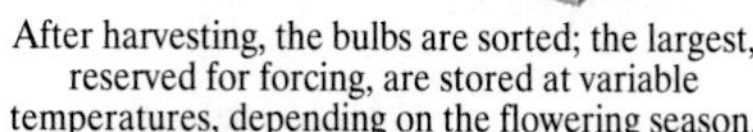

After harvesting, the bulbs are sorted; the largest, reserved for forcing, are stored at variable temperatures, depending on the flowering season.

Acidanthera
Related to the gladiolus, it is cultivated to be sold as a cut flower.

Freesia
Another, very fragrant, variety is also sold as a cut flower.

The tulip fields turn the Dutch countryside into a vivid patchwork of color. In Amsterdam a visit to the flower market is a must. It is held from Monday to Saturday along the Singel ▲ *187*.

DUTCH CHEESES

The cheese market at Alkmaar is a picturesque affair.

The Dutch cheese tradition developed thanks to a few essential advantages that favored the breeding of dairy cattle: the type of soil, the climate, the quality of the grass and of the water. As early as the Middle Ages the method for producing long-lasting pressed cheeses was perfected. Edam and Gouda are still produced essentially in the same way. Today a third of the area of the Netherlands is devoted to dairy-farming and they have become the leading exporters of cheese worldwide. Ultra-modern techniques have been developed, resulting in highly efficient dairy-farming methods, a successful dairy industry, and careful control of dairy products.

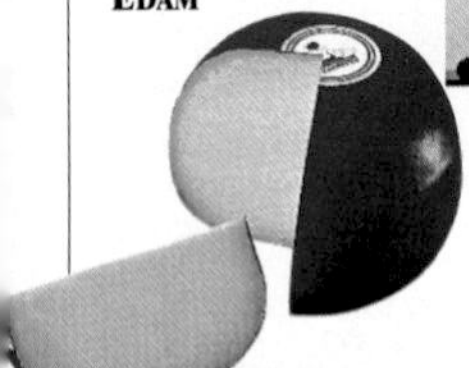

DUTCH BLACK AND WHITE

More than sixty types of cattle, including the Prime Holstein, have been developed from this remarkable dairy breed, which is today the most widespread throughout the world.

GOUDA

MIMOLETTE

EDAM

A lactic fermenting culture and rennet are added to the milk in a huge vat.

The curd, cut and stirred, is separated from the whey to obtain a mass of curds, which is then shaped.

After pressing, which gives the cheese its shape, it spends several days immersed in brine.

History and language

Chronology, *28*
Cartography and urban development, *34*
From intolerance to tolerance, *38*
The Dutch language, *42*

ANTIQUITY

1ST CENTURY B.C. The Romans occupied the marshy regions between the Rhine and the North Sea, home of the Batavi. In 69 AD, under the leadership of Julius Civilis, the Batavi rebelled. Civilis stirred up his fellow citizens' love of war and made them swear allegiance to him. In the 3rd century the Batavi were assimilated by the Franks, who dominated western Europe.

THE MIDDLE AGES

800
Charlemagne is crowned emperor of the Western world.

843
The Treaty of Verdun settles the division of the Carolingian empire.

962
Constitution of the Holy Roman Empire.

600–1200. THE BISHOPRIC OF UTRECHT. In 695, after the establishment of Christianity, Willibrord, an Anglo-Saxon missionary, became bishop of Utrecht, which was an important regional authority. Boniface was one of his first successors. In the 10th century, after the death of Charlemagne and the division of his empire, Utrecht was the only remaining seat of power, but the counts of Flanders gradually formed a territory at the expense of the bishopric of Utrecht. The county of Holland was established in the 12th century, its frontier with Utrecht forming the future site of Amsterdam.

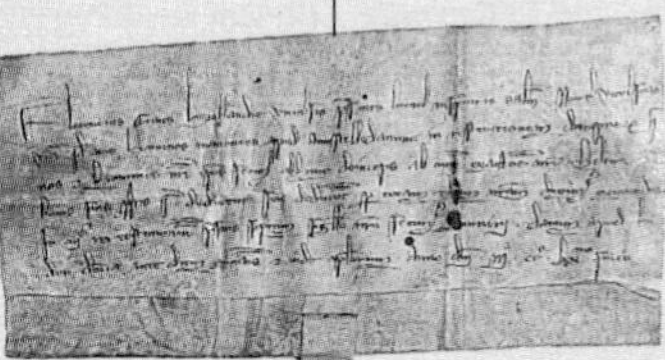

The first official document mentioning Amsterdam in 1275.

1200–1500. FOUNDATION OF AMSTERDAM. Legend has it that the site was discovered by two Frisian fishermen, accompanied by their dog, whose boat ran aground at the confluence of the IJ and the Amstel. It was on this spot that the city was founded, around the 13th century. To protect themselves against floods, the early inhabitants built a dyke (*dam*) across the Amstel, which gave the name Amstelledamme, then Amsteldam and later Amsterdam. The earliest archeological finds date back to 1225. Amsterdam, in the heart of the county of Holland, is mentioned for the first time in 1275, in a document issued by Count Floris V of Holland exempting the city from tax. The city received its charter of independence in 1300. Six years later work began on the first religious edifice, later known as the Oude Kerk. In 1323 the count of Holland decreed that a toll would be applied to all goods entering the city, which was a busy trading center. The miracle of the communion wafer, discovered intact in 1345 ▲ *127*, attracted pilgrims to the city. In 1428 Holland passed into the hands of Philip the Good, duke of Burgundy. Several fires devastated Amsterdam in the 15th century. The city's "Great Privilege" was confirmed in 1477 by Mary of Burgundy, the future wife of Maximilian, the Austrian. Twelve years later Maximilian granted the city the right to add the imperial crown to its coat of arms in return for a loan.

1271
Marco Polo's first voyage.

The Oude Kerk, built in the 14th century beside the Oudezijds Voorburgwal.

1453
Fall of Constantinople.

SPANISH DOMINION. In 1515, through a series of alliances, Charles V became the sovereign of Holland and of the Holy Roman Empire. Twenty years later the millenarian Anabaptist movement, which had spread from Germany, gained a following in Holland. It did not recognize the validity of baptizing children, and was severely repressed. In 1556 Charles V abdicated, leaving the throne to Philip II of Spain, who remained king until 1598. He waged war on the Protestants, who were led by the Calvinists.

Charles V (1500–58).

1492
Christopher Columbus discovers America.

1509
Birth of John Calvin.

1517
Lutheran Reformation.

RELIGIOUS QUARRELS AND UPRISINGS. In 1558 Margaret, duchess of Parma, became regent of the Spanish Netherlands and took up residence in Brussels. In 1566 Protestant worship was authorized in public for the first time. But in April a

Naval battle between the Dutch and the Spanish near Haarlem on May 26, 1573, by H.C. Vroom.

petition called the Request (*Doleanti*) was presented to the regent by the lesser nobles, who were keen to obtain further reforms. This "beggars' revolt" (*geuzen*: Calvinist; *gueux*, French for beggar) forced Margaret to accept a certain religious freedom. Following a second petition, however, a wave of iconoclasm swept the Netherlands. The Dutch rose up against the Spanish after 1568, entering into a war that was to last eighty years. The German prince William of Orange (1533–84), known as William the Silent, appointed as stadholder (representative of the lords of the provinces) by the seventeen provinces of the Netherlands, joined the "beggars' revolt" against Spain in 1572. William managed to save Leiden, but Haarlem fell into the hands of the Spanish after a long siege.

"Be he William of Orange or be he not, may God let him grow up. Preserve this little fellow from death."

THE UNITED PROVINCES. In 1578 Amsterdam, which had until then remained neutral, finally joined the camp of the Protestants and William of Orange: the Catholics were expelled and their institutions dismantled (the Alteration). The following year, after the Protestant Union of Utrecht was formed, a union of the seven northern provinces was created. The Hague became the seat of the court and of the States-General. In 1581 the Spanish sovereign Philip II ceased to be recognized by the United Provinces. Amsterdam then received a flood of immigrants, rich merchants from Antwerp and Jews from Portugal, all of whom were fleeing persecution.

1588
Defeat of the "Invincible Armada" (end of Spanish supremacy at sea).

The theologian Voetius (1588–1676) attacked the Remonstrants and Descartes.

1600-1700 : THE GOLDEN AGE

The port of Amsterdam in the 17th century.

A PERIOD OF WEALTH. At the turn of the century Dutch prosperity was so great that for decades Amsterdam remained the storehouse of Europe. After the expeditions of the late 16th century, ships set off on a second voyage to India, Japan, Ceylon and Indonesia. The year 1602 saw the foundation of the Dutch East India Company (V.O.C.), which enjoyed tremendous commercial and military power. And in 1609 Henry Hudson attempted to find a western passage and explored the area around what was to be New Amsterdam, founded by Peter Stuyvesant in 1625; forty years later it became New York. That same year the Twelve Years' Truce was signed with Spain. It was marked by the beginning of clashes between Protestants, Remonstrants and Counter-Remonstrants. The population of Amsterdam increased greatly as a result of intensive immigration throughout the century: in 1622 the city had a population of 105,000; this had risen to 120,000 by 1630 and to 200,000 by 1675. Plans to extend the city were therefore drawn up. Amsterdam had entered an unprecedented period of wealth, and 1611 saw the inauguration of the Corn and Financial Exchange. In 1622 the Dutch West India Company was established. Four years earlier the synod of Dort had intervened, contrary to the constitution, in the religious conflicts within each state and had decided in favor of orthodox Calvinism against the Remonstrants. The representative of the States-General (the stadholder) Maurice ordered the execution of Oldenbarnevelt, the council pensionary of Holland (head of the administration), who was an advocate of peace with Spain and religious pluralism. In 1630 freedom of worship was instituted. Rembrandt settled in Amsterdam the following year, as the city was transformed into a vast art market. In 1642 Abel Tasman discovered Tasmania, the future Australia and New Zealand. The Dutch navy was then at the height of its power. In 1648 the Treaty of Münster put an end to the war with Spain, and two years later the great pensionary of Holland, whose seat was in

Marie de' Medici's arrival in Amsterdam in 1638.

1609
The Dutchman Hugo Grotius advocates the principle of the freedom of the seas in De Mare Liberum.

1628
Descartes in the Netherlands.

Peter Stuyvesant (1592–1672).

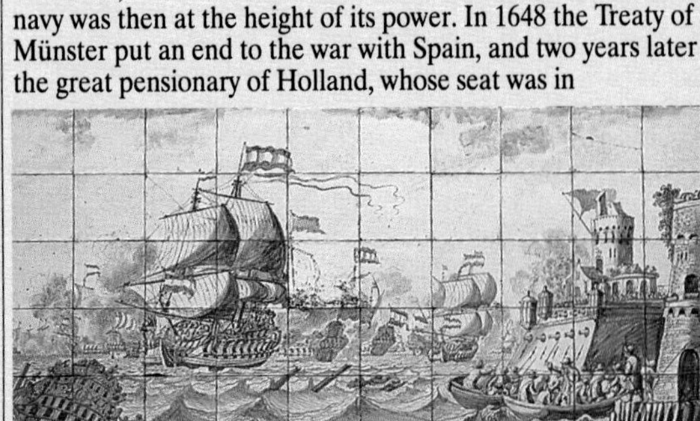

Naval battle between the Dutch and the English.

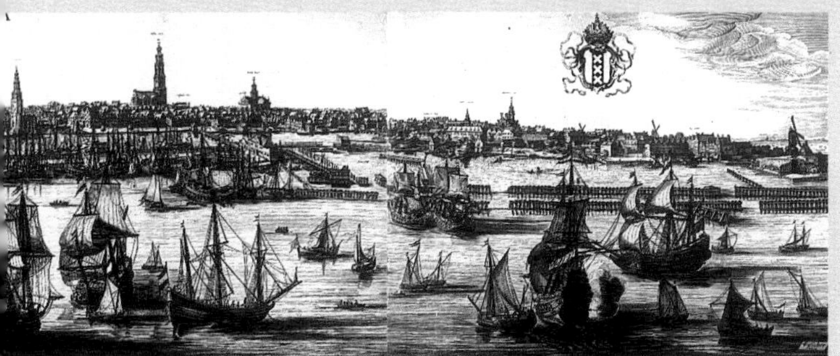

Amsterdam, decided not to maintain an army any longer. The stadholder William II, who was opposed to this decision, invaded the city, but died three months later. The new council pensionary, Johan de Witt, turned down the appointment of stadholder in 1654.

WARS WITH ENGLAND. That same year, England passed the Navigation Act, which favored the English navy, provoking the first war against the United Provinces, and then in 1665 a second conflict. Admiral de Ruyter set fire to the English fleet, which was based on the Thames. In 1667 the two countries signed the Peace of Breda: England and the United Provinces divided up their colonial territories. The peace did not last long, and by 1672 the Dutch were once more at war with the English. At the same time the United Provinces were invaded by Louis XIV, whose army was brought to a standstill 15½ miles outside Amsterdam by opening the locks on the Amstel. The French Protestants took refuge in Amsterdam from 1685, following the revocation of the Edict of Nantes. In 1697 Tsar Peter the Great made his first trip to Holland incognito, with the principal aim of learning about ship-building.

Johan de Witt (1625–72).

Meeting of the States-General in The Hague in 1651 (left).

THE 18TH CENTURY: DECLINE

FOREIGN HEGEMONY. Despite competition from France and England, which were becoming increasingly powerful, Amsterdam continued to thrive for a time, especially as a result of her prosperous colonial trade. Brotherhoods and societies of scholars developed, particularly with the opening of Felix Meritis in 1788. During the war of 1780–84, however, the English destroyed the Provinces' fleet, intending to put an end to the competition once and for all. A patriotic party was formed in Amsterdam at this time, inspired by the American Revolution. It was helped by the French, who formally recognized it in 1782. In 1787 Frederick William II, king of Prussia, occupied Amsterdam to support his brother-in-law, the prince of Orange, forcing the patriots to flee to Paris. Shortly afterward they returned, escorted by the French revolutionary troops, who, after the battles of Wattignies and Fleurus (1795), invaded the country and set up the Batavian Republic, under stringent French control. Numerous constitutions followed, ending with the kingdom of Louis, brother of Napoleon, between 1806 and 1813. During this period Amsterdam had to pay heavy tribute to France.

1689
Stadholder of the Netherlands, William of Orange becomes king of England (William III).

1787
Adoption of the American constitution.

The Prussians enter Amsterdam on October 10, 1787, via the Leidsepoort.

1789
Beginning of the French Revolution.

THE 19TH AND 20TH CENTURIES

October 8, 1811: Napoleon is given the keys to the city.

1815
Battle of Waterloo.

The first steamship enters the port of Amsterdam in 1816, as seen by N. Baur.

FROM EMPIRE TO INDEPENDENCE. At the dawn of the 19th century the French empire dominated Europe and the Netherlands. From 1806 to 1810 Louis Bonaparte, now king, installed himself in the Town Hall on Dam Square. His main task was to maintain the blockade against the English, which proved an economic disaster. Napoleon visited Amsterdam on October 8, 1811, to inspect the ports and the beaches as part of his preparations for the invasion of England. In 1813 the city rose up against France, ridding itself of the occupying forces to become capital of the kingdom of Belgium and the United Provinces. William of Orange was chosen as king under the title of William I. In 1830 Belgium became a kingdom in its own right.

ECONOMIC AND SOCIAL CHANGE. Amsterdam was slow to adapt to the Industrial Revolution, revealing a certain economic backwardness compared with other major European powers. From 1824 to 1876 a canal project to link the city to the North Sea was gradually completed. This meant that ships no longer had to sail round northern Holland and the Zuiderzee, and steamships could complete the journey in just four hours. After 1850 the economy recovered, and there was a significant increase in the city's population, and between 1854 and 1873 the municipality stopped giving assistance to the poor. Luxury industries, such as chocolate, beer, diamonds and eau-de-Cologne, maintained the city's reputation. A development project of 1882 included plans for the Central Station, the Rijksmuseum and the Concertgebouw, and the council reverted to a policy of assisting the poor. Ferdinand Domela Nieuwenhuis played a crucial part in the development of Dutch socialism, which gained increasing support among the workers (12 percent of the votes in 1901). In the early 20th century the working-class population of Amsterdam grew, and the municipality developed public town planning schemes. A law on town planning and housing was passed in 1901; gradually the characteristic style of the Amsterdam School began to emerge. Although they had remained neutral during the First World War, the Netherlands were still affected by food rationing after 1918. In 1932 the north Zuiderzee dyke was finished, transforming the Zuiderzee into an interior sea. During the 1930's the Netherlands suffered from the worldwide recession. In 1934 Jordaan, a working-class district, rose up in protest against conditions of poverty and unemployment. A new development scheme for extending the city was drawn up.

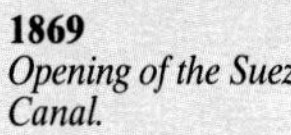

1869
Opening of the Suez Canal.

Ferdinand Domela Nieuwenhuis (1846–1919).

Wilhelmina (1880–1962) reigned from 1890 to 1948.

«OVER THE CENTURIES, THE MAP OF AMSTERDAM HAS BECOME INCREASINGLY COMPLEX, A CHINESE IDEOGRAM [...] WHOSE SIGNIFICANCE IS UNCHANGING. THE EARTH IS THE PAPER, THE WATER, THE INK.» CEES NOOTEBOOM

1940. SECOND WORLD WAR. Despite the fact that the Netherlands had remained neutral, Rotterdam was bombed on May 10, 1940, and the country was occupied by the Germans. Queen Wilhelmina escaped into exile in London. On February 25, 1941, in the midst of occupied Amsterdam, the dockers and transport workers went on strike to protest against the mass deportation of the Jews. In 1942 the Japanese invaded the Dutch colonies in Asia. And on July 15, 1944, the young Anne Frank was arrested. She never returned from deportation. In 1945 the ravaged Netherlands were liberated belatedly by the Allies: a few days before the German capitulation Amsterdam was free once more. In 1949, after two years of war, Indonesia obtained independence.

1948
Juliana (born in 1909) becomes queen of the Netherlands after the abdication of Wilhelmina.

May 5, 1945: the Allied troops enter Amsterdam.

THE POST-WAR YEARS. The 1950's saw a return to prosperity, again in conjunction with a population explosion in the Netherlands. Amsterdam expanded, and in 1963 the population reached an all-time peak of 868,000. The social policy of the municipality was not sufficient to satisfy the many socialist movements, spearheaded from 1964 on by the Provos (provocateurs)▲ *243*, a movement founded by Roel van Duyn. In March 1966 they launched their attack on the established order by demonstrating against the marriage of Princess Beatrix (born 1938), the future queen of the Netherlands, to a German. Around this time the Provos succeeded in gaining a seat on the city council, which debated such key issues as over-population and immigration. In the 1970's Amsterdam's liberal policy toward drugs made it the world capital of the hippie lifestyle. Violent demonstrations took place in 1975 against plans to build a subway, which would entail the destruction of the Jewish quarter, and against development schemes around the Waterlooplein. At the beginning of the 1980's a movement encouraging the occupation of buildings left empty by speculators gathered support: the squatters dominated the news. The year 1986 saw the opening on the controversial Waterlooplein site of a new Town Hall and opera house, which soon became known as the "Stopera". In 1990 there was serious talk of new urban development schemes for the north of the city, and a casino was opened on the site of a prison. The following year was the centenary of Van Gogh's death, and a highly successful exhibition was held to mark the occasion. In March 1992 Amsterdammers voted in favor of traffic restrictions in the historic center, though only the inhabitants of the city center voted to ban cars completely. The very low turnout cast doubt on the validity of the result, however.

1949
Independence of Indonesia.

1957
The Netherlands sign the Treaty of Rome, establishing the European Community.

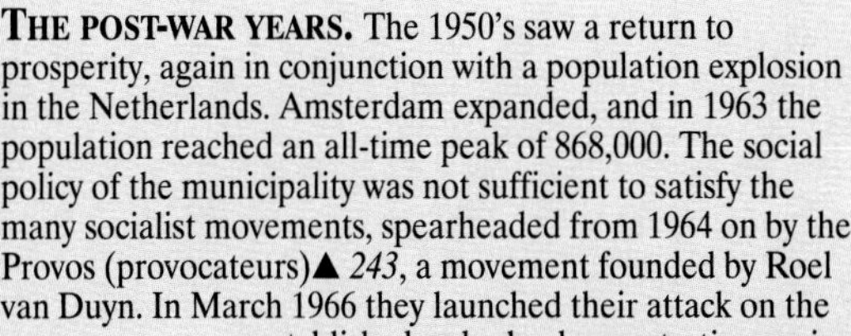

The floods of 1953. Almost all the Netherlands is affected (left).

Demonstration by the Provos in the 1960's.

Queen Beatrix, ruler of the Netherlands since 1980.

Amsterdam c. 1550, as represented by Antonie van den Wyngaerde (right).

The evolution of cartography, one of Amsterdam's specialties, was largely inspired by the major publishers of atlases, the most famous of whom was Jan Blaeu ● 41. The numerous plans and overall views produced ▲ 168 since the 16th century faithfully trace the various stages in Amsterdam's highly structured urban development, which, unlike any other European city of comparable size and importance, has always been controlled by its citizens.

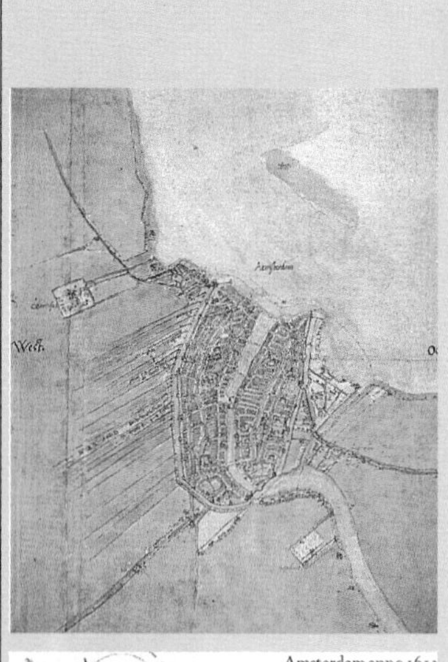

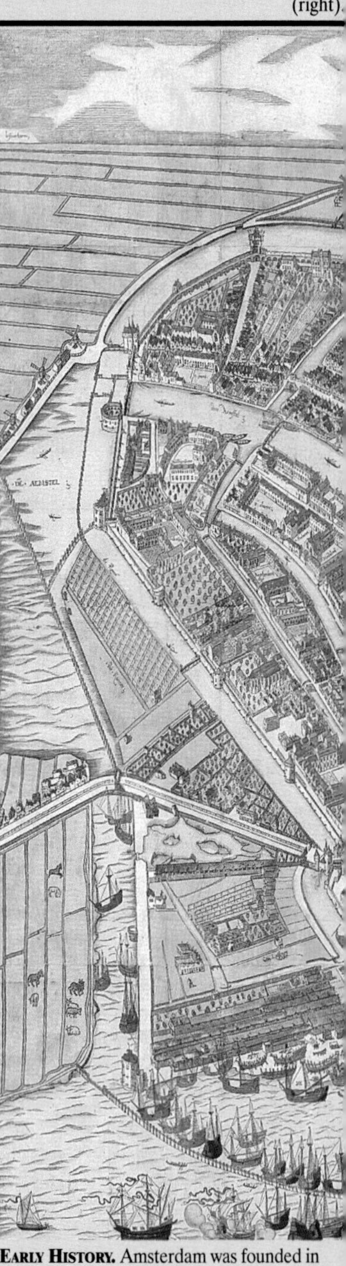

EARLY HISTORY. Amsterdam was founded in the early 13th century. The first village settlement, Amstelledamme, stood at the confluence of the Amstel and IJ rivers. Zeedijk, Nieuwendijk and Haarlemmerdijk grew up to the east and west of the village, followed by the Oudezijds in the east, with its Oude Kerk (Old Church), built in 1306, and the Nieuwezijds in the west, with its Nieuwe Kerk (New Church), built in 1408. During the first quarter of the

15th century new canals were dug along the eastern (Gelderskade and Kloveniersburgwal) and western (Singel) boundaries. The oldest surviving map of Amsterdam was drawn in 1538 and engraved in 1544 by Cornelis Anthonisz (c. 1499–1556). It shows the city surrounded by ramparts constructed in the late 15th century. A map of Amsterdam and the surrounding area (left) drawn c. 1560 by Jacob van Deventer (c. 1500–75) clearly shows the ditches, which later became the Jordaan canals, to the west of the ramparts. From 1585 onwards the city spread along the Oude Schans (old fortification) and over the next three-quarters of a century was extended in successive phases. The first stage, in 1593, involved the construction of new canals (some of which have since been filled in) linking the city to a new district centered around the present-day Waterlooplein – later the Jewish quarter.

FROM THE 17TH CENTURY TO THE PRESENT DAY. The second stage in the city's expansion was begun in 1610. Development of the west and south of the old city involved the construction of Amsterdam's three most famous canals: the Herengracht (Gentlemen's Canal), Keizersgracht (Emperor's Canal) and Prinsengracht (Prince's Canal). The new districts thus created were protected by a double defensive barrier of canal and ramparts: the Singelgracht. In the early 17th century, the Brouwersgracht was built to the north-west, while the Herengracht, Keizersgracht and Prinsengracht were subsequently extended as far as the Leidsegracht. Work was finally completed around 1660. The extension of the three main canals created a new residential district for the upper classes, while the area of Jordaan, constructed outside the new city boundary, was primarily working-class.

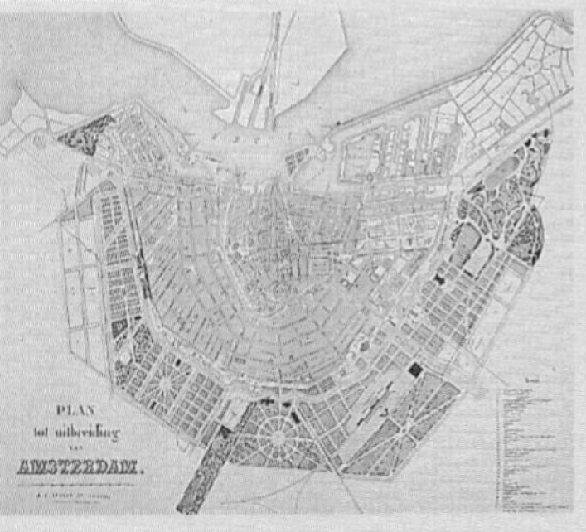

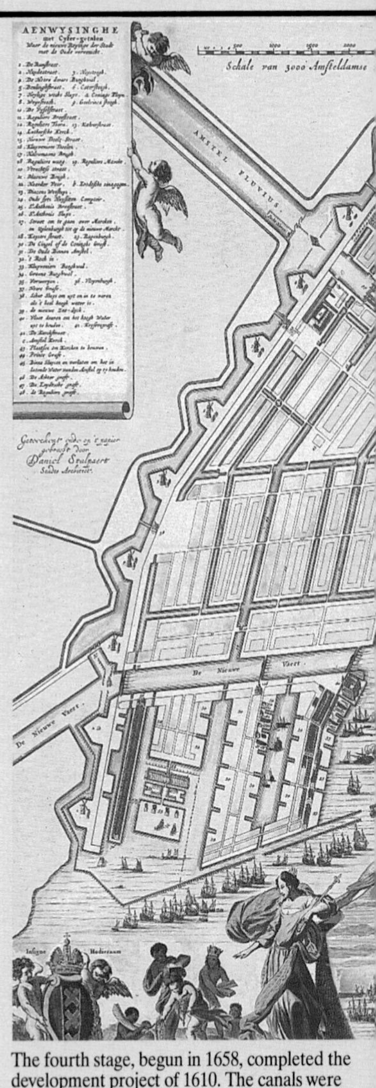

The fourth stage, begun in 1658, completed the development project of 1610. The canals were extended to the river Amstel and then as far as the IJ. The map above was drawn by one of the city's architects, Daniel Stalpaert (1615–76), in 1662 and was printed and published by Nicolas Visscher. This engraving on copper clearly shows the fourth stage of the city's development "in progress". For more than two hundred years Amsterdam remained within its crescent-shaped boundaries, until in the 19th century a group of wealthy and cultured citizens decided to inject new life into the city. One of these great pioneers was Samuel Sarphati (1813–66), a prominent figure in the fields of public health, business education and highway maintenance. As a result of his efforts, a plan was put forward in 1867 by the city's engineer J. van Niftrik. It involved developing a

Drawing by P.J. Otten showing the Nordzee Canal (North Sea Canal), dug in 1876, which gave the port of Amsterdam a new lease of life.

broad outer belt around the old city, where houses, factories and public parks would be juxtaposed to create a balanced urban environment (bottom left). In reality the scheme fell far short of the ideal when it was executed according to a plan put forward by Kalff, director of public works, in 1878. Completed in 1877, the Vondelpark, a luxurious extension of southwest Amsterdam, formed the nucleus of a new residential district. At the beginning of the 20th century the capital annexed several neighboring villages, and between 1898 and 1921 it quadrupled its surface area. H.P. Berlage's project for the south of Amsterdam was approved by the town council in 1917 and carried out between 1920 and 1930. This was followed by a municipal plan for the general development of the city, to be completed by the year 2000. All new districts are to include cycle tracks, green spaces, broad avenues and equal proportions of social housing and private residential areas. The map below (1990) shows what has been achieved so far. Today the city covers an area of nearly 50,000 acres.

SPINOZA (1632–77) Famous for theories on the "love of God", he challenged the theological dogmatism that divided religious communities.

As a Catholic and then a Protestant city, Amsterdam has always been a melting pot for many different nationalities and religions. Because they were used to the cosmopolitanism of international commerce and trade, Amsterdammers tended to apply the Calvinist principle of "freedom of conscience". Over the past three hundred years, this has had a profound effect on attitudes and has helped to develop a strong tradition of tolerance. Hence the attraction of Amsterdam for large numbers of foreigners, emigrants and humanist intellectuals, who have sought to integrate themselves into this cohesive diversity.

PIERRE BAYLE (1647–1706). Of French extraction, he supported the atheists against the idolaters in his *Pensées sur la comète.*

FRANCISCUS GOMARUS (1563–1641) A fervent defender of a rigorist Calvinist doctrine of predestination, according to which a small élite achieved salvation only through the grace of God. From 1604 he stood in opposition to Arminius, who advocated a more moderate doctrine.

«FISHERS OF SOULS» A. P. van de Venne (1589–1662) portrays the rivalry during the Twelve-Year Truce (1609–21) in the eighty years of conflict between the United Provinces and Spain. On the left Maurice, prince of Orange, and several of the crowned heads of Europe, including the young Catholic king Louis XIII can be seen among the Protestants. The Catholics are on the right in a small boat.

THE JERUSALEM OF THE NORTH From the late 16th century onwards Portuguese and German Jews settled in the east of Amsterdam, the only city in Europe to allow them freedom of worship. In spite of resistance from Amsterdammers, the Jewish population was decimated in the years 1940 to 1945.

Dispute between Rigorist and Moderate Calvinists (Abraham van der Eyck, 1684–1724). In 1610 the followers of Arminius brought a petition or "remonstrance" before the states of Holland, objecting to the hardline Calvinism advocated by Gomarus, leader of the Counter-Remonstrants. Gomarus' doctrine was finally recognized in 1618 by the Synod of Dort. The sword of the stadholder Maurice, prince of Orange, count of Nassau, whose dazzling attire contrasts with that of the pastors, is said to have influenced the decision ● *30*.

The Huguenots as disseminators of European culture
Holland, an "international crossroads" and seat of learning for many foreign scholars, became the main haven for exiled French Huguenots. They played an important role in making Amsterdam a center for new ideas, by founding such leading European publications as Pierre Bayle's *Nouvelles de la République des Lettres*, founded in 1683.

The Catholics
Amsterdam was a Catholic city until 1578, when the Reformation condemned the religion – symbol of the Spanish invader and papal power – to two hundred years of semi-clandestine existence. Between 1578 and 1815 the Catholics, though tolerated, were forced to exercise the utmost discretion and to worship in secret. They were not allowed to practise freely and in public until the end of the 19th century ▲ *137*.

FROM INTOLERANCE TO TOLERANCE

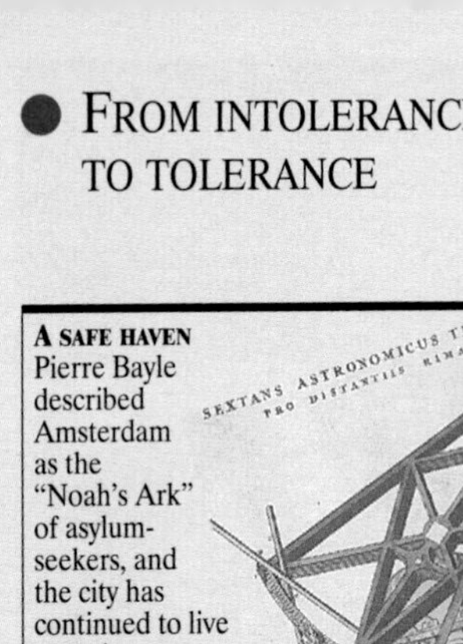

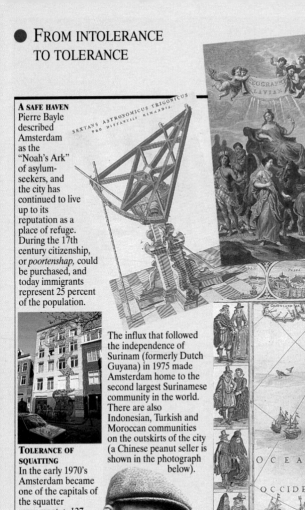

A SAFE HAVEN Pierre Bayle described Amsterdam as the "Noah's Ark" of asylum-seekers, and the city has continued to live up to its reputation as a place of refuge. During the 17th century citizenship, or *poortenshap,* could be purchased, and today immigrants represent 25 percent of the population.

TOLERANCE OF SQUATTING In the early 1970's Amsterdam became one of the capitals of the squatter movement ▲ *127*. Above, no. 201 Spuistraat with its mural.

The influx that followed the independence of Surinam (formerly Dutch Guyana) in 1975 made Amsterdam home to the second largest Surinamese community in the world. There are also Indonesian, Turkish and Moroccan communities on the outskirts of the city (a Chinese peanut seller is shown in the photograph below).

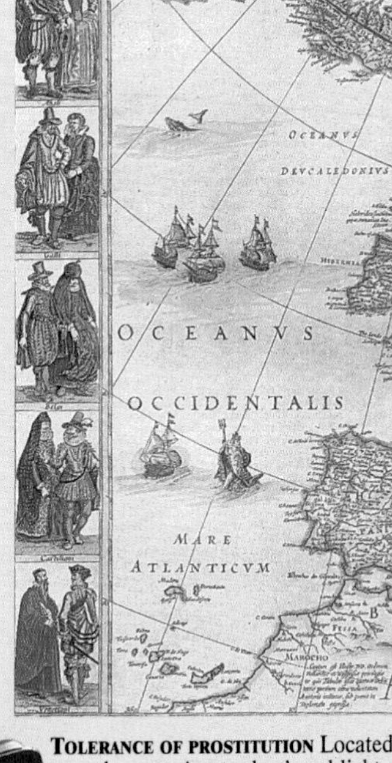

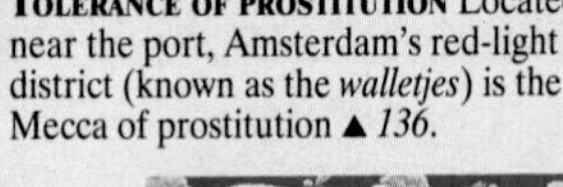

TOLERANCE OF PROSTITUTION Located near the port, Amsterdam's red-light district (known as the *walletjes*) is the Mecca of prostitution ▲ *136*.

«You are the first modern nation to combine freedom and wealth.»

Mirabeau

Tolerance of drugs
Amsterdam adopts a very liberal policy toward drug-users. Soft drugs for personal use are freely available in certain Amsterdam coffeeshops – some even have a "menu" on the counter, while there are free street deliveries of methadone, a hard-drug substitute. The cannabis-leaf sign (left) is now forbidden.

Some extremely powerful publishing houses were established in Amsterdam during the 17th century. The monumental atlases of Jan Blaeu (1598-1673) and the literary classics of Elzevier are just two examples of Amsterdam's cultural influence within Europe ● *54*.

René Descartes
(1596–1650)
"In what other country is it possible to enjoy such complete freedom...?" ● *99*

Free expression
Because 17th-century Amsterdam was the point of convergence for so many different cultures and philosophies, it provided an ideal forum for the exchange of new ideas, which could be rapidly disseminated thanks to Amsterdam's free press. New forms of printed information were also distributed on a large scale. One of these was cartography ● *34*.

Cartouche on an Amsterdam façade: «The Art of Writing».

FROM DUTCH TO ENGLISH
Bons vivants are indebted to the Dutch language for such words as hops from *hoppe* and brandy from *brandewijn* (cooked wine).

MARITIME TERMS
Some interesting words borrowed from the Dutch maritime vocabulary include filibuster or free-booter, a derivative of *vrijbuiter* (a pirate or adventurer in search of booty), scorbutic from *scheurbuik* (i.e. which tears the stomach), meaning afflicted with scurvy, and yacht from *jacht* (*jagen,* to chase).

HISTORY OF THE DUTCH LANGUAGE

A FINE EXAMPLE OF LINGUISTIC PLURALITY. Dutch or, technically speaking, the Netherlandic language, developed from the dialects spoken along the North Sea coast during the Middle Ages. Originally based on Flemish, it gradually spread eastward and was enriched by the dialects of Brabant and old Holland, becoming firmly established throughout the province of Holland during the 17th century. Modern Dutch is therefore a synthesis of these three Germanic dialects.

DEVELOPMENT OF THE LANGUAGE. During the Middle Ages the dialects spoken along the North Sea coast were known locally as *Dietsc* or *Duutsc*. From these came *Deutsch* (the German language) and *Dutch*, the English term for Netherlandic. *Dietsc* means "language of the people" – as opposed to Latin, which was the language of scholarship – but the term conceals the rich diversity of these coastal dialects. For instance, the written languages of Bruges, Antwerp and Amsterdam were all very different from each other. From the 13th century onward, Flemish dialects played a major role in these regions. Given the preeminence and economic power of the Flemish cities of Bruges and Ghent, it is not difficult to understand the prestige of a language that produced such brilliant literary masterpieces as *Reynard the Fox*. During the 15th century Brabant (Brussels, Antwerp, and 's-Hertogenbosch) became increasingly influential and eventually replaced Flanders as a major political and economic center. As a result the Brabant element made an important contribution to the development of these dialects. The religious upheavals of the 16th century resulted in the separation of modern Flemish-speaking Belgium from the southern provinces ● *29*, and a great many people left Flanders and Brabant and moved north, often for religious reasons, during the Golden Age of the United Provinces (17th century). The language cultivated and refined by these "southern" immigrants exerted a strong influence on the dialects of Holland, and it was in this province, where thousands of emigrants from Flanders and Brabant had sought refuge, that the Dutch language acquired its definitive form. At the height of its glory, Amsterdam was a linguistic melting pot from which the Dutch language emerged in the form that we know today.

The influence of Dutch on the English language

The Dutch language has made an important contribution to linguistic exchanges within Europe. The economic success of Flanders during the Middle Ages and Holland during the 17th century has left its mark on several European languages with many words and expressions which are of Dutch origin. English examples include church from *kerk*, bivouac from *bijwake* and stoop(a verandah) from *stoep*. But most of the terms borrowed from Dutch are taken from its maritime vocabulary. The Dutch have always been a seafaring nation, and their shipyards were renowned throughout 17th century Europe.

Dutch names

Exchanging business cards with Dutch friends provides excellent examples of the exoticism of their language. For example, the official identity of the young woman everyone knows as Jo may well be Johanna J.M.D. van Leeuwen-Waterdrinker. There is a clear distinction between the name used by the Dutch on an everyday basis and their official given names; Bas and Dorien are in fact shortened forms of Sebastian and Theodora, for instance. It is also quite common for an official first name to be followed on a business card by three or four other names, often represented by initials. As regards surnames, married women simply add their maiden name to their married name. It is considered good form for women who have successfully completed a university degree to use the title Dra (from the Latin *Doctoranda* , i.e. a person submitting for a doctorate after five or six years of

Dutch-speaking region

Dutch

French

Frisian and Dutch

Dutch in France

Bilingual region

Others

Dutch, known as Hollands (Hollandish) until the 19th century, is a Germanic language lying midway between English and German. Dutch has many regional variations and is spoken outside the Netherlands in Flanders, the northern part of Belgium.

In the classroom Compulsory education, introduced into the Netherlands on July 7, 1900, made it possible to standardize the Dutch language.

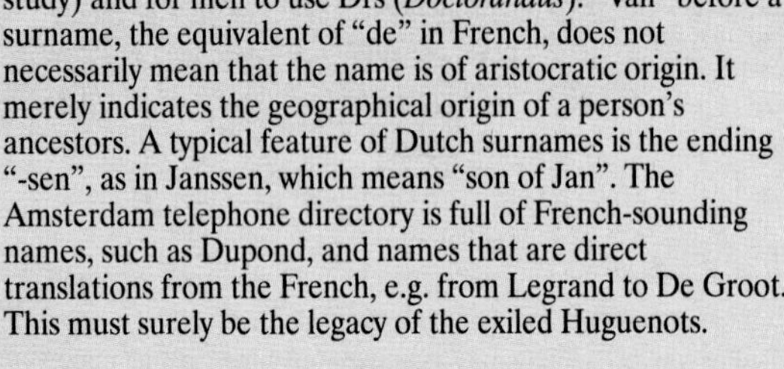

The famous Dutch writer Cees Nooteboom (b. 1933) (below) described the city as an open book, and those who walk through it as its readers.

DUTCH PLACE NAMES
Place names are often historical. Amsterdam's medieval port is called the Oude Schans (old fortification) because it occupies the site of the old city walls ● *34*. Warmoesstraat (which literally means Street of Vegetables) refers to the type of trade that was once there. However, the translation of place names is not without surprises. For example, the Nieuwendijk (New Dyke) is in fact the city's oldest dyke.

LITERATURE
Those who want to improve their knowledge of *Amsterdams* should read G.A. Bredero (1585–1618) ▲ *153* and Simon Carmiggelt (1913–87). Both writers illustrate the verve and vigor of this colorful dialect.

study) and for men to use Drs (*Doctorandus*). "Van" before a surname, the equivalent of "de" in French, does not necessarily mean that the name is of aristocratic origin. It merely indicates the geographical origin of a person's ancestors. A typical feature of Dutch surnames is the ending "-sen", as in Janssen, which means "son of Jan". The Amsterdam telephone directory is full of French-sounding names, such as Dupond, and names that are direct translations from the French, e.g. from Legrand to De Groot. This must surely be the legacy of the exiled Huguenots.

DUTCH AS SPOKEN IN AMSTERDAM ◆ *310*

The dialect of Holland (*Hollands*, or Hollandish) is widely spoken throughout the Netherlands, and many of its characteristics, particularly the very guttural pronunciation, are a feature of the Dutch spoken in Amsterdam. However, it would be more accurate to refer to *Amsterdams* when describing the language of the Dutch capital, which seems to embody a sense of pride and unity shared by all native Amsterdammers. People living in Haarlem, who claim to speak Dutch in its purest form, describe *Amsterdams* as a hybrid dialect, while the inhabitants of The Hague who, in an attempt to refine their language, speak *Bekakt* (i.e. in an affected manner), consider it a common dialect. In fact *Amsterdams*, like the city itself throughout history, has incorporated extraneous elements and uses a great many words and phrases introduced from French, Hebrew and Yiddish by the Huguenots and Jews. Amsterdammers from old, established families refer to their city as *mokum*, from the Hebrew *makom* (sacred place). Without necessarily belonging to the Jewish community, they will tell you about their *mispooche*, from the Hebrew *mischpacha* (family), while the expression *kapsones maken* (to make a fuss) comes from the Hebrew *kapsones* (self-importance). Between 15 and 20 percent of the Dutch and an even higher proportion of the *Amsterdams* vocabulary is of French origin. The Huguenot influence is found in Jordaan ▲ *238*, which may be derived from the French jardin (garden), while in expressions such as *in de merode zitten* (to be in a mess), *merode* comes from maraude (pilfering, looting) and *op zijn ponteneur zijn* comes from the expression *mettre un point d'honneur à* (to make it a point of honor).

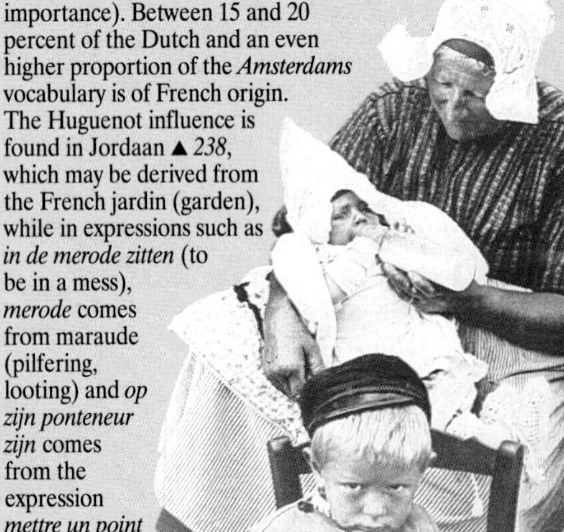

Crafts and traditions

Festivals, *46*

Music, *48*

Cafés, *50*

Traditional shops, *52*

Old books and bookshops, *54*

Furniture and interior design, *56*

Bicycles, *58*

Sport, *60*

Gastronomy, *62*

Specialties, *64*

Most of Amsterdam's major festivals evoke the city's trading past. They are occasions for general celebration which provide an opportunity to organize the most wonderful processions, open-air games and performances. One of the most spectacular of these traditional events, which have been kept very much alive by Amsterdammers, is the occasion of the queen mother's birthday, when the entire city is transformed into one vast market. Another important national festival is the feast of Saint Nicholas, celebrated in memory of the patron saint of merchants, sailors and children.

DECEMBER 6, SINTERKLAAS (FEAST OF SAINT NICHOLAS)
Three weeks before, a tugboat brings Saint Nicholas along the IJ to Amsterdam. He then rides through the streets on his white horse, while his assistants, the Black Peters (*Zwarte Pieten*) throw handfuls of *pepernoten* (small ginger biscuits) to the children in the crowd.

On Saint Nicholas' Eve (December 5) a member of each family puts on a black glove, knocks on the door and leaves in the main room a basket of presents and cakes, and a satirical poem signed by *Sinterklaas*.

FESTIVALS
The 1864 watercolor on the right illustrates the typically Dutch fascination for fairs and folk festivals. Many traditional entertainments are still enthusiastically enjoyed today. One of these is *Kop van jut*, which involves a test of strength, where participants swing a huge hammer onto a

platform; if they hit hard enough a ring moves up a pole and the bell at the top rings. Be it an open-air concert, street theater, a checkers tournament in Dam Square or a water pageant like the one held in honor of Marie de' Medici in 1638 (top), Amsterdammers are always holding some form of festival.

QUEEN JULIANA'S BIRTHDAY

Queen Beatrix of the Netherlands has preserved the traditional festival held on April 30 to celebrate the birthday of her mother, Queen Juliana. The city is transformed into a vast market, which was originally organized by children, and many wear

something orange in honor of the House of Orange. The painting above illustrates the festive atmosphere of this colorful event.

Music plays an important part in the everyday life of Amsterdam, and the city welcomes music-lovers of all kinds: jazz and rock as well as classical music. Every year fourteen thousand concerts are held in various purpose-built concert halls, as well as in museums, churches and in the open air. The streets and canals of Amsterdam provide the backdrop for a continuous performance of classical and modern music, by solo musicians and groups of players of all ages.

BARREL ORGANS
Jordaan ▲ *235* is the home of the magnificent Perlee collection of barrel organs. L. van Leeuwen, the last survivor of a

"dynasty" founded in 1875, collects and lovingly restores these fine old instruments before hiring them out.

CONCERTS
The resident symphony orchestra of the Concertgebouw, built in 1888 and famous for its perfect acoustic, is conducted by Ricardo Chailly. It enjoys an international reputation ▲ *216*, and the first violinist even has a fan club! The Muziektheater or "Stopera", built in 1986, is the home of the national opera and ballet companies, while jazz enthusiasts have a wide choice of venues ◆ *298*.

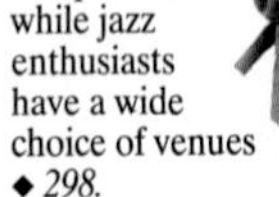

THE ORGANS OF AMSTERDAM
The Westerkerk organ ▲ *179* is protected by a panel painted by Gerard de Lairesse (1641–1711) during the 17th century (detail above). Forty-two large organs are still played in churches throughout Amsterdam, a record number for a city of this size.

«THE LETTER» BY VERMEER
This painting of c. 1666, depicts a woman holding a cither. It illustrates a pastime that is still common today, since most Dutch households possess at least one musical instrument. Amsterdam has always been the home of accomplished musicians, such as the members of the present-day Amsterdam Baroque Orchestra.

Traditional décor in the Eerste Klas, the restaurant and bar at the Central Station ▲ *138*.

The Hooghoudt at no. 11 Reguliersgracht is a typical *proeflokaal*.

Looking out of the 't Smalle café ▲ *237*. It has outside terraces for use in summer.

De Kroon, one of the old cafés on the Rembrandtplein (gouache by Leo Gestel, 190

The Kort, a restaurant and bar at no. 12 Amstelveld, beside the Amstelkerk ▲ *204*.

De Jaren at no. 20 Nieuwe Doelenstraat is on of Amsterdam's most modern cafés ▲ *160*.

De Druif at no. 83 Rapenburgerplein is a stone's throw from the Maritime Museum ▲ *269*.

The Papeneiland at no. 2 Prinsengracht has no changed for over three centuries ▲ *176*.

Cafés in Amsterdam fall into three categories: brown cafés, i.e. old cafés done out in dark wood (hence their name); *proeflokalen* (tasting houses) which are similar to brown cafés but sell only spirits such as genever (juniper-flavored gin); and more modern cafés with a "designer" décor ◆ *296*.

Int Aepjen at no. 1 Zeedijk is in the heart of the red light district ▲ *136*.

De Zeilvaart at no. 106 De Ruyterkade is traditionally a sailors' café overlooking the port.

The Rembrandtplein and the Leidseplein have the highest concentration of cafés in the city.

De Belhamel, a restaurant and bar at no. 60 Brouwersgracht, has a view of the main canals.

«Designer» décor: the Dantzig at no. 15 Zwanenburgwal is the «Stopera» complex café.

Many of Amsterdam's cafés have a table where customers can sit and read newspapers.

Schipchandler at no. 8 Gelderskade is now a private catering business.

De Drie Fleschjes at no. 18 Gravenstraat, near Dam Square ▲ *130*.

Amsterdam is a city with a strong merchant tradition and it proudly preserves the old shops that are a reminder of its glorious past. They are the survivors of a "Golden Age" when the Dutch merchant navy undertook long sea voyages to bring home exotic commodities such as tea, coffee, tobacco, spices, precious silks and porcelain. A few shops have retained the luxurious décor of that period, with their wood panelling, ceramic tiles, velvet hangings and chandeliers. Several family businesses that have been handed down over generations have continued to trade near the old port despite the gradual encroachment of the more titillating shopfronts of the red light district.

PRESERVING OLD TRADITIONS
Every detail of the herbalist's shop *Jacob Hooy* (left), opened in 1743, has been preserved. Jan Beekhuizen specializes in rare pewter (center), and his shop displays the type of goblets and pitchers so often depicted in paintings of the Golden Age, particularly the still lifes of Pieter Claesz. The earthenware factories of Delft were established in the 17th century to imitate fine Chinese porcelain. Antique shops sometimes sell rare early pieces such as this tulip vase (right). Today modern Delftware, an original and extremely well-crafted product, is still very much in demand. It can be found in its simplest form in Amsterdam's many souvenir shops (above).

«THE SHOPKEEPER'S GOLDEN RULE SHOULD BE TO PUT HONOR BEFORE PROFIT.»

GODFRIED UDEMANS

Early 20th-century décor in the salon of P.J. Jansen, hairdresser and collector.

The different blends of tea sold at Wijs en Zonen, are always tested and tasted.

"GAPER"
An apothecary's sign in the form of a man's head.

The illustration on the right (1857) shows an apothecary's shop displaying a gaper. These figures represent a sick person who has come for a diagnosis. Their Moorish appearance reminded customers of the distant origins of the remedies.

Amsterdam's reputation as a city of booklovers dates from the arrival of the Huguenots after the revocation of the Edict of Nantes in 1685. Attracted by the city's reputation for tolerance, they settled and founded publishing houses ● *31*. As early as the 15th century a craftsman from Haarlem, Laurens Janszoon (Coster), was the first person after Johannes Gutenberg to print a book using movable type ◆ *304*. Today Haarlem has about 285 bookshops.

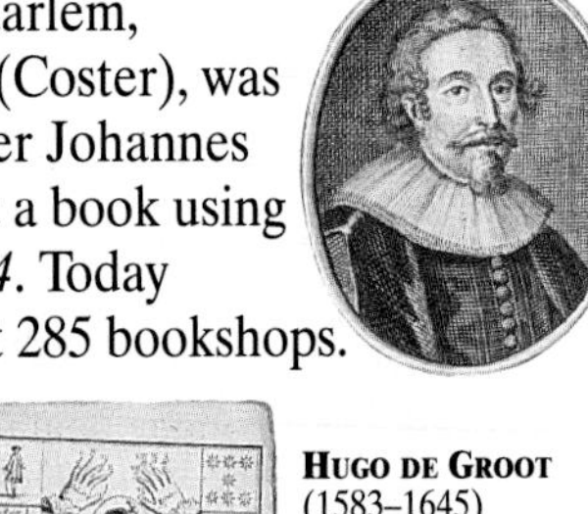

Schryf A. B. C.

A B C D E F G H I K L M N O P Q R S T V W W X Y Z.

A a b c d e f g h i j k l m n o p q r ſ s t u v w x y z.

Klinkletters.

A. E. I. O. V.

Aapschop. Boom. Chinaas-appel. Duit. Eenhoorn. Fakkel. Gatepatiel. Haan. Inschenken. Klok. Ladder. Moolen. Nap. Oven. Peer. Quartel. Rooster. Schaal. Trommel. Viltje. Varken. Waijer. X. Yzer-komvoor. Zandlooper.

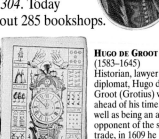

A children's alphabet primer published in Amsterdam in 1759.

HUGO DE GROOT
(1583–1645)
Historian, lawyer and diplomat, Hugo de Groot (Grotius) was ahead of his time. As well as being an active opponent of the slave trade, in 1609 he published the *Mare Liberum*, an apologia for the freedom of the seas.

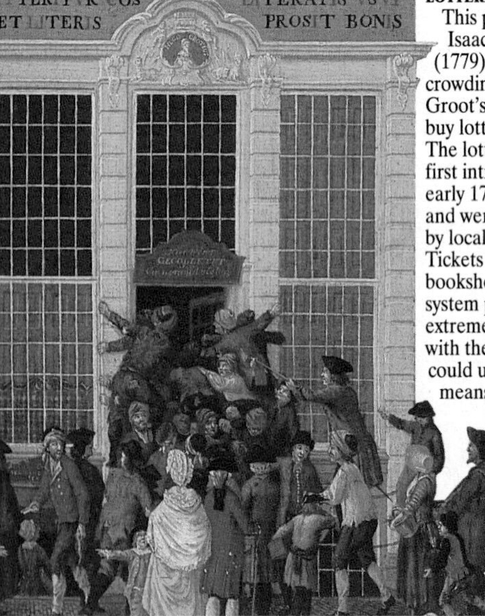

LIBRARIES AND LOTTERIES
This painting by Isaac Ouwater (1779) shows people crowding into Jan de Groot's bookshop to buy lottery tickets. The lotteries were first introduced in the early 17th century and were organized by local magistrates. Tickets were sold in bookshops, and the system proved extremely popular with the Dutch who could use it as a means of acquiring wealth without incurring the wrath of the Calvinists.

The signature of Isaak Elzevier (1596–1651), a member of one of the most prestigious Dutch printing families.

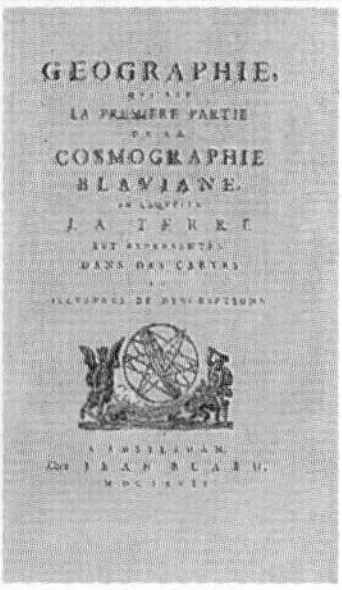

GEOGRAPHIE,

LA PREMIERE PARTIE

COSMOGRAPHIE

BLAVIANE.

LA TERRE

DANS DES CARTES

AMSTERDAM,

Chez JEAN BLAEU.

Cover of *Geography*, the first part of Jan Blaeu's cosmography ● *41* (17th century).

J. CATS

HOUWELYCK.

DAT IS

DE GANTSCHE GE-

LEGENTHEYDT

DES

ECHTEN-STAETS.

TOT DORDRECHT,

Gedruckt by Ian Barentsz. Smient, Boeck-verkooper by de Tol-Brugh, in den vergul-

This anonymous wood engraving (1655) is for the title page of *Houwelijck,* a treatise on marriage by the statesman and writer of moral tracts, Jacob Cats (1577–1660). His work remained extremely popular for almost two centuries, a popularity that was described by one critic as "a national disaster".

LIBRARIES AND BOOK MARKETS

Few visitors to the Rijksmuseum enjoy the privilege of visiting the extraordinary library (left) built at the beginning of the 20th century. Almost as exclusive is the Bibliotheca Hermetica Philosophica in Bloemstraat ▲ *247*.

FURNITURE AND INTERIOR DESIGN

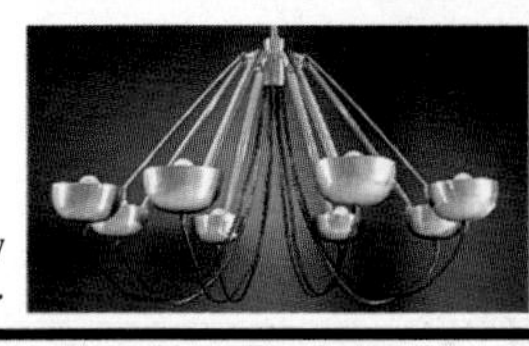
Lampshade by Robert Eckhardt.

Typical early 20th-century drawing room, designed by T.W. Nieuwenhuis in 1909.

During the Dutch Golden Age cabinet-makers produced striking pieces, such as tall cabinets with tiered cornices and furniture with exotic panels. During the reign of Louis XV French influence superseded the popularity of Dutch design, and it took the creative genius of Berlage ▲ *133* to invest Dutch furniture with a new identity. This is revealed in the designs of the Amsterdam School ● *84*, active during the early 20th century, and still survives today in the work of contemporary Dutch designers.

DELFTWARE
Delft tiles could be assembled to create all kinds of everyday scenes in the manner of a fresco: this meal taken on a terrace (1707), for example. Delftware vases were displayed on the tiered cornices of Dutch cabinets. This example of a late 18th-century cabinet, with decorative painted glass panels from China (below), can be seen in the Rijksmuseum.

LINEN CUPBOARD
Impressive rosewood and ebony linen cupboard (1650) typical of the grandiose Dutch style that was superseded a few years later by the increasingly dominant French influence.

The best-known example in this range of chairs by Rietveld is the 1934 zigzag model (on the right).

De Stijl
The artist Piet Mondriaan and the architect Gerrit Rietveld are two of the most famous members of the Dutch art group known as De Stijl ▲ *228*, formed in the 1930's. Their aim was to create an art of rigorous, mathematical precision. Today Dutch creativity is still a powerful force, with such internationally renowned designers as J. des Bouvries, R. Eckhardt, D. Huese, M. Metz and B. Sipek.

Above: Bar stool and chairs (1990) and "upside-down" lamps (1991).

Oak armchair with gilded bronze feet designed in 1923 by architect C.J. Blaauwe in the style of the Amsterdam School.

Equally revolutionary is this oak cupboard inlaid with ivory, designed by Sluyterman (1925).

The Amsterdam School
This movement (1910–30) favored curving designs and challenged the constructivism of Berlage. It is the Dutch equivalent of Art Deco. Its members would not allow "outsiders" to intefere in their work and sometimes designed every detail of a building, from the carpets to the furniture.

"A King of Hugo" armchair by Robert Eckhardt (1989): a typical example of modern Dutch design.

When bicycles first appeared at the end of the 19th century Amsterdammers were quick to adopt the new means of transport, which was ideally suited to the flat terrain. During the 1960's the Provo movement ● *33* exploited the advantages of the bicycle by introducing a fleet of white bicycles for public use within the city. These bicycles could be taken, used and then left for someone else. In 1978 Amsterdam town councillors, concerned by increasing traffic congestion, decided to construct cycle lanes. The plan was enthusiastically received in a city of narrow canalside streets and alleyways. The environmentally aware Amsterdammers have also taken to their bicycles in an attempt to reduce pollution: Today there are over 550,000 bicycles in use in the city.

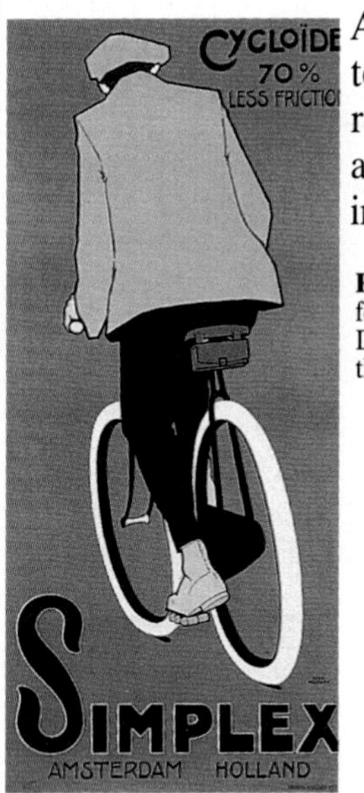

POSTER (1910) An advertisement for Simplex, one of the leading Dutch bicycle manufacturers of the early 20th century.

CARTOON
The dangers of the early bicycles, as illustrated by an English caricature. Although modern bicycles are much easier to handle, cycling is still not an entirely relaxing sport for the unsuspecting tourist, particularly as many Dutch bicycles still use a back-pedalling system as a means of braking. Cyclists in Amsterdam have scant regard for one-way systems and red lights... as many pedestrians have discovered to their cost!

BICYCLES OF EVERY STYLE
The range of bicycles that can be seen in Amsterdam is infinitely varied. More often than not, they are customized: painted in bright colors or fitted with seats and panniers for children and animals. In spite of sophisticated anti-theft devices, they disappear in their thousands every year, and barges can sometimes be seen fishing the remains of abandoned stolen bicycles from the canals. For this reason many people prefer to ride around on cheap, secondhand bicycles.

Bicycle production in the Netherlands

The Netherlands currently manufactures approximately 900,000 bicycles per year. Above: advertising poster of 1886.

Folding and elongated bicycles

Originally designed for soldiers during the First World War, folding bicycles are still available today, although they are made of much lighter materials. Many other variations can be found: tandems, for example, are occasionally seen. Some models are more specialized, e.g. the bicycle with an elongated frame used by messengers to deliver parcels and letters.

Once the water which surrounds Amsterdam had been brought under control and turned to the country's economic advantage, it became the playground of the Netherlands. All year round there is sailing on the IJsselmeer ■ *16*, which provides the setting for some fiercely competitive yacht races, while rowing boats glide along the canals, propelled by the rhythmic cadence of the oars. In winter the water freezes over, and in the 16th century this gave the Dutch the idea for a novel way of getting around. Ice-skating has since become an Olympic sport.

AJAX, THE PRIDE OF AMSTERDAM
Johan Cruijff, the great Dutch footballer of the 1970's, came from Amsterdam, where football is high on the sporting agenda. Its prestigious club, Ajax, was formed in 1900 by a group of friends, who posed for this memorable photograph in 1904 (left).

BOAT RACE ON THE AMSTEL IN THE EARLY 1900'S
Amsterdam's boating lake in the Amsterdamse Bos, to the south of the city, is world-famous. Rowing also takes place on canals and lakes ▲ *195*.

WATER SPORTS
This drawing by Adriaan Aartman (1755) is a reminder that sailing and rowing on the Amstel and Vecht rivers, to the east of Amsterdam ◆ *308*, have always been extremely popular with Amsterdammers.

ICE SKATING
Adam van Breen's painting of 1611 shows that iceskating was already in vogue by the 17th century. Today there are over 1,200 ice-skating clubs in the Netherlands which regularly organize outings and races.

THE OLYMPIC GAMES
When Amsterdam hosted the 1928 Olympic Games it welcomed forty-six competing nations.

THE "ELFSTEDENTOCHT" – ELEVEN-TOWN RACE:
It covers a distance of 125 miles and passes through eleven towns, with the fastest skaters covering the distance in under seven hours. The ice has only been thick enough for it to have been held thirteen times since it was first established in 1909. The last race, held in 1985, attracted fifteen thousand competitors.

DUTCH SPLIT-PEA SOUP

Erwtensoep, or split-pea soup, dates from at least as far back as the Dutch Golden Age. This rich, wholesome and fortifying dish was a favorite with Dutch sailors as they embarked on, and when they returned from, their long voyages around the world. It was also popular because the ingredients were relatively inexpensive. It is still eaten today and has become one of the Netherlands' national dishes, on a par with *boerenkool* (a slow-cooked dish with kale and potatoes served with sausage) and *hutspot* (a meat stew prepared with the vegetables in season).

INGREDIENTS FOR EIGHT PEOPLE: 1 lb 2 oz split peas, 9 pints water, pinch of sugar, ½ – 1 teaspoon dried savory or 2 teaspoons fresh savory, salt, pepper, 5 medium potatoes, 5 leeks (except for the green tops), 1 head celery...

... 2 large pig's trotters, 8 Frankfurters, 10 oz bacon.

1. Peel and cube the potatoes, then clean and finely chop the leeks and celery.

2. Wash the split peas in cold water, remove any impurities and leave them to soak in 9 pints of water for about 12 hours.

3. Using the water in which they were soaked, bring the peas to the boil.

«MANY FAMILIES IN THE CITY [...] WOULD BUY A COW OR A PIG AND, ONCE THE MONTH OF NOVEMBER WAS PAST, PUT IT TO GOOD USE IN THE FORM OF OFFAL, SAUSAGES AND DRIED MEAT TO SEE THEM THROUGH THE WINTER.» SIMON SCHAMA

4. Add the pig's trotters, bacon and salt. Bring the soup back to the boil and skim. Cover and leave to simmer for 3 hours.

5. Add the potatoes, leeks, celery and Frankfurters. Partially cover and leave to simmer for about 30 minutes, stirring from time to time to prevent the ingredients from sticking.

6. Remove the pig's trotters, bacon and Frankfurters, leaving the pan to simmer on a low heat.

7. Remove the bones from the pig's trotters and dice the bacon and Frankfurters before returning them to the pan.

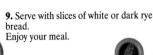

8. Add the savory, some freshly ground black pepper, a pinch of sugar, and salt to taste.

9. Serve with slices of white or dark rye bread.
Enjoy your meal.

Columbus, Struis, Natte and Zatte beers are produced in Amsterdam ▲ *273, 276.*

The famous Edam cheese may be mild (matured for two to three months) or fully mature (matured over a longer period, for up to eighteen months) ■ *26*. The Dutch were the first nation to import tea into Europe. Hollands (juniper-flavored gin), or genever, is distilled from the must of cereals and juniper berries. It is drunk particularly in the *proeflokalen* ● *50* ▲ *240.*

Droste, in Haarlem ◆ *304* , is a famous manufacturer of delicious plain, milk and white chocolate. The Dutch are also very fond of ginger biscuits (below right). Wooden clogs give protection against the cold and damp. They are still worn today by many Dutch farmers and market stall-holders.

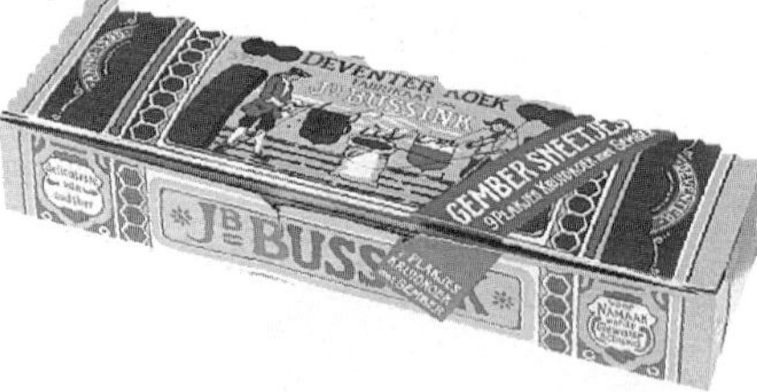

There are several types of *roggebrood* (rye bread). Black rye bread is traditionally eaten with bacon and pea soup ● *62.*

A SELECTION OF DUTCH NEWSPAPERS
De Volkskrant, originally a Catholic paper; *NRC Handelsblad* ▲ *127*, a cultural and scientific paper; *De Telegraaf*, a tabloid paper; *Het Parool*, originally a Resistance paper, now a local daily paper.

At all hours of the day and night you can buy and eat raw herrings, served with gherkins and onions. *Broodje haring* are small herring sandwiches ▲ *145.*

ARCHITECTURE

BRIDGES AND LOCKS, *66*
WINDMILLS, *68*
HOUSE CONSTRUCTION, *70*
GABLED HOUSES, *72*
FROM CLASSICAL MANSION TO ECLECTIC HOUSE, *74*
WAREHOUSES, *76*
RELIGIOUS BUILDINGS, *78*
MONUMENTS OF THE 19TH CENTURY, *80*
FIN-DE-SIÈCLE ARCHITECTURE, *82*
THE AMSTERDAM SCHOOL, *84*
MODERN ARCHITECTURE, *86*

Metal bridge, Amsterdam School.

A great many of Amsterdam's canals were dug to drain and extend the land available for building, as well as to provide an extensive transport system ■ *18*. The number of bridges increased greatly in the 19th and 20th centuries as a result of the growth of the town ● *34* and increasing traffic: there are now more than four hundred. Before 1850 there were three types of bridge in Amsterdam: arched bridges of stone, and fixed and lifting bridges of wood. After 1850 cast iron and steel became the main structural materials, while around 1900 reinforced concrete was combined with brick.

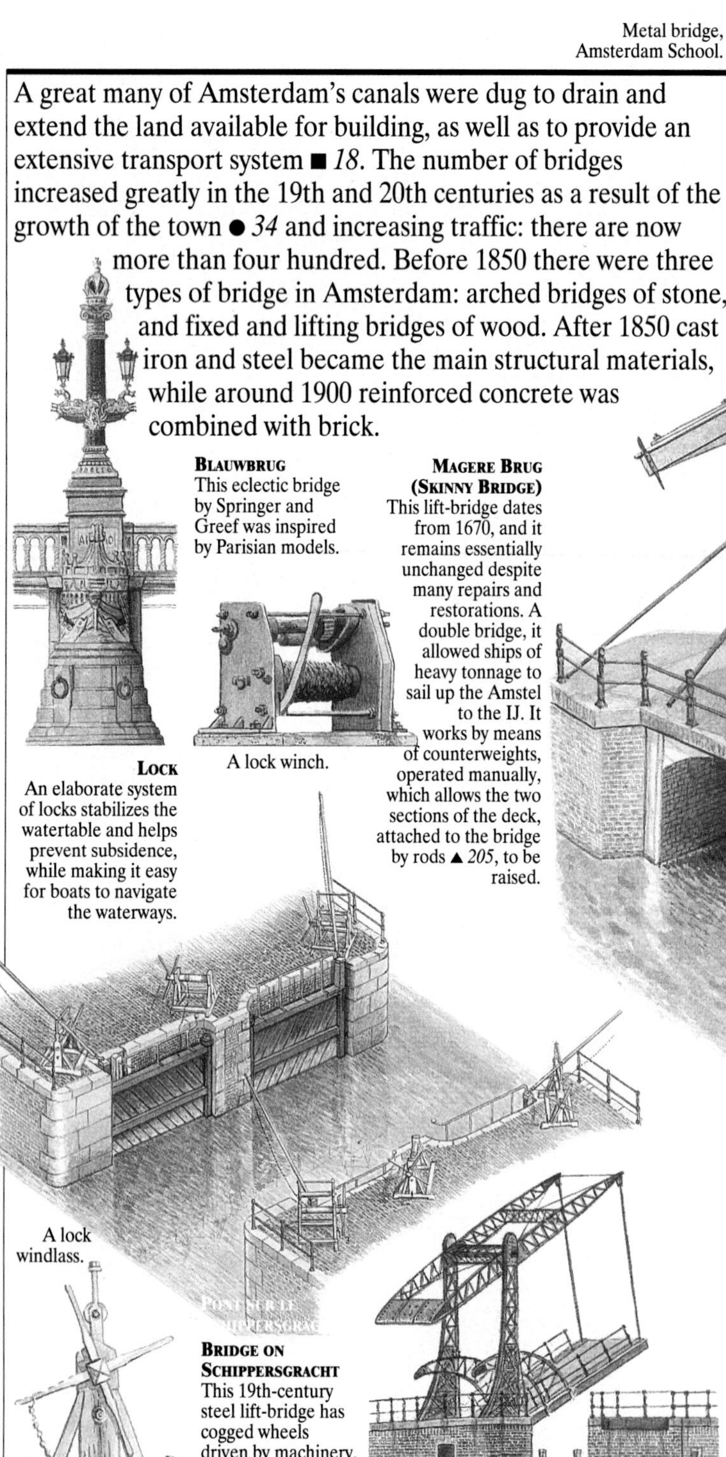

BLAUWBRUG
This eclectic bridge by Springer and Greef was inspired by Parisian models.

MAGERE BRUG (SKINNY BRIDGE)
This lift-bridge dates from 1670, and it remains essentially unchanged despite many repairs and restorations. A double bridge, it allowed ships of heavy tonnage to sail up the Amstel to the IJ. It works by means of counterweights, operated manually, which allows the two sections of the deck, attached to the bridge by rods ▲ *205*, to be raised.

A lock winch.

LOCK
An elaborate system of locks stabilizes the watertable and helps prevent subsidence, while making it easy for boats to navigate the waterways.

A lock windlass.

BRIDGE ON SCHIPPERSGRACHT
This 19th-century steel lift-bridge has cogged wheels driven by machinery.

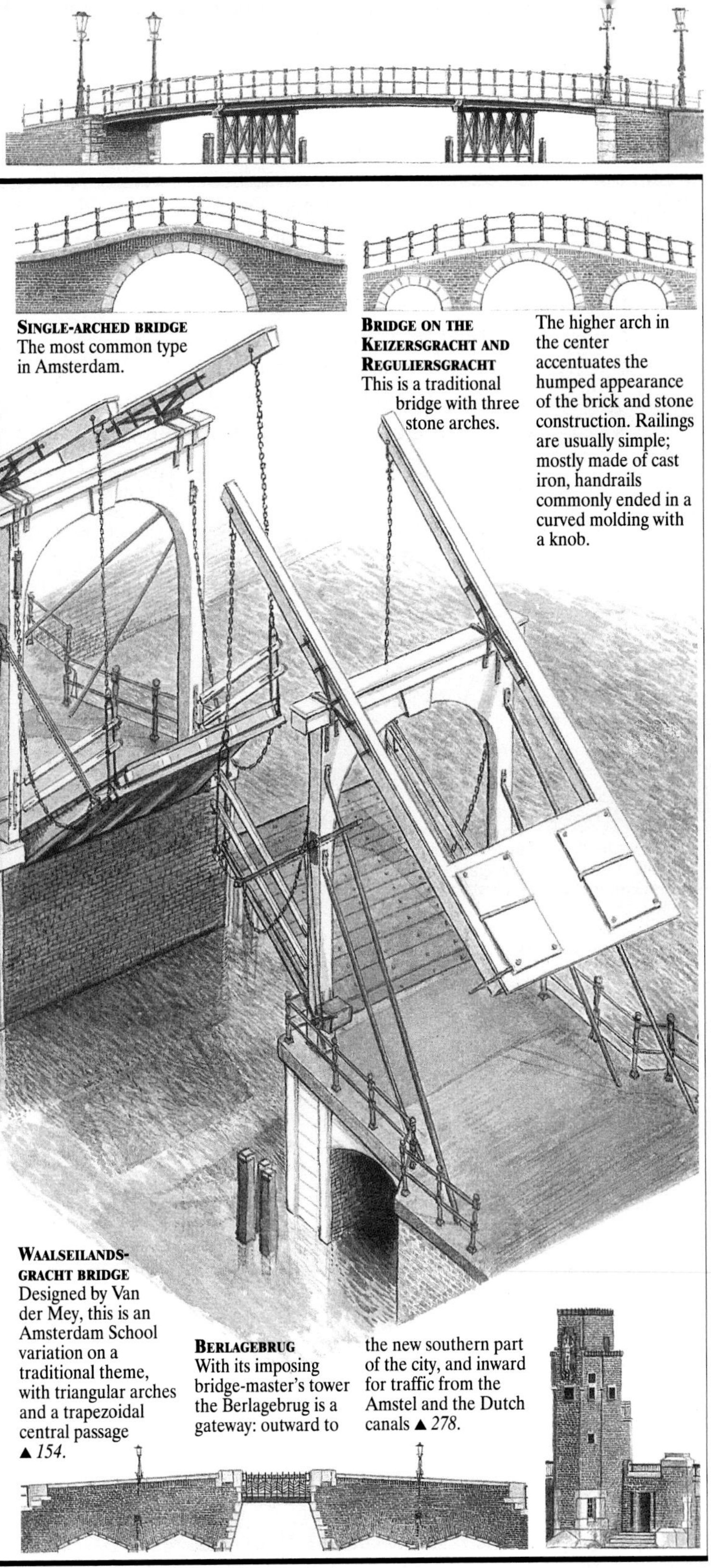

Single-arched bridge
The most common type in Amsterdam.

Bridge on the Keizersgracht and Reguliersgracht
This is a traditional bridge with three stone arches. The higher arch in the center accentuates the humped appearance of the brick and stone construction. Railings are usually simple; mostly made of cast iron, handrails commonly ended in a curved molding with a knob.

Waalseilands-gracht bridge
Designed by Van der Mey, this is an Amsterdam School variation on a traditional theme, with triangular arches and a trapezoidal central passage ▲ *154*.

Berlagebrug
With its imposing bridge-master's tower the Berlagebrug is a gateway: outward to the new southern part of the city, and inward for traffic from the Amstel and the Dutch canals ▲ *278*.

The Tjasker post-mill is the smallest of the land drainage mills.

"WIPMOLEN"
This hollow-post mill is the oldest used for land drainage, raising water through 5 feet.

Once rich in windmills, Amsterdam now has only seven, most having succumbed to increased urbanization. Mills are characterized by their structure, type, function and source of energy, usually wind. Structure is determined by the part of the mill that moves to meet the wind: the cap, the base or the whole structure (a revolving mill with a cap or a revolving base) ◆ *306*.

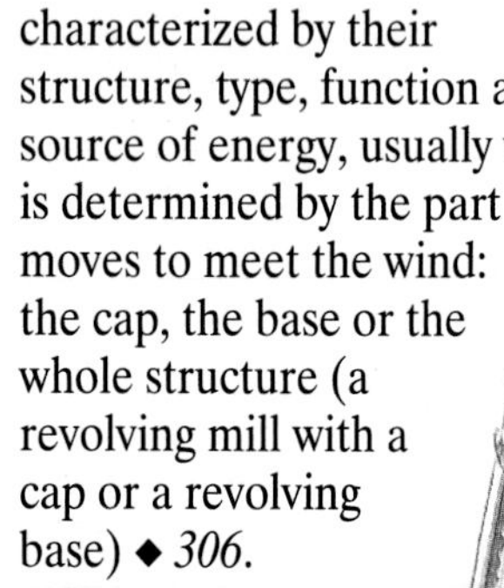

TYPE AND FUNCTION
The external appearance of the mill (post mill, with platform or spider) indicates the type. Used to drain the polders in the 17th century ■ *17*, windmills could also turn wheat into flour, linseed into oil, or be used for paint manufacture or sawing wood.

"PALTROK"
This mill at Zaandam is used for sawing wood. The whole structure, and not just the cap, turns on its base.

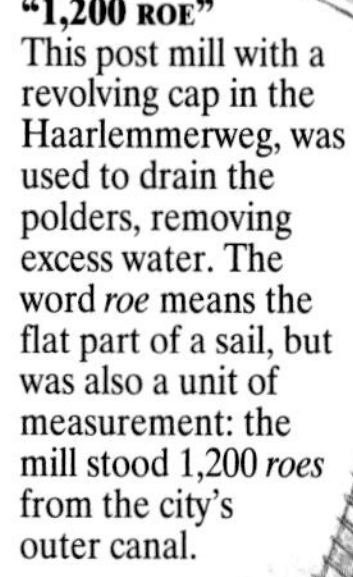
"1,200 ROE"
This post mill with a revolving cap in the Haarlemmerweg, was used to drain the polders, removing excess water. The word *roe* means the flat part of a sail, but was also a unit of measurement: the mill stood 1,200 *roes* from the city's outer canal.

"OLIEMOLEN"
A galleried mill that crushes and presses oil-seeds.

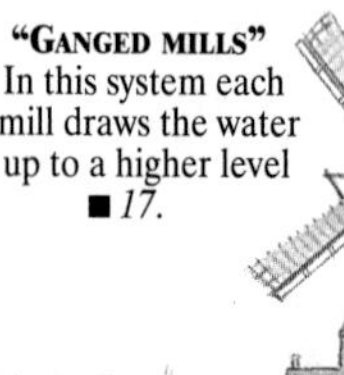
"GANGED MILLS"
In this system each mill draws the water up to a higher level ■ *17*.

THE SAILS
The miller has to set, or reef the sails, to suit the strength of the wind. Systems of self-regulating shutters save him this work.

"DE GOOYER"
This old flour mill (on Funenkade ▲ *273*) with a revolving cap has a more recently added platform (10).

Symmetrical sail

Flemish sail

Shuttered sail

Jib sail

MECHANISM
Built on a brick base (1), the mill consists of an octagonal body, a wooden framework covered with thatch (2), and a cap (3). This is movable by means of the tail-pole (4), a long piece of wood attached to its wooden frame, which holds the windshaft (5). The stocks of the sails (6) are fastened into the cast iron poll-head at its end (7). The vertical shaft, driven by the brake-wheel (8) on the windshaft, transmits power to a pair of millstones (9).

Ball governor for the millstones.

Windlass for moving the cap.

● House construction

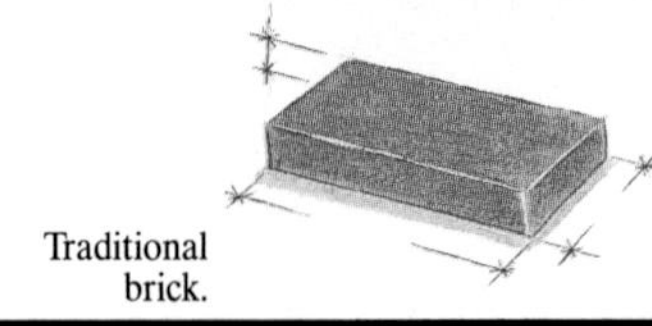

Traditional brick.

First built of wood in the Middle Ages, the Amsterdam canalhouse used stone and, especially, brick after the great fires of the 15th century (first for the side walls, and then for the façade as well). Only the floors and roof structure continued to be made of wood. Houses also grew in height and depth. Although the internal structure changed little during the 17th and 18th centuries, the main façade was influenced by fashion. It is sometimes tilted forward so as to gain extra space, and above all to show off the gable. Façades are most commonly divided into three bays on five floors.

Framework
1. Common rafter
2. Principal rafter

3. Purlin
4. Brace
5. Ridge purlin (see diagram right)
6. Beam
7. Tie beam
8. Stringer
9. Wall plate
10. Joist (below)
The principal rafters (2) support the stringers (8) and the purlins (3), which in turn support the common rafters (1). The joists (10) are connected to the beams (6) by dovetail joints (below).

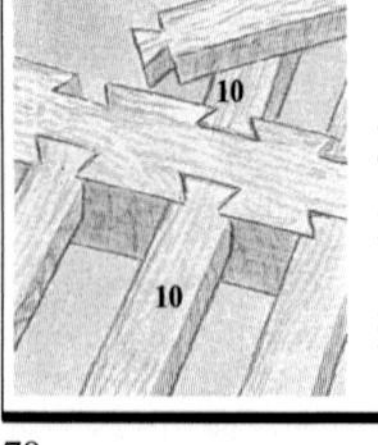

Organization of the house
Houses are traditionally made up of the *voorhuis* (front house) and the *achterhuis* (back annex). Connected by a passageway, they are clearly separated by a walled courtyard (plan opposite, top). The floors consist of a basement, main floor, and then usually two shallower floors and an attic.

Hoist beam
An indispensable fitting in Amsterdam, it is built into the roof timbers, and bears the weight of objects being hoisted to the upper floors.

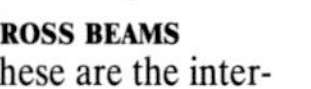

Cross beams
These are the interconnected wooden beams, resting on piles, that provide the foundation for the masonry.

Piles
These long tree trunks were driven 10 to 20 yards into the ground, into the first layer of stable sand ■ *16*.

Basement entrance
This was used by staff and tradesmen. The kitchens were often located in the basement.

The traditional canalhouse plan is made up of the *voorhuis* and the *achterhuis*, which extended the house toward the back.

Roof
Battens nailed to the rafters support the typical Dutch curved tiles.

The tiles are fixed to the battens with pegs.

Walls and ties
The anchors attached to the transoms (above ritght) counter the outward pressure on the walls exerted by the roof structure. Anchors on the façade (right) are embedded in the masonry. The walls are built of brick. A brick laid lengthways is called a stretcher; one laid to show only its end, a header. The most common bond alternated rows of headers with rows of stretchers.

Masonry on the cross beams
The foundation of the wall is constructed of brick on a cross beam, gradually narrowing from a broad base (below).

Windows
From the 18th century onwards casements were replaced by sash windows divided into panes with crossbars.

FROM SIMPLE GABLE TO BELL GABLE
Façades were crowned with gables, which also gave access to the attic. The house on the far left (1) has one of the first brick façades, which replaced the wooden versions: it has a plain gable. Placed over the central bay, neck gables were straight-sided with decorative additions(2 and 3). Bell-gables had curved sides (5 and 6).

Straight-sided, pointed gables in wood or stone existed as early as the Middle Ages. The step gable, also medieval in origin, became popular in the Renaissance. The neck gable, which appeared around 1630, predominated for almost two centuries; supplemented with volutes from 1660, it developed into the bell gable. The gable with cornice and pediment was adopted from 1670, particularly for houses with wide façades ● *74*. At the same time decoration became more sober. By the late 18th century only the classical type with cornice was used, and in Napoleonic times many neck and bell gables were straightened to appear more fashionable.

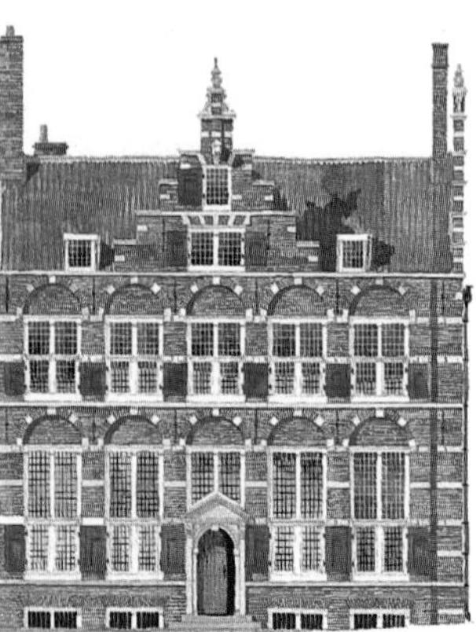

THE HOUSE ON THE THREE CANALS
Standing at the confluence of the canals, the house (1610) has three step gables built in the sober style of the Dutch Renaissance ▲ *142*.

EAST INDIA HOUSE
This building attributed to Hendrick de Keyser at no. 24 Oude Hoogstraat dates from 1605. Its façade is richly decorated. The use of red brick for the walls and of yellow sandstone for the decoration is typical of the work of this great architect ▲ *156*. The very tall gable, with its windowframes in volutes and topmost balustrade, is exceptionally well designed ▲ *145*.

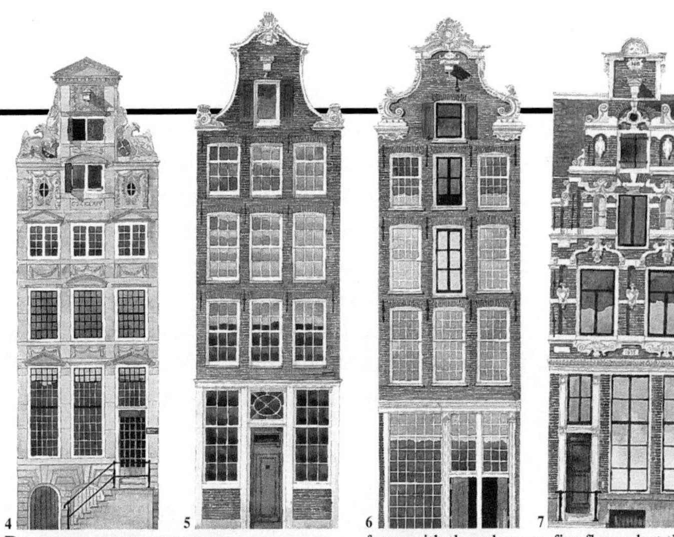

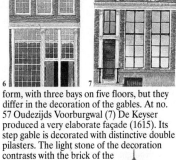

Different styles of gables
The House of Eagles (4) at no. 91 Rokin is the work of architect Philip Vingboons (1608–75), who, like his brother Justus, specialized in designing houses for Amsterdam. The façade is in stone ▲ *140*. Nos. 60 and 36 Leliegracht (5 and 6) ▲ *172* have bell gables. Both are built in the classic form, with three bays on five floors, but they differ in the decoration of the gables. At no. 57 Oudezijds Voorburgwal (7) De Keyser produced a very elaborate façade (1615). Its step gable is decorated with distinctive double pilasters. The light stone of the decoration contrasts with the brick of the rest of the façade.

The House of Heads This double house (1662) is the work of Pieter de Keyser, who was inspired by the Bartolotti House ▲ *170* built five years earlier by his father Hendrick. Its large gable is ornamented by columns and obelisks ▲ *118, 173*.

Begijnhof house
No. 34 is one of the last two wooden houses in Amsterdam, which are reverently preserved. All the houses in the Begijnhof were built around the same time (1460), but with the exception of this one they were rebuilt in the 17th and 18th centuries. All except no. 34 now have brick façades, while the party walls were rebuilt in stone to halt the spread of fires ▲ *122*.

● From classical mansion to eclectic house

"The Art of Building" Cartouche from above the door of no. 390 Singel.

Door (1740) The transom window with its exaggerated tracery is characteristic of the Rococo style (no. 284 Nieuwezijds Voorburgwal).

Buildings with more than three bays and a cornice with or without pediment represent another type of Amsterdam house, from the 17th century. The most important variations are represented by Jacob van Campen's classicism, Adriaan Dortsman's sobriety, and the French influence of the 18th century, seen in attic stories with or without ornamented cornices. The next century saw the triumph of eclecticism.

Trippenhuis Eight fluted Corinthian pilasters support the entablature and pediment of this imposing stone house ▲ *151*.

Narrow house This simple two-bay house at no. 323 Herengracht has an attic floor framed by two brackets. The sculpture contrasts with the austerity of the façade.

Jacob's Ladder This elegant mansion (Jacob's Ladder) by P. Vingboons ● *73*, finished in 1655, has five bays. The center of the façade is ornamented with Doric and Ionic pilasters, and topped by a pediment with an *oeil-de-boeuf* window surrounded by festoons. The perfect symmetry of the design is strongly characteristic of Vingboons' work (no. 316 Oudezijds Voorburgwal).

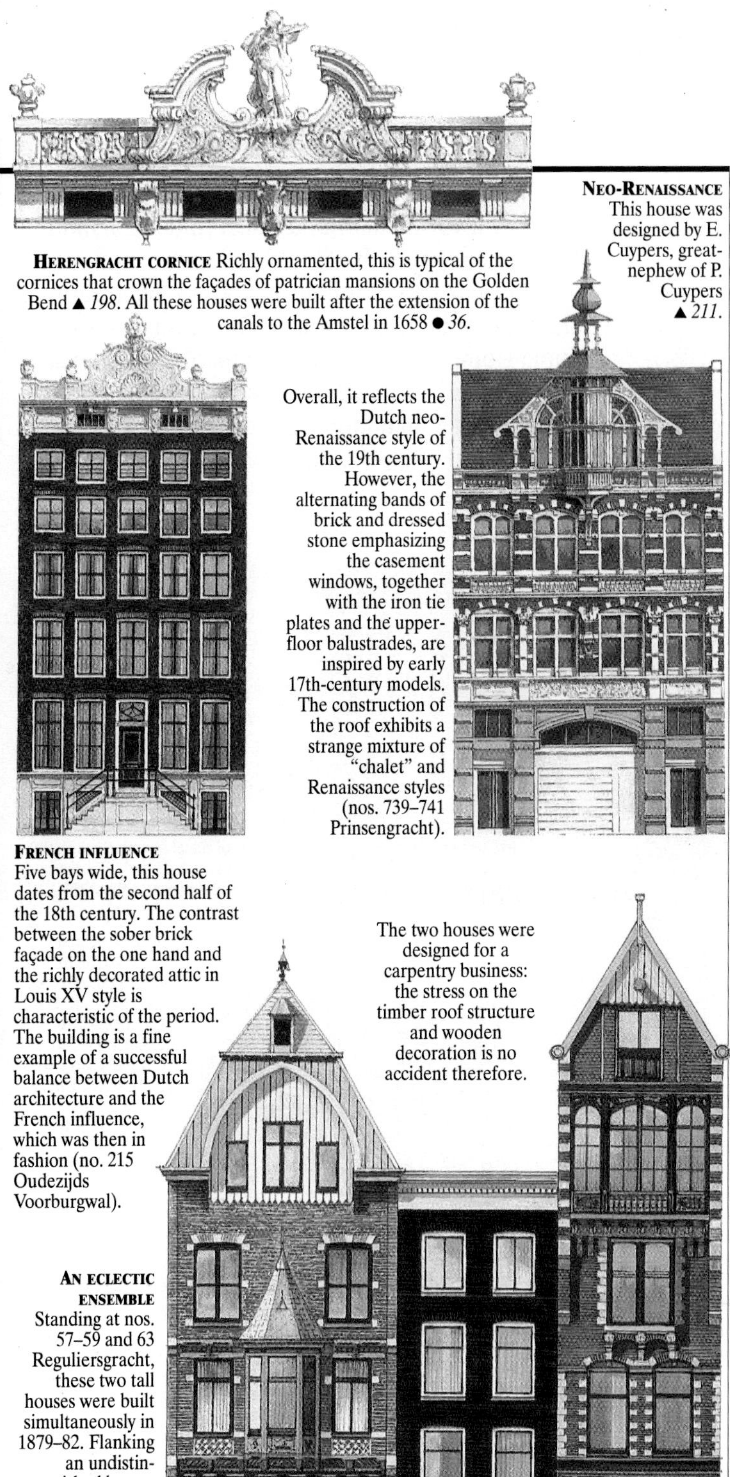

Herengracht cornice Richly ornamented, this is typical of the cornices that crown the façades of patrician mansions on the Golden Bend ▲ *198*. All these houses were built after the extension of the canals to the Amstel in 1658 ● *36*.

Neo-Renaissance This house was designed by E. Cuypers, great-nephew of P. Cuypers ▲ *211*.

Overall, it reflects the Dutch neo-Renaissance style of the 19th century. However, the alternating bands of brick and dressed stone emphasizing the casement windows, together with the iron tie plates and the upper-floor balustrades, are inspired by early 17th-century models. The construction of the roof exhibits a strange mixture of "chalet" and Renaissance styles (nos. 739–741 Prinsengracht).

French influence Five bays wide, this house dates from the second half of the 18th century. The contrast between the sober brick façade on the one hand and the richly decorated attic in Louis XV style is characteristic of the period. The building is a fine example of a successful balance between Dutch architecture and the French influence, which was then in fashion (no. 215 Oudezijds Voorburgwal).

The two houses were designed for a carpentry business: the stress on the timber roof structure and wooden decoration is no accident therefore.

An eclectic ensemble Standing at nos. 57–59 and 63 Reguliersgracht, these two tall houses were built simultaneously in 1879–82. Flanking an undistinguished house, they exhibit a highly fantastical neo-medieval style ▲ *203*.

By the end of the 16th century Amsterdam was a rich city involved in international trade ● *30*, and today it has a wealth of buildings once used for storing goods and for housing the administration of the great trading companies (Dutch East and West India Companies). The appearance of warehouses was usually dictated by the civil architecture of the same period, but they tend to be marked in addition by solidity and sobriety, with arched windows and brightly colored wooden shutters.

NATIONAL NAVAL STOREHOUSE
Near the National Arsenal stands this square building with an internal courtyard, built in 1656 by Daniel Stalpaert. Originally the central stores of the republican Navy, it was restored to its full splendor after the fire of 1791. The two projections in the center, as well as the projecting dormers, were added later. The plaster is decorated with false joint-lines. The simple pediments and the rhythmical composition of doors and windows make this a building of great sobriety ▲ *269*.

CONVERSION
Today more and more warehouses are being converted into apartments ▲ *175*.

MARITIME MUSEUM With the transfer of naval installations to the North Sea coast, in the 20th century the Arsenal fell into disuse. Restored from 1974 to 1981, the building now houses the Maritime Museum.

CITY PEAT HOUSES
The two straight gables separated by a trapezoidal gable, in brick edged with dressed stone, are in the Renaissance style (1610). Nearby peat for heating was distributed to the city's paupers.

«MANY BUILDINGS HAVE BEEN GIVEN A NEW FUNCTION: THIS IS THE CASE FOR MOST OF THE WAREHOUSES, WHICH HAVE BEEN CONVERTED INTO APARTMENT BUILDINGS [...] WHILE LOSING NOTHING OF THEIR CHARACTERISTIC APPEARANCE, WITH THEIR HEAVY WOODEN SHUTTERS.» MAX VAN ROOY

DOCKERS' GUILD
This cartouche can today be found in the courtyard of the Historical Museum.

PULLEY AND WINDLASS
The system for lifting loads up to each floor of a warehouse is remarkable for its efficiency and simplicity of design. The rope outside is fastened to the axle of a large wooden wheel, which drives the mechanism.

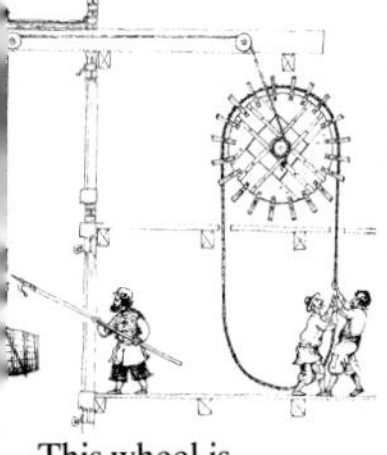

This wheel is provided with forked cogs through which a ring of rope passes, and is operated from the floor beneath by pulling on the rope. It obeys the principle of mechanical advantage, which allows a small number of men to lift heavy loads. On each floor a roller fixed to the lintel of the window helps the load to slide past if it catches in the opening while being hoisted.

Dutch West India Company.

Krom Boomssloot ▲ *155*.

Greenland warehouse ▲ *174*.

DECORATION
Small works of art, these zinc canopies serve both as a decorative element on the façade and as protection for the hoist beam. Façades are differentiated by their use of dressed stone alongside the brick, and by stone-carved volutes or spirals, which decorate the sides of the gables.

Dominated initially by Northern Gothic, Amsterdam chose a new style and form of building after the adoption of Protestantism in 1578 ● *29*. After the Zuiderkerk, a pseudo-basilica with a triple-nave, and then the Noorderkerk, with its centralized plan in the shape of a Greek cross, Hendrick de Keyser ▲ *156* created a combination of these two plans in the Westerkerk. The city's synagogues were similarly well designed.

NIEUWEKERK
Unlike the Oudekerk ▲ *134* this transept basilica (late 14th-century) in the Late Gothic style was built on a regular symmetrical plan. It offers a contrast between the central nave, with its wooden barrel vault, and the side aisles, with their rib vaults in stone. The main spire, by Jacob van Campen, remains unfinished ▲ *131*.

NOORDERKERK
The sober façades display astonishing balustraded gables.

Built in 1620, the Noorderkerk is the most highly developed example of the central plan adopted by De Keyser ▲ *239*.

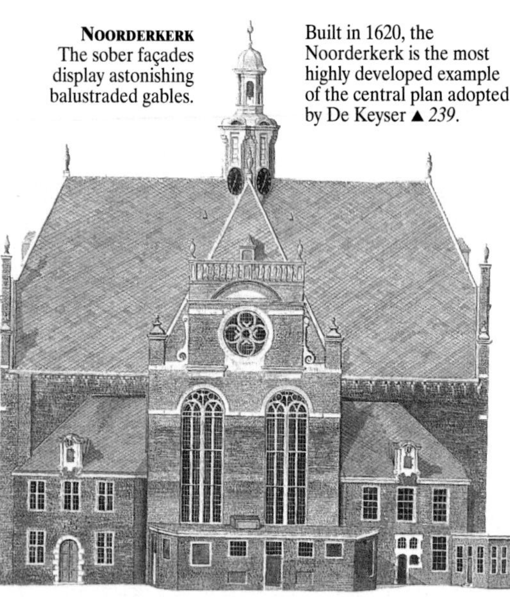

THE 19TH-CENTURY CATHOLIC RENAISSANCE
Catholic churches, tolerated after 1578, were forbidden to display any distinctive signs: they remained semi-clandestine ● *39*. It was not until the 19th century that Catholics were permitted to build official churches, and the style they adopted was mostly neo-Gothic, though a Classical style, inspired by Antiquity and the Renaissance, was also popular.

CHURCH OF SAINT ANTHONY OF PADUA ("MOSES AND AARON")
Designed in the classical style, it has wooden towers modeled on those of Saint-Sulpice in Paris ▲ *159*.

It was built between 1837 and 1841 by the architect T.F. Suys.

KRIJTBERG CHURCH
Neo-Gothic (1881), at no. 446 Singel.

PORTUGUESE SYNAGOGUE
The division of the façades with pilasters and tall arched windows is typical of the style of Elias Bouwman, who in this case created a building on a monumental scale (1675) ▲ *158*.

SAINT NICHOLAS CHURCH
Baroque and neo-Renaissance elements combine here(1887) ▲ *137*.

WESTERKERK
The ingenious design, juxtaposing two Greek crosses, combines a centralized plan, better suited to Protestant worship, with the volume of the Gothic nave (1620). The style is not without some Mannerist elements ▲ *179*. Its 280-ft spire (1638) bears the imperial crown from the city's arms.

VONDELKERK
Cuypers' masterpiece (1880) combines the longitudinal axis of the basilica with an octagonal structure around the transept crossing. This plan lends the exterior a centralized appearance which results directly from the structure ▲ *233*. The tower was rebuilt after a fire in 1904.

ZUIDERKERK ● *94*
This church inspired the style of the Westerkerk.

The raised arms of the Westerkerk's two transepts are probably a modification on De Keyser's original conception, but do nothing to destroy the elegant and gentle lines of the design.

Detail of the Zuiderkerk spire (1603) ▲ *156*.

Central Station: detail of one of the pavilions.

In the 19th and 20th centuries Amsterdam grew significantly, extending the territorial responsibilities of the city council ● 36. Transport, commerce and the arts thus required a new architecture. This led to considerable changes in the city, especially in the late 19th century: between 1885, with the inauguration of the Rijksmuseum, and 1903, the year that marked the opening of Berlage's Exchange, new public buildings multiplied.

The Central Station stands on an artificial island. Its structure is very similar to that of the Rijksmuseum.

CONCERTGEBOUW The style is a compromise between neo-Dutch Renaissance elements (windowframes, blocks and bands of dressed stone) and a more international neo-classicism (Corinthian colonnade with pediment). The whole (1888), by A. L. van Gendt, is nonetheless well-balanced, in spite of the modern entrances opened at the side ▲ *216*.

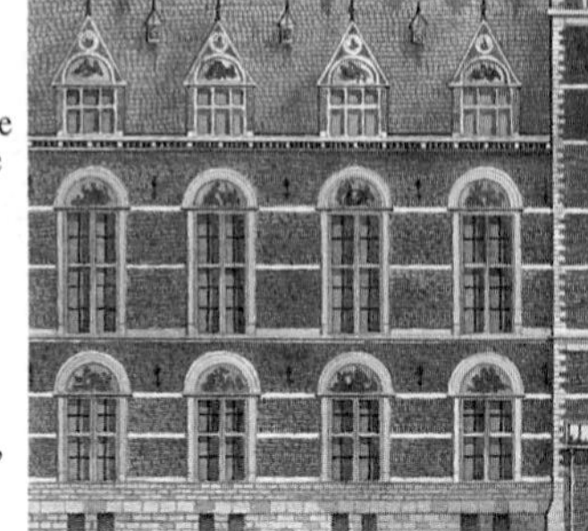

RIJKSMUSEUM Protestants found the design too Gothic, and therefore too Catholic for a national museum. So Cuypers (himself a Catholic) changed the ogives of the arcade into semicircular arches. The building (1885) ▲ *212* remains, like the Central Station, a mixture of Gothic and Renaissance elements.

Old Central Post Office (1889) C. H. Peters, an architect of public buildings, designed the structure with pilasters, stringcourses in stone, sculpture and ornaments; it draws its inspiration directly from the Dutch Renaissance, despite its Gothic outline. The little round-arched galleries in the gables are of Romanesque influence ▲ *130*.

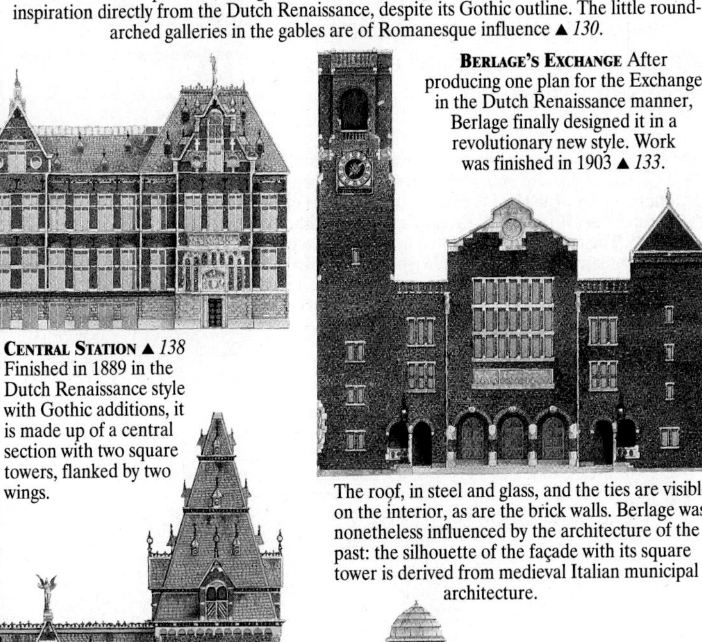

Berlage's Exchange After producing one plan for the Exchange in the Dutch Renaissance manner, Berlage finally designed it in a revolutionary new style. Work was finished in 1903 ▲ *133*.

Central Station ▲ *138*
Finished in 1889 in the Dutch Renaissance style with Gothic additions, it is made up of a central section with two square towers, flanked by two wings.

The roof, in steel and glass, and the ties are visible on the interior, as are the brick walls. Berlage was nonetheless influenced by the architecture of the past: the silhouette of the façade with its square tower is derived from medieval Italian municipal architecture.

A.N.D.B. building In this case Berlage left the brick bare both inside and out. Here again the Italian influence is clear ▲ *266*.

Detail of the windows in the façade of the "American" Hotel, surrounded by pinnacles.

Continuing the architectural renewal of Amsterdam begun in the 19th century with the construction of the great public buildings ● *80*, turn-of-the-century architects displayed much inventiveness and imagination under the influence of such diverse intellects as Cuypers and Berlage. Major buildings were designed combining elements of Art Deco, Art Nouveau and the Amsterdam School ● *84*, and many bear witness to a taste for experimentation, which led to distinctive and often highly successful results.

DE UTRECHT Standing at nos. 28–30 Damrak, this building is one of the rare examples of American influence in Amsterdam. Designed by J.F. Staal (future architect of the "Skyscraper" ▲ *280*) and A. J. Kropholler, it was finished in 1905. The narrow bays separated by flattened columns accentuate the impression of height, as the building is fairly narrow. The sculptures above the doors are by Mendes da Costa.

"AMERICAN" HOTEL
In this building on the Leidseplein, built 1898–1902, W. Kromhout combined Berlage's concerns (aspect and structure) with Art Deco elements. This hotel was a source of inspiration for the Amsterdam School and for Functionalism. The gallery and arcade of the façade evoke the Exchange and foreshadow the work of the Amsterdam School ▲ *191*.

E.H.L.B. BUILDING Constructed in 1905 on the corner of the Keizersgracht and the Leliegracht, this was originally the offices of an insurance company. Van Arkel designed an Art Nouveau ensemble, the imposing façade of which, with its bow windows, is decorated with turrets and mosaics. The entrance hall is also highly decorated ▲ *172*.

TUSCHINSKI CINEMA This cinema, dating from 1918–21, is decorated in an exuberant Art Deco style with stained glass windows, turrets and lamps ▲ *208*.

ASSCHER Influenced by Berlage, G. van Arkel designed this diamond-cutting house with Art Nouveau elements in 1907 (Institute of Technology, no. 127 Tolstraat).

ABN-AMRO BANK Built between 1919 and 1926 from plans by De Bazel, the polychrome façade of alternating granite and syenite stands ten floors high and stretches for 330 feet. The building stands out with its highly geometric composition and rhythmical decoration (nos. 66–80 Vijzelstraat).

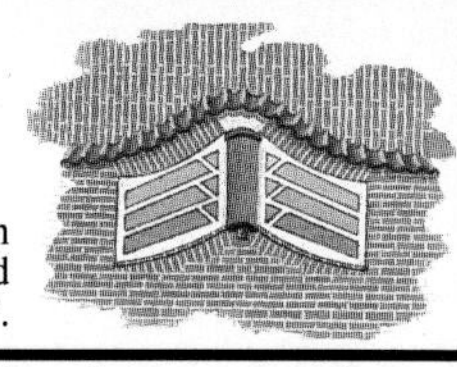

Window detail from the inner courtyard of the "Ship".

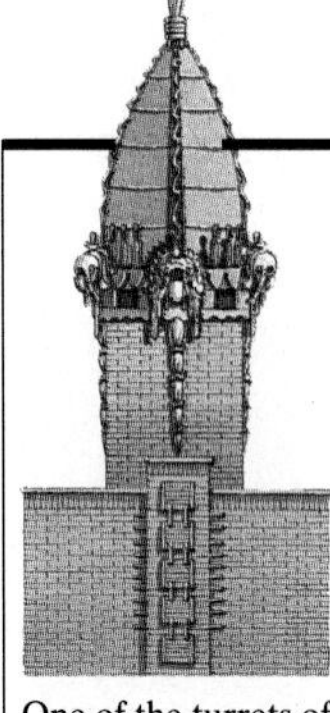

One of the turrets of the Scheepvaarthuis, covered in zinc and lead.

Marked by expressionist tendencies, a taste for ornament and the strict use of brick, the style of the Amsterdam School (1912–40) reached its zenith around 1920. At the same time the Functionalist movement heralded by Berlage ● *82* advocated the use of glass, concrete and steel. The city's architectural commission preferred the Amsterdam School, which left its mark on the south of the city (even though it was planned by Berlage ● *37*) and the west. The Functionalists came into their own after the war.

The staircases were set in vertical cylinders covered with tiles. Windows, doors and stair rails are decorated with small imaginative details.

SPAARNDAMMERPLANTSOEN

Designed by Michel de Klerk, this social housing block, financed by the Eigen Haard Association, was built between 1913 and 1915; it was one of the first large buildings in which brick played a decorative role ▲ *256*.

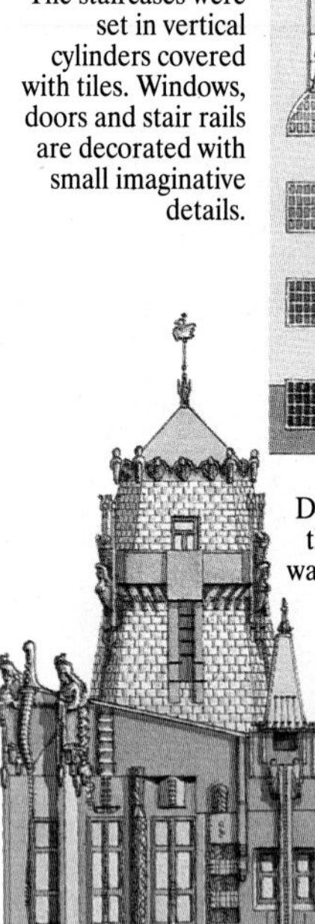

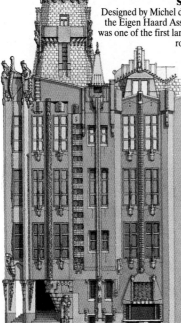

SCHEEPVAARTHUIS

In the Maritime House J.M. van der Mey created the first Amsterdam School building (1911–16). It is in a highly expressionist style, which accentuates the verticality of the narrow bays. The structure is crowned by a pentagonal lantern. The many sculptures represent the oceans and their heroes, a reference to the Netherlands as a nation of seafarers. The Scheepvaarthuis housed the offices of a firm of ship-owners ▲ *154*.

A small window on one corner of the "Ship".

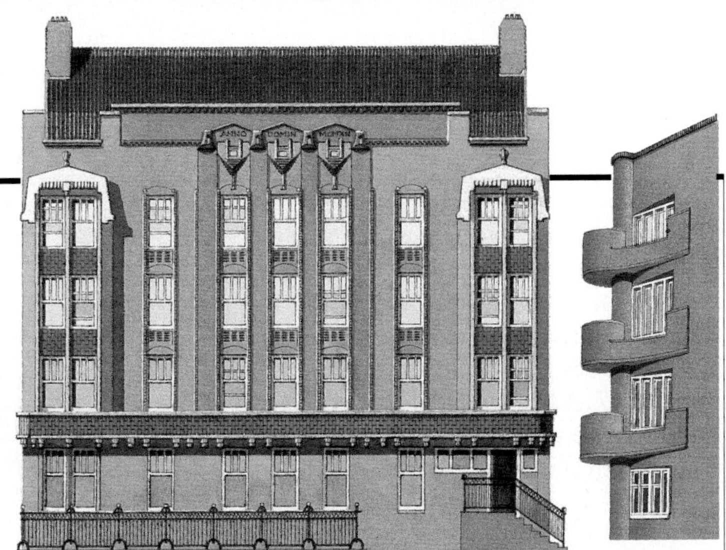

Hillehuis Built in 1911–12 on the Vermeerplein, near the museums, this was the first important building by Michel de Klerk. Its lines are boldly vertical, but although there are some decorative motifs, it still lacks the expressive quality that is so characteristic of the Amsterdam School.

Holendrechtstraat Many works of the Amsterdam School incorporate sinuous forms in brick, like these balconies.

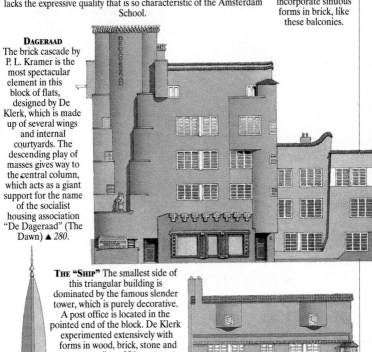

Dageraad The brick cascade by P. L. Kramer is the most spectacular element in this block of flats, designed by De Klerk, which is made up of several wings and internal courtyards. The descending play of masses gives way to the central column, which acts as a giant support for the name of the socialist housing association "De Dageraad" (The Dawn) ▲ *280*.

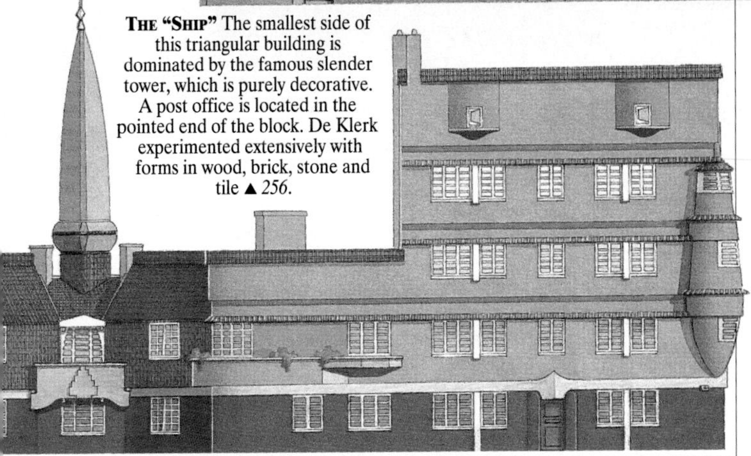

The "Ship" The smallest side of this triangular building is dominated by the famous slender tower, which is purely decorative. A post office is located in the pointed end of the block. De Klerk experimented extensively with forms in wood, brick, stone and tile ▲ *256*.

Modern architecture

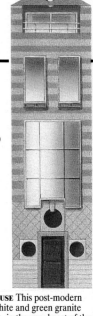

Post-war architecture is characterized above all by an opposition between the traditionalists of the Delft School and the Functionalists. When the latter began to make an impression, a counter-tendency appeared that was opposed to large-scale designs inspired by the past. A. van Eyck ▲ *267* and H. Hertzberger were its main leaders. Since then architects have been free, each in their own way, to develop their style and innovative ideas.

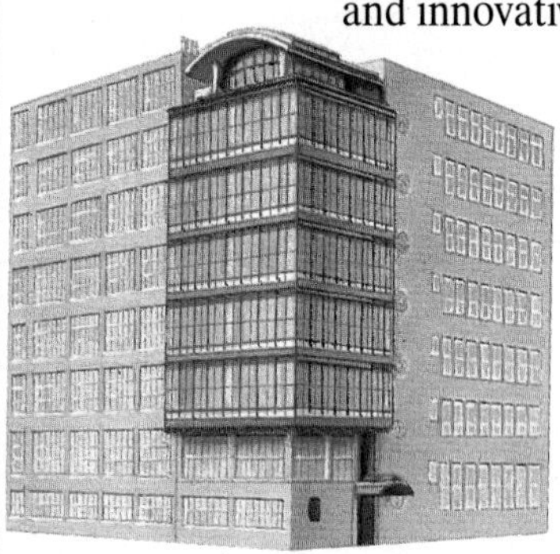

Modern gable house This post-modern façade in brown, white and green granite stands at no. 99 Rokin, in the very heart of the city ▲ *140*. Built in 1990, the building has the traditional narrow façade of the Amsterdam house ● *70* and respects the lines of its neighbors. At the top the stylized triangular form evokes the traditional gable.

Joodse Invalide Continuing with the style of the "Skyscraper" ▲ *280*, the very opposite of the Amsterdam School, this building, with its large glass surfaces, was designed in 1935 by J. F. Staal. The corner of the building is crowned by a rounded roof, which was very unusual for its time: the little columns seem to be its only supports.

NMB Bank
Finished in 1987, the head office of this bank, with its irregular plan, thoughtfully combines interior layout and external forms to provide a more comfortable environment for the people working there.

West Warehouse On the eastern islands ▲ *272* there are recent examples of social housing projects financed by non-profit-making associations. Built in Cruquiusweg in 1992, this building partly overhangs the canal, creating a linear play with the water surface.

AMSTERDAM AS SEEN BY PAINTERS

In the 17th century the Amsterdam bourgeoisie commissioned the painters of urban landscapes (a school first established in Delft primarily by Vermeer and Pieter de Hooch) to produce countless views of the port on the river IJ, to which they owed their wealth. Ludolf Backhuysen (1631–1708), who excelled in this field, painted *The Port of Amsterdam* (2) in 1674 ▲ *260*. Backhuysen's spectacle of a busy, thriving port contrasts with the drawing *View of the IJ and of Amsterdam* by Lambert Doomer (1624–1700), a pupil of Rembrandt, which depicts a scene of heavenly tranquillity (3). The master himself no doubt spent hours walking around Amsterdam, as we can see from his many drawings and sketches of the suburbs, nearby villages and surrounding countryside. His ink drawing *View of Amsterdam* (1641) (1) shows the IJ in the foreground to the left ▲ *218*. In the 19th century George Breitner (1857–1923) developed an Impressionist style with bold forms, broad, sweeping brushstrokes and lack of detail. *The Dam by Night* (previous page) is a fine example of his work ▲ *258*.

A native of Haarlem, Geritt Berckheyde (1638–98) painted *The Flower Market* (2) between 1670 and 1675. To the left is the Nieuwezijds Voorburgwal canal, which has since been filled in and made into a street. The rear of the Royal Palace on Dam Square can be seen on the right. The composition is

governed by the interplay of sunlight and shadow. Jan Wynants (c. 1630–84) was a landscape artist of the Haarlem school. His *View of the Herengracht* (1) is the only urban scene he painted. Wynants focuses on the canal itself ▲ *194*, rather than the neighboring houses. Painted in 1633, *Annual Procession of Lepers on Copper Monday* (3), an imposing canvas by Adriaan van Nieulandt (1587–1638), depicts the hustle and bustle of the Dam on this holiday ▲ *128*.

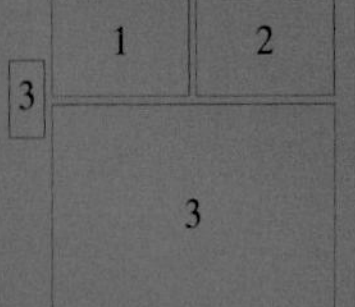

«AMSTERDAM IS A REMARKABLE CITY, BUSTLING AND UNPREDICTABLE; I HOPE TO RETURN THERE.»

CAMILLE PISSARRO

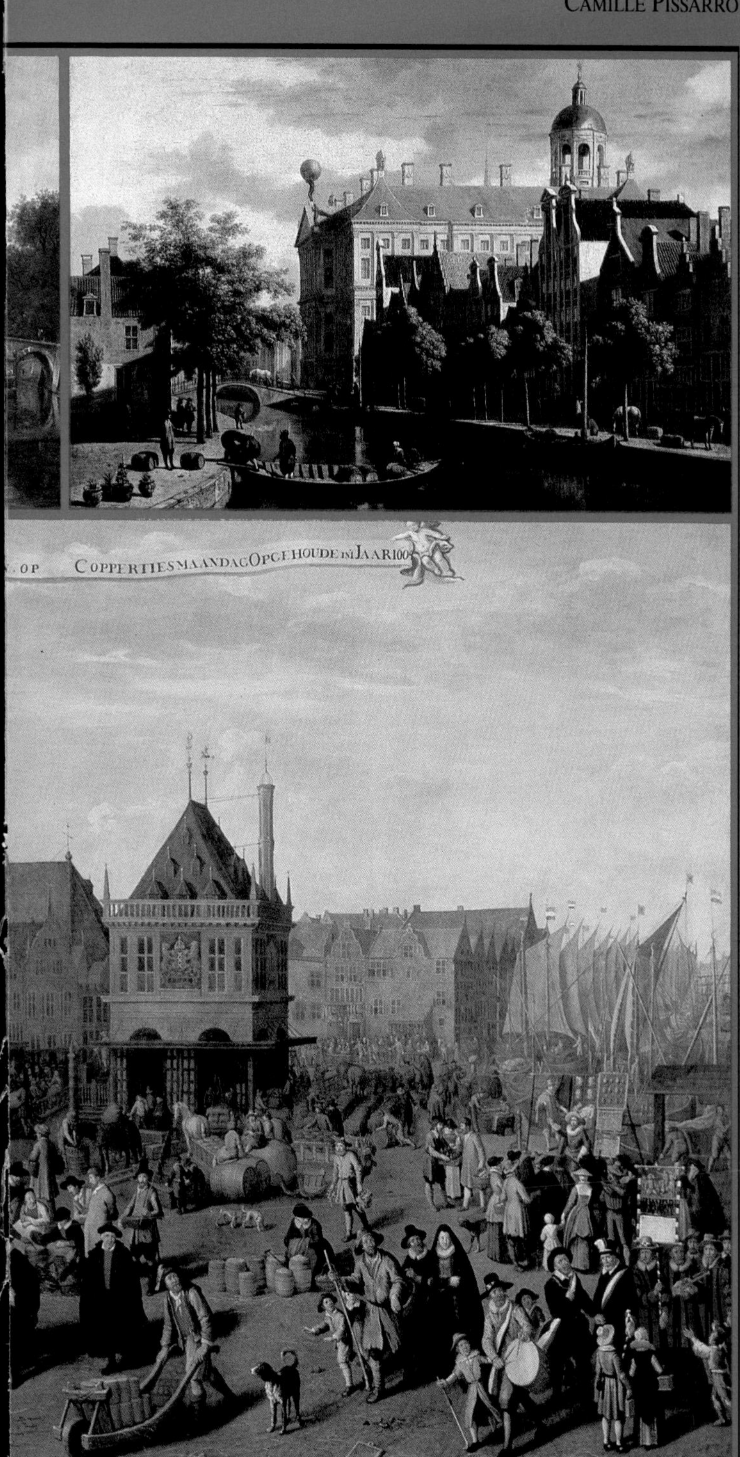

«THE DUTCH SCHOOL CAN FLOURISH AND WORK FOR A WHOLE CENTURY; HOLLAND IS CAPABLE OF SATISFYING THE INSATIABLE CURIOSITY OF HER PAINTERS, FOR AS LONG AS THEIR LOVE OF HER REMAINS ALIVE.» EUGÈNE FROMENTIN

In 1945 Karel Appel (born 1921, above) painted this broad view of the IJ (1) in a style which is very different from the one he later developed in the CoBrA movement ▲ *230*. An excellent painter of ports, ships, the sea and naval battles, Willem van de Velde the Younger (1633–1707) settled in London in 1672 as a court painter. His 1686 painting of *The Port of Amsterdam* (2) suggests great depth through its brightly lit sky filled with scudding clouds.

The Herring Tower (3) by Abraham Storck (1635–1704) presents another aspect of the port, with the tower on the right (later destroyed) and, in the background, the Admiralty building of the Dutch East India Company ▲ *146*.

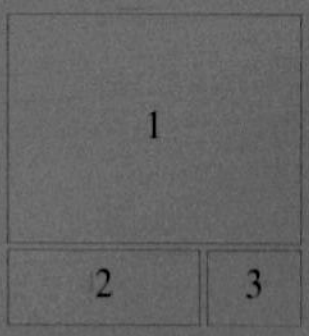

1

2 3

In the 19th century many foreign artists, especially French, visited Amsterdam. They included Boudin, Daubigny, Manet and Pissarro. Another visitor was Claude Monet, who came to Holland at least twice, some time around 1870, in search of subjects for his work. There are two versions of his painting *The Zuiderkerk in Amsterdam seen from the Groenburgwal* (1871–4). The springtime version, below, is dominated by blues, while the autumn one favors ochers and browns.

In the 17th century Gabriel Metsu (1629–67) was considered a highly talented painter. At that time the elegance of his work, the rich and harmonious palette and graceful forms were greatly valued. Today he is a somewhat neglected artist. His most famous work is *The Vegetable Market* (c. 1660), which is set on the Singel. The painter's love of detail is clearly evident.

AMSTERDAM AS SEEN BY WRITERS

A FREE AND OPEN CITY

A HAVEN FOR PHILOSOPHERS

With the Golden Age Amsterdam acquired a reputation as the literary capital of Europe. It was in this thriving creative atmosphere that Bayle, Descartes, Voltaire, Montesquieu, Rousseau and Diderot bypassed French censorship by sending their manuscripts to be printed in Amsterdam. On May 5, 1631, René Descartes (1596–1650), the French philosopher, wrote to his friend Jean-Louis Guez de Balzac.

❝In this big city where I find myself at present, where there is no man, except myself, who is not a trader, everyone is so obsessed with profit that I could spend the rest of my life here without ever being noticed by anybody. I stroll about every day among the noise and bustle of a great nation, with as much freedom and tranquillity as you have among your avenues of trees, and I pay as little attention to the men I see, as I would to the trees in your forests or the animals that graze there. The commotion of their comings and goings does not disturb my train of thought any more than would the babbling of some stream. And if I should happen to reflect on their activities, I derive the same pleasure as you would gain from watching the peasants tilling their fields. For I see that all their efforts serve to embellish my place of residence, and to ensure that I lack for nothing. For if there is pleasure in watching the fruit ripening in your orchards, and to be surrounded by abundance up to your ears, do you not think that there is equal enjoyment in watching ships entering port laden with produce from the Indies and all that is rare in Europe? Where else in the world are all life's commodities and all conceivable curiosities to be found as easily as here? In what other country can one find such absolute freedom, can one sleep more peacefully, where there are always armies standing ready to defend us; where are poisoning, betrayal and calumny less frequent, and where can be found more of what remains the innocence of our ancestors?❞

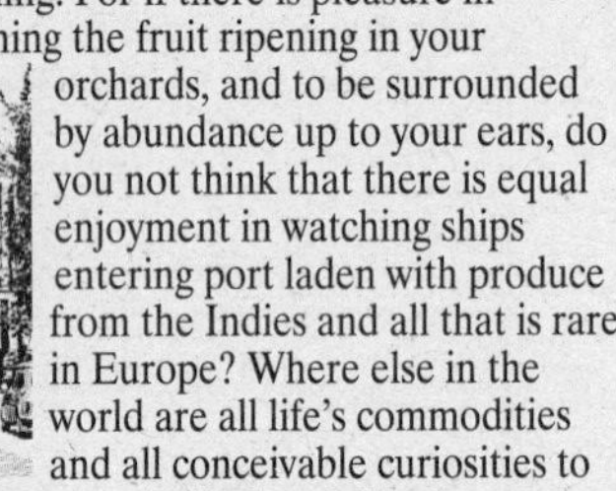

RENÉ DESCARTES, *CORRESPONDENCE*, 1631

THE FRUITS OF FREEDOM

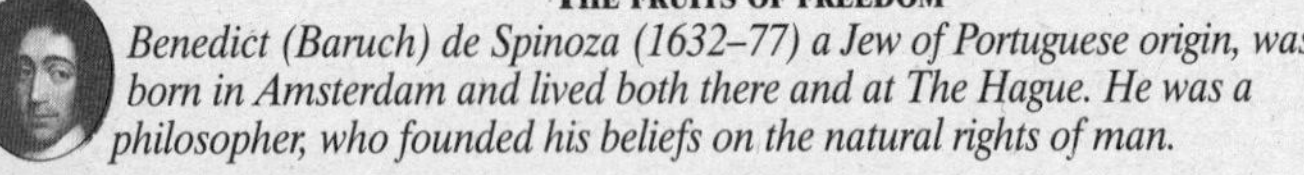

Benedict (Baruch) de Spinoza (1632–77) a Jew of Portuguese origin, was born in Amsterdam and lived both there and at The Hague. He was a philosopher, who founded his beliefs on the natural rights of man.

❝In order to prove that from such freedom no inconvenience arises, which cannot easily be checked by the exercise of the sovereign power, and that men's actions can easily be kept in bounds, though their opinions be at open variance, it will be well to cite an example. Such an one is not very far to seek. The city of Amsterdam reaps the fruit of this freedom in its own great prosperity and in the admiration of all other people. For in this most flourishing state, and most splendid city, men of every nation and religion live together in the greatest harmony, and ask no questions before trusting their goods to a fellow-citizen, save whether he be rich or poor, and whether he generally acts honestly, or the reverse. His religion and sect is considered of no importance: for it has no effect before the judges in gaining or losing a cause, and there is no sect so despised that its followers, provided that they harm no one, pay every man his due, and live uprightly, are deprived of the protection of the magisterial authority.❞

SPINOZA, *TRACTATUS THEOLOGICO-POLITICUS*, 1670

Protection for the poor

John Evelyn (1620–1706) spent much time traveling in Europe in his twenties and kept a diary recording his impressions. The following extract, from 1641, describes some ways in which shelter was provided in Amsterdam for those who could not take care of themselves.

“As we returned we stepp’d in to see the Spin-house, a kind of Bridewell, where incorrigible and lewd women are kept in discipline and labour, but all neate.–We were shew’d an Hospital for poor travellers and pilgrimes, built by Queene Eliz. of England; and another maintained by the Citty. . . . I went to see the Weese-house, a foundation like our Charterhouse, for the education of decay’d persons, orphans and poore children, where they are taught several occupations. The girls are so well brought up to housewifry, that men of good worth who seeke that chiefly in a woman, frequently take their wifes from this seminary. Hence we went to see the Rasphouse, where the lusty knaves are compell’d to worke, and the rasping of Brasill and Logwood is very hard labour. Thence to the Dull-house, for madmen and fooles. But none did I so much admire as an Hospitall for their lame and decrepid souldiers, it being for state, order, and acom’odations, one of the worthiest things that the world can shew of that nature. Indeede it is most remarkable what provisions are here made and maintain’d for publiq and charitable purposes, and to protect the poore from misery, and the country from beggers.”

Diary of John Evelyn, 1818

Tolerance and reform

Simon Schama is the author of the much-acclaimed “Embarrassment of Riches” which examines Dutch culture in the Golden Age, as well as most recently a study of the French Revolution, entitled “Citizens”.

“The site of the building into which the children disappear, clutching swim fins and gaudy towels, was once the Convent of the Sisters of Saint Clare, the Klarissenklooster. From its lobby, sounds of spacious hooting and whiffs of chlorine confirm it as one of Amsterdam’s public swimming pools. And it was here, so travelers reported in the seventeenth century, that men were faced with a stark choice: drown or be Dutch.

After Erasmus, Netherlandish humanism was short on jokes, so that it seems unlikely that the metamorphosis of the drowning cell into the swimming pool would have amused the city fathers. Certainly, there is nothing lighthearted about the sculpture that they placed at the entrance of the house in the Heiligeweg. The forbidding group atop the roof, showing Amsterdam dishing out castigatio (punishment) to heavily manacled and fettered delinquents–a constabular version of Michelangelo’s prisoners–was added in the late seventeenth century. The alarming flail she held in her right hand has, quite recently, mysteriously disappeared, as perhaps out of keeping with Amsterdam’s present ethos of relaxed liberalism...It should come as no surprise, then, to learn that the door in the Heiligeweg once greeted new inmates for the city’s first House of Correction: Tugthuis. A very similar work of penal iconography by de Keyser can still be made out through the sooty masonry of the door on the Oude Zijds Achterburgwal Spinhuis, where, from 1597, “fallen women” – vagrants, whores and thieves – were sent for stiff doses of improvement at loom and wheel.

These grim hostels were founded at the end of the sixteenth century through the recommendations of earlier inspectors for vagabondage. Lodged on the sites of the dissolved religious orders, they signified the change from voluntary ecclesiastical alms to the aggressive social intervention that characterized humanist reform, both Catholic and Protestant. Around the middle of the sixteenth century, magistrates in

many of the larger European cities sought to deal with the rapidly increasing hordes of beggars, destitute rural migrants and what they perceived as whole armies of petty criminals by means other that the indiscriminate brutalities – brandings, mutilations, floggings and bloody executions – that constituted traditional punishment and deterrence. The two purposes of economic relief and penal reform united in an ambitious correctional program designed to reform the malefactor as well as punish him...
Criminals, beggars, vagabonds, men without occupation or abode... were by definition outsiders against whom the community had to defend itself. But were

there groups whose ethnic origins precluded full and authentic admission to the host culture? I have already argued that immigration itself was no bar at all to assimilation, and during the last quarter of the sixteenth century the northern Netherlands received as many as 150,000 refugees from the Spanish conquest of the south....What of another immigrant group that added the complication of a different religion: the Jews? Traditionally, the response of the Dutch to Jews in their midst has been thought the locus classicus of benign pluralism: an exceptional case of tolerance in a Christian Europe that either ejected or confined them in humiliating and degrading circumstances. There is much to support this optimistic scenario. There was no Amsterdam ghetto, no yellow badge, horned hat or lock-up curfew behind gates and walls. The costume of the Sephardim from the Iberian world in particular was indistinguishable from that of gentile Amsterdammers and, most significantly, the demonological exaggeration of physical features disappears from the depiction of Jews in their artistic rendering by Rembrandt and Lievens. Instead, the Semitism of their physiognomy was actually mobilized to enhance the narrative immediacy of scripture painting, so that Rembrandt gives us not only a David but a St. Matthew and a Jesus with the features of his Jewish neighbors on the Breestrat.❞

SIMON SCHAMA, *THE EMBARRASSMENT OF RICHES*, 1987

"NOT THE FAULT OF THE DUTCH"

Different races and civilizations have always lived peacefully side by side in Amsterdam. Countless works of Dutch literature recall how this tolerance was damaged by the Nazis. In this extract from Anne Frank's famous diary of June 24, 1942, Anne, whose family had fled to the Netherlands after Hitler came to power in Germany, pays tribute to Dutch solidarity. Thanks to the help and heartfelt sympathy of the Amsterdammers, many Jews managed to survive in this city, which they called "Mokum". Of the Frank family, however, only Anne's father lived through the war. He found Anne's diary and published it in 1947, whereupon it became an international bestseller.

❝Dear Kitty,
It is boiling hot, we are all positively melting, and in this heat I have to walk everywhere. Now I can fully appreciate how nice a tram is; but that is a forbidden luxury for Jews – shanks's pony is good enough for us. I had to visit the dentist in the Jan Luykenstraat in the lunch hour yesterday. It is a long way from our school in the Stadstimmertuinen; I nearly fell asleep in school that afternoon. Luckily, the dentist's assistant was very kind and gave me a drink – she's a good sort.
We are allowed on the ferry and that is about all. There is a little boat from the Josef Israelskade, the man there took us at once when we asked him It is not the

Dutch people's fault that we are having such a miserable time.
I do wish I didn't have to go to school, as my bicycle was stolen in the Easter holidays and Daddy has given Mummy's to a Christian family for safe keeping. But thank goodness, the holidays are nearly here, one more week and the agony is over."

THE DIARY OF ANNE FRANK, TRANS. B.M. MOOYART, 1947

PORTRAIT OF A PEOPLE

AN EASY-GOING ENVIRONMENT

Adam Hopkins, a 20th century travel writer, journalist and broadcaster, has completed books on Crete and Holland. Here he writes about the attitudes of modern Amsterdammers.

"Amsterdam...makes its disclosures openly. Elegant and scruffy, distinguished and whorish, sophisticated and gauche, international in outlook but its historic centre tiny by comparison with Rome or Paris, Amsterdam is the embodiment of the seventeenth-century Dutch Republic which rose on a mixture of pride and modesty and practised the art of tolerance more thoroughly than any other state in Europe. Amsterdam has retained its ability to accommodate, to provide what people want; and it is this which has given it its name for open sex, the ready availability of drugs and its capacity to put up with any kind of do-as-you-please behaviour. But the truth is that the image has outlasted the reality. It was the 1960s and 1970s which saw the furthest reaches of tolerance, as if the city was an escape hatch for all the pressures in Dutch society and a playground for the young of many nations. Today there is a realization that tolerance, as recently practised, had allowed some people's freedoms to limit the freedoms of others. The city remains accommodating and easy-going. It continues to put up with its very outré red light district but hard drugs are now reckoned a menace and dealing in hard drugs a criminal activity. You can still see plenty that is surprising, sometimes shocking, sometimes funny; you can still get your car broken into in a flash on the apparently safest of canal sides. But some kind of corner has been turned. From the visitor's viewpoint the mixture of canals and canal houses, of intellectual and artistic liveliness, the flower market along the Singel canal, the old 'brown' pubs with quiet talk and sometimes carpets on the tables, the unexpected as well as what one may have planned for – all this makes Amsterdam a place to wander endlessly. It is an admirable city, but not quite the city of popular folklore."

ADAM HOPKINS, *HOLLAND*, 1988

An upright and industrious character

A social chronicler of the 17th century, William Aglionby had a high opinion of the Dutch, on the whole.

"*Of the Manners and Dispositions of the Inhabitants.*
The old *Hollanders* were formerly despised by their Neighbours, for the grossness of their temper, and the simplicity of their life. They were us'd to be call'd *Block-heads, and eaters of Cheese and Milk*: but as they formerly had the reputation of silly, so now they are esteemed as subtil and understanding a Nation as any is in *Europe:* as may be well evidenced from their Treaties and Alliances made with Strangers. This I think proceeds from that Commerce they drive through all the world, and from the mixture made amongst them by divers Strangers that had setled in these parts; for above half those that do inhabit the Towns are either Strangers, or descended from them. . . . They are not so much upon the punctilio of honor, as the other Nations, but are rather given to Trade and getting, and they seem as if they had suck'd in with their milk the insatiable desire of acquiring. They never complain of the pains they take, and go as merrily to the *Indies,* as if they went to their Countrey Houses. They are of a strong Constitution, tall proper men, and very capable of whatsoever they undertake.
Those amongst them that prefer the study of Liberal Arts to the desire of growing rich, do succeed as prosperously; for without doubt or flattery, *Holland* has produced as many learn'd and ingenious persons as any Province in *Europe.* Others follow the Art of Painting, and transport themselves into *Italy,* where are the best Masters of the world; and by these means good Pictures are very common here, there being scarce an ordinary Tradesman, whose House is not adorn'd with them. If there be any body that has any new invention or discovery, he shall be sure to find money for it here, if it will yeeld any.
Above all things the *Hollanders* hate all Quarrels and Duels; as likewise they abhor all treacherous actions, blasphemy, swearing &c. They are no wayes bloody-minded, but much more enclin'd to compassion than their Neighbours. . . . The married Women and Maids are very fair and chaste. They have a great care of their House, and keep all their Cupboards, Cabinets, even the Floors, extream neat: some of them are so curious, as not to let you come into their rubb'd Rooms, without putting on a pair of Slippers, or making your own Shooes very clean. The Women do enjoy as much liberty as their Husbands; and it is an unpardonable fault to beat them. I have often heard them say, that if a Husband does beat his Wife, he is bound to give his Neighbours a Gammon of Bacon; and if she beat him, she is bound to give two. Every day they rub and wash the lower Floors, and straw them with fine Sand, and make them so neat, that Strangers often make a scruple of spitting in them. . . . They are a little too indulgent to their

Children, and are punished for it; for many of them rebell against their Parents, and at last go away to the *Indies,* the ordinary vent of these *Provinces.* When any body tells them of their fondness to their Children, the presently say, *Does any body spoil their own Face, or cut off their own Nose?*"

WILLIAM AGLIONBY, *THE PRESENT STATE OF THE LOW COUNTRIES*, 1669

UNHEALTHY CLIMATE, HEALTHY OPTIMISM

William Temple (1628–99) was a statesman and author. He visited Holland in 1666 to arrange the Triple Alliance between England, Holland and Sweden, and then again in 1674 to organize the marriage of William of Orange and Mary.

"They are generally not so long-lived, as in better airs; and begin to decay early, both men and women, especially at *Amsterdam.* The diseases of the climate seem to be chiefly the gout and the scurvy; but all hot and dry summers bring some that are infectious among them, especially into *Amsterdam* and *Leyden*:these are usually fevers, and lie most in the head, and either kill suddenly, or languish long before they recover. Plagues are not so frequent, at least not in a degree to be taken notice of, for all supress the talk of them as much as they can, and no distinction is made in the registry of the dead, nor much in the care and attendance of the sick: whether from a belief of predestination, or else a preference of trade, which is the life of the country, before that of particular men. . . . Strangers among them are apt to complain of the spleen, but those of the country seldom or never: which I take to proceed from their being very busy, or easily satisfied."

WILLIAM TEMPLE, *OBSERVATIONS UPON THE NETHERLANDS*, 1672

BUSINESSMEN AND DREAMERS

In 1954, Albert Camus (1913–60) stayed briefly in Amsterdam: one day and one night. But it was a very full day, and a whole night spent storing up images which he was to make use of a year and a half later in "The Fall".

"Besides, this country inspires me. I like this crowd of people swarming on the pavements, wedged into a little space of houses and canals, hemmed in by fogs, cold lands, and the sea steaming like wet washing. I like it, for it is double. It is here and elsewhere.

Yes indeed! From hearing their heavy tread on the damp pavement, from seeing them move ponderously in and out of their shops full of gilded herrings and jewels the color of dead leaves, you probably think they are here this evening? You are like everybody else; you take these good people for a tribe of syndics and merchants counting up their gold crowns together with their chances of eternal life, whose only lyricism consists in occasionally, without doffing their broad-brimmed hats, taking anatomy lessons? You are wrong. They walk along with us, to be sure, and yet see where their heads are: in that fog compounded of neon, gin and peppermint emanating from the red and green shop-signs above them. Holland is a dream, Monsieur, a dream of gold and smoke – smokier by day, more gilded by night. And night and day that dream is peopled with Lohengrins like these, dreamily riding their black bicycles with high handle-bars, funeral swans constantly drifting throughout the whole country, around the seas, along the canals. Their heads in their copper-colored clouds, they dream; they ride in circles; they pray, sleep-walking in the fog's gilded incense; they have ceased to be here. They have gone thousands of miles away, towards Java, the distant isle. They pray to those grimacing gods of Indonesia with which they have decorated all their shop-windows and which at this moment are floating aimlessly above us before alighting, like gorgeous monkeys, on the signs and stepped roofs, to remind these homesick colonials that Holland is not only the Europe of merchants but also the sea, the sea that leads to Cipango and to those islands where men die mad and happy."

ALBERT CAMUS, *THE FALL*, TRANS. JUSTIN O'BRIEN, 1957

LIFE ON THE WATER

RESPECT FOR RESOURCEFULNESS

Peter Mundy (1596?–1667) was a traveler who kept journals of his voyages to India, China and Japan; he also visited Denmark, Russia and Prussia. "The Travels of Peter Mundy in Europe and Asia" were published in several volumes.

❝Wantts and inconveniences suplied and amended.
The number off other shippes which perpetually Ebbe and Flow to this Citty, etts., is incredible, By which meanes, as by their Industry and labour, they have made off this land, which naturally off itt selffe is unproffitable and unuseffull For Man or beast, And, as some say, where all the Foure elementts are currupted, *viz*., the Earth Marshy, Muddy; the water brackish, stincking (I mean their wells); in some places the Aire participates off both by his vicinity; and For Fire, their Cheiffest Fewell beeing turffe. This is objected [adduced]. I will not stand to answear in particuler. Only thus Much in generall termes I say, thatt Notwithstanding all these inconveniences, they have by their engenious labours and cleanlinesse soe correcteed them, that they have made a place where they live in health and wealth, ease and pleasure. For allthough the land, and thatt with Much labour, is broughtt only to pasture, and thatt butt in summer Neither, yett by Meanes off their shipping, they are plentifully suplied with whatt the earth affoards For the use off Man, As Corne, pitch, Tarre, Flax, hempe, etts. From Dantzicke, Cuningsberg [Königsberg], etts. in the Balticke Sea; Masts, timber, Fish, etts., From Norway; From Denmarcke, Cattle; and From any part off the world beesides, either in Europe, Asia, Affricke or America, where any trade is, with the Most pretious and Ritche Comodities off those parts, with which supplying other Countries they More and More enritche their owne.❞

PETER MUNDY, *A PASSAGE FROM ENGLAND OVER INTO HOLLAND*, 1639–47

LAND RECLAMATION RIDICULED

Andrew Marvell (1621–78), lyric poet, patriot, satyrist and foe to tyranny, possibly worked as a spy in Holland in 1662–3. This poem is anti-Dutch propaganda with a strong English prejudice.

❝*Holland*, that scarce deserves the name of Land,
As but the off-scouring of the *British Sand*;
And so much Earth as was contributed
By *English Pilots* when they heav'd the Lead;
Or what by th' Ocean's slow alluvion fell
Of shipwrackt Cockle and the Muscle-shell;
This indigested vomit of the Sea
Fell to the *Dutch* by just Propriety.
Glad then, as Miners that have found the Ore,
They with mad labour fish'd the *Land* to *Shoar*,
And div'd as desperately for each piece
Of Earth, as if't had been of *Ambergreece*,
Collecting anxiously small Loads of Clay,
Less than what building Swallows bear away,
Or than those Pills which sordid Beetles roul,
Transfusing into them their Dunghill Soul.

How did they rivet with Gigantick Piles,
Thorough the Center their new-catched Miles,
And to the stake a struggling Country bound,
Where barking Waves still bait the forced Ground,
Building their *watry Babel* far more high
To reach the *Sea*, than those to scale the *Sky*.”

ANDREW MARVELL, *THE CHARACTER OF HOLLAND*, 1681

THE POET'S IMAGINATION SETS SAIL

LUXURY, CALM AND PLEASURE

In 1847 Charles Baudelaire (1821–67) wrote “L'Invitation au Voyage” for his collection of poems part of “Les Fleurs du Mal” (“The Flowers of Evil”). These lines from the prose version of the same subject evoke a dreamlike, mythical vision of a city that must be Amsterdam, though it is not named and the poet never set foot there.

“There is a wonderful country, a country of Cocaigne, they say, that I dream of visiting with an old love. A strange country lost in the mists of the North and that might be called the East of the West, the China of Europe, so freely has a warm and capricious fancy been allowed to run riot there, illustrating it patiently and persistently with an artful and delicate vegetation.
A real country of Cocaigne where everything is beautiful, rich, honest and calm; where order is luxury's mirror; where life is unctuous and sweet to breathe; where disorder, tumult, and the unexpected are shut out; where happiness is wedded to silence; where even the cooking is poetic, rich, and yet stimulating as well; where everything, dear love, resembles you.
On shining panels or on darkly rich and gilded leathers, discreet paintings repose, as deep, calm and devout as the souls of the painters who depicted them. Sunsets throw their glowing colors on the walls of dining-room and drawing-room, sifting softly through lovely hangings or intricate high windows with mullioned panes. All the furniture is immense, fantastic, strange, armed with locks and secrets like all civilized souls. Mirrors, metals, fabrics, pottery, and works of the goldsmith's art

play a mute mysterious symphony for the eye, and every corner, every crack, every drawer and curtain's fold breathes forth a curious perfume, a perfume of Sumatra whispering come back, which is the soul of the abode.
These treasures, these furnishings, this luxury, this order, these perfumes, and these miraculous flowers, they are you! And you are the great rivers too, and the calm canals. And those great ships that they bear along laden with riches and from which rise the sailors' rhythmic chants, they are my thoughts that sleep or that rise on the swells of your breast. You lead them gently toward the sea which is the Infinite, as you mirror the sky's depth in the crystalline purity of your soul; – and when, weary with rolling waters and surfeited with the spoils of the Orient, they return to their port of call, still they are my thoughts coming back, enriched, from the Infinite to you.”

CHARLES BAUDELAIRE, *PARIS SPLEEN*,
TRANS. LOUISE VARESE, 1951

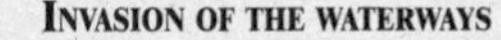

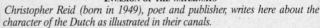

INVASION OF THE WATERWAYS

Christopher Reid (born in 1949), poet and publisher, writes here about the character of the Dutch as illustrated in their canals.

“Amsterdam is a city famous for having long defended itself against hostile elements by accommodation with them. Built in defiance of the sea, it allows water into its very heart through its canals, and so exploits what would most threaten it. I'm inclined to think that much the same ruse has been applied to that elemental force of modern times, the tourist invasion. According to this scheme, foreign visitors, flooding into the city, find themselves conducted, so gently and efficiently that they hardly notice it, along certain channels of public behaviour; the whole thing is managed in such a way as to bring the least possible inconvenience, as well as a measure of profit, to those who live and work there; and it's an arrangement designed to gratify both parties – for the tourist, who at every turn meets nothing but the staunchest courtesy from his Dutch hosts, really has little cause to complain. Except that...
Except that, as one prowls about, the suspicion grows that real life, however defined, is being lived elsewhere, out of sight. A genial inscrutability comes to seem the predominant local trait.[...]
Amsterdam's canals provide an illustration. In this respect, a comparison with Venice – which no one dares to call 'the Amsterdam of the south' – is telling. There the waterways are still employed for serious traffic, while here they are set aside for almost exclusively frivolous usage. Typical craft are the glass-topped canal cruiser for sightseers, and that frankly ludicrous invention, the *grachtenfiets,* or canal bike. A sort of aquatic cousin to the golf-buggy, powered by pedalling, it seats four. It is a vehicle in which it must be virtually impossible to carry oneself with any semblance of dignity. A common sight between bridges is the canal bike whose operators have given up the ungainly legwork required to keep it in motion, and who have adopted an air of being quite content to float awry in midstream, grimly fascinated by whatever may happen to lie visible on the nearest bank. There is a touch of the theme-park about all this, a quality utterly alien to Venice, whose most generous concession to the outsider keen to muck about in a boat takes the uncompromisingly ancient and stately form of the gondola.”

CHRISTOPHER REID, *DEPARTURES*, 1993

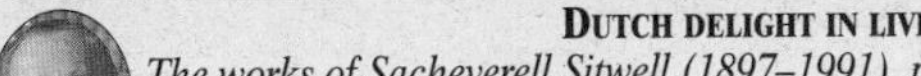

Dutch delight in living

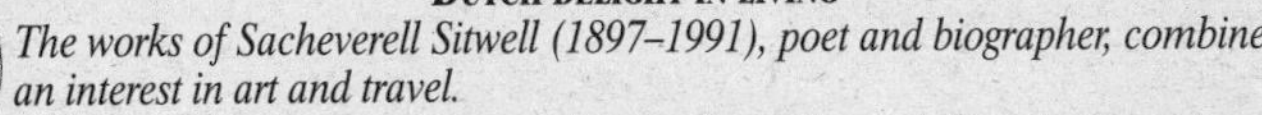

The works of Sacheverell Sitwell (1897–1991), poet and biographer, combine an interest in art and travel.

❝If we would enquire into the difference between Amsterdam and London, it is that Amsterdam has no fogs, only sea mists, and that in the working class suburbs there are flowers in every window. It is, in the first place, the immensity of London that appals the foreigner. Amsterdam is a much lesser town than London. Its fine old houses are confined to a small area, almost, we might say, to the Keizersgracht and Heerengracht. But the interior mystery of London has often intrigued the foreigner. . . . One of the few and fast diminishing old London interiors, a solicitor's office, shall we say, somewhere near Lincoln's Inn Fields or Bedford Square, the part of London most akin to Amsterdam, would show . . . typical reticence and understatement in the 'Adam' mantelpiece, or the classical motifs or urn and honeysuckle in low relief upon the stucco ceiling. There is nothing, here, of the Dutch delight in living. For this, we shall find in Holland, is what lies hidden, unsuspected.❞

SACHEVERELL SITWELL, *THE NETHERLANDS: A STUDY OF SOME ASPECTS OF ART, COSTUME AND SOCIAL LIFE*, 1974

Grachts and canals

Karel Capek (1890–1938), the Czech novelist and dramatist, also wrote short stories, science fiction and travel books, including "Letters from Holland", in 1933. His writings are full of social and political satire and foreshadow totalitarianism. Here he writes about the waterways of Holland.

❝Now this is the way of it: where we have streets between the houses, in Holland there is merely water; this is known as a gracht, and when the water flows from town to town it is a canal. And this restful water is not bordered with an embankment and a parapet, but with tall, restful trees and restful frontages of houses with shiny windows; and all of it is restfully mirrored in the water. We are told that these grachts are really waterways, and that in olden times the Dutch used to carry goods on them all over the town. . . . From the look of things I should be inclined to say that in olden times the Dutch built their towns of houses and water chiefly because in that way they could produce two towns at a single blow, so to speak: one on top and the other mirrored in the water. As, owing to the size of their country, they could not broaden out very much, they doubled their dimensions vertically: by relection in the water. As, on their sand, they could not to any extent stretch upwards, they simply reversed the process and produced a looking-glass effect downwards. It is the people who live on top, restfully and staidly; underneath, it is their shadows which move, even more restfully and staidly. I should not wonder if the surface of the grachts still reflected the shadows of people from bygone centuries, men in broad ruffs and women in mob caps. You see, there grachts are very old and consequently somehow unreal. The towns appear to be standing, not on the earth, but on their own reflections; these highly respectable streets appear to emerge from bottomless depths of dreams; the houses appear to be intended as houses and, at the same time, as reflections of houses.❞

KAREL CAPEK, *LETTERS FROM HOLLAND, 1933*

SNAPSHOTS OF THE CITY

LOW LIFE AND LECHERY

James Boswell (1740–95), essayist, diarist and philanderer, traveled throughout Europe and kept a candid journal of his impressions.

❝Holland certainly has a very harsh climate, dangerous to strangers who have been brought up in a temperate region. There are horrible fogs and excessive cold, but especially a continuous dampness, except in the summer months." Thus a discontented man might describe the United Provinces, and, I confess, with considerable justice. But when one has actually made the experiment of living there, one finds that there is no great difference between Holland and other countries; that is to say, if a stranger lives well, eats well, drinks well, and dresses well–and also takes a good deal of exercise, which in Holland is absolutely necessary to give a brisk circulation to the blood and consequently an agreeable liveliness to the mind. If one lives after that fashion and has a suitable occupation, one can be very well satisfied. I speak positively for I speak from experience.
At five I went to a bawdy-house. I was shown upstairs, and had a bottle of claret and a *juffrouw.* But the girl was much fitter for being wrapped in the blankets of salivation than kissed between the sheets of love. I had no armour, so did not fight. It was truly ludicrous to talk in Dutch to a whore. This scene was to me a rarity as great as peas in February. Yet I was hurt to find myself in the sinks of gross debauchery...
I resolved to go to a *speelhuis* but had no guide. I therefore very madly sought for one myself and strolled up and down the Amsterdam streets, which are by all accounts very dangerous at night. I began to be frightened and to think of Belgic *knives.* At last I came to a *speelhuis,* where I entered boldly. I danced with a fine lady in laced riding-clothes, a true blackguard minuet. I had my pipe in my mouth and performed like any common sailor. I had near quarrelled with one of the musicians. But I was told to take care, which I wisely did. I spoke plenty of Dutch but could find no girl that elicited my inclinations. I was disgusted with this low confusion, came home and slept sound.❞

JAMES BOSWELL, *DIARY*, MAY 26, 1764

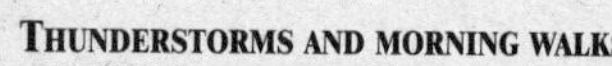

THUNDERSTORMS AND MORNING WALKS

Vincent van Gogh (1853–90) spent a year in Amsterdam while studying theology. His letters to his brother Theo in that period contain vivid descriptions of the city The complete collection of letters was published by Theo after the artist's death, and provide a deeply moving document of his deteriorating state of mind in the last decades of his life.

❝This morning at a quarter to five there was a terrible thunderstorm here; shortly after, the first gang of workmen came through the gates of the yard in the pouring rain. I got up and went out into the yard, taking a few copybooks with me to the summerhouse. I have been sitting reading there, looking out over the whole yard and dock; the poplars and elderberry and other shrubs were bowed down by the heavy storm, and the rain poured down on the piles of wood and on the decks of the ships. Boats and a little steamer were sailing back and forth, and in the distance, near the village across the IJ, one saw swift-moving brown sails and the houses and trees on Buitenkant and the more vividly colored churches. Again and again one heard the thunder and saw the lightning; the sky could have been from a picture by Ruysdael, and the sea gulls were skimming the water. It was a grand sight and a real relief after the oppressive heat of yesterday. It has quite refreshed me, for I felt very tired when I went upstairs last night.”

“I got up early and saw the workmen arrive in the yard while the sun was shining brightly. You would be intrigued by the sight–that long line of black figures, big and small, first in the narrow street where the sun just peeps in and later in the yard. Then I breakfasted on a piece of dry bread and a glass of beer–that is what Dickens advises for those who are on the point of committing suicide, as being a good way to keep them, at least for some time, from their purpose. And even if one is not in such a mood, it is right to do it occasionally, while thinking, for instance, of Rembrandt's picture, “The Men of Emmaus”. Before I went to Stricker's, I walked through the Jewish quarter and along the Buitenkant, the Old Teertuinen, Zeedyk, Warmoes Straat, and around the Oudezijds Chapel and the Old and the South churches, through all kinds of old streets with forges and coopers' shops, etc., and through narrow alleys, like the Niezel, and canals with narrow bridges, like those we saw that evening at Dordrecht. It was interesting to watch the start of a new day's work there.”

Complete Letters of Vincent van Gogh, Vol 1, pub. 1958

Trapped in port

In the late 19th century the canals froze over and prevented Captain Joseph Conrad (1857–1924) of the British Merchant Navy from leaving Amsterdam. The author of “Lord Jim” here gives an account of his escapades on shore, which bring him to the glass-roofed building that is now the Hotel Krasnapolski. This anecdote illustrates the importance of Amsterdam's port.

“Notwithstanding the little iron stove, the ink froze on the swing-table in the cabin, and I found it more convenient to go ashore, stumbling over the Arctic wasteland and shivering in glazed tramcars in order to write my evening letter to my owners in a gorgeous café in the center of the town. It was an immense place, lofty and gilt, upholstered in red plush, full of electric lights, and so thoroughly warmed that even the marble tables felt tepid to the touch. The waiter who brought me my cup of coffee bore, by comparison with my utter isolation, the dear aspect of an intimate friend. There, alone in a noisy crowd, I would write slowly a letter addressed to Glasgow, of which the gist would be: There is no cargo, and no prospect of any coming till late spring apparently. [...] Almost each morning a letter from my owners would arrive, directing me to the charterers and clamor for the ship's cargo; to threaten them with the heaviest penalties of demurrage; to demand that this assortment of varied merchandise, set fast in a landscape of ice and windmills somewhere up- country, should be put on rail instantly, and fed up to the ship in regular quantities every day. After drinking some hot coffee, like an Arctic explorer setting off on a sledge journey towards the North Pole, I would go ashore and roll shivering in a tramcar into the very heart of the town, past clean-faced houses, past thousands of brass knockers upon a thousand painted doors glimmering behind rows of trees of the pavement species, leafless, gaunt, seemingly dead for ever.”

Joseph Conrad, *The Mirror of the Sea*, 1906

A BOURGEOIS PASSION FOR ORDER

Henry James (1843–1916) was educated in New York, London, Paris and Geneva and he settled in Europe in 1875."Transatlantic Sketches" was an early work, published in that year, in which he collects a number of short pieces describing his impressions of Europe and broaches a theme which was to recur throughout his later work: the contrast between the older civilization of Europe and that of America.

"Amsterdam, where I took my first Dutch walk, is a stately city, even though its street-vistas do look as if they were pictured on a tea-caddy or a hand-creen. They have for the most part a broad, sluggish canal in the middle, on either side of which a row of perfectly salubrious, but extremely attenuated trees grow out of a highly cultivated soil of compace yellow bricks. Cultivated I call it by a proper license, for it is periodically raked by the broom and the scrubbing-brush, and religiously manured with soap-suds. You lose no time, of course, in drawing the inevitable parallel between Amsterdam and Venice, and it is well worth drawing, as an illustration of the uses to which the same materials may be put by different minds. Sky and sea in both cases, with architecture between; winding sea-channels washing the feet of goodly houses erected with the profits of trade. And yet the Dutch city is a complete reversal of the Italian, and its founders might have carefully studied Venetian effects with the set purpose of producing exactly the opposite ones. It produces them in the moral line even more vividly than in the material. It is not that one place is all warm color and the other all cold; one all shimmer and softness and mellow interfusion of every possible phase of ruin, and the other rigidity, angularity, opacity, prosperity, in their very essence; it is more than anything that they tell of such a different view of life. The outward expression on one side is perfect poetry, and on the other is perfect prose; and the marvel is the way in which thrifty Amsterdam imparts the prosaic turn to things which in Venice seem the perfect essence of poetry. Take, for instance, the silence and quiet of the canals; it is almost impossible to express. In the one it is the stillness of order, and in the other of vacancy–the sleep of idleness and the sleep of rest; the quiet that comes of letting everything go by the board, and the quiet that comes of doing things betimes and being able to sit with folded hands and say they are well done.

In one of George Eliot's novels there is a portrait of a thrifty farmer's wife who rose so early in the morning to do her work that by ten o'clock it was all over, and she was at her wit's end to know what to do with her day. This good woman seems to me an excellent image of the genius of Amsterdam as it is reflected in the house-fronts – I penetrated no deeper. It is impossible to imagine anything more expressive of the numerous ideas represented by the French epithet bourgeois than these straight façades of clean black brick capped with a rococo gable of stone painted white, and armed like the forehead of the unicorn with a little horizontal horn – a bracket and pulley for hauling storable goods into the attic. The famous Dutch cleanliness seems to me quite on a level with its reputation, and asserts itself in the most ingenious and ludicrous ways. A rosy serving-maid, redolent of soap-suds from her white cap to her white sabots, stands squirting water from a queer little engine of polished copper over the majestic front of a genteel mansion whose complexion is not a visible shade less immaculate than her own. The performance suggests a dozen questions, and you can only answer them all with a laugh. What is she doing, and why is she doing it? Does she imagine the house has a speck or two

which it is of consequence to remove, or is the squirt applied merely for purposes of light refreshment – of endearment, as it were? Where could the speck or two possibly have come from, unless produced by spontaneous generation? There are no specks in the road, which is a neat parquet of scoured and polished brick; nor on the trees, whose trunks are to all appearance carefully sponged every morning. ...Of a dozen harmlessly fictitious necessities of the same sort, the canal-sides at Amsterdam offer lively evidence. Nothing could be more thoroughly in keeping with the bourgeois spirit than the way in which you everywhere find this brilliant cleanliness and ceremonious thrift playing the part, not of a convenience, but of a restriction; not of a means, but of an end.”

Henry James, *Transatlantic Sketches*, 1875

Rembrandt and Amsterdam

Robert Lowell (1917–77), the American poet, spent some time in Amsterdam in 1951–2 with his second wife, the writer Elizabeth Hardwick.

Rembrandt

His faces crack...if mine could crack and breathe!
His Jewish Bridegroom, palm spread on the Jewish Bride's
bashful, taffetta-leveled bosom, is faithful;
the fair girl, poor background, gives soul to his flayed steer.
Her breasts, the snowdrop, last into the storm;
often the Dutch were sacks, their women a sack,
obstinate, undefeated hull of the old scow.
But Bathsheba's ample stomach, her heavy, practical feet,
are reverently dried by the faithful servant,
his eyes dwell lovingly on each fulfilled sag;
her unfortunate body is the privilege of his service,
loose radiance of his spirit void of possession....
One sees, if one sees at all, through a red mist
the strange new idol of the marketplace.

Robert Lowell, *History*, 1973

Dutch Art

Karel Capek (1890–1938)analyses the character of the Dutch as seen in their art.

“...They are called 'small masters' also because they painted, not St. Sebastians and Assumptions and Holy Families and Dianas and Venuses, but the small things in life, such as a slaughtered duck, a worthy uncle on the mother's side, peasants at a beanfeast, cows at pasture or a ship at sea. As regards the St. Sebastians, just go and have a look inside the Dutch cathedrals. Calvinism stripped them of all idols, whether graven, carved or painted, and left them as bare as vessels without a cargo, high and dry on the beach; sculpture hasn't got over this even yet, and painting had to apply itself to earthly matters; hounded out of the cathedrals, it found its way into the kitchen, the tavern, the world of clodhoppers, shopkeepers, old ladies and charitable societies, and made itself remarkably snug and contented there. As regards the Dianas and Venuses, it was perhaps Dutch puritanism or perhaps also the Dutch climate which kept them away; such damp and rheumaticky surroundings are not exactly in the best interests of nudity. [...]

Dutch art is the work of seated painters for sedentary townsfolk; an urban art which sometimes paints peasants, but does so with the condescending banter of sedate urban shopkeepers. They are fond of still-lifes. They are fond of pictures which tell a story; stories provide entertainment for sedentary people. These pictures were not painted for galleries where people walk about, but for rooms where they sit down. Dutch art revealed a new reality by betaking itself home and sitting down there.

The world in which it sits is restful, talkative and easy-going, it is cosy, matter-of-fact, sociable and rather given to tittle-tattle; it notices the things nearest to it, and this is really how it reveals them; it observes at close quarters and with enjoyment. Make an excited man sit down; immediately he drops his heroics and all his grandiose posturings. Nobody can preach sitting down permanently on its wicker footstool, Dutch art banished all high-flown heroics from itself and the world which it portrays; it began to look at things more from close quarters and from below. Until at last we come upon Rembrandt, an awesome and tragical figure, swathed in the dim and ruffled mantle of twilight. [...]

Rembrandt or the exception. It is true that afterwards he was copied by others, by a much larger school, in fact, than you probably supposed, but they failed to get at his secret. It was a personal secret. It was the conflict between a tragical romantic and the world of staid burgesses. One of the first romantics in the world and he had to be born in that bright, humdrum, shallow Holland, of all places. They still show you his house on the fringe of the Amsterdam ghetto. This is not merely Rembrandt's address, but part and parcel of his inner destiny. Flight from Protestant restraint. Unhappiness and social derangement. The search for darkness, the search for the Orient. A man in whom brooding, sensualism, effusiveness and stark realism were strangely mingled. The warm gloom of his pictures glimmers with gems and the body's decay, the bearded heads of Talmudists, and the moist eyes of Susanna. The Son of Man and the countenance of man; but chiefly and above all else, the troublous, the dire, the mournful, the ineffable Soul of man. The greatest irony which he encountered was that, judging from the number of his satellites, he must have had quite a considerable success in his own country. Nevertheless he died in a state of bankruptcy; and for two hundred and fifty years his next-of-kin have, with all due formalities, been applying for the bankruptcy proceedings against the painter Rembrandt Harmensz van Rijn to be suspended.

Worthy folk from all over the world piously throng in front of his pictures which are fashioned of gloom and lustre; but these pictures remain inscrutable. And the pilgrim who desired to behold and to fathom the secret of a small nation, at least from its art, was confronted by an even queerer secret: the riddle of a great artist.”

KAREL CAPEK, *LETTERS FROM HOLLAND*, 1933

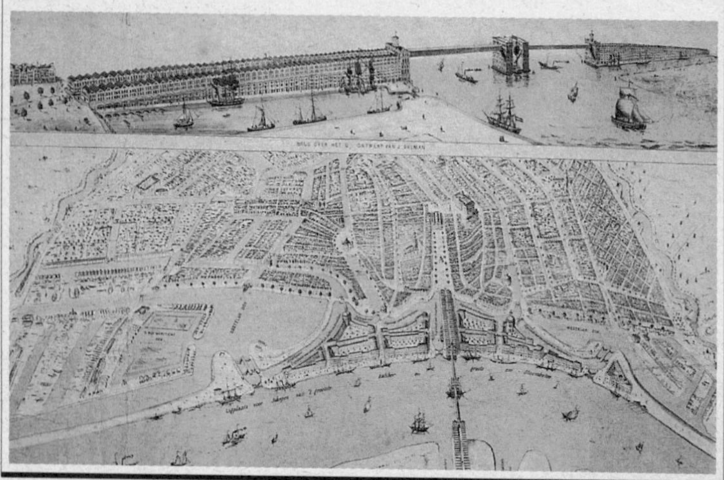

Itineraries

City center west, *119*
City center east, *139*
Northern canals, *161*
Southern canals, *189*
Around the museums, *209*
Jordaan, *235*
Old Port West, *249*
Plantage, *263*
De Pijp
and the South, *275*

▲ Ancient gables and cornices on the Keizersgracht.

▲ Summer and winter alike, bicycles can be seen everywhere.

▲ The sloping roofs of old Amsterdam, hidden behind façades and gables.

▼ Streets in the red light district, and the brightly lit windows of the Oudezijds Voorburgwal.

▲ The town of tolerance even broadcasts its views on the waterfront.

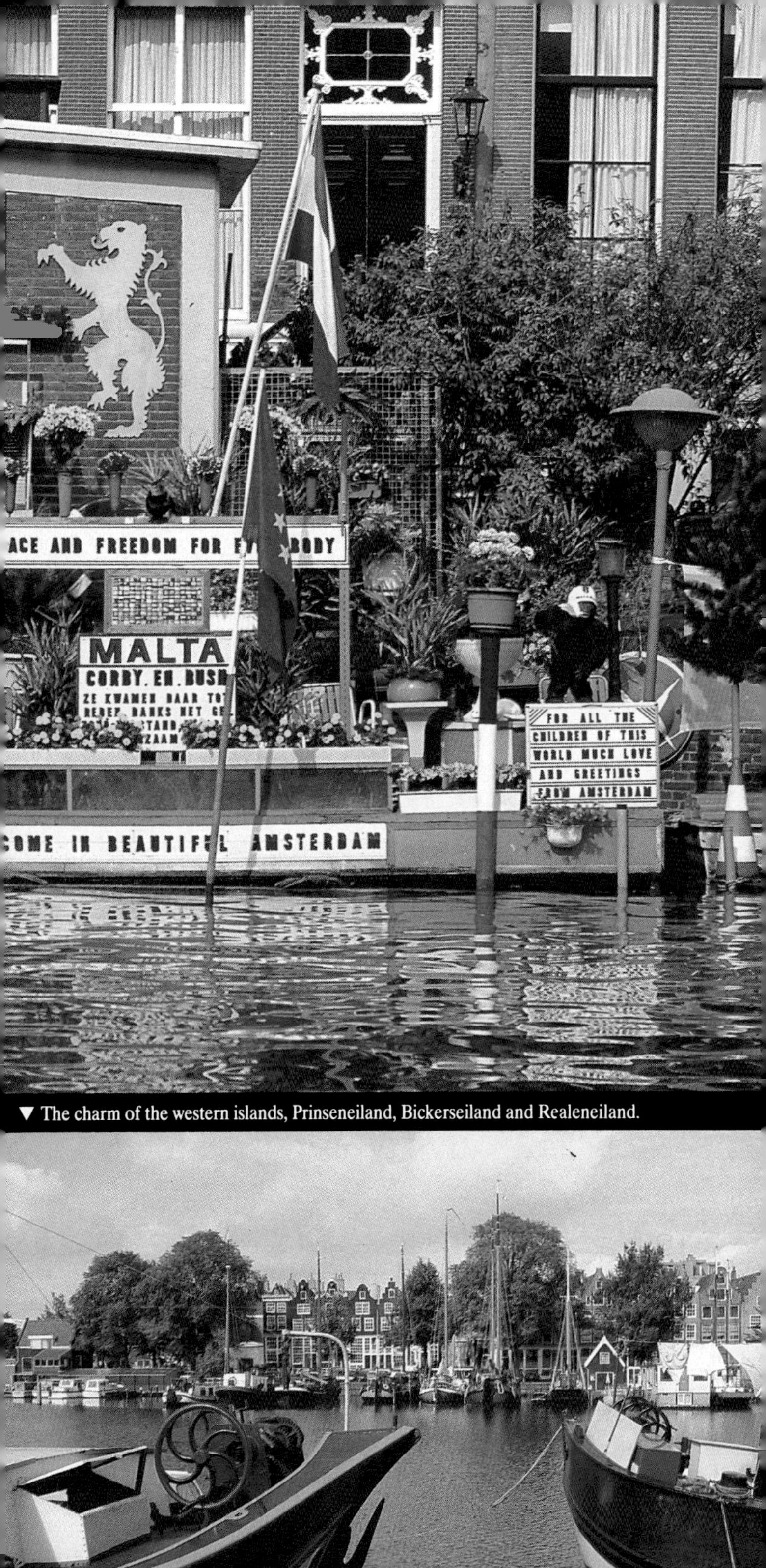

▼ The charm of the western islands, Prinseneiland, Bickerseiland and Realeneiland.

The House of Heads on the Keizersgracht, built in the 17th century.

City Center WEST

Muntplein, *120*
Koningsplein, *121*
Heiligeweg and Kalverstraat, *121*
Oude Lutherse Kerk, *121*
Spui, *122*
Begijnhof, *122*
Historical Museum, *123*
Militia Companies, *126*
Squats and squatters, *127*
Dam, *128*
Royal Palace, *128*
Nieuwe Kerk, *131*
Story of the Stock Exchange, *132*
Berlage's Exchange, *133*
Oude Kerk, *134*
Red light district, *136*
Amstelkring Museum, *137*
Sint-Nicolaas Kerk, *137*
Central Station, *138*

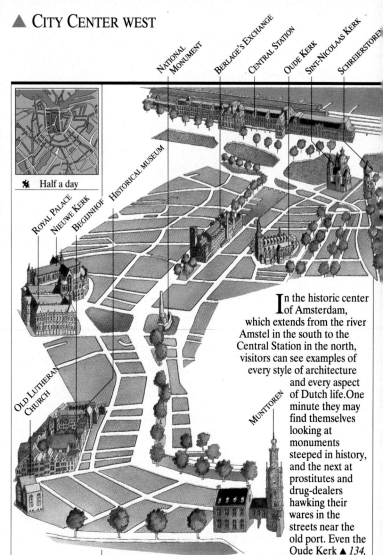

NATIONAL MONUMENT
BERLAGE'S EXCHANGE
CENTRAL STATION
OUDE KERK
SINT-NICOLAAS KERK
SCHREIERSTOREN
Half a day
ROYAL PALACE
NIEUWE KERK
BEGIJNHOF
HISTORICAL MUSEUM
OLD LUTHERAN CHURCH
MUNTTOREN

In the historic center of Amsterdam, which extends from the river Amstel in the south to the Central Station in the north, visitors can see examples of every style of architecture and every aspect of Dutch life.One minute they may find themselves looking at monuments steeped in history, and the next at prostitutes and drug-dealers hawking their wares in the streets near the old port. Even the Oude Kerk ▲ *134*, the oldest church in the city and one of the most beautiful, is overlooked by prostitutes' windows.

A Gaper, the traditional sign of the pharmacist, in Kalverstraat ● *53*.

FROM MUNTPLEIN TO SPUI ★

MUNTPLEIN. Mint Square stands at the confluence of the Singel and the Amstel. The MUNTTOREN (Mint Tower) which rises above the hurly-burly of the Muntplein, is the western corner tower of the old REGULIERSPOORT (Regulars' Gate), which was built around 1490. When the gate caught fire in 1618 only the lower part survived, and the city council asked the architect Hendrick de Keyser ▲ *156* to design a wooden superstructure which could be built on top of the remaining stone section. This led to the creation of the tower we see today. The carillon, located in the octagonal lantern, is largely the work of the Hémony brothers ▲ *128*. The monument takes its name from a period (in 1672–3) when money was minted there because Dordrecht, the town where this had previously taken place, was being threatened by Louis XIV's French troops.

KONINGSPLEIN. This square, standing on the Singel, was originally organized around the HEILIGEWEG GATE, but this was demolished in 1663. When the city was extended in 1593 ● *34* the Singel became an internal canal called the Koningsgracht (King's Canal). Since then, the square has been known as King's Square, even though the name of the canal has fallen out of use.

HEILIGEWEG AND KALVERSTRAAT. A short but busy shopping street, Heiligeweg leads into the equally busy Kalverstraat, which runs between Muntplein and the Dam. These two streets are very closely connected historically. In the 14th century the Chapel of the Holy City was built on Kalverstraat to commemorate the Miracle of Amsterdam (1345) ▲ *127*. At the same time the monks built a road for pilgrims that led to the Kalverstraat, and which was called the Heiligeweg (Holy Way). At no. 19 Heiligeweg, a gatehouse dating from the early 17th century and attributed to Hendrick de Keyser is a reminder that the Rasphuis (workhouse) once stood here. Its function was to return beggars and delinquents to the straight and narrow by attempting to "civilize" them. The institution was created as a result of measures taken by the magistrates, from 1595 onward, in an attempt to counter the increasing level of begging and crime in the city. The male inmates were made to undertake unpleasant tasks, reducing brazilwood to powder to obtain a coloring agent used in the dyeing industry, for example. The Rasphuis was demolished in 1896 following the construction of a new prison in 1892.

OUDE LUTHERSE KERK. Arriving from Germany after 1600, the Lutherans converted a warehouse, De Vergulde Pot (Gilded Pot), into a church. In 1631 the city council authorized them to demolish this building and replace it with another, on condition that the new building's façade resembled that of the original warehouse. And so in 1632–3 the Old Lutheran Church (Oude Lutherse Kerk) was built on the corner of the Singel and the Spui. It took its present name when the new Lutheran Church ▲ *165* was built. On Sundays Lutherans still hold their church services here. During the rest of the week the building, which has been bought by the University of Amsterdam, is a place for viva voce examinations, seminars and inaugural lectures given by professors appointed by the queen.

THE MINT TOWER
It marks the confluence of the Singel and the Amstel.

THE RASPHUIS
The gatehouse at no. 19 Heiligeweg has been preserved: it is decorated with a bas-relief showing a cart, drawn by wild animals, loaded with wood for rasping (top). On the left is the Old Lutheran Church, as seen by Pierre Fouquet in the 17th century.

THE OLDEST HOUSE. This wooden façade with its pointed gable stands in the Begijnhof. It dates from 1460 and is the oldest house in Amsterdam ▲ *73*.

THE GATE OF THE BEGIJNHOF Opening onto the Spui, it is crowned by a statue of Saint Ursula. Above, a contemporary naïve painting by Lotte Funke showing the Begijnhof.

SPUI ★

The very busy Spui (Sluice) Square lies between the Singel and Rokin ▲ *140*. It is famous for Hoppe ◆ *296*, an OLD BROWN CAFÉ dating from 1670 that is a favorite haunt of Amsterdammers: in the evenings it is often impossible to get in. Its more recent neighbor the Luxembourg Café, decorated in 1930's style, is also very popular ◆ *296*. At 14 Spui the ATHENEUM bookshop has an Art Nouveau façade; it offers a wide choice of titles (including many in English), in the book-loving tradition of the city ● 54. Its sister shop next door, the Atheneum Nieuwscentrum (news world), is open every day.

BEGIJNHOF ★

On the left of the Spui, across the Nieuwezijds Voorburgwal, a small gateway crowned by a statue of Saint Ursula leads into the Begijnhof or Beguinage(Beguine Convent). The setting and atmosphere are striking: the Begijnhof is so well cared for and painstakingly restored that it looks like a film set. A walled community made up of old houses and a small church surround lawns planted with age-old trees. Even the sound of the car horns, the trams and

CARTOUCHES FROM THE BEGIJNHOF
The Flight into Egypt, martyrs, and the disciples at Emmaus.

the noisy streets does not penetrate. The Begijnhof was established in 1346 on land that at that time marked the outer limit of the city. The NIEUWEZIJDS VOORBURGWAL, then the defensive canal, curved round to enclose the Beguines' orchard. "The pulse of history, particularly that of the social history of the city, can also be heard beating in the dead silence that characterizes the secular *hofjes* which are so numerous in the old town. They are oases of peace, enclosed by a circle of little houses, all alike, real doll's houses, usually with a small front garden. Built with the proceeds of donations from private individuals and associations, these groups of houses arranged around an inner courtyard reached through an arched gateway, were the first old people's homes in Amsterdam. The eldest sister, and very finest of these *hofjes,* is the Begijnhof" (Max van Rooy). The Beguines, who were not, strictly speaking, nuns, nonetheless made a (revokable) vow of obedience to God, and, if they were not elderly themselves, devoted their energies to the care of old people. The great fires of 1421 and 1452 ● *28* left nothing of the original enclosure. Most of the existing houses date from the 17th century. Although it has been restored, one house, no. 34, still has a wooden façade. The oldest house in Amsterdam, it was built in 1460 ● *73.*

TWO CHURCHES. The church in the center of the courtyard was built around 1400 in the Gothic style. It was confiscated from the Beguines by the city during the Alteration (1578). For a while it stood empty and was then used as a warehouse, before being given to the English community in Amsterdam in the 17th century for Presbyterian worship.The building was enlarged in the 17th century and is still the city's Presbyterian Church, with ministers appointed by the Church of Scotland. Among the other houses is a (once clandestine) Roman Catholic church dating from 1671 ● *39* ▲ *137.*

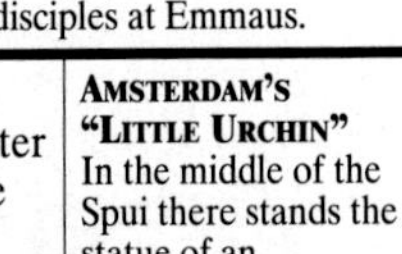

AMSTERDAM'S "LITTLE URCHIN"
In the middle of the Spui there stands the statue of an Amsterdam street urchin (*Het Lieverdje*), the work of sculptor Carel Kneulman. In the late 1960's this lanky character became a symbol of the Provo movement. The Provos were often active on the Spui and particularly liked to organize "happenings" around this statue. ● *33* ▲ *243.*

HISTORICAL MUSEUM ★ ● *34* ▲ *124*

At the northern edge of the Begijnhof, the Historical Museum (Historisch Museum) contains impressive collections of paintings, books, maps and all sorts of objects illustrating the history of the city.

In the early 16th century the Begijnhof lay on the edge of the city. In the foreground is the present-day site of the Spui.

After rallying to Calvinism in 1578 ● *29*, the city established a municipal orphanage in the cloisters of Saint Lucy's Convent. It was enlarged in the 17th century by the architects Hendrick de Keyser and Jacob van Campen. The orphanage remained in existence until 1960, when the premises were restored by the city authorities to provide a museum of the history of Amsterdam. The greatest innovation was the construction, on the site of a small canal, of the Schuttersgalerij, a "museum street" displaying portraits of the militia companies ▲ *126*.

THE NOORDERKERK AROUND 1644
This painting by Abraham Beerstraten (dates unknown, but thought to be active 1635–65) shows the church, shortly after its construction, seen from the Brouwersgracht ▲ *175* in winter. The artist came from a family of painters: his father and brothers produced several seascapes and winter landscapes.

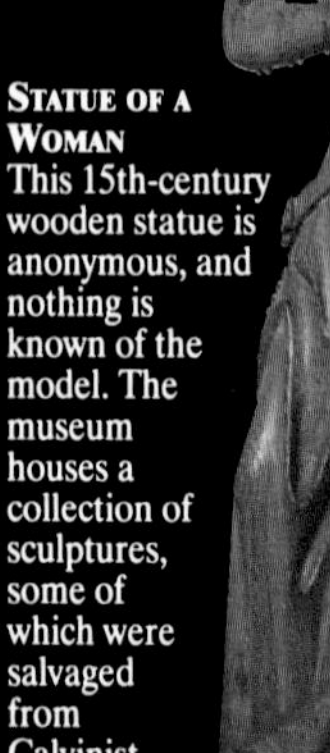

STATUE OF A WOMAN
This 15th-century wooden statue is anonymous, and nothing is known of the model. The museum houses a collection of sculptures, some of which were salvaged from Calvinist iconoclasm.

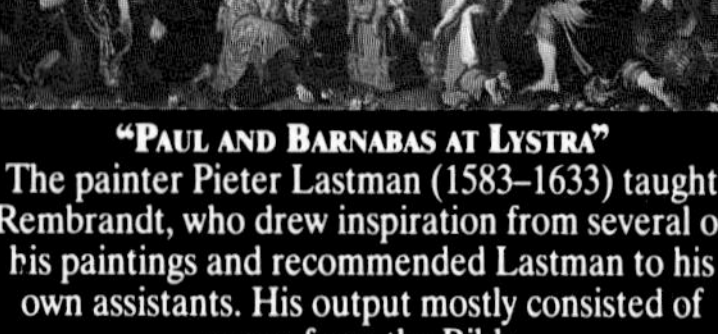

"PAUL AND BARNABAS AT LYSTRA"
The painter Pieter Lastman (1583–1633) taught Rembrandt, who drew inspiration from several of his paintings and recommended Lastman to his own assistants. His output mostly consisted of scenes from the Bible.

"HET FRANSCHE PAD"
This painting by Willem Hekking (1796–1862) shows the Goudsbloemgracht in Jordaan .

Silver clasp
The clasp on the left decorated the coffin of a member of the Guild of Grain-Porters.

Escaped
A fragment of a painting by Pieter Aertsz, or Aertsen (1508–75); it is almost certainly part of an *Adoration of the Magi* destroyed by iconoclasts in 1566 or by the fire at the Town Hall in 1652.

"Tavern with Merry Drinkers"
Painting by Adriaen van Ostade (1610–84). Early works by this artist, who produced almost nine hundred paintings, are characterized by picturesque figures and scenes from everyday life.

Cartouches
A great many cartouches, taken from demolished house façades, have been installed in the wall at the Sint Luciensteeg entrance to the museum (above). On the right, a milkmaid with her two pails.

"Goliath"
This statue, dating from the 17th century, originally stood in a Prinsengracht garden. Today it can be seen in the museum restaurant.

Elderly man
Engraving by J.C. van der Vliet (c. 1610).

A squat at nos. 214–16 Spuistraat, bought by its inhabitants. Its painted façade has become famous.

THE AMSTERDAM MILITIA COMPANIES. From the time of the foundation of Amsterdam, its inhabitants had to contribute to the defense of their city. This collective obligation led them to form corporations, or militias. After 1578, the year when Amsterdam went over to Protestantism ● *29*, a new form of organization appeared: each of the eleven districts had its own company under the leadership of a captain, the head of the district, who was assisted by three lieutenants and three sergeants. In 1580 these companies were transformed into civic guards and shooting associations controlled by the city council. The whole was led by a colonel-in-chief, and each company was divided into four sections. One of these sections was commanded by Frans Banningh Cocq, who later became famous thanks to Rembrandt's representation of him in *The Night Watch* ▲ *218*.The *doelen*, or shooting ranges, slowly changed in character. Their buildings were enlarged, and were used more and more for banquets and receptions. The great pictures commissioned by these organizations demonstrate their militaristic and hierarchical development: social differences are expressed through dress and armor. The members of the militia companies were generally burghers who had attained a certain social standing, although the officer ranks were staffed exclusively by members of the great patrician families. Over the centuries the militia companies gradually lost prestige, partly because of the decadence of their celebrations and banquets, and partly because it was possible to buy one's way out of doing military service. Transformed into a national guard in 1813, the militia disappeared unmourned. The national guard itself was subsequently dissolved in a military reorganization in 1907. The Golden Age, when the Netherlands enjoyed enormous prosperity, was also the great period of the militia

View of the Royal Palace from the western canals.

THE HANDELSBLAD-GEBOUW SQUAT
A hundred or so people live in these apartments in an area where avant-garde art galleries and shops do a thriving trade. The occupants enjoy a unique view of the Royal Palace from the roof terraces.

companies. A multitude of group portraits were painted by the greatest artists of the day, among them Rembrandt, Hals and Van der Helst, showing the men in full dress uniform or carousing at table ▲ *218, 224*.

STAMP MARKET. Near the Historical Museum, on Nieuwezijds Voorburgwal, a stamp market has taken place regularly, every Wednesday and Saturday, since 1927. The vendors occupy tiny stalls.

SQUATS AND SQUATTERS

THE SQUATTER MOVEMENT. "The unlawful occupation of an empty dwelling does not entail criminal sanctions [under current law]", the Amsterdam city council noted in 1923. The city called in vain for severe penalties to be imposed on "families who move into unoccupied dwellings without permission". An eviction order entailed a complicated procedure, and it was only in 1986, with the passing of a law concerning unoccupied premises, that the council saw its wish granted. Until then homeless people consistently took advantage of the legal loophole in order to squat. In the 1970's squatting even became a mass phenomenon, particularly among young people. This organized collective movement was an extension of the political activities of the Provos ● *33* ▲ *243*; cafés, legal advice, newspaper small ads and various squatting manuals all assisted people wishing to take the plunge. ▲ *183, 234*. Today squatters are fewer and older, but squatting is still very much a part of Amsterdam life.

SQUATTING IN AN OLD NEWSPAPER OFFICE. After its amalgamation with the *NRC* (*Nieuwe Rotterdamse Courant*) in 1975, the liberal daily *Handelsblad* ● *64* moved from its premises at no. 230 Nieuwezijds Voorburgwal, which it had occupied since 1831, leaving behind a warren of office buildings between Nieuwezijds Voorburgwal, Paleisstraat, Spuistraat and Keizerrijk. Three years later the first squatters moved into the premises, which were still unoccupied. In April 1980 the city acquired the group of buildings, but it took six years of negotiations to reach an agreement on rents and rebuilding work. Today the first inhabitants are still there; the walls have escaped demolition, and after years of neglect gaping holes have given way to renovated apartments.

ROKIN
Rokin, as seen by Breitner ● *88* at the end of the 19th century (below), and in the 17th century (bottom).

MIRACLE OF THE COMMUNION WAFER
On Rokin near the Dam stands a monument commemorating a miracle: in 1345 a wafer that a sick person could not swallow at mass was thrown into the fire but did not burn. It was found intact in the ashes. This event prompted numerous pilgrimages to the spot ● *28*.

Tympanum of the Royal Palace.

DAM ★

● *90*

The city's central square, located at the intersection of Rokin and the Damrak on the course of the Amstel, is known as the Dam, which means a dam or dyke. This square in turn gave its name to the city, as the meaning of Amsterdam is "dam on the Amstel". The original Dam was built around 1270 between the two dykes along the banks of the Amstel (now Nieuwendijk and Warmoesstraat), to prevent floods caused by storms blowing from the north. The medieval square, which was built over the vaulted lock, used to provide the location for the city market. On the square stood the Public Weighhouse (which has now gone), the Town Hall (now the Royal Palace) and the Nieuwe Kerk (New Church), which together made up the "Holy Trinity" of the Dutch commercial spirit. The Dam has always been a very lively place, and has been painted by a great many artists over the years ● *87*. It was the scene of the Anabaptist riot in 1535 and, in 1628, of the revolt over the booty of the "Silver Fleet" ▲ *252*. Political disturbances have occurred on several occasions, as well as scuffles during popular festivals. The Dam witnessed riots in 1918 (because of a potato shortage) and in 1934 (because of reductions in unemployment benefit) ▲ *238*, and then clashes with the police in the 1960's and 1970's by the Provos ▲ *243* and the Damslapers ("Dam sleepers", young people who spent the night in the square). There were also demonstrations against the Vietnam War and during the enthronement of Queen Beatrix at the Nieuwe Kerk ● *33* ▲ *244*. Nowadays, gatherings tend to be more peaceful: Remembrance Day celebrations (May 4), and musicians and funfairs (in May).

THE HÉMONY BROTHERS
The carillon of the Royal Palace was cast by François and Pierre Hémony (1610–67 and 1620–80). From Levécourt in the Lorraine, they emigrated to Zutphen (1642) during the Thirty Years' War. They established their workshop on the Keizersgracht, near the Molenpad, and are buried in the Nieuwe Kerk.

ROYAL PALACE ★

In 1648 construction work began on a new Town Hall to replace the old building, which dated from the 14th century. The architect Jacob van Campen (1595–1657) was responsible for introducing the classical style to Amsterdam, with its solid lines, great richness of ornament and fine Bentheim stone. Van Campen departed from the somewhat fantastical

The former Town Hall, the oldest part of which was built in the 14th century, was destroyed by a fire on July 7, 1652. Painting by P.J. Saenredam (1597–1665).

forms of the Dutch Renaissance and built in a plainer, more substantial style. At the time, the result was something of a surprise. Supported on 13,659 piles, the building is 262 feet in length and 184 feet in breadth. It was the symbol for the outside world of the prosperity of a city devoted to business. Inside, the reception room (Burgerzaal) is the most imposing of the many rooms. Although the foundation stone was laid on October 29, 1648, progress was soon delayed: should the Town Hall be finished first, or the tower of the neighboring Nieuwe Kerk? A misunderstanding arose between Jacob van Campen and Daniel Stalpaert ● *36*, appointed city architect in 1648, who wished to make changes to the original plans. This culminated in Van Campen's final departure in 1654. But matters were speeded along by a fire at the old Town Hall just next door in 1652, and on July 9, 1655, the city's leaders were finally able to move into their new building. In the second half of the 17th century and throughout the 18th century the city administration was based here, as well as the magistrature. In 1808, however, everything changed: while King Louis was resident in Amsterdam, he chose to live at the Town Hall, and the city council was therefore obliged to move (as they had done in the

The National Monument
Inaugurated on May 4, 1956, at the center of the Dam, it is the place where those who died in the Second World War are honored each year in the presence of the royal family and members of the Government. The monument is the work of the architect J.J.P. Oud and sculptor J. Raedecker. The Dam also serves as a meeting place for young people (left). Musicians play in the open air, and small fairs are also held there.

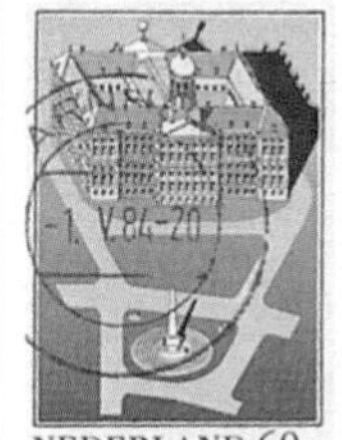

The construction of the new Town Hall, portrayed by J. Lingelbach (1622–74). The Public Weighhouse occupies the center of the square, which is busy with the market.

Behind the Royal Palace, the old Post Office (below left) has been converted into a shopping center ● *80*. The old De Drie Fleschjes café (below right, and right) stands in Gravenstraat.

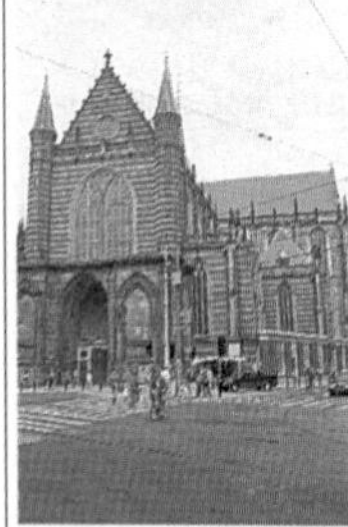

THE ROYAL CHURCH
From William I in 1814 to Beatrix in 1980, kings and queens have all been enthroned in the Nieuwe Kerk (above). As well as the De Ruyter mausoleum, the church contains the tombs of Jan van Galen, killed in a naval battle against the English in 1653, of Admiral van Kinsbergen (1735–1819) and of J. C. van Speyk (1802–31), whose ship was sunk at Antwerp during the Belgian war of independence. Also buried here are the mayors C.P. Hooft ▲ *162* and Jan Six ▲ *206*, Dr Tulp ▲ *182*, the painter Jan Lievens, the engraver Reinier Vinkeles, the architect J.J. Bilhamer, the poet and historian P.C. Hooft ▲ *186*, Professor Caspar van Baerle ▲ *143*, the great economist Pieter de la Court and, finally, the diplomat R.J. Schimmelpenninck (1761–1825).

years 1652–5) into the Prinsenhof ▲ *144*. Napoleon's brother made alterations to the interior of the palace, and a balcony was added to the façade.

TOWN HALL OR ROYAL PALACE? After the 1813 Revolution, the palace was given to William of Orange, now King William I. In 1873 a group of leading citizens asked the city council to recover the building so that it might once more be used as the town hall. An agreement was concluded on December 19, 1935. The city gave up all its claims to the building in exchange for a payment from the state of ten million guilders, which was to provide for the construction of a new city building: the "Stopera" ▲ *160*, finally built in the 1980's, at a far higher cost. The Royal Palace still belongs to the sovereign, whose principal residence is in The Hague, the seat of the Dutch parliament and government. In the Middle Ages the States General, the representative body of the Dutch provinces, used to meet in The Hague, at the palace of the counts of Holland. The United Provinces continued with this arrangement, which explains why the political institutions are to be found in The Hague, and not in Amsterdam, which is nonetheless the capital of the country. The queen only occasionally occupies the palace on the Dam, notably for official receptions.

NIEUWE KERK ★

● 78

The Nieuwe Kerk (New Church), adjoining the Royal Palace, was built in the 15th century. On November 15, 1408, the bishop of Utrecht authorized the inhabitants of Amsterdam to build a second parish church, the first being the Oude Kerk ▲ *134*. The town was beginning to grow, and its burgeoning wealth permitted this new construction. In 1421 part of the town burned down, and the as yet unfinished church was damaged. Work continued until 1452, the year of the terrible fire of Amsterdam: only the Oude Kerk and the surrounding area escaped the blaze ● *28*. Built in the Gothic style, the Nieuwe Kerk was beautifully decorated but in 1578 the church came into the hands of the Calvinists, who cleared it of statues and altars. Only the porch escaped the ravages of iconoclasm. The church survived a fire in 1645, but was eclipsed by the construction of the Town Hall, and its great bell tower was never built. As the three bells cast by François Hémony were small, it was possible to hang them in the small tower at the intersection of the roofs. At the end of the 17th century a mausoleum was built in the church for Michiel Adriaansz. de Ruyter (1607–76), the Netherlands' greatest admiral ▲ *148*.

JOHANES BLAEU
From 1666 to 1672 the Blaeu family's map-printing house stood in the Blaeu Erf, near the Nieuwe Kerk, until it burned down ● *41*.

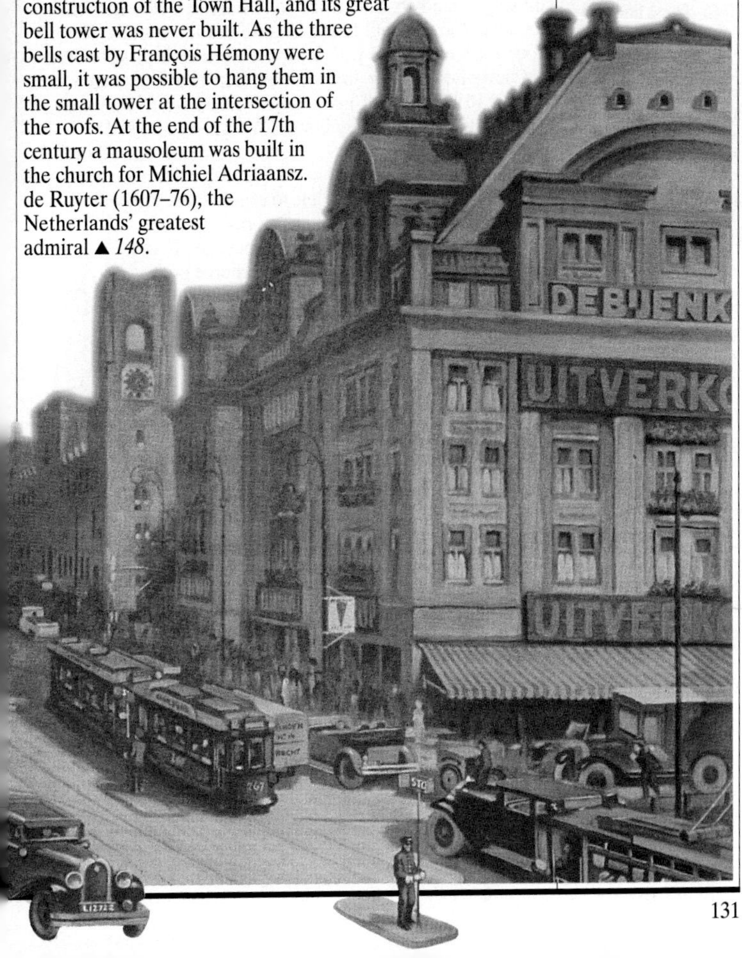

The Damrak, which runs between the Dam and the station, in the 1930's.

Zocher's Exchange, built in the 19th century.

View of the Exchange in 1668 by Job Adriaensz. Berckheyde (1630–93).

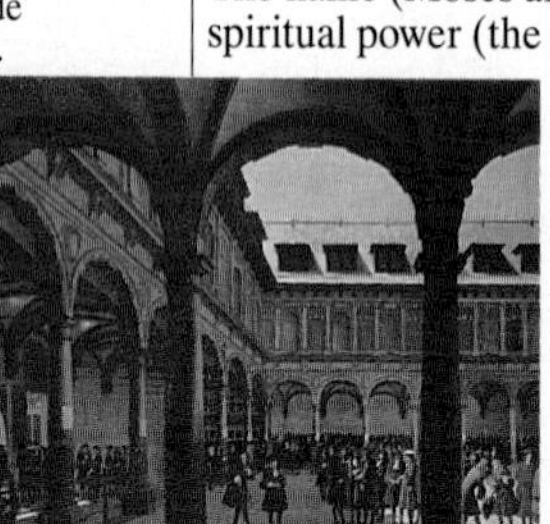

MOZES EN AARONSTRAAT. This street runs from the Royal Palace and the Nieuwe Kerk to the Nieuwezijds Voorburgwal. The name (Moses and Aaron) represents both temporal and spiritual power (the old Town Hall and the church). Between 1942 and 1945 the street was known as Poststraat as the Germans did not wish to retain the names of Jewish biblical figures.

STORY OF THE STOCK EXCHANGE

From the Middle Ages, when trade first began to develop in Holland, the merchants used to meet together regularly to conduct business. They naturally congregated near the port, close to the mouth of the Amstel, on the Damrak and Rokin. These meetings originally took place in the open air on Warmoesstraat between the Sint Olofspoort and Oudezijds Armsteeg. When the weather was bad, the merchants would shelter beneath the canopies of the houses. By the 16th century other great European cities such as London and Antwerp already had their indoor exchanges. Hendrick de Keyser ▲ *156* was sent to the English capital to study the Stock Exchange there with a view to gaining inspiration from it in designing one for Amsterdam. "The new Exchange was built on Rokin in 1608, just a stone's throw from the Town Hall and the Public Weighhouse (Waag) – symbols of patrician jurisdiction over the economy. Confined within the fine courtyard with its Mannerist Flemish colonnade, the Exchange was more or less left to regulate itself. It was not a matter of the city thinking up rules for the Exchange, but of creating a barrier between it and the commerce of the town. And this was

THE PRIDE OF AMSTERDAM
The Exchange in 1665. These lines are inscribed in a medallion on one of the façades: "The glory of Ephesus was the temple, Tyre had its market and its port, Babylon its walls of stone, Memphis its pyramids, Rome its Empire: the whole world praises me."

a barrier of time, as well as a physical barrier. The Exchange was the only place authorized for such business, and dealing could only take place between midday and two o'clock. Opening and closing times were strictly marked by the great clock tower that dominated the courtyard, and members who arrived after the fixed times were fined. If paintings such as those of Job Berckheyde and Emmanuel de Witte portray the meetings as peaceful affairs, written accounts give a rather different picture of behavior at the Exchange." (Simon Schama, *An Embarrassment of Riches*). Built over the Amstel, the Exchange stood on top of five arches, the main one being sufficiently large for boats with masts to pass beneath. In 1835 the original Hendrick de Keyser building was demolished, and ten years later Jan David Zocher (1791–1870) designed a new Exchange. Zocher is rather better known as a landscape painter than as the architect of this classical building, which was described by Jacob van Lennep ▲ *197* as "a little Ionic portico giving onto a little Doric temple". Not suitable for its purpose, this Exchange quickly proved unsatisfactory, and toward the end of the century Hendrik Berlage came up with some proposals for a new one.

BERLAGE'S EXCHANGE ★ ● *81*

On a block of land obtained by the compulsory purchase of building plots near Warmoesstraat and by partially filling in the Damrak, a canalized part of the Amstel, Hendrik Petrus Berlage (1856–1934) ▲ *279* built Amsterdam's new Exchange, which was completed in 1903. The design of the building, which stretches along the whole length of the Damrak, was a great influence on early 20th-century Amsterdam architecture and it is also remarkable for the simplicity of its materials. It is mainly constructed in brick, but the use of iron, notably in the roof spans of the three halls, is a novel element. Several other artists contributed to the decoration of the building: there are sculptures by Lambertus Zijl and Mendes da Costa, murals by Jan Toorop and R.N. Roland Holst, as well as stained glass by Professor A.J. der Kinderen. The poet Albert Verwey contributed some of the inscriptions on the clocks (*Beidt Uw Tijd* and *Duur Uw Uur*, meaning "Bide your time" and "Last your hour") and on the façades of the building. The Exchange now houses two delightful concert halls (it is the home of the Netherlands Philharmonic Orchestra) and is used for various exhibitions, meetings and lectures. "From the architectural point of view, the Exchange is the most interesting building in Amsterdam. I pass the Exchange at least once a week and I go into it regularly. I never fail to knock on the massive wood of the doors and to stroke the pale red brick with my fingers, this incomparable Dutch brick, produced by baking the rich, greasy clay dug beside the towpaths on the banks of our rivers" (Max van Rooy.)

HENDRIK PETRUS BERLAGE
A pupil of Cuypers ▲ *211*, Berlage was an architect whose influential building style led to a considerable renewal of ideas in the Netherlands and in Europe generally at the turn of the century. His most famous project, the Amsterdam Exchange, is flanked by a clock tower ornamented with sculptures, which dominates the Damrak (left and below). The great hall (bottom) has a roof of glass and metal.

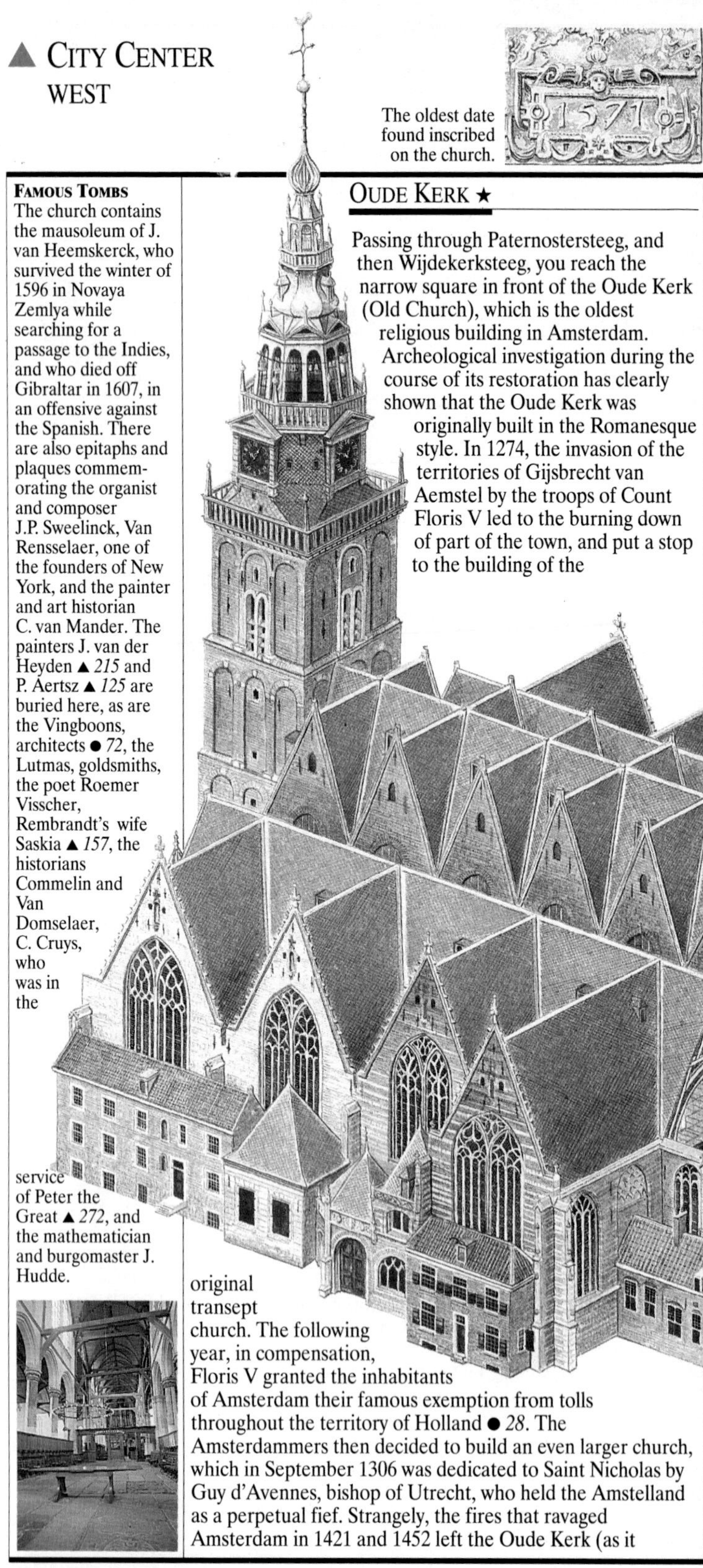

The oldest date found inscribed on the church.

FAMOUS TOMBS
The church contains the mausoleum of J. van Heemskerck, who survived the winter of 1596 in Novaya Zemlya while searching for a passage to the Indies, and who died off Gibraltar in 1607, in an offensive against the Spanish. There are also epitaphs and plaques commemorating the organist and composer J.P. Sweelinck, Van Rensselaer, one of the founders of New York, and the painter and art historian C. van Mander. The painters J. van der Heyden ▲ *215* and P. Aertsz ▲ *125* are buried here, as are the Vingboons, architects ● *72*, the Lutmas, goldsmiths, the poet Roemer Visscher, Rembrandt's wife Saskia ▲ *157*, the historians Commelin and Van Domselaer, C. Cruys, who was in the service of Peter the Great ▲ *272*, and the mathematician and burgomaster J. Hudde.

OUDE KERK ★

Passing through Paternostersteeg, and then Wijdekerksteeg, you reach the narrow square in front of the Oude Kerk (Old Church), which is the oldest religious building in Amsterdam. Archeological investigation during the course of its restoration has clearly shown that the Oude Kerk was originally built in the Romanesque style. In 1274, the invasion of the territories of Gijsbrecht van Aemstel by the troops of Count Floris V led to the burning down of part of the town, and put a stop to the building of the original transept church. The following year, in compensation, Floris V granted the inhabitants of Amsterdam their famous exemption from tolls throughout the territory of Holland ● *28*. The Amsterdammers then decided to build an even larger church, which in September 1306 was dedicated to Saint Nicholas by Guy d'Avennes, bishop of Utrecht, who held the Amstelland as a perpetual fief. Strangely, the fires that ravaged Amsterdam in 1421 and 1452 left the Oude Kerk (as it

The coat of arms of Maximilian of Austria and of Philip the Fair.

became known during the building of the Nieuwe Kerk) untouched. This explains why a great part of the original architectural structure has survived. As the south porch is decorated with the arms of Maximilian of Austria and of his son Philip the Fair, it is possible that these sovereigns made a considerable contribution to its construction. By the middle of the 16th century the imposing church had been largely completed, and in 1565 it received its bell tower, which can still be admired, as can the carillon cast by François Hémony (1658) ▲ *128*. The octagonal tower was probably the work of Joost Jansz Bilhamer. The church is characterized by its triple nave and elaborate vaulting, which from the outside gives the roof a highly distinctive appearance, particularly for the Netherlands. In the year after the tower was finished, Calvinist iconoclasm raged in Amsterdam, leading to serious damage being done to the altars: in 1578 Amsterdam went over to the Protestant party, and the church came into Calvinist hands ● *29*. Its interior is therefore particularly sober, except for the organ added in the 17th century. From the beginning, the Oude Kerk was the principal church in Amsterdam, and it remained so despite the wishes of the inhabitants of the newer part of the city ● *34*, who in the 15th century hoped to make their parish church, the Nieuwe Kerk ▲ *131*, the principal church. Although it was enlarged and given a south entrance on the Dam, it did not succeed, initially, in supplanting the Oude Kerk, which after the Reformation remained the most important religious edifice.

Organ concerts
The austerity of the Oude Kerk interior, a result of Reformation taste, was alleviated by the installation of the great organ in the 17th century. Today concerts are often held in the church, and the carillon chimes every day ◆ *294*.

"Amsterdam is intersected in all directions by a multitude of interlinking canals, which break the city up into hundreds of islands connected to each other by around five hundred bridges. This alone, it seems, would be enough to assure it of a status more or less unique in the world. But, what is even more typical, what makes it especially distinctive, is that it has retained all its age-old finery."
Henry Havard, *La Hollande à vol d'oiseau*

In the 17th century, the diaconate moved into a new building on Gravenstraat, just next door to the Nieuwe Kerk. The church council, which already divided its summer and winter meetings between the two churches, now established itself permanently at the Nieuwe Kerk. King William I was crowned there, and so the rivalry was at last over: since the 19th century the Nieuwe Kerk has been the national church of the Netherlands. Since the beginning of the 20th century the Old Church has been looked after by the Oude Kerk Foundation, which has been restoring it since 1955. Concerts are often held there, which offer an opportunity to appreciate the great organ ● *49*.

WINDOWS
Be they windows with red lights, or just shop windows, in this area they are often an enticing sight!

RED LIGHT DISTRICT ▲ *114*

The square around the Oude Kerk is right next to the official prostitution district. The visitor is therefore forced to switch abruptly from looking at the oldest church in Amsterdam, or from hearing a concert of organ music by Bach, Schütz or Sweelinck, to the sight of prostitutes' windows. These occupy some of the houses on the square and the whole of the neighborhood, which used to be frequented above all by sailors, when the port was only a stone's throw away. The Belgian singer Jacques Brel expressed the atmosphere of the area in his song *Amsterdam*: "There are sailors who sing/Of the dreams that haunt them/When they are off Amsterdam [...] In the port of Amsterdam/There are sailors who drink/And drink again./They drink to the health of the prostitutes of Amsterdam,/Of Hamburg or elsewhere." The working port has now moved west, to the edge of the town, but the official prostitution district is still here, on Oudezijds Voorburgwal and Zeedijk, which runs between Saint Nicholas' Church and the Nieuwe Markt ▲ *152*. It is impossible to avoid the prostitutes' windows, with their red lights above, when walking through the narrow streets. This area is also frequented by drug-dealers, and here too are found the great majority of Amsterdam's marijuana-selling coffee shops ● *41*. "This is the Zeedijk, the sailors' quarter. It is here that at the end of their long and dangerous voyages the Dutch sailors come to rest from their labors and get drunk on love and gin. There is nothing more curious, or less edifying than to walk through

THE CHAPEL OF THE OLD QUARTER
An 18th-century view of the chapel, which stood on Oudezijds Armsteeg.

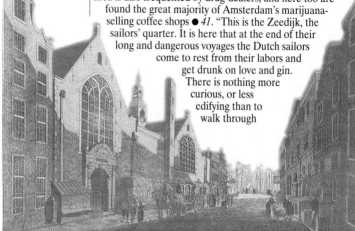

this neighborhood, full of crowded bars, clubs and *Tapperijen*, where the sign *Zeeman-logement* clearly indicates the kind of tenants they are looking for, while the girls, oiled, pommaded and made up, displaying their repugnant graces on the doorsteps of their dwellings, inform us that the traveler will find there a good bed 'and the rest', as La Fontaine put it." So wrote Henry Havard at the end of the 19th century. A century later, very little has changed!

AMSTELKRING MUSEUM ★

In the midst of this sordid environment, a few yards from the Oude Kerk at no. 40 Oudezijds Voorburgwal, stands one of the smallest museums in Amsterdam, and also one of the most attractive. In 1663, at a time when only Calvinist Protestantism could be openly practised ● *39*, these early 17th-century commercial premises were converted into a private Roman Catholic chapel dedicated to Saint Nicholas, patron saint of Amsterdam. It was enlarged in the course of internal renovations and transformed into a secret church. Mass was said on the upper floor, giving rise to the popular name for the church: *Onze Lieve Heer op Zolder* (Our Lord in the Attic). The church functioned until 1887, when a larger church dedicated to Saint Nicholas was built opposite the Central Station. After 1888 the Church of "Our Lord in the Attic" was converted into the Amstelkring Museum, which attracts visitors because of its historical interest and its collections of religious art. Just before the Second World War the building was completely restored. One can wander through the different levels and visit the various rooms that make up this astonishing museum, from the priest's bedroom to the church itself, where there is a partly collapsible altar. In an emergency, if Protestants arrived, it vanished behind panels.

STEP GABLE
This house at no. 14 Oudezijds Voorburgwal dates from 1605. Above, a detail from the decoration of the façade.Left, the chapel in the Amstelkring Museum.

"Look, only a few streets away there is a museum called 'Our Lord in the Attic'. In those days they put their catacombs up under the roofs. What else can you do, the cellars around here are flooded. But today, you can be sure, their Lord is neither in the attic nor in the cellar. They have put him on a bench, in their innermost hearts, and they thump on, above all they judge, they judge in his name. He spoke gently to sinners: 'Neither do I condemn you,' "
Albert Camus, *The Fall.*

SINT-NICOLAAS KERK ● *79*

Standing on Prins Hendrikkade, the Roman Catholic church of Saint Nicholas is one of the more recent churches to have been built in the city center and provides a landmark just outside the station. This imposing building, in neo-Renaissance style, is characterized by a cupola and two great frontal towers. It was designed by A.C. Bleys (1842–1912), who also designed the house at no. 508 Keizersgracht ▲ *196*. It was consecrated in 1888.

The station façade, looking toward the city, stretches for several hundred yards. Its style is very similar to that of the Rijksmuseum ▲ *212*.

CENTRAL STATION ● *80*

When the government was considering the development of the railways after 1860, the Den Helder-Alkmaar-Amsterdam line was planned to allow connections with other existing or proposed means of transport.

ARGUMENT ABOUT THE SITE. There began a debate about where the station should be built. Some were in favour of a site on the Leidseplein ▲ *190,* linked to the building of a bridge over the Amstel for the line to Utrecht; others argued the need for a line running along the southern side of the city, which was rapidly expanding at that time. Then there were those who argued for a line to the north of the city, with a central station on the IJ. In 1864 the prime minister Johan Rudolf Thorbecke (1798–1872) ▲ *207* invited the city council to give its opinion. They came out unanimously against a station on the IJ and opted for a site behind the Leidsepoort ▲ *191*. But the state engineer preferred a station on the IJ, and his point of view prevailed thanks to government pressure.

SEVEN YEARS' WORK. The construction of the railway and of the station totally cut off the city's access to the IJ: this was the principal complaint against the project, and the maritime capacity of Amsterdam suffered considerably because of it. In addition, the station, which opens onto Damrak, has considerably accentuated the monocentric nature of the city center, organized along the Damrak-Dam-Rokin-Rembrandtplein-Leidseplein axis. Construction began in 1882, based on plans drawn up by P.J.H. Cuypers (1827–1921) ▲ *211* and A. L. van Gendt (1835–1901) ▲ *216*. On October 15, 1889, the station, which rests on three artificial islands and 8,700 piles, became operational.

SINT OLOFSPOORT
CENTRUM

SINT OLOFSPOORT
This lane off Prins Hendrikkade near Saint Nicholas' Church, is in the oldest part of Amsterdam. Nearby the little Oudezijds Kolk canal lies alongside the church; before the construction of the station it ran directly into the IJ.

The Open Havenfront canal separates the station from Saint Nicholas' Church (below, an early 20th-century view).

CITY CENTER EAST

ROKIN, *140*
ALLARD PIERSON MUSEUM, *141*
LANGEBRUGSTEEG, *142*
NES AND KUIPERSSTEEG, *142*
HOUSE ON THE
THREE CANALS, *142*
AGNIETEN KAPEL, *143*
OUDEMANHUISPOORT, *144*
PRINSENHOF, *144*
WALLOON CHURCH, *145*
HEADQUARTERS OF THE DUTCH
EAST INDIA COMPANY, *145*
THE DUTCH EAST INDIA
COMPANY, *146*
KLOVENIERSBURGWAL, *151*
TRIPPENHUIS, *151*
NIEUWMARKT, *152*
SCHREIERSTOREN, *153*
SCHEEPVAARTHUIS, *154*
MONTELBAANSTOREN, *155*
SINT ANTONIESBREESTRAAT, *156*
ZUIDERKERK, *156*
REMBRANDTHUIS, *156*
JONAS DANIEL
MEIJERPLEIN, *158*
SYNAGOGUE OF THE
PORTUGUESE JEWS, *158*
SYNAGOGUE OF THE
GERMAN JEWS, *158*
MOZES EN AARONKERK, *159*
WATERLOOPLEIN, *160*
"STOPERA", *160*

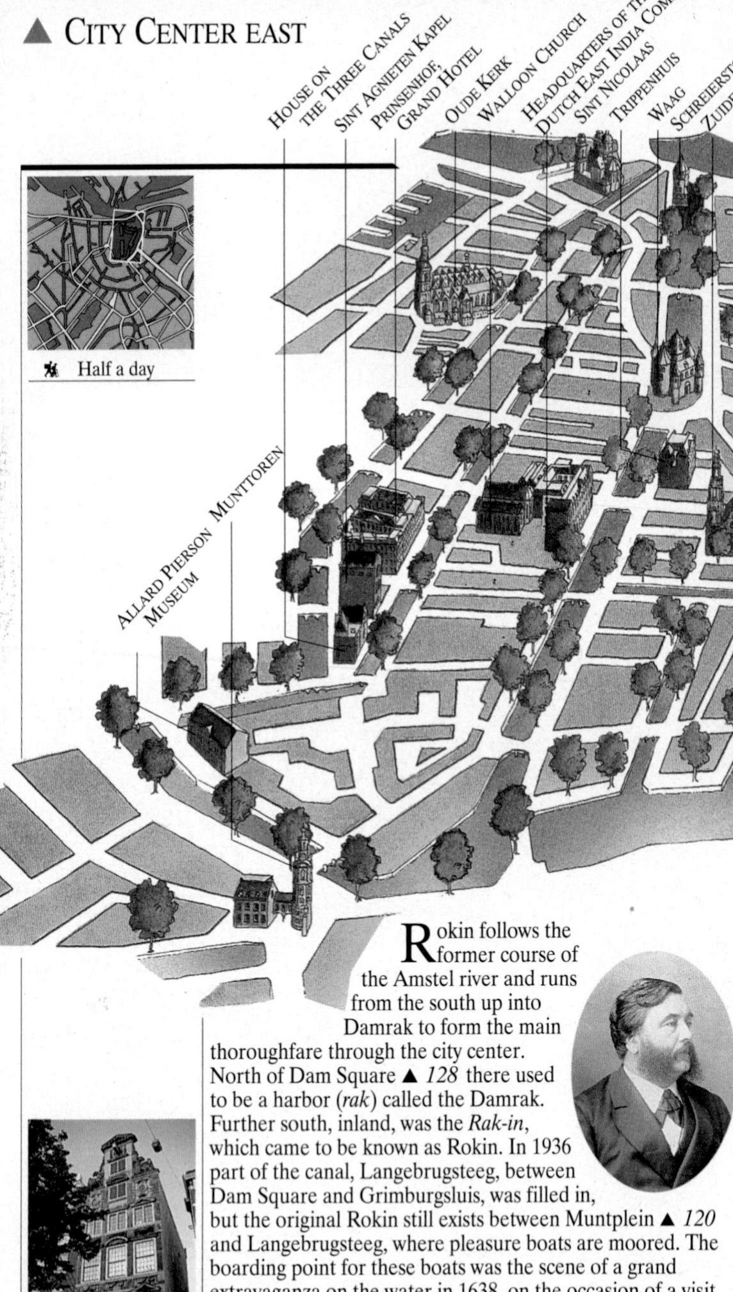

Rokin follows the former course of the Amstel river and runs from the south up into Damrak to form the main thoroughfare through the city center. North of Dam Square ▲ *128* there used to be a harbor (*rak*) called the Damrak. Further south, inland, was the *Rak-in*, which came to be known as Rokin. In 1936 part of the canal, Langebrugsteeg, between Dam Square and Grimburgsluis, was filled in, but the original Rokin still exists between Muntplein ▲ *120* and Langebrugsteeg, where pleasure boats are moored. The boarding point for these boats was the scene of a grand extravaganza on the water in 1638, on the occasion of a visit to Amsterdam by Marie de' Medici, the French queen mother ● *30, 46*.

OFFICES AND SHOPS. Today Rokin is lined with large office buildings, between which a few ancient houses have survived, especially at the quieter end. These residences have neck gable façades designed by Vingboons. The most eye-catching examples are at nos. 91 and 141-7 ● *72*. At the corner of SPUI ▲ *122*, which formed the southern boundary of the town until the end of the 14th century, a large commercial and artists' center has grown up around the EQUESTRIAN STATUE OF QUEEN WILHELMINA; it includes the Maison de Bonneterie (nos.140–2), and the headquarters of the ARTI ET AMICITIAE

ANCIENT GABLES
Among the new buildings in Rokin, a few ancient houses have survived. At no. 91 the gabled façade, designed by Vingboons, is decorated with eagles ● *72*.

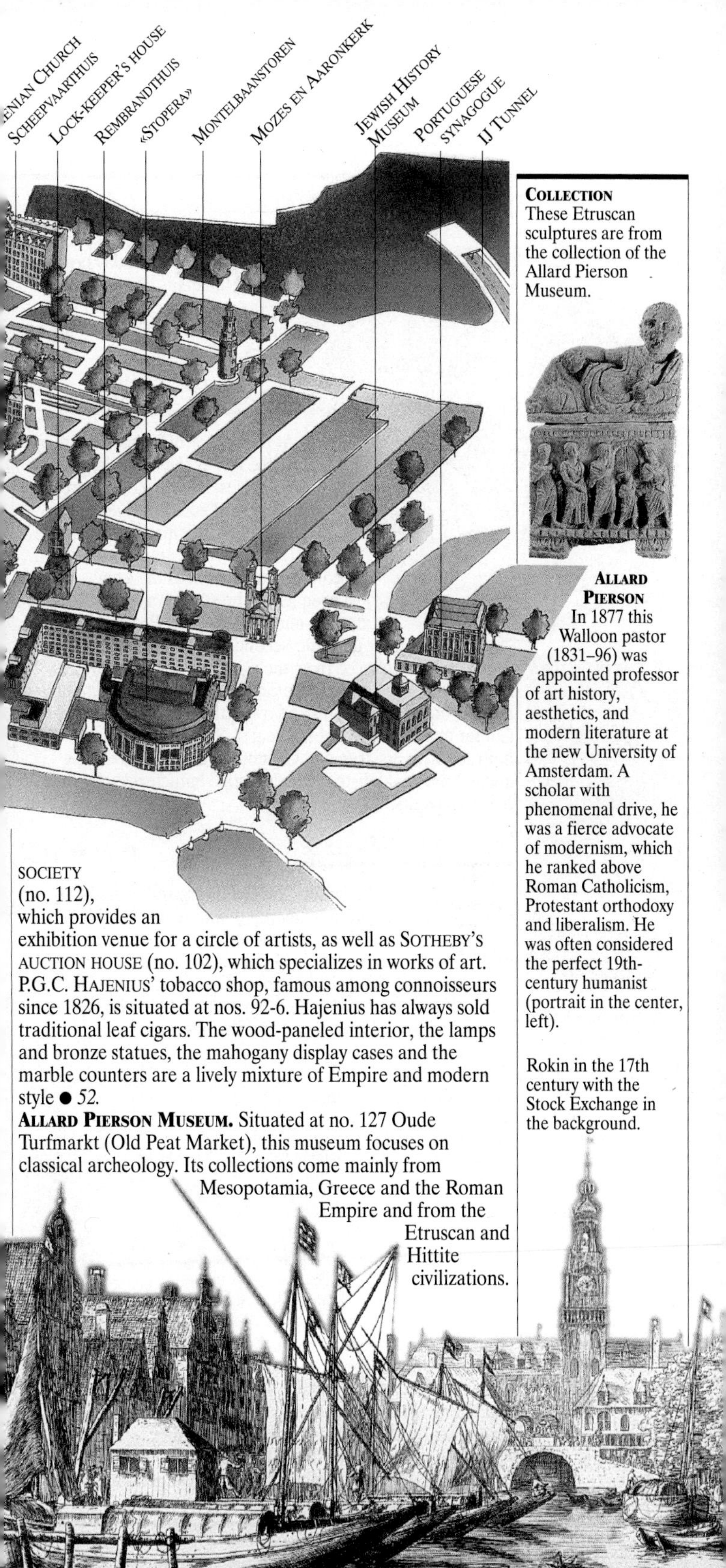

COLLECTION
These Etruscan sculptures are from the collection of the Allard Pierson Museum.

ALLARD PIERSON
In 1877 this Walloon pastor (1831–96) was appointed professor of art history, aesthetics, and modern literature at the new University of Amsterdam. A scholar with phenomenal drive, he was a fierce advocate of modernism, which he ranked above Roman Catholicism, Protestant orthodoxy and liberalism. He was often considered the perfect 19th-century humanist (portrait in the center, left).

Rokin in the 17th century with the Stock Exchange in the background.

SOCIETY (no. 112), which provides an exhibition venue for a circle of artists, as well as SOTHEBY'S AUCTION HOUSE (no. 102), which specializes in works of art. P.G.C. HAJENIUS' tobacco shop, famous among connoisseurs since 1826, is situated at nos. 92-6. Hajenius has always sold traditional leaf cigars. The wood-paneled interior, the lamps and bronze statues, the mahogany display cases and the marble counters are a lively mixture of Empire and modern style ● *52*.

ALLARD PIERSON MUSEUM. Situated at no. 127 Oude Turfmarkt (Old Peat Market), this museum focuses on classical archeology. Its collections come mainly from Mesopotamia, Greece and the Roman Empire and from the Etruscan and Hittite civilizations.

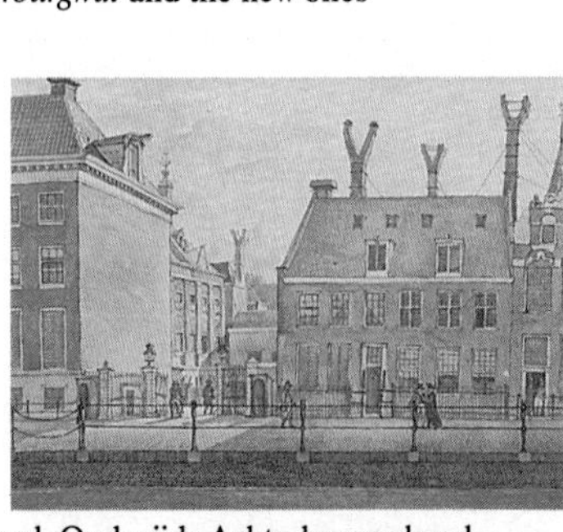

LANGEBRUGSTEEG

This little street leads to GRIMBURGWAL. The former buildings of the central hospital today house faculties of the University of Amsterdam, including the political science building, the cultural center and a university refectory, the *Atrium*.

NES AND KUIPERSSTEEG

At the corner of Langebrugsteeg, on the left, is the beginning of the Nes, a long, narrow street, the name of which derives from *Nesse*, meaning "marshy field". In the 15th and 16th centuries several convents were built in the area; subsequently the street was taken over by craftsmen and shopkeepers. From the 19th century until the Second World War it was famous for the sale of tobacco from the East Indies, especially at Frascati's. Nes was also a center of culture, entertainment and leisure, noted for *De Brakke Grond*, the Flemish Cultural Center and De Engelenbak theater. The little passage between Kuiperssteeg and Grimburgwal is typical of this ancient medieval district which is still characterized by the many convents.

THE THREE CANALS ★ ■ 18 ● 60,72

GRIMBURGWAL CENTRUM

In the 14th century the Grimburgwal formed the city's southern boundary (*grim* means "muddy ditch"). Before 1385 the river Amstel divided the city into two almost equal halves: the old side (*oude zijde*) and the new side (*nieuwe zijde*). Each was demarcated by a moat. When new moats were dug, around 1385, the existing ones were called *Voorburgwal* and the new ones *Achterburgwal*.

SINT AGNIETEN KAPEL
Saint Agnes Chapel once served as an Admiralty warehouse, used to store trade goods in particular (top).

OUDEMANHUISPOORT
A passage between Oudezijds Achterburgwal and Kloveniersburgwal, Oudemanhuispoort (above) was built around 1600. When Amsterdam University was founded, the buildings became part of the university complex. Right, a view of the Oudezijds Voorburgwal.

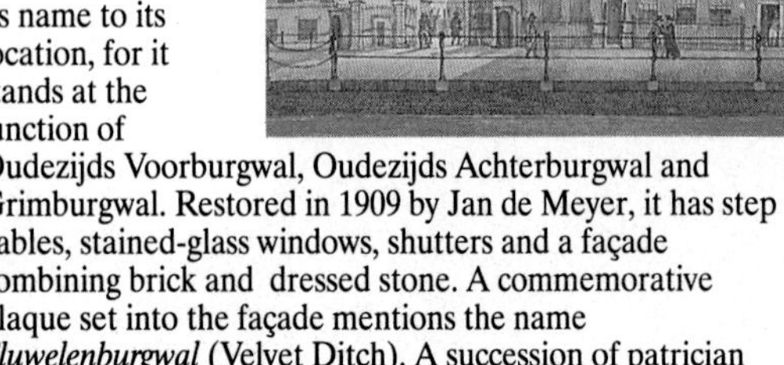

HOUSE ON THE THREE CANALS ★ ● 72.
One of the most beautiful residences of the city, the Huis op de Drie Grachten owes its name to its location, for it stands at the junction of Oudezijds Voorburgwal, Oudezijds Achterburgwal and Grimburgwal. Restored in 1909 by Jan de Meyer, it has step gables, stained-glass windows, shutters and a façade combining brick and dressed stone. A commemorative plaque set into the façade mentions the name *Fluwelenburgwal* (Velvet Ditch). A succession of patrician families lived here, including the Reael, Oetgens, and Roeters. Nowadays it is a bookshop.

Agnieten Kapel. At no. 231 Oudezijds Voorburgwal is the only chapel, built in 1397, of a medieval convent that has been preserved intact. After being burned to the ground, the convent was rebuilt in 1470. In 1578, when Calvinism was at its height ● *29*, the building was given a new function as an Admiralty warehouse. In 1632 it became the Atheneum Illustre (Illustrious Atheneum) devoted to higher education ▲ *197*, and from the middle of the 17th century it was the focus of scientific life in the capital, also housing the municipal library until 1838. The first two professors of the Illustrious Atheneum were famous scholars from the University of Leiden: Caspar van Baerle (Barlaeus) and Geeraerd Vossius. Barlaeus gave an opening speech on the "Mercator sapiens" (Wise Merchant), and Vossius discoursed "De Historia Utilitate" (On the Usefulness of History). The two men had to work hard to gain acceptance: their reputation was initially tarnished by the fact that they were considered to be exponents of liberal ideas. In 1877 the Latin School of the Illustrious Atheneum was replaced by the municipal University of Amsterdam, which was granted the right to confer the distinction of Doctor. The restoration of the chapel was carried out under the supervision of the architect A.A. Kok (1881–1951), who succeeded in preserving the

Kuiperssteeg
This is the site of the former Convent of Saint Claire. In the 17th century it was a cooperage. The cartouches of no. 3, above, depict craftsmen.

Langebrugsteeg
There are several shops specializing in objects made of precious metals in this little street. Left, the window of a jeweler's shop.

Tropical fanlights
In Rusland one house has doors which feature fanlights of tropical inspiration, probably influenced by the Netherlands' colonial past.

An early 20th-century photograph of the northern part of Oudezijds Achterburgwal.

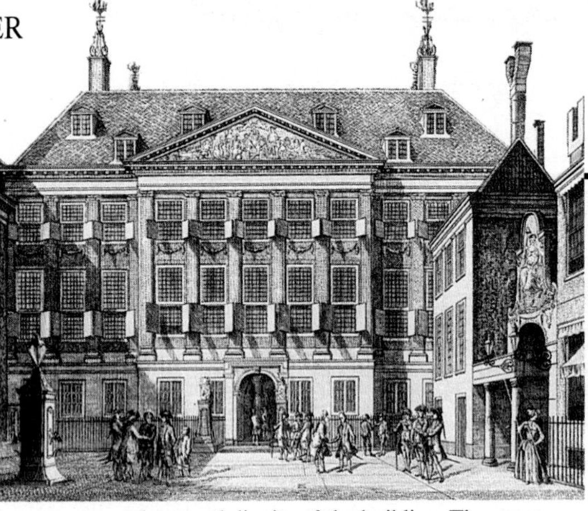

This view of the Admiralty headquarters was painted in the 17th century by Pierre Fouquet. The courtyard of the Prinsenhof is almost unchanged, and today it is a prestigious

hotel, The Grand, with a 20th-century façade overlooking the canal (detail above).

beauty, atmosphere and dignity of the building. The steep, Gothic-style roof is adorned with a slender turret and the various turning points in the Atheneum's history are recorded on the gates.

OUDEMANHUISPOORT ★. Between Oudezijds Achterburgwal and Kloveniersburgwal there used to be an almshouse for elderly men which was built around 1600. It later became part of the University of Amsterdam. Secondhand book stalls now line the passage, which leads to a lovely interior courtyard.

RUSLAND. This name, contrary to expectations, has nothing to do with Russia. It is a somewhat distorted reference to the name of Willem Russchen, who owned this plot of land according to an act passed in 1403. In the 16th century a stream ran across the land. Houses were built on its banks, and it was subsequently filled in. That is why Rusland is wider than the other thoroughfares in the old city.

Notables gathering at the Prinsenhof for a meal in 1597.

THE STATE PAWN SHOP. After 1578 the Calvinist Protestants were strongly opposed to the Lombard usurers, who played an important part in trade. To assist citizens whose income was limited or sporadic, it was decided that, to circumvent the usurers, the municipality itself should act as a moneylender. That is how the STADSBANK VAN LENING (State Pawn Shop), situated at no. 300 Oudezijds Voorburgwal, came to be founded. This period is evoked by two neighboring streets called Enge and Wijde Lombardsteeg (meaning narrow and wide Lombard Streets). At no. 274 Oudezijds Voorburgwal, the former Vleeshal (Meat Market) is surmounted by stone cattle heads, recalling the building's original function.

This mural by Karel Appel, in the former canteen of the City Hall, did not find favor with the municipal employees who worked there.

PRINSENHOF ★

Opposite, on the right bank of the canal, the Prinsenhof was built on the site of the former Convent of Saint Cecilia. After 1578 it became a royal residence before being renovated to host meetings of the Admiralty. When Louis-Napoleon decreed that the City Hall on Dam Square should be transformed into the Royal Palace (1808) ● *32* ▲ *128*, the Prinsenhof became in turn the seat of Amsterdam's municipal council. Following the construction of a new City Hall, the "Stopera" ▲ *160*, in the 1980's, it was converted into a luxury

"I LIKE WALKING THROUGH THE CITY AT NIGHT, WARMED BY GIN. I WALK FOR WHOLE NIGHTS AT A TIME, DREAMING OR TALKING ENDLESSLY TO MYSELF."

ALBERT CAMUS

OUDE ZIJDS VOOR BURGWAL
CENTRUM

hotel, The Grand. The courtyard retains the original style. The early 20th-century Amsterdam School exterior, especially the main entrance and the façade, has been well preserved. The most radical alterations were made in the 1920's. The board room is from this period, as are the Art Deco banqueting hall and the marble staircase with its decorative stained-glass windows. In the lobby of the former City Hall workers' canteen, which is now the Café Roux, Karel Appel ● 93 ▲ 230 painted a fresco in 1949, an almost abstract modernist work entitled *Vragende Kinderen* (*Children Questioning*).

HERRING WITH GIN
At no. 18 Oude Doelenstraat, Jan Hendriks' fish shop sells its own special herring. Washed down with Korenmout gin, the herring is prized by Amsterdam gourmets ● *64*.

WALLOON CHURCH

At the end of Oude Doelenstraat, the *Pillenbrug* (a nickname meaning "bridge of pills and drugs") on the Oudezijds Achterburgwal is famous for its trade in illegal or semi-illicit substances. Beyond the bridge on the right, slightly set back from the canal, the Oude Walenkerk (Walloon Church) is the last remnant of the medieval convent of the Brethren of Saint Paul. In 1586 the municipality gave the remains of the ancient chapel to the Walloon Protestants, who had arrived as refugees in 1540, enabling them to continue their Protestant worship in French ● *38*.

OUDE WALENKERK
The old Walloon Church is the last vestige of the medieval convent of the Brethren of Saint Paul. In front of the church is the little Walloon Square (Waalsepleintje), which is quiet and secluded.

EGLISE WALLONNE
CULTE PROTESTANT EN FRANÇAIS
TOUS LES DIMANCHES

HEADQUARTERS OF THE DUTCH EAST INDIA COMPANY

At no. 24 Oude Hoogstraat, and along the Kloveniersburgwal, stands the former headquarters of the Company, which was established there in the 17th and 18th centuries. The history of Amsterdam and the Netherlands is closely bound up with its rise and fall.

The Oude Walenkerk can be seen below on an 18th–century document.

▲ The Dutch East India Company

Building a VOC ship (1647).

From the end of the 16th century the Dutch navy was trading with southeast Asia. In 1602 a number of trading companies in Amsterdam joined forces to organize a trading monopoly under the banner of the *Verenigde Oost-Indische Compagnie* (VOC) ● *30* ▲ *150*. The Dutch East India Company acquired powerful rights of sovereignty, including the power to make war and peace, and opened a number of trading posts in Japan, the East Indies, Ceylon and Tasmania. After tremendous prosperity in the 17th century, which benefited Amsterdam, the Company declined as a result of competition from England and France, and was bankrupt by the end of the 18th century.

Admiral Cornelis Tromp (1629–91)
Son of the great admiral Maarten Harpertsz Tromp (1598–1653), he helped build up the naval power of the VOC.

"Return from the Second Voyage to the East Indies"
In 1595 the Dutch organized their first expedition to the East Indies. Then in May 1599 a second returned. It is the second voyage that forms the subject of this painting by Hendrick Cornelis Vroom (1566–1640).

The headquarters of the Dutch East India Company
Situated on the corner of Kloveniersburgwal and Oude Hoogstraat, this building, a former arsenal and munitions depot, was rented to the Company from 1605. Ships could berth at the quay. For two centuries the *Oost-Indisch Huis* was the nerve center of the entire administration of the VOC, whose warehouses and offices were dotted throughout the city.

View of Batavia (Jakarta) by Andries Beeckman (1658).

François Valentijn, Dutch naturalist (1656–1727)
He was the author of *Oud en Nieuw-Oostindie*, on the flora and fauna of the East Indies (1724–8), with illustrations from his shell collection.

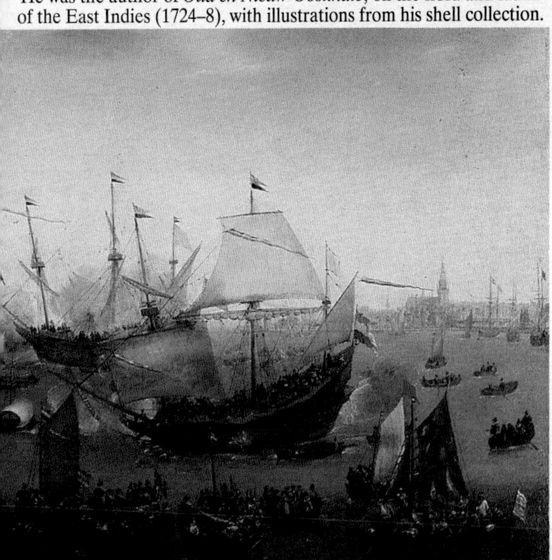

Trading negotiations with the Japanese
To increase its dividends and strengthen its monopoly, the Company extended its operations into eastern Asia as far as Japan, importing tea, sugar, silk, porcelain and lacquerwork.

An excess of wealth
The directors grew wealthy at the expense of their Asian trading partners. Dividends averaged between 18 and 20 percent; 1662 was a record-breaking year with dividends of 50 percent. The cost of the fourth war against the English (1780–4) and the partners' high incomes were partly responsible for the decline of the VOC.

Tea bush
Hendrick d'Acquet Collection ▲ *149.*

Singhalese script
N. Witsen's notes (1641–1717) are shown bottom left.

"Dutch Plantation in Bengal"
(H.V. Schuylenburg).

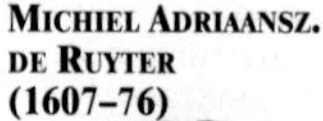

MICHIEL ADRIAANSZ. DE RUYTER (1607–76)

He sailed the seas from the age of eleven as a merchant seaman and climbed the rungs of the naval hierarchy in the service of the Republic, distinguishing himself in successive wars against the English. Admiral de Ruyter died fighting against the French fleet in the Mediterranean off Naples.

A FACTORY
The VOC in Bengal, right, painted by H.V. Schuylenburg in the 17th century.

THE DUTCH EXPLORERS
W. Janszoon reached the shores of Australia first in 1606, and Abel Tasman discovered Tasmania in 1642; the Dutch territories were colonized by the English in 1788.

MARITIME MUSEUM
Old VOC warehouses have been converted to a museum ▲ 270.

CHINESE PORCELAIN SALT BOX (17TH CENTURY)
Salt boxes at the time were made of wood. The VOC called on the expertise of Chinese ceramicists to produce porcelain boxes in conventional European shapes (below left).

"SQUADRON OF THE DUTCH EAST INDIA COMPANY"
(Ludoft Backhuysen, 17th century ● *88*)
The Company's archives record only 5 percent of ships lost. Fewer men died in shipwrecks or mutinies on board ship than through sickness as a result of poor hygiene, polluted water, food shortages and changes of climate. Attempts at improving hygiene by scrubbing with vinegar or smoking with juniper berries did not eliminate scurvy, typhoid fever or dysentery. And nothing could be done about the psychological effects of sea voyages known as "the great melancholy", which could lead to madness or suicide.

PASSION FLOWER
Seemingly crowned with thorns, nails and a hammer, symbols of Christ's Passion, the passion flower got its name in the 17th century.

ERYTHRINA ORIENTALIS
Herbert de Jager (1642–1706), in *Plants of Java*.

GRAPEFRUIT
Adriaan van Lee (1624–1715). These three drawings are from Hendrick d'Acquet's collection (1632– 1706). Mayor and alderman of Delft as well as a keen naturalist, he ordered the sailors and functionaries of the VOC to bring back anything of interest, and so built up a remarkable collection.

THE COURTYARD OF THE COMPANY HEADQUARTERS
At no. 24 Oude Hoogstraat is an entrance porch leading to the little courtyard of the former headquarters of the VOC. The perfectly preserved building, attributed to the architect Hendrick de Keyser, dates back to 1605. The gable above the façade, with its subtle, rounded shapes dominated by a balustrade, is unusual for Amsterdam ● *72* ▲ *146*. The building is now occupied by the Institute for Sociological Studies.

HISTORY OF THE DUTCH EAST INDIA COMPANY ● *30***.** Established in 1602, the Company brought together several trading firms. It was the brainchild of Johan van Oldenbarnevelt (1547–1619), by far the most influential politician in the young Republic. As he was responsible for signing the Treaty of Antwerp with Spain ● *29*, the orthodox Calvinists accused him of betraying his country, and he was executed in The Hague in 1619 at the age of seventy-two. The all-powerful VOC could sign treaties and maintain a fleet and an army. Divided into six chambers (Amsterdam, Middelburg, the Meuse estuary represented by Rotterdam and Delft, and West Friesland by Hoorn and Enkhuizen), the Company had sixty-three directors from the previous individual firms, headed by a board of directors comprising seventeen members, called the *Heren XVII* (Seventeen Magistrates). These directors were chosen from among the rich bourgeoisie of Holland, and their power was absolute. The sole aim of the Company was to profit through trade. This led to dissension between advocates of harmonious and widespread colonial development (particularly those who were not part of the VOC) and partisans of the monopoly maintained in accordance with the strict rules that had been laid down (the directors of the VOC). To strengthen its authority and improve cooperation between its very scattered trading posts, the Company became very centralized, appointing a single head: the governor general. The first governor, from 1609 to 1614, was Pieter Both, who

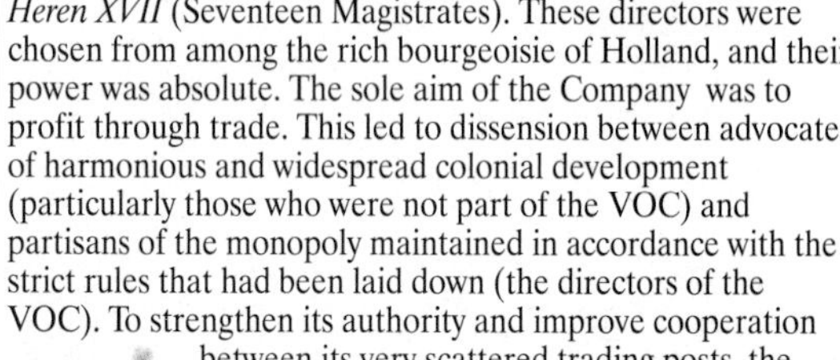

selected by the Council of the East Indies (consisting of five people). The seat of power was originally located at Banten (to the extreme west of Java) and then at Batavia (present-day Jakarta), founded by Jan Pieterszoon Coen on the ruins of the former Jacatra. To maintain its monopoly, the Company first had to extend its field of operations as far as Japan (Decima island), with the result that, in addition to spices from Indonesia, Amsterdam imported lacquer, tea, silk and porcelain from Japan and China, while India supplied cotton fabrics. The Company prospered until the end of the 18th century, before being officially disbanded on March 17, 1798, under the Batavian republic established by the French revolutionaries ● *31*.

TRIPPENHUIS
Home of the Tripp brothers, this building housed the sessions of the legislative assembly during the French occupation. The Royal Institute of Sciences and Fine Arts, inaugurated by Louis–Napoleon, was then established and a collection of paintings, including *The Night Watch* by Rembrandt, was kept there before the opening of the Rijksmuseum.

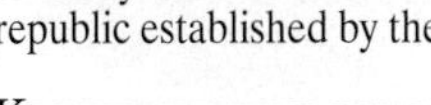

KLOVENIERSBURGWAL ■ *18* ● *60, 72, 74*

This canal takes its name from the militia men (*kloveniers*) who set up their associations and training grounds here ▲ *126*. Further up the canal is BETHANIENSTRAAT, named after the former Convent of Saint Mary Magdalen of Bethany (Bethanienkloster) which was built on this site around 1450. The district has some excellent examples of urban renewal. At nos. 6–8 Kloveniersburgwal the Brouwhuis Maximiliaan is a café-restaurant where malt and hops are prepared in red copper vats. The resulting sweet malt wort, or infusion, is then mixed with yeast and left to ferment in vats. According to ancient documents, the Bethany Convent used to run its own brewery here (1567). At no. 12 is the former grocer's shop *Jacob Hooy & Co.*, dating back to 1743; nowadays a herbalist sells his wares there ● *52*. In Barndesteeg the former Bethany Convent, which has been partially restored, is now used as a concert hall and conference center.

TRIPPENHUIS ★ ● *74*

The brothers Lodewijk and Hendrik Tripp became very rich thanks to their lucrative trade in iron, copper, lead, weapons, and even warships. In 1660 they commissioned Justus Vingboons to build their residence. It stands at no. 29 Kloveniersburgwal, an impressive greystone building in the classical French style. There are eight engaged Ionic columns on the façade, with pilasters, a large number of sculptures, and, on the roof, huge chimneys in the shape of mortars. It now serves as The Royal Dutch Academy of Sciences.

"JACOB HOOY & CO."
The fragrance of the herbalist's aromatic products wafts from no. 12 Kloveniers-burgwaal, the site of the former grocer's shop *Jacob Hooy & Co.* (1743).

SINT ANTONIESPOORT The first Saint Anthony's gate, built in 1488, was enlarged and embellished with towers and loopholes to become the monument that can still be seen today. After being integrated into the inner city, the gate became the public weighhouse, where traders came to weigh their goods.

This painting of 1765 entitled *The Nieuwmarkt with St Anthony's Weighhouse* is by Isaak Ouwater. In the foreground women vendors are selling paintings and pottery.

NIEUWMARKT ★

Resembling a medieval fortress, the WAAG building (public weighhouse) used to be one of the gates of the city: St Anthony's Gate. Its round heavy towers have loopholes that betray the original function of the structure. In 1614 the gate became part of the inner city, and a section of the Kloveniersburgwal was filled in to extend St Anthony's Market (present-day Nieuwmarkt). The upper floor of the Waag also housed some of the trade guilds: the blacksmiths, the painters, the builders and the surgeons. Each guild had its own entrance. The surgeons' entrance still bears the inscription *Theatrum Anatomicum*. It was in the meeting room of their guild that Rembrandt painted *The Anatomy Lesson of Dr Tulp* ▲ *182*. Hendrick de Keyser decorated the builders' entrance. Here the stonemasons, roofers, tilers and plumbers would meet. The painters shared a guild with the glaziers and sculptors and their patron saint, Saint Luke the Evangelist, is depicted above the door leading into their meeting room. In the 17th and 18th centuries Nieuwmarkt was divided into specialized markets, including a fish market. Boats came right into the square along the Geldersekade, a canal which comes straight from the port on the IJ.

SCHREIERSTOREN ★. From the Waag, looking north you can see a small semi-circular brick tower standing at the corner of Prins Hendrikkade and Geldersekade. It is a vestige of the old medieval city wall.

The name of the tower (Tower of Tears) is a reference to the weeping of the women who saw their husbands off to sea from this point. Among the many famous navigators who left Amsterdam from the Schreierstoren was the Englishman Henry Hudson, who set sail in 1609 aboard his ship the *Halve Maen* (Half Moon) in the service of the Dutch. He sailed westward and was responsible for discovering the Hudson River on the American coast, on which present-day New York stands ▲ *252*.

GERBRAND ADRIAENSZ. BREDERO. On Nieuwmarkt, opposite Geldersekade, a statue sculpted by Professor Esser depicts an amorous 17th-century couple similar to those written about by Gerbrand Adriaensz. Bredero (1585–1618). This major writer grew up in a milieu characterized by both Amsterdam and Flemish rhetoric. He was born in a house on the Nes, in the city's great convent district at the end of the Middle Ages ▲ *142*. His father earned a living there as a cobbler. In the same district the immigrants from Brabant had their meeting hall, known as the "White Lavender". Thus

Center left, an overgrown houseboat on Geldersekade, which has become a haven for swans.

"THE NORTH"
An old tourist poster advertising the North, showing the Schreierstoren. At the foot of it the skaters glide by on the frozen Geldersekade.

AN UNUSUAL STYLE
The interior and exterior décor of the Scheepvaarthuis, built between 1911 and 1916, is an early example of the Amsterdam School ● *84.* A glass roof covers the stairway and entrance hall, and the two main façades are intricately decorated with details inspired principally by Art Nouveau and typical of the early 20th-century Amsterdam School (top right).

WHERE THE CANALS MEET
The Montelbaanstoren was built in the 16th century. The original small tower (shown center as it was in 1544) was later enlarged. At the beginning of the 17th century a light wooden superstructure was added, probably following a design by Hendrick de Keyser. The canals running alongside it are very busy as they are close to the port (right).

Bredero became familiar with the dialect of Antwerp, which had fallen into the hands of the Spanish army in 1585 ● *29.* His best-known play, *De Spaanse Brabander* (*The Spanish Brabanter*) was inspired by the famous Spanish work *Lazarillo de Tormes* which was translated into Dutch in 1609. It tells the story of a child of the common people who enters the service of a poor nobleman. Through this character Bredero was able to criticize the growing xenophobia that had accompanied the arrival of large numbers of immigrants from the south of the Netherlands. Bredero, author of a great many plays and of a collection of burlesque songs and poems, created a faithful and accurate image of the life of the city's common folk. He was also a painter and a good pupil of the fencing master, doctor and architect Gérard Thibaut. He died at the age of thirty-three. Bredero's motto was *t'kan verkeeren* (luck can change) ● *44.*

SCHEEPVAARTHUIS ★ ● *84*

Taking Binnen Bantammerstraat or one of the streets running parallel to it through the Chinese quarter brings you to Waals Eilandsgracht. This canal is crossed by an unusual bridge, which is typical of the Amsterdam School ● *67.* It was designed by the architect Johan Melchior ven der Mey (1878–1949), whose works also include the Scheepvaarthuis (Navigation Center) overlooking the canal on the corner of Waals Eilandsgracht and Prins Hendrikkade. In the tapering construction of the Sheepvaarthuis, Van

de Mey wanted to suggest the bow of an approaching ship. The sculptures on the façades were created by Hendrik Albertus van den Eijnde (1869–1939). Since 1916 the Scheepvaarthuis has been used as the headquarters of various shipping companies and today it is home to the offices of the municipal transport company.

Lastage
At no. 42 Recht Boomssloot a cartouche (above right) bears the name Lastage. This is what the district was called in the Middle Ages, and is probably a reference to the French word *lest* (ballast), as there were once shipyards, warehouses and rope factories here. In 1593 this little area outside the city was integrated into Amsterdam and in 1930 substantial renovation work was carried out. At 61 Krom Boomssloot there is a cartouche depicting a tiger (top, center).

Montelbaanstoren ★

This tower was built in the 16th century at the junction of Waals Eilandsgracht and the Oude Schans (Old Entrenchment) to guarantee the district's defense. The origin of the name remains rather obscure. Historian Jan Wagenaar tentatively suggests that the term may be linked to the Château of Montauban in Guyenne (southwest France). Another theory is that there was a house called Montalbaan in the district: a number of houses do in fact have plaques commemorating Renaut de Montalbaen, one of the four characters who fought Charlemagne on the magnificent steed Bayart ● *194*.

Armenian Church. Following the left bank of the little Recht Boomssloot canal, you cross its twin, the Krom Boomssloot on your left. At no. 22 a warehouse was converted to a church in 1714; it has since been restored and is still in use.

Door of the Armenian Church at 22 Krom Boomssloot.

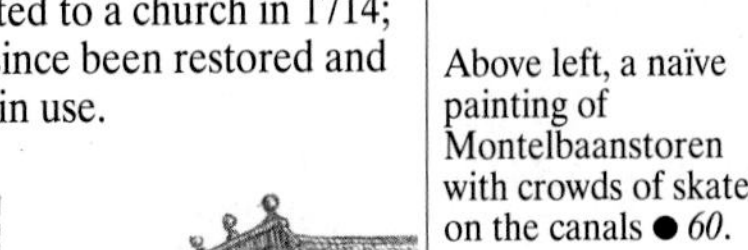

Above left, a naïve painting of Montelbaanstoren with crowds of skaters on the canals ● *60*.

In the 16th century Cornelis Pieter Boom, owner of a shipyard near the port, had two small canals dug in the heart of the district to create a link between his shipyard and Lastage. These canals are named after him.

Self-portrait by Rembrandt drawn in 1630 (right).

TRANSFORMATIONS
Contrasting views of the Zuiderkerk from Sint Antonies-breestraat, in the 17th century (bottom right) and today (below), reveal the intrusion of modern life into this street. The Pintohuis at no. 69, a beautiful house built in 1651 by the banker Isaac de Pinto, has survived the development of the area intact. It has been converted to a library annex.

SINT ANTONIESBREESTRAAT.
At the southern end of Krom Boomssloot a short street called Snoekjessteeg runs into Sint Antoniesbreestraat, one of the main thoroughfares of the old city of Amsterdam. This is the old Jewish quarter of the city, which extended from Nieuwmarkt to the synagogues of J.D. Meijerplein to the east. There were around one hundred thousand Jews living in Amsterdam before the Second World War; most of them were deported during the German occupation. The Jewish quarter, partly destroyed by the Germans and very run down, has been totally transformed by major rehabilitation and modernization works, as well as by the construction of a subway in the 1970's. That is why Sint Antoniesbreestraat, a very ancient street, is lined with modern buildings. The redevelopment aroused protest, leading to serious clashes between the police and demonstrators who objected to the transformation of their district, the historic heart of Amsterdam ● *33*.

ZUIDERKERK ★ ● *79, 94*

Slightly set back from Sint Antoniesbreestraat, on the edge of a little pedestrian square flanked with modern buildings, the Zuiderkerk (Southern Church) is a relic of bygone days. The square (Zuiderkerkhof) is reached through the gate of a former cemetery, which runs along the length of the street. The Zuiderkerk, built in 1611 to designs by Hendrick de Keyser, was the first Protestant church in the Netherlands. It resembles the Westerkerk, which is by the same architect: the bell tower, similar in style, dominates the area just as the bell tower of the Westerkerk dominates the four main parallel canals ▲ *179*.

HENDRICK DE KEYSER
This architect (1565–1621) is particularly famous for the Bartolotti house ▲ *171*, the Munttoren ▲ *120*, and the Westerkerk ▲ *179*. His son Pieter (1595–1676) was also an architect.

REMBRANDTHUIS ● *110*

Crossing the bridge of the Zwanenburgwal lock and the Oude Schans, it is possible to glimpse the little wooden LOCK-KEEPER'S HOUSE ★ to one side. This has now been turned into a delightful café. The huge

Memorial to the Jews
In 1988 a column by Joseph Glatt was erected on the Zwanenburgwal lock bridge to commemorate the deportation of the Jews from Amsterdam during the Second World War.

Diamond-cutters
The diamond-cutters of the Coster firm hard at work in the 19th century recall the past importance of Amsterdam's diamond market, especially in this district. The Gassan diamond-cutting factory (formerly Boas) is close to the Nieuwe Uilenburgerstraat.

concrete block of the university building (known as the Maupoleum) along Jodenbreestraat is due to be demolished as it is unusably dangerous. Although this street is another that underwent a major transformation in the 1970's, the Rembrandthuis still stands here at no. 4. The painter spent some happy times in this district with his wife Saskia, though his livelihood was seldom secure. At that time it was only through commissions from rich patrons such as Six that painters were able to survive ▲ *206*.The early years of economic decline brought together in the district several people facing poverty or imminent ruin. And it was here that Rembrandt lived, among his chisels and awls, brushes and palettes. Here he found the models for his biblical paintings, bearded Jews from eastern Europe and aristocratic Jews from Portugal, all of whom had settled in Amsterdam hoping to find peace and freedom. The painter would also go for long walks along the Amstel and in the Waterland ● *89*, later composing his canvases from what he had seen during the day in old Amsterdam. In 1633 he painted, among other well-known figures, the great Remonstrant, theologian and advocate of firm tolerance, Johannes Uyttenbogaert (1567–1644). In this house, restored in 1908 and turned into a MUSEUM ★, engravings, etchings and drawings are displayed in tribute to the painter. Rembrandt's house has been furnished as it would have been during the painter's lifetime.

On the left in the 17th-century picture above stands Rembrandt's house on Jodenbreestraat. In the background, the Zuiderkerk.

The towers of the Moses and Aaron Church were modeled on those of Saint-Sulpice in Paris.

THE JURIST JONAS DANIEL MEIJER Between 1819 and 1823 Meijer's greatest work, *The Spirit, Origin and Progress of the Legal Institutions,* was published in six volumes.

JONAS DANIEL MEIJERPLEIN

At the end of Jodenbreestraat, after the modern crossroads of Mr Visserplein, is Jonas Daniël Meijerplein. In October 1873 the city of Amsterdam honored the jurist Daniël Meijer (1780–1834) by naming this square after him. From a family of bankers, he was captivated by the slogan of the French Revolution: "Liberté, Egalité, Fraternité". When the Batavian republic was proclaimed, he played a part in introducing humanitarian legislation and became the first Jewish lawyer in the Netherlands. After Louis-Napoleon came to power in 1806, J.D. Meijer, on his orders, carried out a study of the Jewish community of Amsterdam and revealed its poverty. He also played an important part in introducing French law into the Netherlands, and from the beginning of the sovereign kingdom, in 1813, Meijer was a trusted advisor to King William I ● *32*.

SYNAGOGUE OF THE PORTUGUESE JEWS ★ ● *79*

This synagogue is the largest and most majestic of the three synagogues on Jonas Daniël Meijerplein. In 1590 the first Sephardic exiles from Portugal and Spain sought refuge in the Netherlands. Soon there were many of them. At first they held their religious services in a little synagogue on the Houtgracht. After moving a few times, in 1671 they settled into the present building, designed by Elias Bouman and inspired by the Temple of Solomon. It took four years to build this edifice, which faces southeast toward Jerusalem. The synagogue was consecrated in 1675 in the presence of the burgomaster and the aldermen of Amsterdam. The heart of the Jewish community, it is still a synagogue today and has some six hundred members. There were more than seven thousand members on the eve of the Second World War. The library, *Ets Haim*, founded in 1616, is considered one of the largest synagogue libraries in the world.

SYNAGOGUE OF THE GERMAN JEWS

The "Great Synagogue" is in fact the smallest of Jonas Daniël Meijerplein's three synagogues, though it is the oldest. In 1825 it became the main synagogue of the Dutch Jewish

THE MOST BEAUTIFUL OF THE "HOUSES OF GOD" The splendid Synagogue of the Portuguese Jews (right), which took four years to build, faces southeast, toward Jerusalem. It is honored on a postage stamp (above).

community. The building, of classic austerity, was designed by Daniel Stalpaert and erected in 1670–1. Originally, the building was called "the old synagogue of the High-German Jews". The latter had fled central Europe, in the face of the atrocities of the Thirty Years' War, during the first quarter of the 17th century. Around 1635, in this new district, the first Jewish community developed. Then in 1649, as a symbol of tolerance, the first synagogue was inaugurated by the burgomaster and aldermen of Amsterdam. The Jewish community grew so rapidly that by 1670 the building was already proving too small. In 1752 a NEW SYNAGOGUE, designed by G.F. Maybaum, was built next door to it. Inspired by the Great Synagogue, it was executed with more attention to detail than its model. Partly destroyed by the Nazis and severely affected by the financial hardship suffered by the Jewish community in the wake of the war, the two synagogues closed down. The complex has now been completely renovated and turned into a MUSEUM of Jewish history.

In this painting of 1680 Emmanuel de Witte (1617–91), who specialized in painting interior views of religious buildings, indicates the fabulous wealth contained in the Portuguese Synagogue. The mysterious figure with his back to us in the foreground also appears in other works by de Witte.

Silver plate belonging to the Portuguese Synagogue.

MOZES EN AARONKERK ● *78*

This Roman Catholic church (of Moses and Aaron) on the Waterlooplein dates back to the 19th century. It was originally called Saint Anthony of Padua. The building, with two openwork towers and four columns in front of the entrance, has a long history. When the Catholics were not allowed to practice their religion openly, they decided to set up clandestine churches

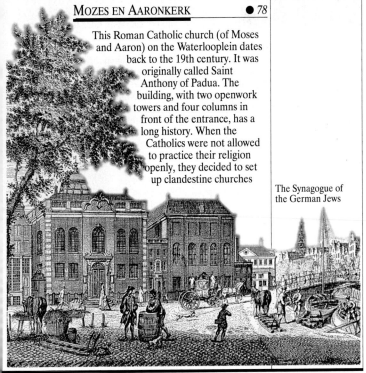

The Synagogue of the German Jews

The Amstel in the 19th century, showing, on the left, the district where the new City Hall and opera house were to be built in the 1980's.

● *39* ▲ *137*. To this end, a priest named Boelens bought the Mozes and Aaron House on Jodenbreestraat. At the time, it belonged to a rich Jewish merchant who had decorated the façade with little statues representing Moses and Aaron. The present church was consecrated on October 26, 1841. The MOZESHUIS (Moses House) and the Moses and Aaron Church are now used as training centers for immigrant workers. Exhibitions, concerts and plays are also put on there.

WATERLOOPLEIN

ALL TOGETHER
The "Stopera", seen from the Amstel above, includes a concert hall. The sculpture in the lobby of a cellist rising out of the ground shows the modernity of the complex. Behind the "Stopera", Waterlooplein hosts an open-air flea market where secondhand clothes, records, furniture and stamps are sold. One of Amsterdam's most modern cafés, the Dantzig, is located on the ground floor of the "Stopera". Its picture windows and, in summer, its outdoor terrace, offer an excellent view of the city center ♦ *297*.

"STOPERA" ● *33*. Since 1986 this large square has been the site of the new CITY HALL (Stadhuis) and the MUZIEKTHEATER, a concert hall where opera and ballet are performed ● *33*. The complex has been nicknamed the "Stopera", a contraction of the words Stadhuis and opera. The impressive building was designed by the Viennese architect Wilhelm Holzbauer, who won a competition organized to select the best design, and by his Dutch colleague Cees Dam. The building of the City Hall, on the banks of the Amstel, was much criticized because the entire old quarter was completely destroyed in the process, and not everyone finds the "Stopera" aesthetically pleasing.

MONUMENT TO THE JEWS. In front of the "Stopera", at the junction of the Amstel and the Zwanenburgwal, a stela dedicated to the memory of the Jewish resistance against the Nazis was erected in 1988. In the inner passage of the City Hall, the headquarters of several municipal services, there are transparent vertical pipes that make it possible to observe the level of the waters surrounding Amsterdam and several other areas throughout the Netherlands ■ *16*. During discussions about the renovation of the area, from the late 1960's onwards, the public works department suggested turning the narrow streets into broad thoroughfares. Following furious opposition to this plan, which was already being implemented by this time, for example in Jodenbreestraat, the works were brought to a halt. The results can be seen if you compare the width of Jodenbreestraat with that of Sint Antoniesbreestraat. On the other side of the Zwanenburgwal, Staalstraat runs into the Groenburgwal, which offers a marvelous view of the Zuiderkerk (shown above, at the beginning of the 20th century) ● *94*. In Nieuwe Doelenstraat, on the other side of the Kloveniersburgwal, the ultra-modern café-restaurant De Jaren has two terraces overlooking the Amstel ◆ *297*.

Northern Canals

Singel, *164*
Lutheran church, *165*
The Swan House, *165*
Multatuli Museum, *166*
Blauwburgwal, *166*
Torensluis, *166*
The Dolphin House, *167*
Amsterdam,
"Venice of the North", *168*
Herengracht, *170*
Leliegracht, *172*
Keizersgracht, *173*
Warehouses and whales, *174*
Brouwersgracht, *175*
Prinsengracht, *176*
Houseboats, *176*
Anne Frank's House, *178*
Westermarkt, *179*
Westerkerk, *179*
Anne Frank, *180*
Nicolas Tulp's House, *182*
"Big Keijser", *183*
Felix Meritis Theater, *184*
Old Lutheran Church, *187*
Flower Market, *187*
Transverse Streets, *188*

✱ Half a day

CORNELIS PIETERSZ HOOFT (1547–1626)
A former mayor, he lived at no. 122 Singel, as did his son Pieter Corneliszoon, the famous poet and historian ▲ *186*.

THE DANGER OF CANALS
Because so many people were falling into the canals and drowning, in 1812 the occupying French ordered that ropes should be tied along the quays. However these were not enough to contain the hollands-drinkers who lingered in the district after dark. At the start of the 20th century an inhabitant of Jordaan, Dirk Rietveld, covered himself in glory by saving more than a hundred involuntary "divers". Today a low barrier runs along the quaysides, protecting pedestrians, cyclists and above all cars.

NEW LAYOUT
This map, made by Claes JanszVisscher in 1612, shows the three new parallel canals as originally constructed in 1609, stopping at Leidsegracht. They were extended in 1660.

FELIX MERITIS THEATER

Starting at the IJ, a girdle of canals encloses the old center ▲ *119* on the western side. The architectural cityscape of the four large parallel canals, designed in the 17th century, remains apparently unchanged, but the area is still lively thanks to the lifestyles of Amsterdammers. Taking a zigzag route through the districts that make up this essential part of Amsterdam, the visitor can observe how the inhabitants live and share in the activities they enjoy: stopping in cafés and shops and wandering along the canals, sitting down on a bench every now and then to admire a particular façade or to watch the bicycles wheeling along the quaysides. This is the best way to enjoy the peaceful surroundings.

HISTORY

● *34*

The canals in the northern part of the area were built up during the 16th and 17th centuries when the city was expanding toward the west. They stretch from the old city to the Jordaan district ▲ *235*, some of them delineating its border, others even crossing it. In 1585 the fall of Antwerp to the Spanish unleashed a demographic, economic and social explosion in Amsterdam. The city became a place of refuge for thousands of Protestants, a great number of whom were merchants. Until this time the city limits had been marked to the west by the Singel, the moat round the old city walls.

CONSTRUCTION OF THE CANALS. In 1586 the municipal council decided to annex the Singel and to make it into an inner canal

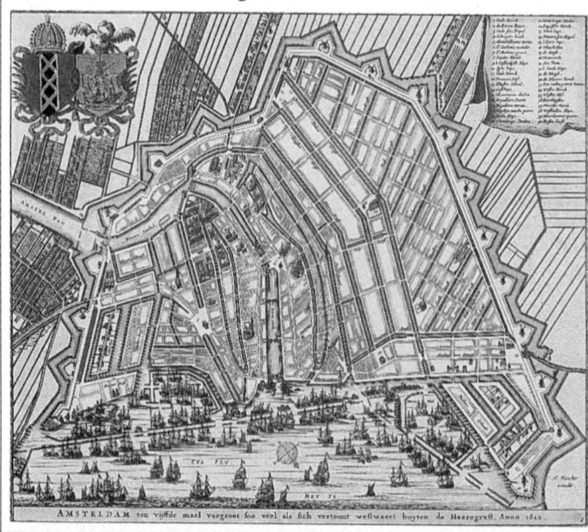

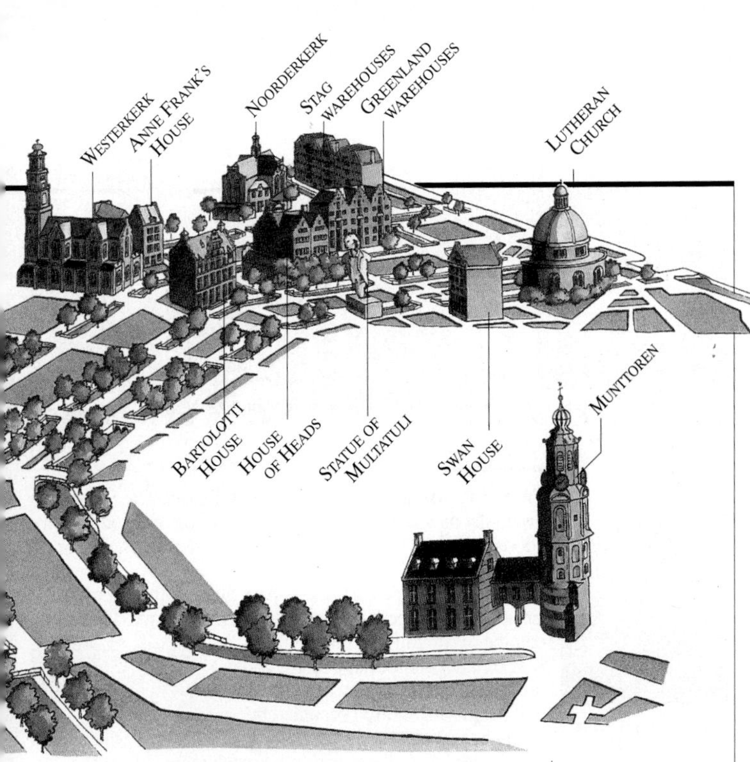

by widening it and building quays along its west bank. A new quay was built beyond, on what was to become the HERENGRACHT, which was dug as part of Hendrick Staets' plan, begun in 1609, to create three new parallel canals leading down to the LEIDSEGRACHT (Leiden Canal). After 1660 the prosperity of Amsterdam and its wealthy inhabitants made it possible to extend the ring of canals round to the east as far as the river Amstel ▲ *205*. The quays on Singel were originally built of wood before being reinforced with brick. The division of the new land into separate plots immediately established a difference in value and use between the canalside plots and those that lay behind them. On the former, more expensive plots, houses for the rich merchants were built, together with warehouses that benefitted by being directly accessible from the canals. These warehouses were used as sites for workshops and rented accommodation. But the plots were often further split up by their first buyers, creating pieces of land that differed widely in size. After the canals had been built, Cornelis Pietersz Hooft, a herring merchant and former city mayor renowned for his integrity, was appointed head of a works commission, the role of which was to try to halt speculation on land values. Hooft suggested that the plots should be valued, whether for selling or compulsory purchase, according to their development potential. The houses, churches, bridges and warehouses on Singel and on the other three canals that were later added to it constitute an architectural group that spans four centuries of history. Since the early 20th century, residents of the area have set up several organizations for the study, restoration and preservation of the canals, one of which is the "Hendrick de Keyser" association ▲ *246*.

❝You stand by the canals, on the footbridges over the Amstel, or at some other busy point in this labyrinth of water all cluttered with boats, pontoons, overloaded little craft, polished clogs with swollen bellies and chubby sterns, a cross between junks, furniture and barrels.... You sadly hum through the hours in the atmosphere of the pale sky. The men come and go between the banks, over the slender bridges. The observer watches all this life going by, and lives.❞

Paul Valéry, *Retour de Hollande*

SINGEL ★

■ 18

FROM A COMMERCIAL TO A RESIDENTIAL QUAY. The Singel was originally devoted primarily to trade and the transportation of goods by water. It did not acquire its residential character until much later. For a long time it was the quay used by large freight ships, which had first to pass through the Haarlem Lock (Haarlemmersluis) at its northern entrance. With the coming of the railway, however, this type of navigation disappeared. Today the canal is used only by local traffic, and its quays are often occupied by permanently moored houseboats ▲ *177*. Singel – which should not be confused with the Singelgracht, last of the series of canals to the west – is called Cingle (Belt) on old documents and maps. The left bank, formerly a moat adjoining the old city ▲ *119*, is in places lined with houses that are lower, more austere and older than those on the right bank. Singel is certainly the canal with the fewest warehouses in this district; some of them have completely disappeared. Nos. 19 to 27 used to form a single building which until 1647 housed a brewery named De Os (The Ox), situated in Ossepooksteeg (Oxen Alley), a tiny street running from the Kattengat to the Sonesta

SINGEL
CENTRUM

THE HAARLEM LOCK
This is one of the locks that protected the city from the tides before the Zuiderzee was enclosed. Boats passed through it into the Singel. From the 18th century onwards it was opened in order to clean the canals.

VIEW OF SINGEL
The view above shows several façades (from no. 44 to no. 16), the oldest of which date from the 17th century. Gradually, more recent buildings have slipped in among the old gables.

THE CANAL AROUND 1760
Engraving of the Singel by Jan de Beijer (1703–80). The boat with the flag in the foreground ferried goods and passengers to other towns via the canals and lakes.

Koepelzaal (Lutheran Church) on the Singel. Today, nos. 19 to 21, which came into being when the brewery was split up, form one long restored house; it combines a French-style roof with a neck gable. On its façade are written the words *Vita hominum similis naviganti*, meaning "The life of man is like that of a sailor".

Lutheran Church. This church, built by Adriaan Dortsman between 1668 and 1671, burned down in 1822 but was subsequently rebuilt. In February 1993 another fire damaged the dome, which is an unusual feature in the Netherlands, where spires are more often found on churches ● *78*. At the top perches the Lutheran swan. Today this church, like many others in Amsterdam, is used not for religious worship but for conferences and concerts, particularly of chamber music, which are held every Sunday morning ● *48*.

Architectural diversity. Over time some houses were converted into warehouses. They are noticeable as soon as you enter Singel. No. 2, De Spaanse Gevel (Spanish Gable) café, with its *De Kruiwagen* (Wheelbarrow) cartouche, was used for storage around 1650 by its owner, a ship's chandler. On both banks of the Singel there is a lively mix of tall, narrow buildings, with gables, roofs, doors, windows, steps and basements of widely varying forms. Within, one can imagine the steep and narrow staircases, the highly individual arrangement of the rooms and the hidden gardens behind. Though it may not have the aristocratic character of the Herengracht or Keizersgracht, or the vivacity of the Prinsengracht, Singel has managed to create a harmonious balance between community and commercial life. No. 36, known as Zeevrugt (Shellfish), was built in 1736. Its links with the sea are illustrated by the vessel carved above the door and the presence of Mercury, god of trade, in the cornice, with a purse in his hands and a cockerel at his side. Looking at nos.

Post house
The mail coach between Amsterdam and The Hague left from no. 74 Singel. The service began in 1660 and also carried passengers.

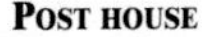

A boat moored by the banks of Singel gives shelter to the local cats.

The Swan House
No. 83 Singel bears a cartouche with a swan representing the owner's name (Zwaan). The house was built in 1651 and in fact consists of two juxtaposed buildings.

View of Singel: nos. 82 to 54.

62 and 64 you can see how the architects of the second half of the 19th century derived inspiration from the style of the 17th-century canal houses ● *72*. The house on the left has an 18th-century façade with a step gable in the Renaissance style of 1638. This has been copied and taken even further in the 19th-century house on the right, which is built in the neo-Renaissance style.

MULTATULI MUSEUM ★. In his novel *Max Havelaar,* published in Amsterdam in 1860, the poet and novelist Multatuli depicted the narrowmindedness of his colleagues and the racism of the colonizers toward the indigenous people of Java. This work greatly influenced the anti-colonialist movement. An interesting little museum and library are devoted to Multatuli in Korsjespoortsteeg ▲ *248*.

BLAUWBURGWAL ★. At the corner of no. 108, Blauwburgwal, a small transverse canal, affords a view to the west. It probably owes its name to the blue bridge that was built when the canal was dug in 1614, though it may refer to the dyeworks that was once located here. The sign "NVSH" at nos.7 to 9 indicates an organization typical of Holland, the Dutch Society for Sexual Reform. Dating from before the Second World War, this center provides sex information. It includes a shop and club that have little in common with the windows of the red light district ▲ *136* and do not attract the same crowds. At the end of this short canal the aristocratic façades of the Herengracht ▲ *170* can be glimpsed.

TORENSLUIS. Bridges have always been places for commercial and social activity and the exchange of goods in the often residential world of the canals. There used to be a market held on the wide Torensluis (Tower Lock) bridge, the arches of which now house a picture gallery. Ships unloaded their cargoes on the neighboring quay, then called Rouaanse Kade (Rouen Quay).

THE SMALLEST HOUSE. No. 166 Singel, built in 1634, looks as though it must be Amsterdam's smallest dwelling. However, behind its tiny façade it has a broader section that runs along an alleyway ◆ *294*.

WINDMILL AND BOAT
In the 16th century a windmill must have stood on the site where the house at no. 188 Singel was later built. The ship (right) can be seen on the façade of no. 8 Blauwburgwal. Below right, the gable of no. 116 Singel and its pulley, which is still in use today.

THE JAN ROODENPOORTSTOREN
This tower, which was built in the 17th century, became a military prison. It once stood on Singel's widest bridge (46 yards), which was therefore called the Torensluis. The prisoners were locked away in cells under the bridge

which are today occupied by an art gallery. On the site of the tower, demolished in 1829, there is now a wide esplanade where a statue of Multatuli stands.

LEANING FAÇADE. At no. 182 the façade leans forward, following a construction method, officially established in 1565, that meets both aesthetic and functional requirements. The narrow, jutting façade could be seen in its entirety from the quayside, and its angle meant that the rope did not catch on it as loads were being hauled up. Even today, residents use the rope and pulley to get furniture into their homes, because the stairways are too steep and narrow.

FACULTY OF ARTS. These modern buildings, erected in 1984, provide an example of successful integration with the older buildings along Singel. Combining iron with grey, yellow and white glass, they blend in with the other frontages of the canal, incorporating the house on the corner of Raadhuisstraat, which was built in 1900. These university buildings are also called P.C. Hoofthuis, as the poet used to live on one of these sites in the 17th century ▲ *186*.

THE DOLPHIN HOUSE ★. The double house at nos. 140 to 142 was built around 1600 by the architect Hendrick de Keyser (1565–1621). It originally belonged to Hendrik Laurensz Spieghel (1549–1612), the writer and author of the first Dutch grammar ● *42*. The dolphins that originally figured in the frieze were an allusion to one of his works.

EDUARD DOUWES DEKKER
This Amsterdam civil servant (1820–87) used the pseudonym Multatuli, a Latin word meaning "I have suffered greatly".

THE DOLPHIN HOUSE
In 1630 the house, depicted here by Abraham Stork (1684) ● *93*, became the property of Mayor Overlander's daughter, wife of Captain Frans Banningh Cocq. The hero of Rembrandt's *The Night Watch* (1642) ▲ *218*, Cocq, nicknamed Lord Purmerland, was a doctor of law and immensely rich.

▲ AMSTERDAM, "VENICE OF THE NORTH"

This cartouche at 9 Stromarkt is a reminder that a spice merchant once lived here. He displayed the lion of St Mark on his house, a sign of trading relations with Venice.

"And by reason of the air, the water and the seat of the place, and for convenience and the great number of canals, which are to be found down almost every street, and for other reasons, this city is similar almost to that of Venice. [...] This city will rightly become the Venice of the North." In 1582 the great Florentine traveler Lodovico Guicciardini was the first to use the phrase "Venice of the North" in relation to Amsterdam, in his *Description of all the Netherlands*. There are many similarities, both real and imaginary, between the two cities. Besides the water and canals, both rely on maritime trade, banking and printing, and share the qualities of tolerance and cosmopolitanism; both are renowned for republicanism and painting.

"At the time when I was living in Amsterdam, it seldom happened that I uttered the name of this large and beautiful city before a foreigner without hearing the latter immediately call it the Venice of the North. Certainly, for those who have a deep knowledge of the history of Holland and that of Venice, who have lived in both countries, studied the character of their inhabitants, penetrated their manners and customs and explored their traditions, there are striking similarities between Amsterdam and Venice."

Henry Havard, *Amsterdam and Venice*.

Above, a late 16th-century view of Venice by G.B. Arzenti.

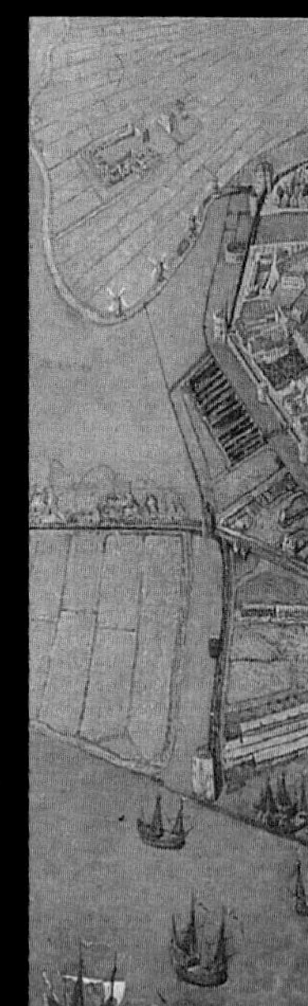

Dutch "vedutisti". The long Dutch tradition of buying Italian works favored the Venetian paintings market. However the leading vedutists of Rome and Venice were Dutch: Matthias Withoos (1627–1703) and above all Caspar Adriaensz van Wittel (Amersfoort 1653 - Rome 1736), famous under the name of Vanvitelli, who originally painted Venice from engravings, then went there for the first time between 1690 and 1694. Above, his Bacino di San Marco, painted in 1710, shows a broad, panoramic view of the Grand Canal and the Salute. His work paved the way for Canaletto (portrait below right).

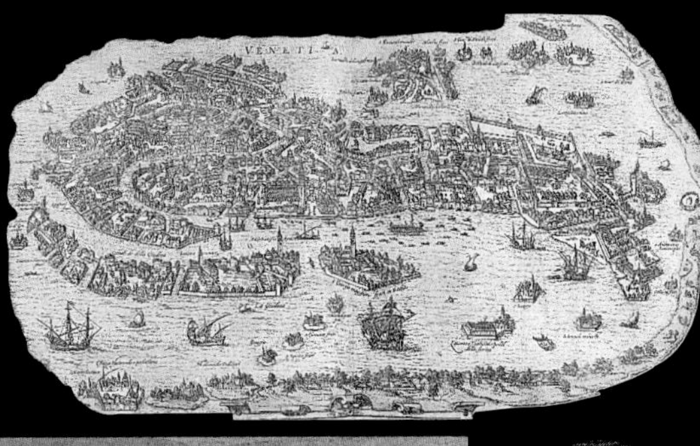

Active ports Images of the two cities between the 16th and 18th centuries always show the bustling maritime activities of their ports. Left, a map of Amsterdam by Cornelis Anthonisz (1538). Above, a view of la Serenissima from the early 17th century. Below, Amsterdam at the same period.

The shopping arcade on Raadhuisstraat.

THE CLEARING
This painting by George Breitner ● *88* ▲ *258* depicts work being carried out on

Raadhuisstraat between 1894 and 1896. This street was primarily created to allow trams to cross the canals from Jordaan to the Royal Palace. A shopping arcade, designed at the same time by the architect A.L. van Gendt ▲ *216*, runs along the street between Herengracht and Keizersgracht. Above, an external detail from the arcade.

Like the Bartolotti House and the House of Heads ▲ *173*, both designed by de Keyser and his son, this was a double house with both the usual *voorhuis* (front house) and a second large reception room. The family lived on the floors above, and the top story was used as a warehouse. The kitchen was in the basement. The gables form a most spectacular decorative element, combining brick and white stone with pilasters, obelisks and volutes.

THE HOUSE OF THE RISING SUN. The house at no. 118, built in the 17th century, was sold to Mennonites of what was called the "Sun" congregation, hence the nickname of "House of the Rising Sun". The sun can be seen on the cornice.

THE LEOPARD HOUSE. In 1617 no. 138 was the scene of serious confrontations between Remonstrants and Counter-Remonstrants ● *38*. Here lived Rem Egbertsz Bisschop, Calvinist merchant and supporter of the theologian Arminius, who taught that people had power over their own destinies. The Counter-Remonstrants, sometimes called "monkeys", came here to break up what they believed to be a public gathering of their enemies. The house was ruined before the authorities could intervene.

HERENGRACHT ★

HISTORY. The Herengracht (Gentlemen's Canal) was the first of the new canals, begun in 1585. It was later incorporated into the 1609 plan ● *34* and continued beyond Leidsegracht after 1660. The construction work and land sales were carried out almost simultaneously in order to fill the city's coffers and finance the project. To attract rich merchants, the new canal offered much larger plots than those on Singel, but the height of buildings was limited to 30 feet over two-thirds of each plot and to 10 feet on the rest. On the other hand they could dig down to a depth of 190 feet. Each buyer had to pay for the brick wall on the quayside that corresponded to his plot. Artisans were not permitted to carry out their activities in this zone. Bascule, or swing, bridges were not permitted; all bridges had to be fixed. These regulations were also to apply to the Keizersgracht (Emperor's Canal), begun in 1614, after that of Prinsengracht (Princes' Canal).

VAN BRIENEN HOUSE. This house (no. 182) was bought at the end of the 18th century by Jan van Brienen, a Roman Catholic banker. His son Willem Joseph Brienen van de Groote Lindt was appointed mayor at the time of Holland's incorporation into the French Empire. His was the delicate task of presenting the keys of the city to Napoleon in 1811 when the latter visited Amsterdam ● *32*.

THE BARTOLOTTI HOUSE AND THEATER MUSEUM ★. The dwelling on the opposite bank of the canal, seen from Driekoningenstraat, which now houses the Theater Museum, was built by Hendrik de Keyser between 1617 and 1618. Its

Cartouche on the façade of the Bartolotti House.

owner, an administrator of the Dutch West India company ▲ *252*, was in fact called Van den Heuvel, but he took the Italian name Bartolotti in exchange for an inheritance from his father-in-law, a Calvinist of Bolognese origins. Bartolotti was involved in all kinds of trade, signing an exclusive contract with Russia for importing wheat in the mid-16th century. By 1631 he was already said to be the second richest man in the city. The façade shares the decorative style of the Dolphin House ▲ *167* and the House of Heads ▲ *173:* windows framed by pilasters surmounted by decorative motifs and a step gable. There are mottos in the lateral cartouches: *Ingenio et assiduo labore* ("Through ability and hard work") and *Religione et probitate* ("Religion and rectitude"). Today you enter the museum and the Bartolotti House through no. 168, known as the "White House" because of the color of its sandstone façade. Michiel Pauw, one of the founders of the Dutch West India Company ▲ *252*, commissioned it in 1638 from the architect Philip Vingboons (1607–78) ● *73*. Vingboons created what was probably the first façade with a neck gable decorated with a vase and volutes. The interior was transformed in 1730 by the owner, who had a monumental staircase built from cellar to attic, a rare feature in these houses, which are always rather narrow. Of note in the hall are sculptures by Ignatiuszoon (1733) and ceilings by Jacob de Wit (1696–1754) ▲ *206*, whose characteristic grisailles with their designs of pale lines on a white background have been nicknamed *Witjes*. Crossing the corridor takes you to the Bartolotti House at nos. 170–2. The two outer doors form a double entrance: no. 172 for the daytime and no. 170 for the evening. The present-day decoration of this floor was carried out by successive owners of the house. Jacob de Wit decorated the doors and ceilings with gods and goddesses. Wall panels by Moucheron in the style of Louis XIV, installed

THEATER MUSEUM
This contains costumes, displays about the photography of artistes and about the stars of the 1930's, above. Baron van Slingelandt's miniature theater (1781), left, can also be seen here.

PATRICIAN HOUSES
In 1688 Jan van der Heijden (1637–1712) ▲ *193* painted the three houses at nos. 168 to 174 Herengracht. The house on the left was completely altered at the end of the 18th century. However, the Bartolotti House still occupies the center of this bend in the canal.

in the 19th century, can also be admired here. In the garden the Germans established a fortified command post during the Occupation which is still visible.

THE "MESSINA". In the 17th century the house at no. 164, which has been greatly altered over the years, was inhabited by a rich silk merchant, Philip de Flines. He had a fine collection of paintings, which included several by Giorgione, Titian and Poussin, as well as Italian Renaissance engravings. The Rijksmuseum ▲ *212* also has on display a few grisailles by Gerard de Lairesse (1640–1711) from this collection (opposite).

LELIEGRACHT ★

Leliegracht (or Lily Canal; many of the transverse canals in Jordaan ▲ *235* have the names of flowers, plants or trees ▲ *236*) was dug at the instigation of the first buyers of plots along its planned route, who did not want a road created there. Its two functions were navigation between Jordaan and the center and, by means of a lock, the linking of the two water supply systems of the canals: the one known as the "blue" system, supplying the three central canals, which are completely separate from the rivers, and the "red" supply to the Prinsengracht, which is linked to the Amstel. Leliegracht enabled the water to be cleansed by pouring reserves from the red system into the blue system, but it fell into disuse with the transformation of the Zuiderzee ■ *18, 20.* Today Leliegracht is a lively thoroughfare full of shops and cafés. Gradually this small canal has become one of the best places for lovers of books, both new and second-hand. An architectural book fair is held every year in June ● *54*.

This Art Nouveau building of 1905 housed a life insurance company ● *82*. Inside, a ceramic represents the granting of exemption from the toll in 1275 ● *28* and, at the top of the façade, another shows a kind of guardian angel, symbolizing the company's responsibilities. The ecology organization Greenpeace has now set up its headquarters here, with a souvenir shop.

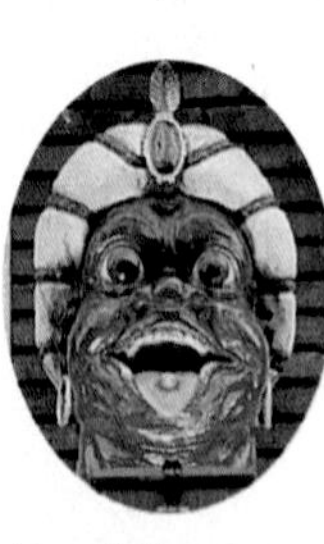

At no. 7 Herenstraat a yawning man with a pill stuck to his tongue is the traditional sign of Amsterdam pharmacists ● *53*, ▲ *120*.

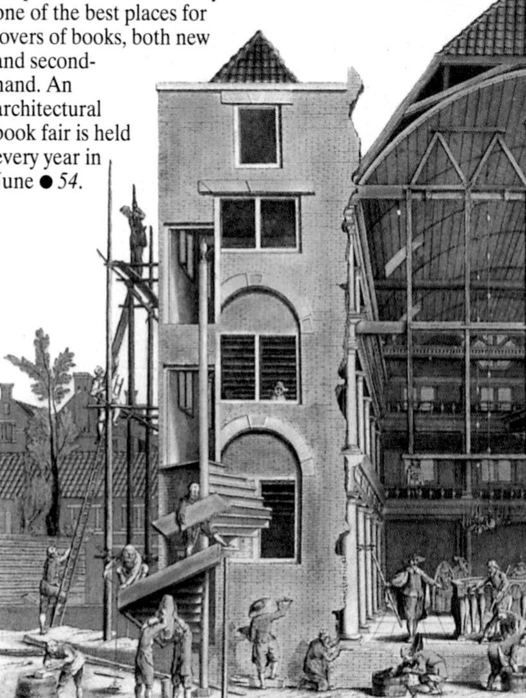

Keizersgracht ★

The Emperor's Canal, which is named after Maximilian, the German Holy Roman emperor, dates from 1612.

The House of Heads ★ ● *73.* Recently restored (no. 123), this dwelling is a third example of the decorative style of Hendrik de Keyser. He died in 1621, and it is thought that his son Pieter probably completed the building in 1622. Its first owner was Nicolaas Sohier, who was related to the Bartolotti family by marriage and must have known their nearby house ▲ *170*. He was followed by a rich merchant, Louis de Geer, who traded in arms and iron with Sweden and its King Gustavus Adolphus.

De Rode Hoed ★. *De Rode Hoed* (Red Hat) at no. 102, is named after the hatter's cartouche at no. 104. In the 17th century it used to house a semi-clandestine church of Remonstrants, supporters of Arminius and critics of Calvinist doctrine ● *38*, in the building shown under construction below. The internal framework and beautiful columns in different kinds of wood are quite magnificent. The present-day brick façade dates from the last century. The building is now used variously as a café, recording studio and concert hall.

Gasparus van Houten's chocolate factory was established at no. 22 Leliegracht in 1812. The cocoa beans were first roasted then ground in a mill driven by men.

The House of Heads
One evening the owner Nicolaas Sohier went out with all his family, leaving a servant in the house. From the kitchen she heard men's voices and, arming herself with a sword, went down to the cellar. The windows had been forced open and a man's head was poking through one of them. She cut it off. Six more heads appeared, which she cut off one after the other. When her master came home, she sent him down to the cellar. Astounded, he is said to have immortalized this feat by having the six heads carved on his façade.

WHALING
Whales were hunted using harpoons fired from a *sloep*, a small ship with a single vertical mast. The carcass was then cut up on shore, and the blubber (the fatty part) was boiled to extract the oil. After 1642 the whales left Spitzbergen and went further north. This migration forced the fleets to withstand terrible winters. Often nearly 250 boats were hunting at the same time. At its height in 1721, whaling employed nearly ten thousand men.

WAREHOUSES AND WHALES. In the past this section of the Keizersgracht marked the limit of the industrial and commercial zone from which the city drew its economic strength. Many of the old buildings still remain, although their functions have changed frequently over the years. This is particularly true of the warehouses, which are otherwise not typical of this largely residential canal. The Dutch discovered schools of whales while seeking a northern route to India at the end of the 16th century and the Dutch Northern Company, set up in 1614, held the monopoly on whaling until 1642. Whale oil was sought after for soap manufacture, lubrication and lighting. It was also used for treating leather and wool and was an important ingredient in the paint and tar applied to ships. It was graded according to its quality and stored in vast tanks made of brick on the ground floor of the GREENLAND WAREHOUSES at nos.40 to 44 Keizersgracht. Each of the three main buildings had five tanks divided into four vats. The whalebones (used to make knives, corsets and boxes) were stored on the upper floors. These days the warehouses have been converted into apartments. However whales are still to be found as motifs in the decoration of many houses in the district.

NANKY DE VREEZE GALLERY. The function of the building known as De Zaaier (Sower) at no. 22 has changed many times over the years. Originally the inhabited part of a warehouse, it became a JESUIT CHURCH around 1663. Mass was celebrated here on and off, depending on the restrictions which were being imposed on Catholic worship ● *39*. Around 1835 the building began to look like a classic church, with a real façade decorated with Catholic splendor. In 1859 the building was renovated by the architect P.J.H.Cuypers. Abandoned in 1929, it went on to become a warehouse, then a sports hall, until finally in 1992, with assistance from the city authorities, it was converted into an enormous gallery for modern art.

This wrought-iron sign (no. 162 Brouwersgracht) representing two dried fishes can be seen on an 18th-century house on the site of the large "Bergen" warehouse, headquarters of the Dutch Northern Company.

BROUWERSGRACHT ★

■ *18* ● *76*

Brouwersgracht, formerly an industrial and artisan district, has become a peaceful canal with pleasant and affordable housing.

BREWERS' CANAL. Brouwersgracht forms the northwest limit of the girdle formed by the canals. It was dug before the others and occupied a very important position due to its proximity to the port, the IJ and the Spaarne (a waterway once leading to Haarlem). It took its name from the principal local activity, the brewing of beer. It originally ran from Singel to the Herengracht, then on westward after its extension in 1613 ● *34*, and became an important center with huge warehouses and factories. All the polluting processes were concentrated here, while regulations in force on the other canals preserved the peace of their wealthy residents. The main products processed and stored here were saltpeter, powder, leather, whale oil, spices, cocoa, coffee, sugar and grain.

FROM INDUSTRIAL TO RESIDENTIAL DISTRICT. For a very long time Brouwersgracht was simply a dark and smelly industrial zone. Today it is a highly desirable area with its houseboats, its complete warehouses (*Pakhuizen*) converted into apartments, and its shops. Lying between Jordaan ▲ *235* on its southern bank and Haarlemmerbuurt ▲ *251* to the north, it is extremely lively, largely as a result of the youth of its population. The warehouses can instantly be identified by their heavy wooden shutters designed to protect the goods stored there ● *76*. At nos. 174 to 178 SLAGTHUIS was originally three warehouses with step gables; they were converted into a single dwelling in 1894. The district is seen at its best in the evening when people put the lights on in their apartments so you can see the depth of the rooms and their current layout. A school for poor children was built in the last century at no. 198. Today it houses apartments at affordable rents managed by a district housing committee. At nos. 204 to 212 two large warehouses enclose a smaller one; these former grain warehouses, renovated in 1975, are called after stags (*hert*, a word also meaning "heart" in Old Dutch) and their roofs are decorated with stags.

THE GREENLAND WAREHOUSES

In 1621 there were five Greenland warehouses. Today only three remain (nos. 36 to 38).

Below, this imperial crown – emblem of the city – dated 1618 decorates the warehouse at nos. 116–18.

The 17th-century warehouses of Brouwersgracht inspired the naïve painter Zeljko Premerl (left).

These three cartouches decorate the façade of no. 175 Prinsengracht, which must once have housed animals.

A VERY OLD CAFÉ
The Papeneiland (Papists' Island) occupies the ground floor of no. 2 Prinsengracht. Its rustic interior decoration, typical of the brown cafés ● *50*, reflects the building's great age (17th century).

PRINSENGRACHT ★

Prinsengracht (Prince's Canal) takes its name from William the Silent (1533–84), Prince of Orange and hero of the rebellion against the Spanish ● *29*. The last of the historic canals in the girdle, it was designed in 1609 as a thoroughfare lined with housing. It became a focus for all types of activity, from work, represented by warehouses and workshops, to religious worship, since there are several churches on the banks of the canal. At the entrance to the Prinsengracht the very busy quay on the right bank leads to the Noorderkerk, a traditional meeting- and marketplace, built on the edge of Jordaan ▲ *235*. The houses at nos. 2 and 4, where the two canals meet, date from the early 17th century. They belonged to a merchant, who bought them from a potter, and they were also owned for a time by a textile and cheese seller. The step gable surmounting the old Papeneiland café (no. 2) ◆ *296* is typical of Amsterdam, with its combination of brick and white stone, and yet unique, because it is repeated on each of the façades overlooking the canals. These details were brought to light in 1957, after restoration work on the building. In this part of Prinsengracht there used to be many sugar refineries, notably at nos. 13 and 83. Sugar production flourished until the mid-18th century.

VAN BRIENENHOFJE . The term *hofje* refers to a group of Amsterdam institutions that used to house single or elderly women in buildings which were usually arranged around a courtyard (*hofje*) and a small garden. These almshouses can be recognized by the series of numbers displayed on a single entrance ▲ *240*. Van Brienenhofje (nos. 89 to 133 Prinsengracht), built in 1804, is of comparatively recent construction. Legend has it that a rich Catholic merchant, Aernout Jan van Brienen, made a vow of charity after being freed from a strongroom in which he had accidentally been locked up. At that time the land on which the place of his imprisonment stood belonged to a brewery. He bought the site and built an almshouse on it. Its Catholic residents had to submit to very strict regulations, particularly concerning cleanliness.

HOUSEBOATS ★. These unusual dwellings appeared in the 1950's. Their proliferation was linked to the housing crisis, which was worsening at the time, and to the fact that there was reduced navigation on the inner canals in favor of commercial routes. As Franklin Hollander noted in his book entitled *Houseboats*, these floating houses are concentrated primarily on the river Amstel and on the Prinsengracht. But the number of moorings soon became inadequate for the number of craft. In 1973 the city council decided to take action against this illegal form of housing, which they considered to be akin to squatting: those boats already moored, a fleet of about 2,400, were legalized and obliged to pay a modest annual fee.

LIFE ON THE WATER
Most of the houseboats are moored in the area between nos. 187 and 207 Prinsengracht. They differ greatly: from old Rhine barges that have retained their bourgeois solidity, to rafts housing chalet-like constructions, greenhouses, gardens, refuges for cats and artists' studios, all supplied with electricity and water.

«IF ALL THE HOUSEBOATS WERE SUDDENLY TO DISAPPEAR, AMSTERDAM WOULD LOSE MUCH OF ITS CHARM!»

FRANKLIN HOLLANDER

PAVEMENT CAFÉS
Tables set outside in summer attract the clientèle, a mix of regulars and passers-by. Below, 't-Smalle in Jordaan.

A SECULAR TRADE
At no. 180, opposite the Westerkerk, H. Keijzer, tea and coffee merchant since 1839, has a hundred types of tea and twenty types of coffee for sale, all roasted on the premises.

THE GRAND ARMY'S STABLES
General Lebrun, governor general of the city during its occupation by Napoleon, rented warehouses along Prinsengracht to house his carriage and horses.

FRENCH-STYLE CORNICE
This cornice at no. 126, extravagantly decorated in the French style, is of a type rare on Prinsengracht, but more common on Herengracht.

LIFE ON THE PRINSENGRACHT. Whereas Noorderkerk Square is enlivened only by the weekly pattern of market days ▲ *239*, this district, which is made up of small, transverse streets between Prinsenstraat and Leliegracht, is busy every day because of its shops, its bridges and above all its many cafés. In Prinsenstraat activity is greatest at the points where a bridge opens on to the canal. For this reason two brown cafés ● *50*, De Vergulde Gaper (Golden Sign) on the northern corner and De Twee Prinsen (Two Princes) on the southern corner, are particularly lively places. Not far from here, at nos. 60–2, the vegetarian restaurant Bolhoed (Bowler Hat) offers cheap, delicious menus. This establishment has tables outside at lunchtimes, while inside French records of the 1950's to 1970's provide background music. No. 114 is De Twee Zwaantjes (Two Cygnets), a famous café that used to be frequented very early in the morning by workers from the breweries and by porters who unloaded the barges. The clients have a sing-song on Saturday nights.

STABLE-WAREHOUSES. Nos. 187 to 217 are a series of warehouses ● *76*. They used to house a brewery and a sugar refinery, and have evocative names: Hoop (Hope), Liefde (Charity) and Geloof (Faith). Some of their owners also used them as stables.

POORHOUSE. In 1645 the Nieuwezijds Huiszittenhuis (House of the Itinerant Poor) at nos. 235–7 on the canal was established as a place where the needy could find charity. Food (mainly bread and herrings) was distributed to them here. The equipment for preparing this food was located at no. 237, which housed a bakery, a kitchen, a cold store and the administrators' offices. The cartouche on the façade of no. 235 depicts the legend that tells how the site of the future Amsterdam was discovered by two fishermen sailing in a *kogge* with their dog. The building became a firefighters' barracks at the end of the 19th century but was subsequently abandoned and it is now used as apartments for students. Pictures by Ferdinand Bol (1657) and Adriaen de Lelie (1799) showing the six administrators of the Nieuwezijds Huiszittenhuis can be seen in the Rijksmuseum ▲ *212*.

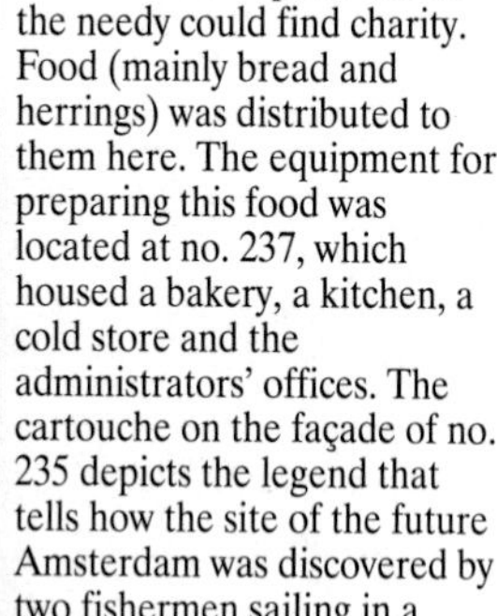

ANNE FRANK'S HOUSE ★. During the Second World War the Frank and Van Daan families lived secretly in the back part of the double house at no. 263 . Today it is a museum and the headquarters of an organization to combat racism and anti-Semitism ▲ *180*.

Cartouche decorating a façade on Prinsengracht.

WESTERMARKT

DESCARTES' HOUSE. René Descartes lived in no. 6 Westermarkt (West Market) during the summer of 1634 ● *98*. In the Europe of the Counter-Reformation, the philosopher, who was also a somewhat unorthodox Catholic mathematician, sought the climate of freedom and tolerance offered by this Calvinist city, which was so open to the new spirit of scientific inquiry.

MONUMENT TO HOMOSEXUAL VICTIMS. The "three pink triangles" monument stands on Westermarkt and Keizersgracht. Unveiled in 1987, this work by Karin Daan commemorates those persecuted for homosexuality, particularly by the Nazis. The triangle was the sign that homosexuals were forced to wear during the Nazi repression.

WESTERKERK ★ ● *78*

The Westerkerk (West Church) and its tower, the Westertoren (West Tower), dominate this part of Amsterdam. Like most of the city's Protestant churches it bears a name derived from its geographical position in the city rather than that of a saint. The building of the Westerkerk was started in 1620, after that of the Zuiderkerk ▲ *156*. It was prompted by the spread of Protestantism, although the Protestant aesthetic developed by the architects, in this case Hendrick de Keyser ▲ *156*, was independent of Catholicism only in its rejection of all forms of decoration. The church tower, 265 feet tall, bears the imperial crown, which Emperor Maximilian granted to the city arms ● *28* and which his son Philip I threatened to withdraw before confirming it in 1497. Visitors are often astonished by the church's simplicity and by the narrowness of its entrance, leading to a nave in the shape of a double Greek cross, which is the largest in all Dutch Protestant churches. The central nave is surmounted by a barrel vault made of wood in order to lessen the weight of the building, which stands on none-too-solid ground. The monumental organ was intended to accompany the singing of the faithful when this practice was finally authorized in the late 17th century. The instrument was commissioned from the organ maker Johannes Duyschot in 1682 and decorated by the painter Gerard de Lairesse, who was well-known for his monumental decorative frescos. His works, and the grisailles in particular, were highly sought after by the patricians who lived in the Herengracht houses ▲ *172*. The artist painted the organ panels, combining biblical themes (such as King David and the Queen of Sheba) with pictures of musical instruments and the Evangelists ● *48*.

REMBRANDT'S TOMB
This drawing of the West Tower (below), attributed to Rembrandt, is in fact said to be the work of one of his pupils. On October 8, 1669, the great master of Dutch painting was buried in the Westerkerk. A plaque describes the event. The church register reads: "8 October, Rembrandt van Rijn, painter, resident at Rozengracht, opposite Doolhof, coffin with sixteen bearers, leaves two children. Monies received: twenty florins".

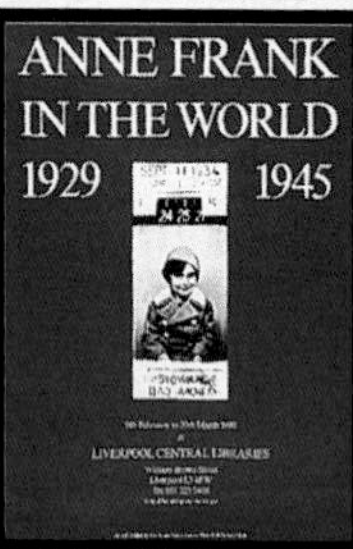

▲ ANNE FRANK

ANNE FRANK
IN THE WORLD
1929 1945

From July 1942 to August 1944 the Frank and the Van Daan families, both Jewish, were forced to live in hiding, in the unoccupied offices of the company run by Mr Frank, in order to escape the Gestapo. It was during this period that Anne began to write her personal diary, in which she noted down the little community's everyday doings with all the wisdom of her thirteen years. On August 4, 1944, they were all arrested and deported. Only Mr Frank survived; he found the diary and published it. The book became a worldwide bestseller ● *33, 100*.

ONRECHT/VERZET
NEDERLAND 50 CT
1985

"INJUSTICE/RESISTANCE" This stamp, issued in Holland in 1985, marks the fortieth anniversary of the end of the German occupation,which decimated the Jewish population of Amsterdam.

May 1942: Anne, aged thirteen, invents an imaginary friend, Kitty, to whom her diary is addressed.

Anne Frank's House
This is one of the most visited places in Amsterdam. There is a canal-bus stop just in front of it.

Hidden in the back of the house
"Our annex is ideal as a hiding place. Although it is damp and oddly shaped, it is a sufficiently comfortable place and unique of its kind. You would not find another one like it in all of Amsterdam" (July 11, 1942).

Hidden door
"Our 'hiding place' now truly deserves the name. Mr Kraler thought we should put a wardrobe in front of our front door (there are many searches because of hidden bicycles), but it would have to be a revolving wardrobe that opened like a door" (August 21, 1942).

Three small rooms to survive in
"It's no fun at all, far from it, living in a hiding place in the fourth year of the war. Will all this carnage ever stop!" (March 14, 1944).

Anti-Jewish round-ups
"Today I have only bad news to give you. Many of our Jewish friends have been gradually taken away by the Gestapo, who do not treat them well" (October 9, 1942).

Anne's family
"My father was already thirty-six when he married my mother, who was twenty-five. My sister Margot was born in 1926 in Frankfurt-am-Main. And I was born on June 12, 1929. As we are 100 percent Jewish, we emigrated to Holland in 1933, where my father was appointed chief executive of Travies N.V. in Amsterdam" (June 20, 1942).

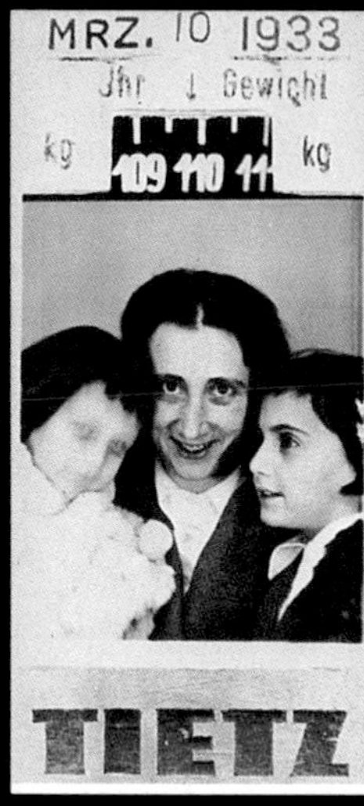

Anne and Margot with their mother.

Symbol
This statue of Anne by M. Andriessen stands on the Westermarkt. Anne has become a symbol of the fight against racism.

ORGAN DECORATIONS
The shutters of the Westerkerk organ were painted by De Lairesse. Here the Queen of Sheba and musical instruments can be seen ● *48*.

A WHITE MARBLE FOOT
This carved foot and sandal, of unknown origin (it may be a fragment of a Roman statue or a 16th- or 17th-century copy) was part of Gerard Reijnst's collection.

A second organ in the church is used exclusively to accompany Bach cantatas. The bells, which were recently restored, are the work of Frenchman François Hémony ▲ *128* and the whole set is made of forty-two separate parts. The Westerkerk, which belongs to the Dutch Reformed Church, holds many concerts, including a carillon concert every Tuesday at 1 pm ◆ *294*. It also houses the tomb of Rembrandt, whose burial here on October 8, 1669, is commemorated by a plaque. The exact location of the tomb has never been determined, however.

AROUND WESTERMARKT

HOUSE OF HOPE. This house at no. 209 Keizersgracht has an attic story dating from 1743. It is decorated with vases and has a carved balustrade. Its pediment is formed by volutes surrounding the statue of a woman holding an anchor, a traditional symbol of hope. The history of the house is marked by an aesthetic awareness in its owners: "In 1634 it passed into the hands of Gerard Reijnst (1599–1658), a merchant who loved art. He built up a magnificent collection, as befitted the spirit of an age founded on the universality of culture. Besides pictures and sculptures, his collection also included fossils and ancient coins" (Melchior Fokkens, *The Canals of Amsterdam*, 1662). Fokkens described the house, which was already considered to be one of the most beautiful in the city, as follows: "A house with an interior worthy of a king's palace, displaying all the decorative variety of India and Ancient Rome ... and all these rarities are worth at least three tonnes of gold, if not more."

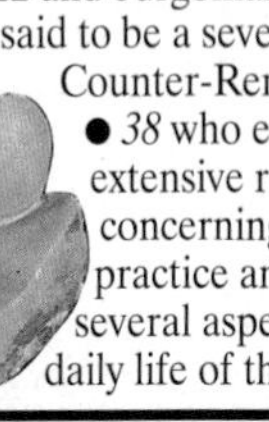

NICOLAAS TULP'S HOUSE. Nicolaas Tulp (1593–1674) is only known to posterity thanks to Rembrandt. Originally called Claesz Pieters, he was a doctor who acquired the nickname of "tulip". This flower, still rare at that time, was the emblem displayed on the house at no. 210 Keizersgracht where he lived until 1637. Nicolaas Tulp became famous in his own lifetime through his dual career as doctor and politician. He was elected an alderman of Amsterdam in 1622 and burgomaster twice after that. He was said to be a severe man and a Counter-Remonstrant ● *38* who established extensive regulations concerning medical practice and other several aspects of the daily life of the city; for

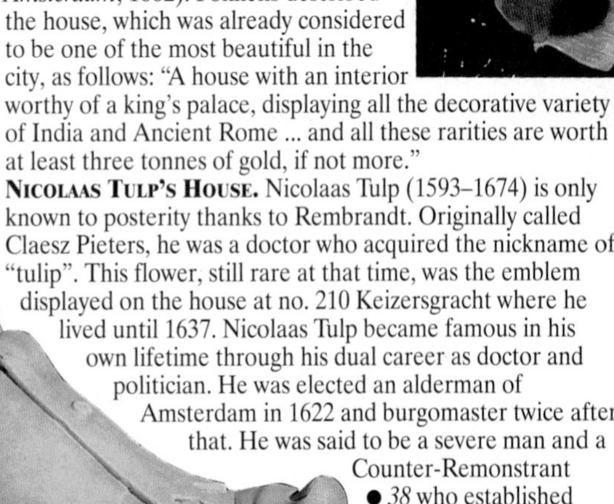

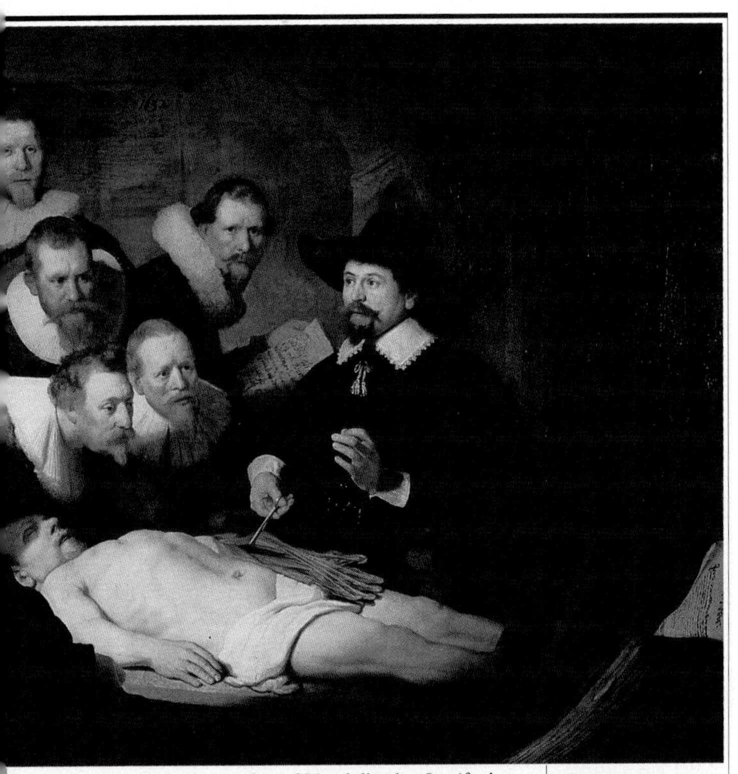

example he forbade the staging of Vondel's play *Lucifer* in 1654. The doctor's image was immortalized in 1632 by Rembrandt in *The Anatomy Lesson of Dr Tulp*. This scene is an example of a traditional genre representing important people and was commissioned by Nicolaas Tulp himself. The work helped to establish Rembrandt's reputation in Amsterdam ▲ *218*.

"BIG KEIJSER". The group of houses from nos. 242 to 252 Keizersgracht, and particularly the building at nos. 242–6, played a special role in the history of a particular aspect of Amsterdam, that of rebellion and tolerance ● *40* ▲ *127*. These houses, long left standing empty, were occupied by squatters in 1979. In December that year, after they had been there for six months, the inhabitants of the five "De Groote Keijser" houses (shown on the right) resisted an eviction order. The eviction order was quashed, and the squatters set up a pirate radio station, "De Vrije Keijser" ("Free Keijser"), which they used to orchestrate a demonstration against the crowning of Queen Beatrix ● *33* on April 30, 1980, before they were finally dislodged. Their slogan was "Geen woning, Geen kroning" ("No housing, No crowning"). Ever since, buildings occupied by squatters have been systematically and immediately cleared by the police.

"THE ANATOMY LESSON"
Rembrandt's painting was little admired in the 19th century. Without the intervention of King William I in 1828, the picture would have been sold to England.

"DE GROOTE KEIJSER IS EVERYWHERE"
This was the favorite slogan of the squatters from the five buildings along Keizersgracht.

As shown in this image of the city of Bordeaux, located at no. 320 Keizersgracht, the Dutch have been importing French wine, and spirits to distill their genever since the 17th century.

FROM REESTRAAT TO KEIZERSGRACHT

PETER THE GREAT
“Now a scholar, now a hero, then a carpenter and navigator, he set his mark on everything and was a perpetual worker on the throne.”
Alexander Pushkin

PEDIMENT OF THE “FELIX MERITIS”
The Felix Meritis Theater, built in 1787, encouraged various forms of knowledge. It included an elliptical concert hall, a model in the small hall of the Concertgebouw ▲ *216*, where Brahms, Saint-Saëns and Grieg played, and a science hall for experiments.

Reestraat comes out on the left bank of the Prinsengracht near nos. 315–75, which were for a long time the site of intense industrial and commercial activity, notably soap manufacture (nos. 325 to 337). In 1644 a vegetable market was established on the other side of Reestraat. There used to be a group of factories at nos. 315 to 331, many of which were renovated in 1968, thanks to a donation from one of the descendants of the founder of the American Pulitzer Prize. These now house a hotel complex, bearing the benefactor’s name, which is famous for exhibitions, art auctions and its restaurant, De Goudsbloem; on leaving the restaurant, you enter the Keizersgracht.

PETER THE GREAT’S VISIT. In 1716, Peter the Great (1672–1725) ▲ *272* made his second visit to the Netherlands for diplomatic reasons, because he wanted to form an alliance with the Netherlands and France. He stayed in his ambassador’s elegant house at no. 317 Keizersgracht, which had been built in 1639. This white house, which has been restored, is remarkable for its narrowness and for the boldness of its vertical decoration, with Doric pilasters supporting the pediments, *oeil-de-boeuf* windows and vases. In his design, the architect Philip Vingboons (1607–78) created a successful compromise between the Amsterdam style and Italo-Dutch influences.

FELIX MERITIS THEATER. This theater, built in 1787, housed the Felix Meritis (“*Happy through Merit*”) Brotherhood, the aim of which, in the climate of the Enlightenment, was social progress through the arts, science and commerce ● *31*. After the Second World War Felix Meritis became the headquarters of the Communist Party of the Netherlands, where its newspaper was produced. In 1968 the experimental Shaffy Theater was set up there, and today the building also houses a foundation for the promotion of European artists.

THEATER OF THE SCIENTIFIC AND CULTURAL ACADEMY. This building at no. 384, which opened in 1637, was inspired by the philanthropic aims of the poet Samuel Coster (1579–1662). Since the late 16th century Amsterdam had attracted many visitors who admired its architecture, canals and city hall, but the city was often criticized for both the buildings and the repertoire of its theater, the Schouwburg. The Marquis de Sade, who visited in 1769, wrote somewhat chauvinistically in a letter: “There are no French plays. A rather bad Dutch company entertains this capital. The theater itself is quite large, but extremely simple, although the ceiling is as high as in our ordinary theaters; it has only two rows of boxes; the floor is covered with benches, and men and women sit together. I was told to expect magnificent decoration; I

THE THEATER BURNS DOWN
On May 11, 1772, the theater of the Scientific and Cultural Academy was entirely destroyed by fire. Some saw it as a punishment from heaven. The fire killed eighteen people, and its flames could be seen from the north of the country.

Amsterdam's houses were not given numbers until Napoleon's occupation. Before this buildings were recognized by their engraved cartouches.. These works reflect their inhabitants' identities in their design by illustrating their professional activity or displaying a symbol chosen by the owner.

Tulip vase
Typically Dutch, this 18th century Delft vase is perfect for displaying flowers bought at the Singel market.

found it very simple. This nation's genius, scarcely extending beyond trade, has not produced a great multitude of poets. Their theater is limited to two tragedies, and during my stay in Amsterdam I was lucky enough to see one of them. It was a compilation of extraordinary incidents without cause or organization." Today all that remains of the Schouwburg theater is its gate and a little courtyard, where stands THE STATUE OF THREE POETS – Pieter Corneliszoon ▲ *162*, Joost van den Vondel and Samuel Coster. The visitor returns to Singel by walking along Huidenstraat, crossing the Herengracht, or else by going north toward Wolvenstraat and Oude Spiegel Straat and then down to Singel.

The Flower Market
It is located on Singel, where the canal ends at the foot of the Mint Tower ▲ *120*, erected by Hendrick de Keyser. A naïve painting by E. Gevaert is shown above, and an engraving by H. Clerget, late 19th century, below.

From Heisteeg to Muntplein

Vogelstruijs ▲ *127*. Besides being decorated with a stone-carved ostrich (*struisvogel* means ostrich, so the founders were making a play on the name), the façade at no. 370 is unusual in being equipped with a surveillance camera. This modern addition, combined with the specially coated synthetic glass windows, is a souvenir of 1980, when the house had to be cleared of squatters three times in three months. The building became a pawn in a power struggle that arose between squatters and the city authorities, when the evictions gave rise to confrontations in the district. Vogelstruijs, which also provides access to no. 329 Herengracht, has remained a target for various forms of action. Continuing toward the southeast, the Spui ▲ *122* is visible to the east, and to the west there is a wonderful view as far as the Prinsengracht.

SINGEL DECORATION
The cartouche of Adam and Eve at no. 367.

OLD LUTHERAN CHURCH. The wooden galleries of the monument at no. 411, built in 1633, are reminiscent of the style of New England churches ▲ *121*.

ODEON. The building at no. 460 was designed by Vingboons. It used to belong to a rich brewer, and the second president of the United States, John Adams, stayed here when he came to negotiate a loan to the young Dutch republic. In 1838 it was converted into a concert hall, when it took its present-day name. Later the Odeon became a film-theater, then a café-discotheque. It was burned out in 1990 but has now re-opened ◆ *299*.

THE ODEON
An interesting feature is the 17th-century neck gable.

"Blond boatmen with the blue of their pipe smoke have eyes drowned by Indonesia, while the tulip sellers are already shouting themselves hoarse for the foreigners."
Louis Aragon, *Le Roman inachevé*

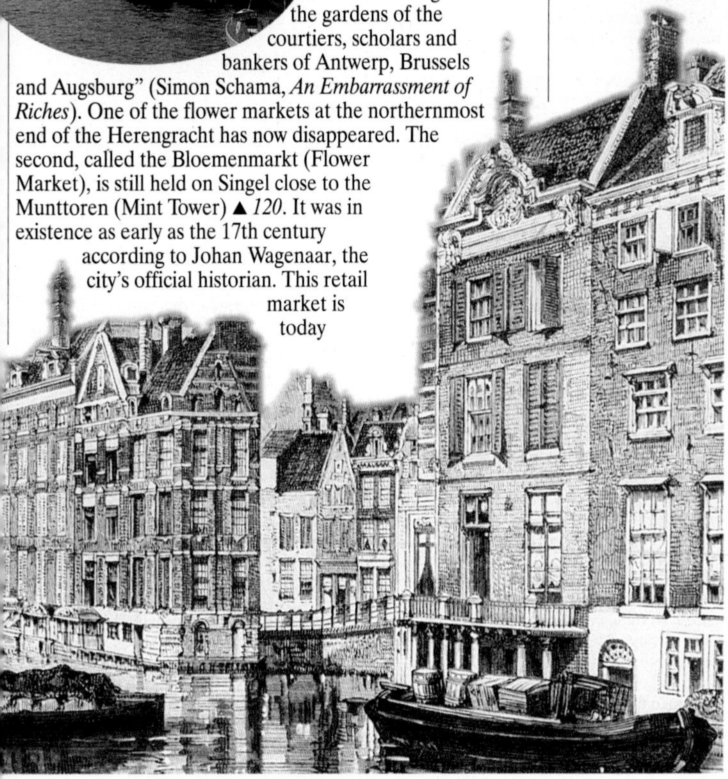

FLOWER MARKET ★. During the 17th and 18th centuries there were about twenty specialized markets in Amsterdam, spread out along the canals ● *96*. At least two of these were flower markets, established to cater for the Dutch passion for tulips ■ *24*. "There is nothing mysterious about the arrival of the tulip in Western Europe. It came to the Netherlands in the 16th century, at a time of flourishing cultural and commercial contacts between the Ottoman Levant and the Hapsburg Empire, despite an official state of war. Ambassador Busbecq observed their cultivation in Andrianople, while in the 1560's agents and diplomats as well as merchants bought bulbs for the gardens of the courtiers, scholars and bankers of Antwerp, Brussels and Augsburg" (Simon Schama, *An Embarrassment of Riches*). One of the flower markets at the northernmost end of the Herengracht has now disappeared. The second, called the Bloemenmarkt (Flower Market), is still held on Singel close to the Munttoren (Mint Tower) ▲ *120*. It was in existence as early as the 17th century according to Johan Wagenaar, the city's official historian. This retail market is today

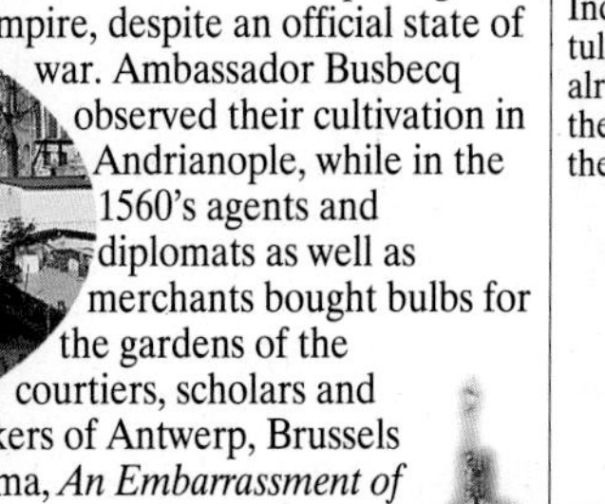

This cartouche on the façade of no. 7 Berenstraat represents the "Prosperity of Amsterdam".

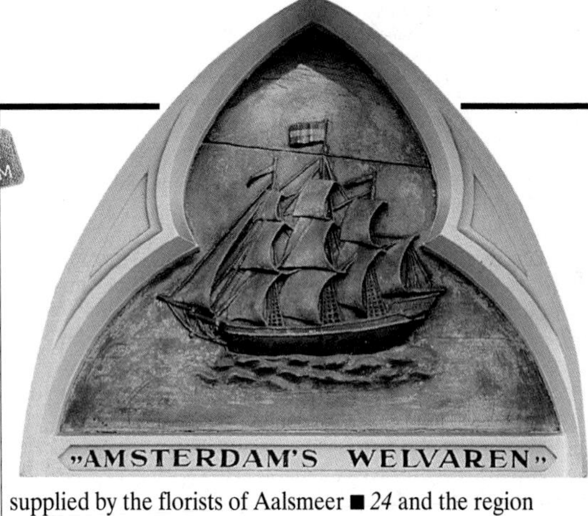

supplied by the florists of Aalsmeer ■ *24* and the region around Haarlem, a city that forms the focus of the tulip's long history. The Bloemenmarkt is unusual in that since 1862 it has been held on boats. Today it occupies about fifteen barges which are permanently moored on the Singel. Its development was linked to the building of the first greenhouses in 1872. Bulbs, cut flowers and plants are all sold here at very reasonable prices. The Amsterdammers have always been great lovers of plants. In Albert Camus' novel *The Fall* the hero says: "In Holland everyone is an expert in painting and tulips." ● *103* ▲ *201*. Besides the multicolored tulips, they are particularly fond of sunflowers, which are often enormous and have to be balanced acrobatically on their bicycles. A procession of flowers ends on these quays every year in September.

An Amsterdam shop near the large canals.

TRANSVERSE STREETS ★

The canals of Amsterdam are crossed and linked together by a series of little streets full of shops which can become particularly busy near the flower market. Most of these streets do not keep their names when they cross from one canal to the next after Prinsengracht. Thus Reestraat becomes Hartenstraat after Keizersgracht, then Molensteeg after Herengracht. The street names are mostly taken from the vocabulary used in the trades of leather processing and selling, which were the two main activities here. One series of names refers to the animals that provide the hides: Huidenstraat (Hide Street), Berenstraat (Bear Street), Wolvenstraat (Wolf Street), Hartenstraat (Stag Street) or Reesstraat (Deer Street). Runstraat refers to the oak bark tannin used to prevent the skins from decaying. Long inhabited by artisans, the ground floors of the houses have gradually been converted over the years into shops selling a wide variety of products. Windows displaying trimmings, secondhand clothes and buttons alternate with florists, secondhand bookshops, cafés and, now a genuine Amsterdam institution, the Pompadour patisserie in Huidenstraat.

❝It is my city, a sign reserved for the initiated. It will never entirely open itself to the foreigner who does not know its language or its history, because it is precisely language and history that preserve the secrets of moods, places and memories. Open city, closed city. One city for us, another for the others. A city by the water, a city of men, a city designed and written by men and by water. A city of stone, wood, water and glass, and of another substance that language cannot name.❞

Cees Nooteboom

SOUTHERN CANALS

LEIDSEPLEIN, *190*
LEIDSEGRACHT, *192*
ARCHANGEL WAREHOUSE, *192*
HERENGRACHT, *194*
BIBLE MUSEUM, *194*
KEIZERSGRACHT, *196*
METZ DEPARTMENT STORE, *196*
THE GOLDEN BEND, *198*
CAT MUSEUM, *200*
REGULIERSGRACHT, *202*
VAN LOON MUSEUM, *202*
AMSTELKERK, *204*
PRINSENGRACHT, *205*
AMSTEL, *205*
WILLET MUSEUM, *206*
REMBRANDTPLEIN, *207*
TUSCHINSKI CINEMA, *208*

Half a day

"In Amsterdam, Gerard went on, you come for a few months, then you leave again. You hang out. At the *Melkweg*, the show changes all the time. It's impossible to know exactly what's going to happen. That's why there's always something happening. You have to come, and wait. Take your time. Do each thing as it comes. Be together. Then withdraw and be by yourself. You've got to realize, he added with a sudden liveliness, that despite the relaxed atmosphere, there's a permanent tension. Far from being dull, people live intensely, because they are doing what they want to do, what they need to do."

Dominique Fernandez, *Amsterdam*, 1977.

As you walk through to the aristocratic "expensive district" of Amsterdam you can trace the family trees of the city's richest families; some remained in the same houses for three centuries, while others moved to the Herengracht. The Deutz, for example, lived on the Herengracht, speculated on the Keizersgracht, and just before the death of the head of the family, the banker Joseph Deutz (1624–84), they built on the Prinsengracht. The branch headed by Jan Deutz (1655–1719) settled on the Keizersgracht, but his eleven children built an almshouse for the elderly on the Prinsengracht, and Willem Gideon Deutz (1697–1757) lived at no. 605 Herengracht. The houses of these families have gradually been acquired by firms and institutions.

VAN LOON MUSEUM
MUNICIPAL THEATER
AMSTELKERK
AMSTEL LOCK
SQUARE THEATER
MAGERE BRUG

STADSSCHOUWBURG Plays and ballets are included in the program of the municipal theater (Stadsschouwburg), designed in the Renaissance style by the architect Springer in 1894.

LEIDSEPLEIN ★

Meetingplace of the Amsterdam crowds, the Leidseplein (Leiden Square) offers a dense concentration of cafés and places of entertainment. In 1774 a wooden-fronted theater nicknamed the "Wooden Box" was opened on the square but it burned down in 1890. The Stadsschouwburg (Municipal Theater) was built a little later, and also served as an opera house until the construction of the "Stopera" ▲ *160*. But this is only one of the Leidseplein's many attractions: there are enough cafés to seat a thousand! Among these are the wonderful Art Deco café of the American Hotel, as well as Eylders and the Hoopman Bodega, which

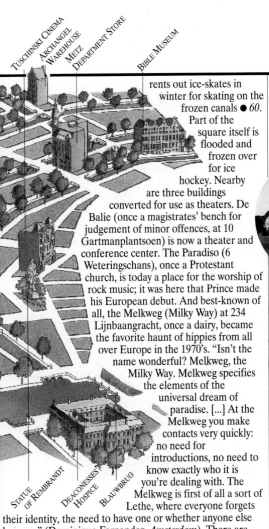

TUSCHINSKI CINEMA
ARCHANGEL WAREHOUSE
METZ DEPARTMENT STORE
BIBLE MUSEUM

rents out ice-skates in winter for skating on the frozen canals ● *60*. Part of the square itself is flooded and frozen over for ice hockey. Nearby are three buildings converted for use as theaters. De Balie (once a magistrates' bench for judgement of minor offences, at 10 Gartmanplantsoen) is now a theater and conference center. The Paradiso (6 Weteringschans), once a Protestant church, is today a place for the worship of rock music; it was here that Prince made his European debut. And best-known of all, the Melkweg (Milky Way) at 234 Lijnbaangracht, once a dairy, became the favorite haunt of hippies from all over Europe in the 1970's. "Isn't the name wonderful? Melkweg, the Milky Way. Melkweg specifies the elements of the universal dream of paradise. [...] At the Melkweg you make contacts very quickly: no need for introductions, no need to know exactly who it is you're dealing with. The Melkweg is first of all a sort of Lethe, where everyone forgets their identity, the need to have one or whether anyone else has one." (Dominique Fernandez, *Amsterdam*). There are several nightclubs around the square, which has often hosted vast gatherings: anti-Nazi demonstrations during the War, and the huge crowds of supporters of the Ajax Amsterdam football club ● *60*. In between the American Hotel and the back of the Melkweg, the visitor enters the Leidsegracht.

STATUE OF REMBRANDT
DEACONESSES' HOSPICE
BLAUWBRUG

THE LEIDEN GATE
The *pleinen* in Amsterdam were the entry-points into the city where travelers would leave their carts or carriages.

Above is the gate (the Leidsepoort) marking the end of the road from Leiden, destroyed in the 19th century.

MELKWEG
Taken over at the height of the Provo

movement ▲ *243*, the center of hippie life in 1970, the Melkweg today is a complex with areas for cinema, exhibitions and concerts. On Saturday nights the walls throb to the rhythms of Reggae, rock and pop.

"AMERICAN HOTEL"
With its Art Deco style, the bar of the American Hotel prefigures the buildings of the Amsterdam School ● *84*. It is one of the Leidseplein's main attractions.

Cornelius Lely
The son of a grain-broker, Lely (1854–1929) was born

at 39 Leidsegracht. An engineer and minister of public works, he directed the building of a dyke to close off the Zuiderzee, and constructed several polders ■ *20*. The isolation of the Netherlands during the First World War and the flooding of northern Holland led to the speedy completion of these works in 1932, three years after Lely's death. His name was given to the new city of Lelystad.

This caricature from the 19th century shows the hectic departure of the audience after a play at the municipal theater.

Leidsegracht ★

The Leiden Canal dates from 1664. For many years flat-bottomed boats called *kagen* traveled along it from the Leidsegracht to Leiden. Many famous people once stayed in this peaceful residential district. Coming from the Melkweg, the visitor arrives on the southern bank of the Leidsegracht at the western end of the canal, near Marnixstraat, on the left. Until 1880 a riding school was sited here, where Mozart gave a concert in 1766. Heading toward the city center, the first canal to be crossed is the Prinsengracht. On the corner, at no. 424, there is a brown café, De Pieper ▲ *50*. Nos. 579-83 on the Prinsengracht housed first a brewery and then in the 19th century, a shop selling cakes and pastries (an old poster for it is shown below). Today the premises, decorated in 19th-century style, are occupied by a piano-dealer, whose shop contains a hall in which concerts and receptions are given. The part of the Prinsengracht that lies between Berenstraat and Leidsegracht has a very distinct character. All along the curve of the canals narrow passages between the houses and small residential lanes are scarce, because such lanes were forbidden by 17th-century regulations. Elsewhere, they provided accommodation for servants, spaces to rent and workshops for small craftsmen. Several are to be found in this section of the Prinsengracht, however: at no. 557 (the home of a cartridge manufacturer), for example, and at no. 497, which once led to a church. Cafés, galleries, and a public library at no. 587 make for a lively neighborhood.

Archangel Warehouse. The building at 88 Leidsegracht is called "Arkhangelsk" in Dutch, from the name of the port at the mouth of the Dvina on the White Sea (Russia). A

These façades are to be found between nos. 66 and 42 on the Leidsegracht (from left to right).

warehouse dating from the 18th century, it has now been converted into apartments. In 1700 an agreement (reproduced below) was signed between Peter the Great ▲ *272* and Egbert Thesingh, the owner of the warehouse. Thesingh expanded the business established by his father, who since 1659 had traveled backwards and forwards from Russia, exporting fabric and importing the wood required for making ships' masts. At a site near Archangelsk, Thesingh built several sawmills following the Dutch design, which were powered by windmills ● *68*. The agreement also granted him a monopoly on the export of books, maps and nautical charts. In fact the Dutch had been producing maps of the Baltic Sea and of all the countries with which they traded since the 16th century.

Calvinism and the Italian theater. In 1681 an Italian theater was established on the site of the houses which stood between no. 42 and no. 56, despite the opposition of the Calvinist church. The theater's promoter, Dirck Stryker, who was the son of the Venetian consul, appointed Jeronimo Sertorio, an Italian engineer, to supervise its construction. The first production opened to the public on December 31, 1681, but the theater closed again a year later.

Leather fighting fire. The attractive, narrow house at no. 4, with a neck gable surmounted by a pediment, survived a fire in January 1684. The blaze was brought under control thanks to the inventor Jan van der Heijden (1637–1712), who in 1672 had introduced the use of leather firehoses connected to pumps: they had the advantage of being flexible and of not freezing in cold weather. Jan, who was at the time the head of the Amsterdam fire service, left an account of the event in his

Archangel Warehouse

Its construction led to rows between the guilds. "The building was put up for the merchant Egbert Thesingh [...]. The building works were supervised by the master mason Reyers Keyms, who hired inexperienced workers from outside the city at half the going rate. He told his client he had paid twice as much. Thesingh had a writ drawn up against the workers by a lawyer [...]. He did nothing but stoke up discontent among the building workers. [...] 134 carpenters and bricklayers resident in Amsterdam submitted a petition to the municipal council" (*The Canals*). They had to wait a year, and then the claim was rejected.

Brandspuitenboek (*The Fire-Engine Book*). A cartouche bearing his portrait can be seen in a tiny street in the western part of the city center, at 5 Koekstraat where he lived. There remains very little of this house, which had a flight of steps with railings in the form of firehoses. In 1669 Jan van der Heijden organized the installation of street-lighting by oil lamp throughout the city. He was also one of the great painters of Amsterdam ▲ *171*.

Bible Museum
This museum at nos. 366–8, presents manuscripts and different editions of the Bible, particularly the *Delft Bible*, the first printed in the Netherlands, in 1477.

HERENGRACHT ★

One of the houses, dating from 1649, leans forward on the corner with Beulingstraat. It is so narrow, and its façade is so typical of Amsterdam with its neck gable and pulley-hoist, that it stands out as if it were part of a stage set. The houses from nos. 362 to 394 form one of the finest architectural groupings in Amsterdam ★, especially the group at nos. 364–370, known by the name of its owner Jacob Cromhout ("vaulted frame"), a rich Catholic who engaged Philip Vingboons as architect. The four façades, which form two pairs, exhibit all the classical elements (pilasters, festoons, *oeil-de-boeuf* windows, pediments) that the Dutch architect had studied, and which were successful in integrating into the limited space available to him on the canal ● *74*. At the end of the 19th century a rumor spread round Amsterdam that the residents on the odd-numbered side of this part of the canal, jealous of those on the other side, had made numerous alterations in order to spoil their view.

Bible Museum. Installed in the patrician Cromhout house, this little museum benefits from a sumptuous décor, for the back part of the dwelling has a ceiling painted by Jacob de Wit (1695–1754) ▲ *171*. Trained at Antwerp, he was the first Catholic painter to receive commissions after the Reformation. Jacob Cromhout had his house altered in 1717, adding a spiral staircase.

The Black Horse. The cartouche on the façade of no. 394 (above) illustrates the legend of the struggle between Charlemagne and the four sons of Aymon: Adelaert, Ritsaert, Writsaert and Renout, who were able to escape thanks to their magic horse. The house, which dates from around 1670, used to have a bread-oven in the basement in the 19th century.

Double plot. The house at no. 386 is the work of Philip Vingboons, who had the advantage in designing it in 1633 on

Corner window
At the intersection of Leidsegracht and Keizersgracht this window, with its wooden frame, is typical of those situated at the crossing of two canals, a strategic commercial location.

From left to right, these are the façades of the houses between no. 30 and no. 2 on the Leidsegracht.

one of the first double plots to be provided for the construction of houses on the canal. The façade, with its five bays, its central entrance and its mixture of stone and brick, marks a turning-point in Amsterdam architecture, which had until then been constrained by the narrowness of the plots provided ● *74*.

Blois or New York on the Herengracht? At the end of the 17th century and during the 18th century, Amsterdam architects were influenced by the French style. At nos. 380–2, for example, J. Nienhuuys, a rich tobacco-planter and founder of the *Nederlandsche Handelmaatschappij* (the successor to the Dutch East and West India Companies) was the owner of two houses in the Louis XVI style. One burned down, and he demolished the other. In 1890 he decided to put up in its place a small château in the French Renaissance style. This building was inspired by his time at the Ecole des Beaux-Arts in Paris and his discovery of the house built between 1879 and 1881 for William Kissam Vanderbilt, son of the American millionaire W. Henry Vanderbilt, at the corner of 5th Avenue and 52nd Street in New York. This New York building has now disappeared. After Runstraat, at 346 Herengracht, an authentic 17th-century house has a façade painted in black and white bands. At no. 395 the architecture of a house built in the neo-classical style at the end of the 19th century combines a gable and a tower containing the staircase; a solution (rarely adopted in Amsterdam) to the difficulties presented by the narrowness of the houses.

Boating on the canals is very common ● *60*.

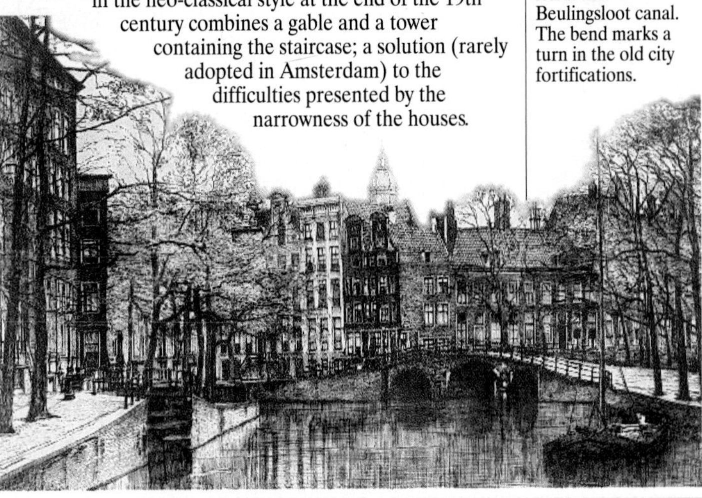

A canal intersection
This engraving shows the Leidsegracht opening onto the Herengracht. To the left is the Beulingsloot canal. The bend marks a turn in the old city fortifications.

At no. 508 stands the Hooft store, once celebrated for its cigars and tobacco (including the famous *Amsterdamer* brand). The bas-relief far right shows cherubs taking part in the different stages of harvesting and transporting tobacco.

KEIZERSGRACHT ★

Heading south along Leidsegracht, the walker arrives at Keizersgracht. The intersection between Keizersgracht and Leidsestraat is given over to commerce, which makes for a certain animation at the meeting-point of these two generally quiet canals. Leidsestraat itself offers many services intended for tourists, notably foreign exchange bureaux and fast food establishments. The two main buildings at the junction date from the last quarter of the 19th century, and were built at a time of demographic and commercial growth in Amsterdam.

On the façade of 401 Keizersgracht, is a cartouche representing the old port at Marseilles.

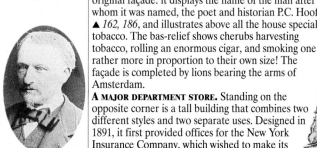

At 453 Keizersgracht, Van Gogh's uncle had a small art bookshop which the painter often visited ▲ *226*.

CIGARS. At no. 508 a building of 1881 exhibits a mixture of Dutch and German neo-Renaissance styles. Its pitched roof is surmounted by a tower, rather than the two traditional right-angle gables. But the interest of this house lies primarily in the cigar and tobacco store that used to occupy the ground floor. THE HOOFT STORE, now a foreign exchange bureau, has retained its original façade: it displays the name of the man after whom it was named, the poet and historian P.C. Hooft ▲ *162, 186*, and illustrates above all the house specialty, tobacco. The bas-relief shows cherubs harvesting tobacco, rolling an enormous cigar, and smoking one rather more in proportion to their own size! The façade is completed by lions bearing the arms of Amsterdam.

A MAJOR DEPARTMENT STORE. Standing on the opposite corner is a tall building that combines two different styles and two separate uses. Designed in 1891, it first provided offices for the New York Insurance Company, which wished to make its presence felt and to emphasize its financial might, here symbolized by eagles. Since then the premises have housed a luxury store, Metz, whose various departments are devoted to products for the home and to beauty. This firm is proud to have supplied the royal household. Its founder, who was of French origin, previously occupied no. 449 Keizersgracht. Decorated with caryatids and eagles, and boasting a dome, the Metz building is strongly marked by Hausmann's Paris style. The owners had the building altered in the 1930's, commissioning the architect Rietvèld ● *57* ▲ *215*, who was world-famous for his geometrical chair, to produce a raised gallery in glass and metal on the top floor. From here visitors can enjoy a panoramic view over Amsterdam. The height of the viewing-point is accentuated by the sight of the

uniformly flat city beneath. The physicist Fahrenheit lived not far from the Metz building, at the southern corner of the intersection.

A QUAY OF WAREHOUSES. After the Leidsestraat, on the right bank, there stands a series of warehouses dating from various periods ● *76*. The oldest are at nos. 483–7. They are named after trees, such as the *Lindeboom* (Lime) and the *Eijkeboom* (Oak), and the first letters of all the names taken together make up the name of their former owners, the Pels brothers. The *Indie* warehouse at no. 495 dates from the 19th century. It is remarkable for its four bays and its width, so different from its neighbors of earlier centuries. This warehouse was originally built for the company that succeeded the old Dutch East India and West India Companies at the beginning of the 19th century, the *Nederlandsche Handelmaatschappij* ▲ *146, 252*. On the opposite bank, PATRICIAN HOUSES have been converted into official buildings and art galleries ▲ *232*. Nos. 524–6 had a garden and a garage, which have been restored. The garden is still visible today through the ground floor.

FRESH WATER. At no. 560 Keizersgracht there lived the writer Jacob van Lennep (1802–68). He is remembered chiefly by the nickname of "Moses in the desert dunes", which was awarded to him after he founded the Dune Water Company to provide Amsterdam with fresh water. This innovation ended the inequality that had previously existed between the rich, who bought fresh water transported by boat, and the poor, who had to take brackish and polluted water from the canals ■ *18*. The widespread pollution of this period inspired Diderot to write the following lines in his *Voyage en Hollande*: "Amsterdam is a stinking city. I do not know what means are used by the inhabitants to purify the air, but I believe they could have saved a good part of the forty or fifty millions they have uselessly spent on it, if they had thought to make the streets wider, to wash them down twice a day with pumps, to make the canals deeper, and expressly to prohibit the washing of clothes and the throwing in of rubbish." Happily, things have changed a lot since then!

At 455 Keizersgracht the Metz store has replaced the New York insurance company, which was the original occupier of this tall building constructed in 1891. Below left, the Hooft tobacco store at no. 508. And left, a detail from the façade of the same store.

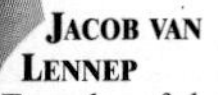

JACOB VAN LENNEP
Founder of the Dune Water Company, Jacob van Lennep lived at 560 Keizersgracht. The secretary of the Illustrious Atheneum ▲ *143*, he wrote plays and novels, translated literary classics into Dutch, and helped with the publication of Multatuli's *Max Havelaar* ▲ *166, 248*.

Left, the Hooft store at no. 508 Keizersgracht .

This cornice stands above no. 487 Herengracht.

THE EXPENSIVE DISTRICT
In the picture below painted in 1685, Berckheyde shows several Herengracht houses (nos. 456–78 and 479–85). He emphasizes the façades, accentuates the bend in the canal and captures a variety of activities, such as the unloading of a boat, the arrival of a carriage, or riders turning into the street. At that time, none of the trees that stand along the canal today had yet been planted.

THE GOLDEN BEND ★ ● *72, 74*

In 1685 Gerrit Adriaensz Berckheyde ● *90* painted the pictureshown below of this bend in the Herengracht, which had just recently been planned and constructed. Here there lived wealthy shipbuilders and merchants, the great beneficiaries of Amsterdam's prosperity during the "Golden Century" ● *30*. "Inside, the houses are full of priceless ornaments, so that they look more like royal palaces than the houses of merchants; a number of them have splendid columns of marble and alabaster, floors inlaid with gold, and the rooms are hung with tapestries of inestimable worth, or with leather stamped in gold or silver and worth millions of florins..." (Melchior Fokkens, *Description de la très renommée cité marchande d'Amsterdam*, 1664). Today, although this part of the canal has retained quite a few of its ancient buildings, it no longer has many private dwellings. These magnificent houses, with their gardens, their broad roofs and their enormous rooms, belong to the banks, to national and international institutions, to publishers, or to museums.

A STRONG FRENCH INFLUENCE ● *74*. The house at no. 450 was built in the French style for the banker Deutz ▲ *190*, some time around 1670, from plans drawn up by Philip Vingboons. Behind the sober five-window façade there is a collection of paintings, among them a self-portrait by Rembrandt. The balustrade that crowns the house at no. 475 (above left) is also marked by strong French influence, by the Louis XIV style in particular. The house was designed in part by Daniel Marot, a French Protestant exiled after 1685. The façade is richly decorated with flowers, acanthus leaves, volutes and children, and at the very top a globe.

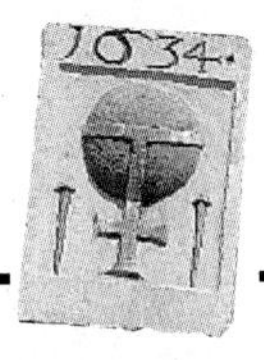

This cartouche is to be found at no. 419 Herengracht.

This painting by Adriaen de Lelie (1755–1820) ▲ *178*, entitled *The Collection of Jan Gildemeester* (1795), shows the interior décor of an art-lover who lived at 475 Herengracht. On the ceiling can be seen a grisaille, and the entablature of the door is decorated in the French manner. The perspective gives a glimpse of the suite of rooms, with the round room probably giving onto the garden.

THE FATE OF THE PICTURE COLLECTIONS. Like most of the rich merchants' houses in this area, the one at no. 485 was built on a double plot. Two-colored, with a central flight of steps, it had a garden "à la française" and a coach-house. In the second quarter of the 20th century it housed the collection belonging to Jacques Goudstikker, a celebrated art-dealer and specialist in Dutch and Italian old masters, as well as the art of his own time. When he died while fleeing the Germans in 1940, his collection fell into Goering's hands. After the war, the pictures were dispersed all over the world. In 1771, no. 462 witnessed the sale of the Gerret Braamcamp estate: 318 pictures altogether, including 2 by Gerard Dou. Catherine the Great of Russia acquired *The Yoking of Oxen* by Paulus Potter, but the painting was allowed to remain in the Mauritshuis Museum in The Hague.

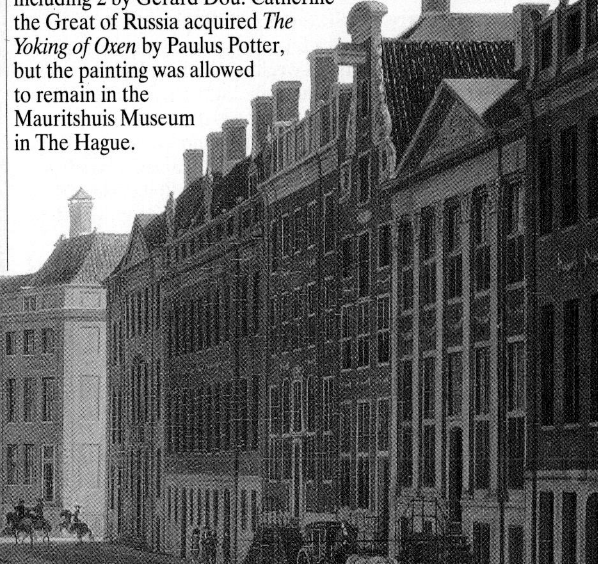

A rich merchant, Jan Six II was sixteen times mayor of Amsterdam.

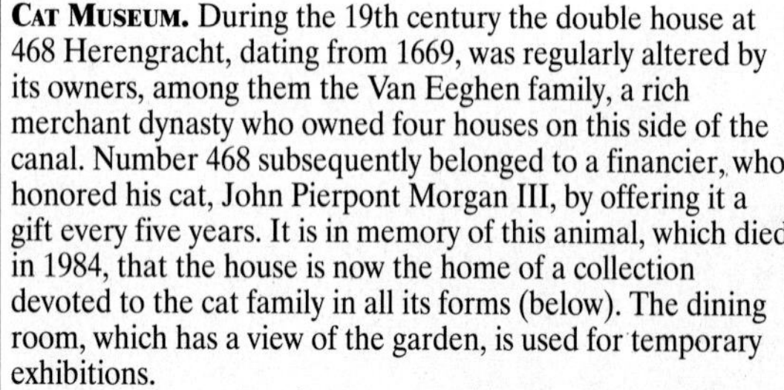

CAT MUSEUM. During the 19th century the double house at 468 Herengracht, dating from 1669, was regularly altered by its owners, among them the Van Eeghen family, a rich merchant dynasty who owned four houses on this side of the canal. Number 468 subsequently belonged to a financier, who honored his cat, John Pierpont Morgan III, by offering it a gift every five years. It is in memory of this animal, which died in 1984, that the house is now the home of a collection devoted to the cat family in all its forms (below). The dining room, which has a view of the garden, is used for temporary exhibitions.

ELEGANT HOUSES ★. Further on at no. 470 Herengracht, a residence which was built in 1669 today houses the Goethe Institute. It demonstrates the typical layout of the Dutch canal house, made up of reception rooms at the front with superb drawing rooms overlooking a garden at the back. Dating from 1670, the house at no. 476 is particularly striking, with its pilasters and mixture of brick and stone. The attic story is crowned by an eagle, the arms of the owners who lived here in the 18th century. It is possible to glimpse its French garden, embellished with statues of the gods of antiquity and a *mappa mundi*. Today the building is occupied by the Prince Bernhard Foundation.

NECK GABLES
The bases of this group of neck gables ● *72* situated between nos. 504 and 510 (opposite, above left) symbolize the power and arms of the owners: dogs with bones, a lion, tritons blowing horns, and sea-gods (details below).

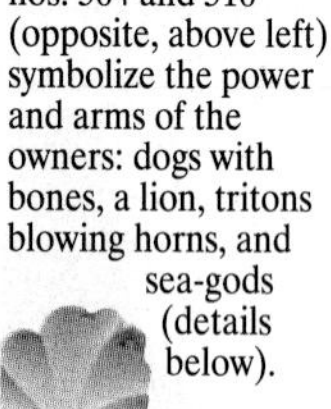

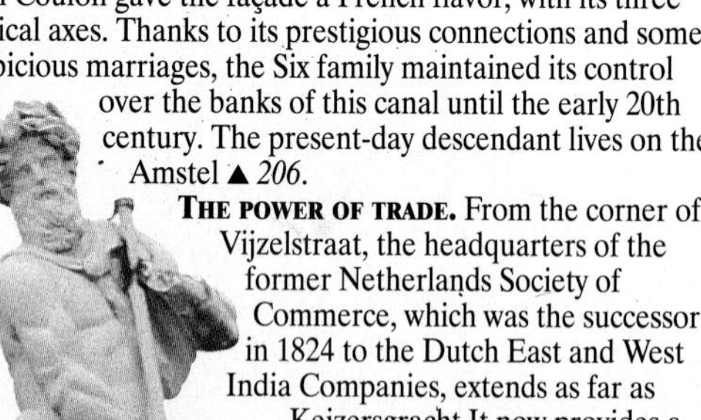

THE SIX DYNASTY. Jan Six II (1668–1750) used to live at no. 495 Herengracht. Son of a financial sponsor who had been painted by Rembrandt, this wealthy merchant had the house completely redesigned in the early 18th century. The architect Jean Coulon gave the façade a French flavor, with its three vertical axes. Thanks to its prestigious connections and some auspicious marriages, the Six family maintained its control over the banks of this canal until the early 20th century. The present-day descendant lives on the Amstel ▲ *206*.

THE POWER OF TRADE. From the corner of Vijzelstraat, the headquarters of the former Netherlands Society of Commerce, which was the successor in 1824 to the Dutch East and West India Companies, extends as far as Keizersgracht.It now provides a hom for the ABN-AMRO bank. Built between 1919 and 1927 from designs by K. de Bazel (1869–1923), it was completed by A. van Gent (1870–1932). The building is ten stories high and the upper two stories are set back, as is often the case in the urban architecture of this

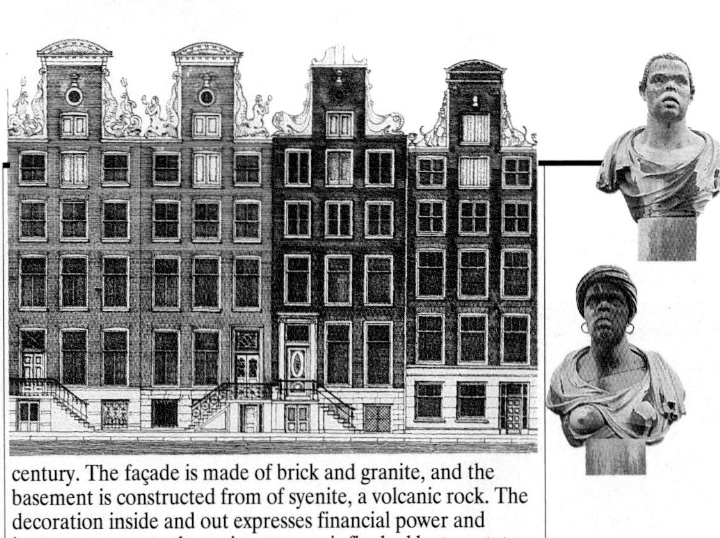

century. The façade is made of brick and granite, and the basement is constructed from of syenite, a volcanic rock. The decoration inside and out expresses financial power and interests overseas: the main entrance is flanked by two statues created by Mendes da Costa which symbolize the two continents of Europe and Asia. Other sculptures invoke commerce, industry and shipping. The staircase celebrates the company's centenary in 1924 with a series of allegorical windows by A. Derkinderen (1859–1925): in them, images of unemployment, idleness, welfare and poverty are opposed by pictures of work, prosperity, peace and harmony ● *82*.

CAMUS AND THE MOORS. The official residence of the mayor of Amsterdam is situated at no. 502 Herengracht. No. 514, a sober house, today a university building, is decorated with two busts of Moors. In *The Fall* Camus has his hero say, mistakenly, that the house once belonged to a slave-trader: "They were bold, saying: 'Look, I hang my sign out in the street, I traffic in slaves, I sell black flesh'. Can you imagine someone today letting it be known that this was their profession? What a scandal! I can hear my Parisian colleagues. They are absolutely intransigent in the matter; they would not hesitate to launch two or three manifestos, perhaps even more!" ● *100*. In fact these busts were intended to evoke the owner's connection with international trade in general rather than the slave trade.

AN IMPERIAL RESIDENCE. No. 527 is built in the French classical style of the 18th century, with its triangular pediment, bearing an eagle, resting on Ionic pilasters which are two stories high. This house has welcomed some famous guests over the years. In 1717 it was leased to the Russian ambassador, who was visited the same year by Peter the Great in the course of his second journey to the Netherlands ▲ *272*. Louis, king of Holland, then bought it as a residence for the Marshal of Holland. According to some sources, Napoleon also stayed in this house when he came to the Netherlands in October 1811 ● *32*.

"The two heads you can see there are those of black slaves. A shop sign. The house belonged to a slave-trader. Ah, you didn't hide what you were up to in those days!"

Albert Camus, *The Fall*.

REGULIERSGRACHT ★

● 66

The Reguliersgracht as seen by Christine Dhanani.

The Reguliersgracht was dug in 1664. It was originally called the "Half-Moon Canal" but its present name comes from the convent of nuns *regular* that existed on the site. This canal was several times the home of the butter market, which was established first of all at the western end, on what is today the Thorbeckeplein, and then still further west again. Perpetually threatened with being covered over, in particular to provide for a tramline, the Reguliersgracht is now permanently protected. This transverse canal is one of the most attractive in the city, thanks to the view it offers of the seven bridges that cross it.The canal's other attractions include the diversity of its architecture and the serene atmosphere, which is sometimes missing in Amsterdam's more monumental residential canals.

CITY OF HAIRDRESSERS? Through the window of no. 45 it is possible to catch a glimpse of a hairdressing salon called Natural Haircuts, which offers personal attention against a musical background. The number of hairdressers of every kind to be found in Amsterdam is quite remarkable.

THE VAN LOON GARDEN
The garden of the Van Loon Museum, seen from a small drawing room, shows how the plots granted after 1660 offered buyers new possibilities. The coach-house opens onto Kerkstraat and could receive carriages entering from that street, between the Keizersgracht and the Prinsengracht. As for the garden itself, it expresses the desire of Amsterdam's residents to remain in contact with nature, even in such a very restricted space.

VAN LOON MUSEUM ★

In 1671 the architect Adriaan Dortsman (1625–82), who drew the plans for the Lutheran Church ▲ *165* and the Walloon Orphanage on the Prinsengracht, was the contractor for the house at nos. 672–4, occupied today by the Van Loon Museum. He was working for a rich merchant, J. van Raey, who had the balustrade decorated with statues of gods representing different aspects of his business: arms, iron and grain (Mars, Minerva, Vulcan and Ceres). After sheltering many different occupants, among them the portraitist Ferdinand Bol (1616–80), the house came into the possession of the Van Loon family, co-founders of the East India Company ▲ *146*, in 1884. They lived there until the end of the Second World War. There is no admission to the basement, which was reserved for the servants, but on the ground and upper floors one can admire the reception rooms, drawing rooms and dining rooms, as well as the family's bedrooms.

"THE FOUR AGES OF MAN". The painting shown opposite, above, by Jan Miense Molenaar (c. 1600–68), forms part of the tradition of genre painting, which raises everyday life to the status of allegory. Often thought of as a pupil of Frans Hals ▲ *224*, Molenaar was the husband of Judith Leyster (c. 1600–60), one of the first important Dutch women painters. He painted a series of studies of domestic life and of the role of the senses. In this painting he unfolds from left to right the

successive ages of life. He is also concerned with the senses, representing them in order of increasing refinement. Thus the children are shown playing and tasting fruit, accompanied by a cat, the symbol of impudence, and a little monkey (on the far left, next to the little girl in red). The young married couple illustrate the sense of smell, in particular through the perfume offered to the wife, Geertruijd van Loon, and the wreath of flowers in her hair. The second couple, who are older, evoke hearing, as they are playing the lute and the spinet. The dog at their feet is the traditional symbol of fidelity. Finally,the more austerely dressed, elderly couple close the cycle, recalling the vanity of life, symbolized by the skull, and illustrating the sense of sight, with the wife touching a Bible and holding her spectacles. According to their descendant, Maurits van Loon, this couple died four years after the completion of the work.The painting also offers information about the changing fashions of dress from generation to generation of the Amsterdam upper classes in the early 17th century. Note, for example, the transition from the ruffs of the older figures through to the simple lace collars of the children (French and Spanish influence is clear here). Similarly, one gentleman wears high boots, while another wears court shoes.

THE VAN LOON GARDEN. This garden, seen from the small drawing room pictured on the left, is typical of the gardens that lie hidden behind the façades, allowing inhabitants, even today, a peaceful place to relax. Governed by a classical sense of order, with its trimmed shrubs and its statues, the garden is a remarkable example of Amsterdammers' need always to maintain a close connection with nature. This even found expression in a certain exoticism, as the historian Renée Kistenmaker tells us: "In the 1700's, a respectable Amsterdam woman was growing pineapples, and in his garden in the country an East India Company administrator had the first coffee and banana plants in the Republic" (*Amsterdam, 1275–1975*).

Born in Haarlem around 1600, dying in Amsterdam in 1668, the painter Jan Miense Molenaar produced this picture entitled [*The Four Ages of Life and the Five Senses*] in 1630.

CARPENTER'S HOUSE
At nos. 57–63 Reguliersgracht there stand two houses built in the last century by the architect T. Gosschalk, for Z. Deenick and Sons, a carpentry firm. This house (on the left, with a detail above) contains both workshop and home. On the balcony (opposite, above right) are carved the tools of the carpenter's trade, such as the plane.

The Market-Crier is a homage to Professor Kokadorus (1867–1934), a market trader.

AMSTELKERK

A Protestant church built of wood, the Amstelkerk (Amstel Church) stands on the corner of Reguliersgracht and Prinsengracht. In this area of the canals, planned after 1660, places of religious worship were initially rare. The construction of the Amstelkerk in 1669 was very likely a temporary remedy for this lack. The church was almost certainly intended as the precursor of a more solid and permanent edifice which was never built. On the Amstelveld (Amstel Field), which was then a meadow liable to flooding, a low-standing church was therefore built, "a great wooden stable with a brick floor in the Dutch manner" (Blokhuis, *The Canals of Amsterdam*). Accommodation for the clergy, a bakery and a coal store were added later. In the 19th century the community made alterations to the interior, giving it a Gothic feel, notably by the introduction of decorated capitals. Recently restored, the building is still a Reformed church, as well as housing the De Keyser Association ▲ *246*. Facing the Café Kort, installed in one of the flanks of the church, the statue of Professor Kokadorus (the nickname of Meijer Linnewiel) recalls a famous and colorful character who harangued the Monday market crowds to get them to buy his goods, which ranged from soap to cigars.

CAFÉ KORT
On one side of the church the Café Kort faces the Amstelveld and the Prinsengracht. When the weather is fine, patrons can enjoy sitting out on the terrace. On Monday mornings a plant market is held on the square.

PRINSENGRACHT

In this section leading to the Amstel, the canal is particularly broad and lively. At no. 756 there stands De Duif (Dove), a Catholic church built in the 19th century, where Plainsong concerts are performed on Sunday afternoons. At No. 808 a ceramic plaque proclaiming the merits of a life insurance company contrasts the improvident going down into darkness with the provident, who achieve happiness.

AMSTEL

The Amstel river, which the four great canals lead into, lies at the heart of the old city and gives Amsterdam its name ● *28*. This river used to flow into the IJ, unobstructed by any dam (*dam*), dyke (*dijk*), or lock (*sluis*). A swing bridge has been built over it, MAGERE BRUG ★ (Skinny Bridge), the most famous in the city (below). Around 1863, as a result of the efforts of Dr Samuel Sarphati ▲ *273, 277*, "the founder of the new Amsterdam", this area awoke from its economic and architectural torpor. A grand avenue was built, the Sarphatistraat: it took the place of the bridge in the background of the painting by Hilverdink (below). On the right bank, opposite the lock, there stands the SQUARE THEATER built in 1887. For a long time the home of Italian opera, today it provides a highly varied program (photo above right).

DEACONESSES' HOSPICE. Dating from 1681–3, this hospice, called the Amstelhof, was for a long time the largest in the city. The two symmetrical wings each contain forty-six rooms, most housing four women. The men were accomm-odated in the basement. This hospice is still in use today.

The Deaconesses' Hospice on the banks of the Amstel.

Painted by Johannes Hilverdink (1813–1902) in 1862–3, the work below shows the confluence of the Prinsengracht and the Amstel. The bridge and the famous Hogesluis (Great Lock) built in 1662 have changed little. This lock was part of the military defences, allowing flooding to prevent invasion.

This fresco by Jacob de Wit dates from 1743 and decorates the ceiling of a room at no. 586 Herengracht. It was commissioned by the new owner of the building, Nicolaas Calkoen the Younger, a merchant and trader in the Levant.

Jan Six I, patron of the arts. Beside the Amstel after the Keizersgracht, the house at no. 218 contains the private collection known as the "Six Collection". This was brought together by the patrician dynasty founded by Jan Six (1618–1700) ▲ *200*. In 1666 he commissioned the architect Adriaan Dortsman to draw up the plans for his fourth house, situated on the right bank of the Herengracht (no. 619). Jan Six belonged to a family of French Protestants who left the town of Saint-Omer, where they had been victims of persecution. He studied at the University of Leiden and did his Grand Tour of Italy in 1640. Mayor of Amsterdam for nine months, he married the daughter of Dr Tulp in 1656 ▲ *182*. Abandoning his business affairs, he then wrote poems and produced his play *Medea*, without any great success. He is remembered above all as the client and protector of Rembrandt.

Herengracht

The Splendor of the De Belmontes ★. At the end of the 17th century the house at no. 586 had only four bays. Its owner leased it to Manuel Isaak Nuñes, the chargé d'affaires of the king of Spain, who became Baron de Belmonte in 1693. This Sephardic aristocrat bought the house in 1700, and lived the high life, entertaining the diplomatic corps. The ceiling of one of the rooms is decorated with a fresco by Jacob de Wit (1696–1754) which represents mythological figures: Pluvius pouring water, Aurora with a torch, and Flora with a basket of fruit (above).

This round room on the ground floor of the Willet Museum opens onto the garden. The woodwork is all in pale green, as was customary in the 19th century. The little table in the center is decorated with French marquetry-work with musical instrument motifs.

Willet-Holthuysen Museum ★. This museum (no. 605) is situated in a double house built in 1687, which, through a succession of alliances, bequests and inheritances became the property of various members of the wealthy Amsterdam families: Jacob Hop, Isabella Hooft, Jean Deutz van Assendelft and Willem Gideon Deutz. In 1855 the house became the property of Pieter Gerard Holthuijsen, a glass merchant and coal-importer. His daughter Sandrina Luisa Geertruida married the art-collector Abraham Willet, and the

On the next floor of the museum, this room was Abraham Willet's office. On the dressing table stands a figurine representing dawn.

couple had a number of alterations made to the house in about 1860. In 1895 the widow gave the house and its collections to the city but it was only in 1962 that it became a museum devoted to Dutch interiors and to objects which had once belonged to rich patricians. This five-window double house has a symmetrical plan. Each floor has a particular function. The basement has the usual offices, cellar and larder and it now contains a reconstruction of an 18th-century kitchen, with its granite sink and original plumbing. The ground floor was the piano nobile with drawing rooms and dining rooms organized around a central passage. The next floor had the living quarters and Abraham Willet's office. The double bed in the bedroom has floral cotton print hangings. The other rooms on this floor contain the collections. In particular, there is a series of Dutch and Italian glasses with biblical and erotic decorations.

THE WILLET GARDEN ★. At the back of the house is a large garden, from which the coach-house and stables have now disappeared. This impressive French garden was designed in the 18th-century Dutch taste. It is ornamented with a sundial and with the usual motifs, in particular statues of Mercury, the god of trade, Flora, goddess of flowers, and Pomona, goddess of gardens. The garden of the Willet Museum is unique in Amsterdam, in that it is visible from the Amstelstraat, there being no building in this street to obstruct the view.

BISCUITS AND THE ARISTOCRACY. Between nos. 579 and 581, standing on an elephant's head, a statue representing the Archangel Michael slaying the dragon offers a quite unexpected sight on the canals. The owner of the house, a manufacturer of biscuits under the trade name "White Elephant", was making a statement about his unusual social status in this largely aristocratic neighborhood. His neighbors and fellow owners in the group of houses between nos. 571–81 were an arms dealer, a shipbuilder and a mayor. The old Reguliersmarkt, the butter market, is now called the Thorbeckeplein, after the statue of Johan Thorbecke (1798–1872) ▲ *138*, liberal statesman and one of those who inspired the 1848 constitution.

The Archangel Michael slays the dragon: this statue decorates the house at no. 579 Herengracht.

"In 1653 Six lent the painter the sum of a thousand florins, and in 1654 the latter painted the portrait which can be found today in the Six Collection in Amsterdam. The painting seems to have marked the end of their friendship. When Six married in 1656, he asked Flinck, and not Rembrandt, to paint the portrait of his wife, and that same year, as if to mark a new break in their relations, he assigned Rembrandt's debt to another person. This was the end of friendship and patronage."
Svetlana Alpers, *Rembrandt's Studio*

REMBRANDTPLEIN ★

For a long time the outermost point of Amsterdam's system of fortifications, as can be seen on the old maps ● *34*, this square changed its role in the late 17th century, after the construction of the "half-moon" of canals. Doubtless as a result of its proximity to the bend in the Amstel, it was used as a location for the butter market. It was at this time that it acquired the name of Reguliersmarkt. All plans of the city show that this broad rectangular square had two important buildings. The first, and older, was the *public weighhouse* (Waag). Compact, and fairly tall, it used to stand in the very middle. The second building, rather smaller, was the MARKET

This statue of Johan Thorbecke, on the Thorbeckeplein, is the work of the artist F. Leenhoff.

A lamp from the Tuschinski Cinema.

HALL itself. This very active market was also for a long time a fairground. The square did not immediately lose its role as a marketplace when it was renamed in honor of Rembrandt in 1876. The public weighhouse no longer exists, and the center of the square is now occupied by a STATUE OF REMBRANDT enveloped in his cloak, his gaze turned toward the Jewish quarter. The picture by Andries Scheerboom (below), painted in 1869, shows the busy commercial activity that animated the Rembrandtplein in the 19th century. In our own day the Rembrandtplein has many places of recreation, such as the cinemas, bars and cafés: these include the Schiller, built in the Art Deco style, and the Monico, a brown café ● *50*. According to legend, it was right on the Rembrandtplein that the famous singer Pisuisse was murdered in 1920, together with his wife, by a jealous lover.

TUSCHINSKI CINEMA ★ ● *83*. At 26 Reguliersbreestraat, a busy street running from Rembrandtplein to Muntplein ▲ *120*, stands the Tuschinski Cinema, surmounted by its two turrets (above left). Abraham Tuschinski, an immigrant Polish Jew and man of the theater, bought an empty plot here at the end of the First World War. He had the cinema built between 1918 and 1921 by the architect H. L. de Jong, who combined the proliferating decoration of the Amsterdam School ● *84* with a Hollywood eclecticism. The foyer (above) is a sort of luxuriant grotto, with its carpets, sofas, tapestries, lamps and stained-glass windows. The Tuschinski has been divided into several cinemas, and so the décor has had to be redone. Screen 1 remains the most authentic.

“One finds the Tuschinski Cinema, this Art Deco monument of a luxury and exoticism unheard of in the Netherlands, which continues to provide a venue for grand premières in the Hollywood tradition. The festive and phantasmagorical interior, dominated by black and dark red, where the least square centimeter seems to have been drawn and colored with quite specific attention, makes up a gigantic picture, warmly glowing, which closes in on the visitor as soft as velvet.”

Max van Rooy

Around the museums

Museumplein, *210*
Rijksmuseum, *212*
Van Gogh Museum , *214*
Stedelijk Museum, *214*
Concertgebouw, *216*
Art collections of Amsterdam, *218*
Vondelpark, *232*
Antique shops
and art galleries, *234*

VONDELPARK
DUTCH RIDING SCHOOL
VONDELKERK
CINEMA MUSEUM
STATUE OF VONDEL

Half a day

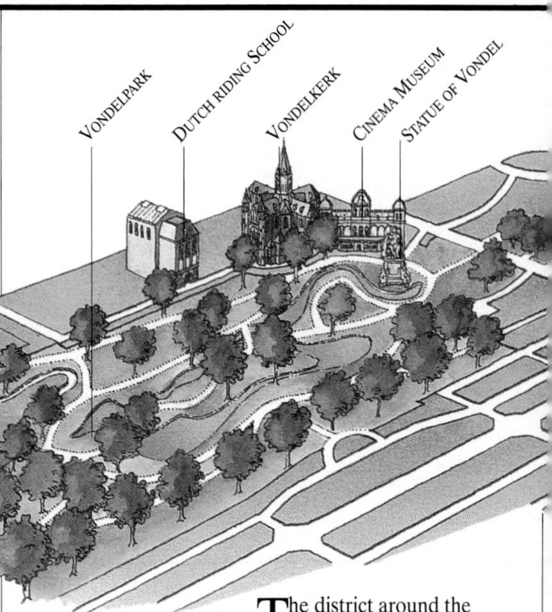

The district around the Museumplein (Museum Square) was founded in the late 19th century on the former Brouwersplein (Brewers' Square), following the draining of a marsh. As well as the houses of the rich Amsterdam bourgeoisie, there are a number of leisure and cultural centers in this part of the city, especially galleries and museums. The major art collections all lie within a short distance of each other.

THE UNIVERSAL EXHIBITION OF 1895
The woman on the poster embodies the city arms (the three

crosses of Saint Andrew) and Dutch power on land (the train), sea (the ship) and throughout the world (the map).

MUSEUMPLEIN

AN ALL-PURPOSE ESPLANADE. The esplanade that stretches south from the Rijksmuseum lay outside the city walls until the early 19th century. The economic revival of the second half of the century led to its transformation and incorporation into the rest of the city around 1880. While expansion to the south of the old city tended to consist of housing projects, often of a social nature, like De Pijp in 1862 ▲ *275*, this esplanade was built with the aim of creating a large residential district dominated by broad avenues. One of the first elements of the plan was the Vondelpark, established in 1877 on the western edge of the new district. The esplanade became an exhibition space and a place where museum visitors could get some air, although paradoxically none of the museums had the benefit of direct access to it. The esplanade figured in the map given to visitors to the 1883 International Exhibition of the Colonies and Foreign Trade. The Museumplein was redesigned in a plan drawn up by J.V. van Niftrick, who hoped

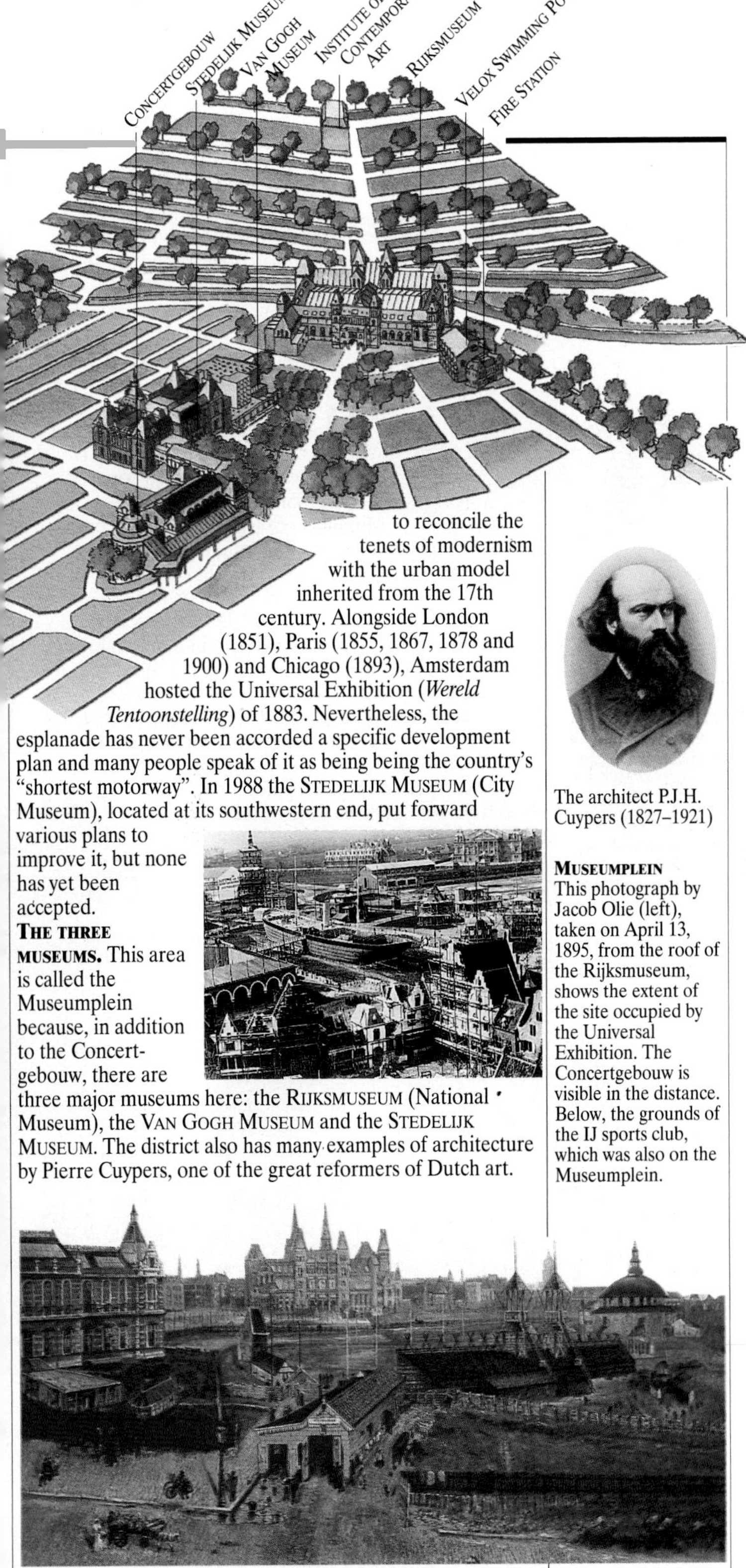

to reconcile the tenets of modernism with the urban model inherited from the 17th century. Alongside London (1851), Paris (1855, 1867, 1878 and 1900) and Chicago (1893), Amsterdam hosted the Universal Exhibition (*Wereld Tentoonstelling*) of 1883. Nevertheless, the esplanade has never been accorded a specific development plan and many people speak of it as being being the country's "shortest motorway". In 1988 the STEDELIJK MUSEUM (City Museum), located at its southwestern end, put forward various plans to improve it, but none has yet been accepted.

THE THREE MUSEUMS. This area is called the Museumplein because, in addition to the Concert-gebouw, there are three major museums here: the RIJKSMUSEUM (National Museum), the VAN GOGH MUSEUM and the STEDELIJK MUSEUM. The district also has many examples of architecture by Pierre Cuypers, one of the great reformers of Dutch art.

The architect P.J.H. Cuypers (1827–1921)

MUSEUMPLEIN
This photograph by Jacob Olie (left), taken on April 13, 1895, from the roof of the Rijksmuseum, shows the extent of the site occupied by the Universal Exhibition. The Concertgebouw is visible in the distance. Below, the grounds of the IJ sports club, which was also on the Museumplein.

Skaters perform risky feats on the Museumplein ● 60 in 1895 (photograph by Jacob Olie ▲ 259).

THE KING AGAINST THE MUSEUM
When he first saw the Rijksmuseum King William III of the Netherlands cried "I shall never set foot in that cloister!" Defending his fellow architects, Berlage ● *80* ▲ *133* replied to the critics, "All these malicious protests come from fellows who are like those little dogs that bark at the starry night sky."

RIJKSMUSEUM ★

● *80* ▲ *218*

The idea of building a national museum in Amsterdam dates from the French presence in the city in 1798. In 1808 a collection which had originally been assembled in The Hague was transferred to Amsterdam. It was first called the Royal Museum, then in 1815 became the Rijksmuseum ("state-run museum"), or National Museum. The name then stuck to this gallery of classical art, although the term *rijks* suggests an administrative status that in fact applies more accurately to other establishments, such as the Van Gogh Museum. The Rijksmuseum was first housed on one floor of the Royal Palace on the Dam ▲ *128*. It received Rembrandt's *The Night Watch* ▲ *218* as a gift from the city. In 1815 the collection moved to the Trippenhuis ▲ *151*, on the canals in the city center, but this building was unable to contain all the gifts and acquisitions that poured in, including a bequest from the collector A. van der Hoop in 1854 ▲ *218*, which enabled the museum to acquire Rembrandt's *The Jewish Bride*. To remedy the space problem, in 1874 four architects were invited by a state commission to submit plans for a new museum.

A "GOTHIC CATHEDRAL". The present building dates from 1885. It is the work of the architect P.J.H. Cuypers, who was born in the Roman Catholic province of Limburg and studied art at Antwerp. When the Catholics were granted complete freedom of worship ● *39* in 1815, he began to specialize in the restoration of Catholic churches. Cuypers contacted A.J.P. Thijm, the famous Catholic man of

letters, who brought him to Amsterdam. The meeting was a decisive one for Cuypers; he was accepted into the Amsterdam intelligentsia, who introduced him to Symbolism, a taste for the Gothic and the cult of the poet Van den Vondel ● *109* ▲ *186*. The Rijkmuseum, Cuypers' first project, was in the neo-Renaissance style; the towers and roofs were designed in brick. But the building also has some Gothic elements, particularly the stained glass of its northern façade; indeed, it was often described as a "Gothic cathedral". It is said that the Rijksmuseum's plan and façade are a virtual replica of the Town Hall, built in 1648 ▲ *128*. The imposing proportions of the façade are clearly reminiscent of an almost identical building, the Central Station, also designed by Cuypers ● *80* ▲ *138*. Images illustrating the history of the Netherlands and of the arts decorate the museum's façades. On the southern side, facing the Museumplein, are mosaics depicting important figures in the cultural life of Amsterdam, such as Vondel, Frederik Hendrik, Tulp ▲ *182* and Huygens. Originally designed to house most of the national collections in its labyrinth of rooms, the museum has undergone numerous alterations. It now has five sections devoted to painting, sculpture and the decorative arts, Asiatic art, the history of the Netherlands and a print room. It covers periods from the 15th century to the late 19th century.

This frieze decorates the top of the Rijksmuseum.

Homage to Monulphus
The mosaic (left) adorns one of the façades of the museum. It represents an episode of late Roman civilization: the foundation around 570 by Monulphus of the Saint Servaas basilica near Maastricht.

Joseph Alberdingk Thijm
J.A. Thijm, Catholic politician and poet, persuaded the architect P.J.H. Cuypers to come to Amsterdam.

Hilverdink
In 1885 the cityscape painter J. Hilverdink (1813–1902) set up his easel to the west of the newly completed museum and painted the then uninhabited area that bordered on the Vondelpark and Museumplein. The bridge on the left is probably the one that used to cross the Paulus Potterkade, today covered by a street.

VAN GOGH MUSEUM ★ ▲ 226

This museum was built on a site donated by the Amsterdam city council as recently as 1973. It was enlarged for the great Van Gogh exhibition which was held in 1991, having originally been designed to house the collection of the painter's brother Theodore van Gogh (1857–91). Theo's widow, and afterwards his son Jo, donated this collection, which includes works by Vincent as well as several by his friends Toulouse-Lautrec, Gauguin and Manet. The original plans for the museum were drawn up by the architect and designer Rietveld (1888–1964) ● 56. Vincent van Gogh's works, including *Self Portrait with Straw Hat*, *The Zouave* and *A Pair of Boots,* are on the first floor up.

A PLACE FOR CROWS AND SUNFLOWERS
The simple, modern structure of the Van Gogh Museum, built in 1973, is surrounded by contemporary sculptures.

STEDELIJK MUSEUM ★ ▲ 228, 230

The Stedelijk Museum (City Museum) opened its doors to the public in 1895 following the donation of Augustus Pieter Lopez Suasso's collection by Sophia Adriana de Bruyn. Amsterdam city council agreed to set up the Sophia-Augusta Foundation, which was responsible for displaying this collection and staging a four-yearly exhibition of works by contemporary painters. The museum's architecture, in the same neo-Renaissance style as the Rijksmuseum, combines brick and stone, turrets and gables. The interior has been modernized under successive directors, and the visitor is immediately struck by the brightness of the monumental staircase and rooms on the first floor up, all of which are painted white.

"HOUSE OF MUSEUMS". Willem Sandberg's (1897–1984) appointment as director in 1945 brought about a revolution. Abandoning the old collection, which was mainly historical, he took inspiration from the Museum of Modern Art in New York in transforming the Stedelijk Museum into a "House of Museums", in which fine art, photography,

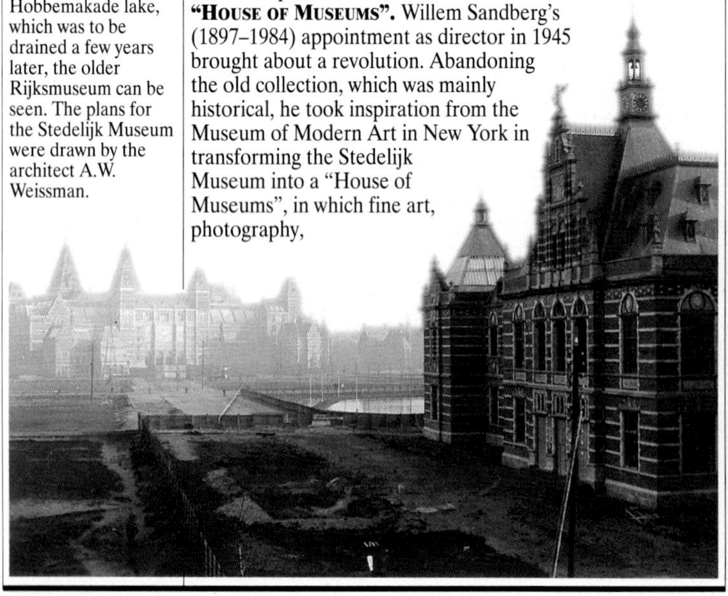

THE BUILDING OF A DISTRICT
This photograph by Jacob Olie ▲ *259*, taken in 1894, shows the newly completed Amsterdam Stedelijk Museum. In the distance, behind the Hobbemakade lake, which was to be drained a few years later, the older Rijksmuseum can be seen. The plans for the Stedelijk Museum were drawn by the architect A.W. Weissman.

"THE PAINTERS... THOUGH DEAD AND BURIED, SPEAK TO THE NEXT GENERATION, OR EVEN TO MANY GENERATIONS, THROUGH THEIR WORKS."

VINCENT VAN GOGH

dance, theater, music and cinema were all represented. Sandberg, himself an artist and typographer, had to defend both his museum and his avant-garde design from an unfavorable response by the critics and a largely conservative public, whom he further antagonized with events and exhibitions regarded at the time as shocking. Nevertheless it is thanks to Willem Sandberg that there is a Dutch audience for modern art today. The museum's highly eclectic collection, which reflects the taste of its creator, is dominated by paintings and sculpture. The 19th century is well represented, with pictures by Van Gogh, Jongkind, Cézanne and Monet, and the museum has many classic works of 20th-century art: Beckmann, Bonnard, Chagall, Dubuffet, Ernst, Kandinsky, Klee, Klein, Matisse, Picasso, Vuillard, Mondrian, Rietveld and the CoBrA movement. A large collection by the Russian Constructivist Kasimir Malevich is also on display, as well as works by most contemporary American artists. A new wing made entirely of glass opens on to Van Baerlestraat.

The clientèle of the Rijwielschool Velox ("Velox cycling school") profited from its proximity to the Vondelpark to practise riding their tricycles ● *58*.

RESIDENTIAL ARCHITECTURE

After passing the Rijksmuseum, where musicians and craftspeople try to attract the attention of passing tourists, you come upon a residential district to the east, built after 1900. Almost all the streets are named after Dutch painters whose works are on display in the Rijksmuseum. The impressive width of the avenues is due to the space available outside the old city walls and to the wealth of the residents.

A SCHOOL FOR CYCLISTS. At the corner of Hobbemastraat and Hobbemakade there is a large brick building dating from 1898 called the Rijwielschool Velox, or "Velox Cycling School". The Rijwielschool was closed from 1904 until 1912, when it was converted into a swimming baths. The large pool was recently restored.

WATER AGAINST FIRE. No. 27 Honthorstraat is a fire station (Brandweerkazerne), also built in 1898 in the Dutch neo-Renaissance style. The Brandweer represented an important step in employing professional firefighters in Amsterdam for the first time, whereas previously they had just used volunteers. The Wildschut Café on Rudolf Hartplein, located on the ground floor of a block built in the style of the Amsterdam School ● *84*, dates from the 1920's. The public library opposite was also constructed during the Amsterdam School period.

BRANDWEERKAZERNE
In 1898 the descendants of the fire brigade led in the 17th century by Jan van der Heyden ▲ *171* benefited from the building of a new barracks, or Brandweerkazerne (left and below).

The décor and chairs of the Wildschut café date from the 1920's.

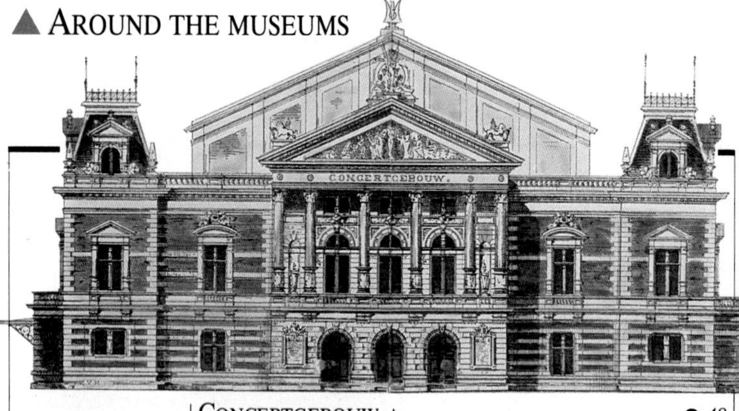

CONCERTGEBOUW ★ ● *48*

The architect A.L. van Gendt.

A NEW CONCERT HALL. The expansion of the city beyond its concentric canals, carried out in the late 19th century, started at the Museumplein. The concert hall (Concertgebouw) was then built on an empty polder further to the south. In the early 20th century it became the center of a new residential district. The idea of the Concertgebouw was formed around 1880 by a group of wealthy music-lovers who were aware of an increasing imbalance between the growth of the art museums and the lack of musical facilities in the city. At that time Amsterdam had only the Parkzaal and the Felix Meritis hall ▲ *184* and it is said that Brahms complained about the dilapidated state of these venues when he visited Amsterdam.

CONCERTGEBOUW PLEIN ZUID

THE SOCIETY IN ACTION. An investment society was set up, which numbered among its members the architect of the neighboring Rijksmuseum, P.J.H. Cuypers. He was influential in the choice of the site, which is located between a candle factory and some children's playgrounds. Despite the unfavorable economic climate, in 1883 Cuypers and four of his colleagues organized a competition to design an oval concert hall with an audience capacity of two thousand. This plan, inspired by that of the Felix Meritis, also included a restaurant, smoking room and garden. A.L. van Gendt (1835–1901), an engineer, architect and businessman, won the competition. He submitted several designs, one of which was greatly influenced by buildings in the French style and by the recently built Gewandhaus in Leipzig. The final project provided for two auditoria, one very large and a second, smaller one for recitals. The façade combined neo-Renaissance elements, the lateral towers echoing those of the Rijksmuseum, with the neo-classical style, which is evident in the central pediment with columns. Despite problems in raising the money, the Concertgebouw was opened on April 11, 1888.

The violinist Joe Cramer opened the Concertgebouw in 1888.

THE WORLD'S FINEST ACOUSTICS ON PILES. It is not the façade of the building but its large auditorium that most impresses the visitor and captivates the listener. Though he was no great music-lover, Van Gendt created a concert hall with excellent acoustics. Originally it had a tiered stage accommodating 120 musicians and a choir of 500, which was dominated by a huge organ in a wooden organ loft. The wind instruments tended to overpower the string section, however, so the slope

These elevations of the north and south façades of the Concertgebouw were drawn by A.L. van Gendt in November 1883.

of the stage was reduced in 1889 and it was subsequently carpeted. The hall was given its polychrome decoration in 1898. The many improvements to the interior did not solve the problem of the building's foundations, however: for the Concertgebouw rests, as indeed does the whole city, on a layer of damp ground sandwiched between two layers of sand ■ *16*. The thousands of wooden piles supporting the building were constantly deteriorating due to the movement of the water around them. In 1983 it looked as though the entire building was in danger of collapse. It was therefore decided to transfer its 10,000 tons, which were resting on 2,186 damaged wooden piles, on to 400 metal tubes, which went deeper and were more robust. A machine called the Tubex sank these new pipes without causing the building to shift, and the old wooden piles were lifted out through them. A concrete base was then created below water level. A new wing was also built, generating fierce opposition as critics claimed that it upset the symmetry and stylistic unity of the building. A gallery of glass and columns, forming a two-story covered promenade, it runs along the side of the main auditorium. It houses a hall, a foyer and some plant equipment. As is the case with many old cultural institutions, the new addition is designed to accommodate larger numbers of visitors and provide them with modern facilities. In particular it makes it possible to separate audiences heading for the small and large halls.

WORLDWIDE PRESTIGE. The Royal Concertgebouw Orchestra is regarded as among the best in the world. Its conductors, both guest conductors and permanent, are some of the most eminent of their generation. One man whose influence marked the history of the hall is Willem Mengelberg (1871–1951), who has remained famous for his performances of the great German symphonic repertoire and particularly for his interpretation of Beethoven's *Egmont* overture. Frans Bruggen, born in 1934 in Amsterdam, made his debut as a flautist here. In 1981 he set up the Orchestra of the Eighteenth Century, an ensemble of forty-eight highly skilled musicians of all nationalities, who perform early music entirely on the original instruments which were in use at the time the music was written.

WILLEM MENGELBERG
This conductor (above) brought the Concertgebouw worldwide acclaim, which is still enjoyed by the orchestra today (left).

Henri Viotta conducted the inaugural concert on April 11, 1888.

REMBRANDT

Rembrandt (1606–69) is today regarded as the greatest Dutch master of the Golden Age and one of the most inspired artists in the history of painting. However he did not enjoy such a reputation in the 17th century. When he first moved to Amsterdam his work was appreciated, and he received many commissions; but as the decades passed his style became increasingly isolated from the taste of his contemporaries, who preferred genre and landscape scenes painted in a more detailed, highly finished style. *The Company of Captain Frans Banningh Cocq and Lieutenant Willem van Ruytenburch*, better known as *The Night Watch* (3) (Rijksmuseum), completed in 1642, provides a good illustration of this isolation. Rembrandt was severely criticized for having ignored the conventions of propriety in the painting. Captain Cocq's company was one of the many groups of riflemen who had ceased to meet except for banquets and marches ▲ *126*. Rembrandt depicted the men as they were preparing to march, but he created such a sense of disorder that the picture appeared to contemporaries to be unseemly. A shot is being fired for no apparent reason, a dog is running around yapping, and a little girl seems to be lost among the men. In contrast to the overall somber tone of the image, the little girl is painted with sparkling brightness, giving her an unreal air.

The Syndics of the Drapers' Guild (1662) is one of Rembrandt's finest group portraits (2), and *The Jewish Bride* (c. 1665) is another of his masterpieces (1). He creates strong contrasts of light and shadow and uses bright colors, but it is the brushwork that reveals his true genius. In places, particularly on the bride's sleeve, the paint is very thickly applied. It was on seeing a similarly inspired painting in 1920 that the German-born artist Hans Hartung claimed that he finally understood the legitimacy of abstract art (Rijksmuseum).

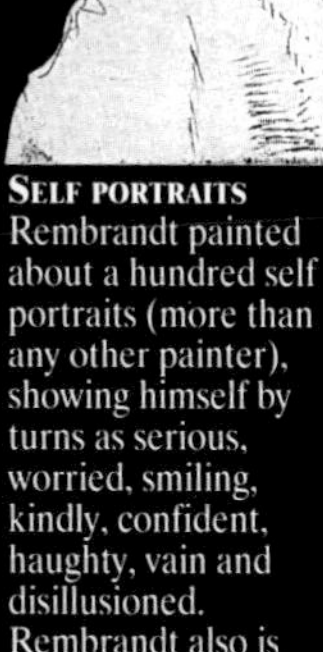

SELF PORTRAITS
Rembrandt painted about a hundred self portraits (more than any other painter), showing himself by turns as serious, worried, smiling, kindly, confident, haughty, vain and disillusioned. Rembrandt also is undoubtedly the most famous of all etchers. This self portrait (4) was drawn when he was twenty-seven years old (Rembrandthuis ▲ *156*).

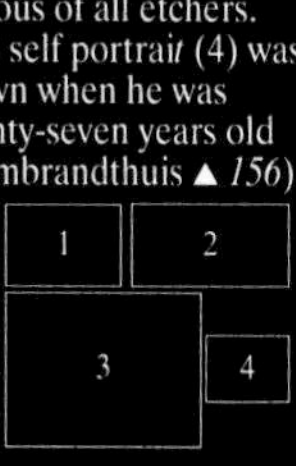

1	2
3	4

"The Adoration of the Golden Calf"
In Moses' absence, the Jews rebelled and adopted a golden calf as an idol which they then worshipped (3). When Moses came down from the mountain, he smashed the Tablets of the Law in his rage.

The influence of Italian Mannerism
In the 16th century Jan van Scorel(1495–1562) and his most important pupil, Maarten van Heemskerck (1498–1574), were among the first painters to introduce the Italian style to the northern Netherlands. They were inspired by Mannerism, adopting its acidic colors, tormented poses and sensual qualities according to their individual tastes. The signature of the famous engraver Lucas van Leyden (1489 or 1494–1533) can be found on some paintings, including the *Adoration of the Golden Calf* (3), a triptych completed in 1525. The confusion of the scene expresses the Jews' moral disarray in the absence of Moses: one man is devouring a ham while another fondles a woman sitting on his knee. Behind them an orgy is taking place.

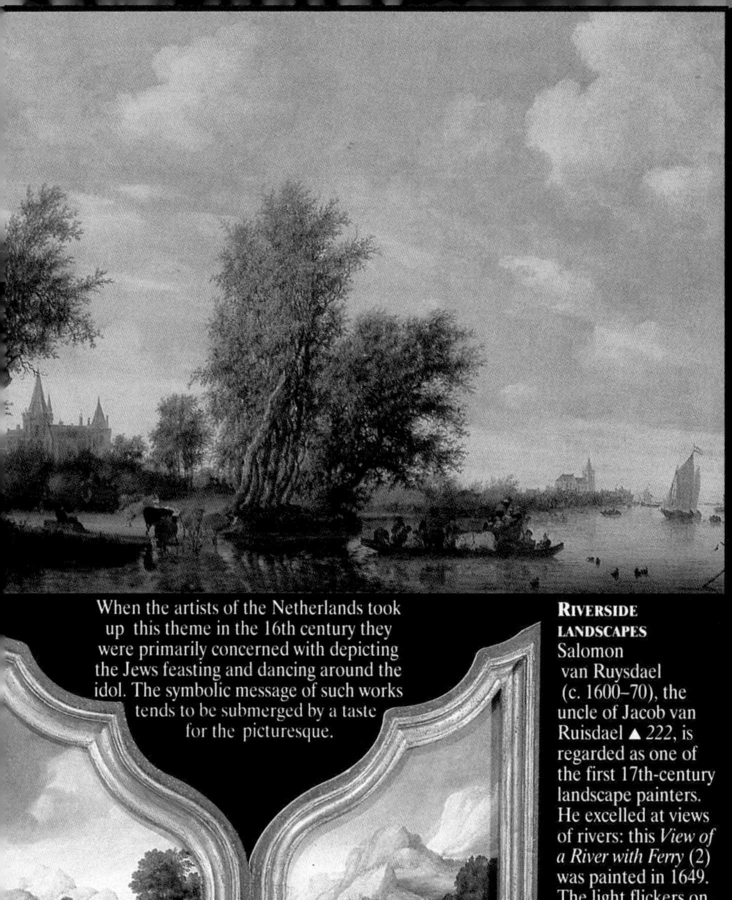

When the artists of the Netherlands took up this theme in the 16th century they were primarily concerned with depicting the Jews feasting and dancing around the idol. The symbolic message of such works tends to be submerged by a taste for the picturesque.

Riverside landscapes

Salomon van Ruysdael (c. 1600–70), the uncle of Jacob van Ruisdael ▲ *222*, is regarded as one of the first 17th-century landscape painters. He excelled at views of rivers: this *View of a River with Ferry* (2) was painted in 1649. The light flickers on the water and filters through the precisely detailed clouds and foliage. The work of Aert van der Neer (1603–77) reveals the maturity of Dutch landscape painting. In his *View of a River in Winter* painted in 1650 (1) the artist conveys the subtle play of winter light through cloud. (All these pictures are on display in the Rijksmuseum.)

1	2
3	

The 17th-century Dutch landscape painters

These artists followed in the footsteps of 16th-century Flemish painters such as Pieter Bruegel, Bril and Van Coninxloo. The most famous and most original landscape painter of the period was Jacob van Ruisdael (1628/9–82).

Windmill at Wijk (2), painted in 1670, is representative of his work as a whole; it combines qualities of solitude, melancholy and grandeur. "All Ruisdael is here: grandeur of aspect, little charm except by chance, a great appeal, a gradually revealed intimacy, accomplished skill and very simple means" (Eugène Fromentin, *The Masters of Past Time*). *Riverside Landscape with Boar Hunt* (3), painted in 1610 by the Antwerp artist Joos de Momper (1564–1635) is, as is often the case, an imaginary composition. Hendrick Avercamp (1585–1634) specialized in winter scenes, where crowds of figures dart about on frozen lakes and canals, as in this *Winter Landscape with Skaters* (4) completed in 1618. Countless painters worked in this highly narrative genre, some stressing the atmosphere, others the picturesque aspects of a scene.

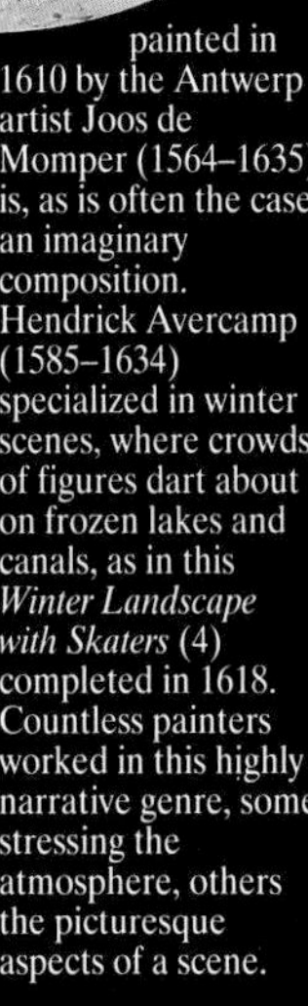

The Hague School

This late 19th-century movement was inspired by the Barbizon School and also by French Impressionism. It shared similar aims, in seeking to breathe new life into the landscape tradition. One of its chief exponents, Anton Mauve (1838–88), painted the elegant *Horseride along the Beach at Scheveningen* around 1875 (1). (These pictures can all be seen in the Rijksmuseum.)

1	3
2	4

FIGURES AND PORTRAITS

Dutch group portraits of the 16th and early 17th centuries often show frozen, monotonous rows of people, tenuously connected by a common activity. These portraits of the many scientific, military, charitable and trade organizations were used to decorate their meeting rooms ▲ *126*. Examples of the style include *The Anatomy Lesson of Dr Sebastian Egbertsz* (1) (Historisch Museum) painted in 1628 by an artist named Thomas de Keyser (1596–1667) who was very fashionable but lacking in genius, and *Distribution of Bread at the Chaplain's House* (detail, 5) (Historisch Museum), painted in 1627 and attributed to Werner van den Valckert (c. 1585–1627). *Banquet of the Civic Guard to Celebrate the Conclusion of the Peace of Münster* (3) (Rijksmuseum), painted in 1648 by Bartholomeus van der Helst (1613–70), dispenses with this monotonous formality, following the example of Frans Hals and the brilliant works of Rembrandt, who had revolutionized the genre with the famous *Anatomy lesson of Dr Tulp* (1632) ▲ *182*. *The Merry Drinker* (2) (Rijksmuseum), painted in 1628 by Frans Hals (1580/85–1666), is characteristic of his work, which is full of life, strength and elegance, and rich in impasto effects and bold brushwork. Hals, like Rembrandt, rejected a highly "polished" style of painting.

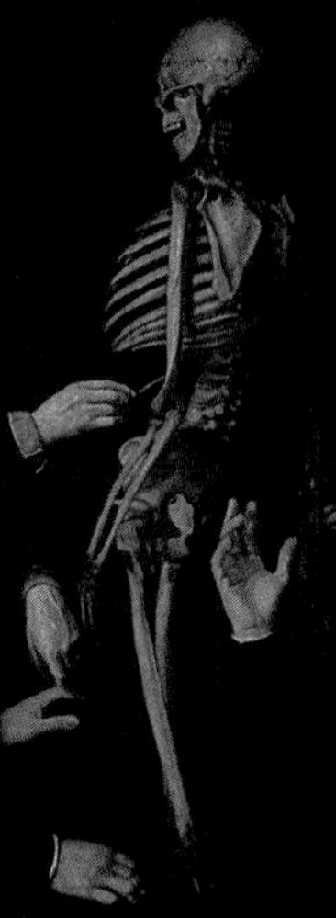

2 3
1 4 5 6

«WHAT BEAUTIES ART GIVES US! AS LONG AS YOU CAN REMEMBER WHAT YOU HAVE SEEN, YOU ARE NEVER EMPTY, NOR TRULY LONELY, NOR EVER ALONE.»

VINCENT VAN GOGH.

THE PAINTERS OF INTIMACY
Pieter de Hooch (1629–84) and Johannes Vermeer (1632–75) were the most eminent genre painters of their period. They were able to capture insignificant moments and scenes from everyday life and to transform them into a beautiful dream. The play of light enlivens the colors and lends an intense, silent inner life to physical objects. De Hooch's *The Messenger* (4), completed in 1670, and Vermeer's *Woman in Blue Reading a Letter* (6), both in the Rijksmuseum, are wonderful examples of this kind of work.

Vincent van Gogh (1853–90) produced his entire oeuvre in less than ten years: his first canvas dates from 1881, and by his death he had painted 879 pictures. His creative intensity can be divided into several phases, progressing toward work of immense power. His distinctive style, full of vigorous, graphic brushstrokes, first emerges in *Leaving the Church at Nuenen* (4), painted in January 1884. In 1887, after his arrival in Paris, he painted *Woman in the Café du Tambourin* (3), a work that demonstrates his discovery of bright colors. After his long stay in Paris, where he absorbed first Impressionism and then Pointillism, Vincent wrote to his sister: "I plan to go away, as soon as possible, and spend some time in the South, where there is even more color, more sun." And it was in Arles that the style of Van Gogh, who was passionately dedicated to the search for artistic and human truth, fully

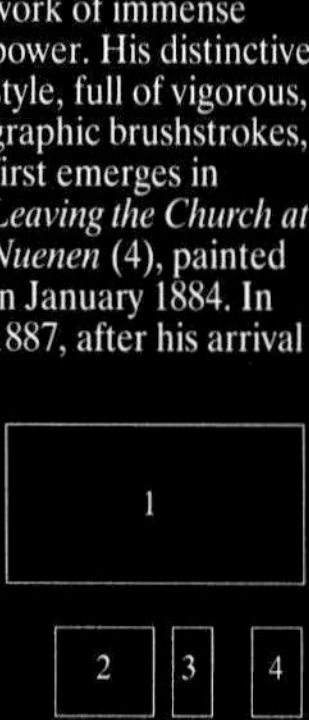

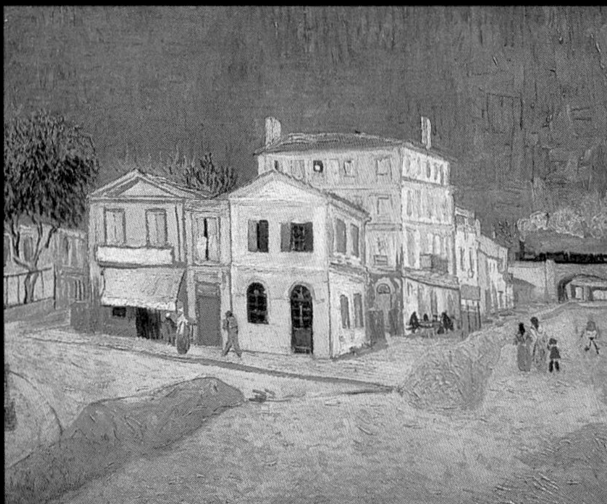

1

2 3 4

matured with *The Yellow House in Arles* (1888) (2). He invited Paul Gauguin to join him in Arles, hoping to build an artists' community in which all property would be held in common. But after only a few months the coexistence of these two strong temperaments became fraught with difficulties, resulting in Vincent's breakdown and self-mutilation. Van Gogh left Provence in 1890 and moved to Auvers, staying with his friend Doctor Gachet, whom he hoped would cure him. His use of color in *The Château of Auvers-sur-Oise* (1) continued to reflect his Mediterranean style, as the landscape of the area fired his stormy imagination.. "When he describes the landscape he is painting [...] he never says there are fields, trees, houses, mountains... but yellow and blue, red and green, and the drama of the relationship between them..." (Octave Mirbeau, *Vincent van Gogh*). In July 1890 the painter committed suicide. Since that time art lovers have never ceased to respond to the powerful message of his works.

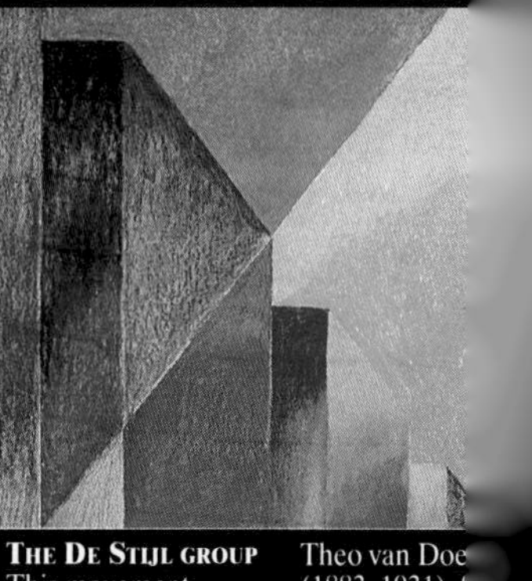

The De Stijl group This movement, consisting of pioneering Dutch abstract artists, took its name from that of a magazine of the same name, founded in Amsterdam in 1917.

Its new concept, derived from Cubism, applied not only to painting, sculpture and architecture, but also to interior decoration and to furniture design. Piet Mondriaan (1872–1944) (8), the group's principal exponent, painted his *Composition in Red, Black, Blue, Yellow and Grey* (7) in 1920. Mondriaan pushed the principle of formal purity to its extreme, working for ten years with only the three primary colors.

Theo van Doe
(1883–1931), t
of the review a
talented theor
painted *Comp*
Counter (4) in
These works a
display at the
Museum.

4 3 2 1
5 8 7
6

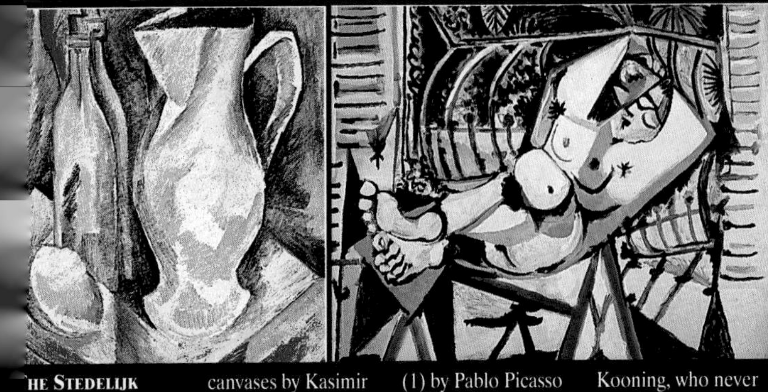

The Stedelijk Museum
This eclectic collection includes a Cubist *Still Life* (2), painted in 1909 by Georges Braque (1882–1963). There are also several canvases by Kasimir Malevich (1878–1935), including *The Englishman in Moscow* of 1924 (5). The best example from the post-war period is *Woman Resting in her Garden* (1) by Pablo Picasso (1881–1973), painted in 1956, while American Expressionism is represented by *Woman Singing* (1966) (6), by the American Willem de Kooning, who never completely broke with figurative painting. An abstract composition by the Italian Salvo, *Untitled* (1986) (3), is reminiscent of works by the De Stijl group.

At the end of the Second World War a new artistic movement was born in the Netherlands. Young artists sought to give their creativity an immediate, raw and unrefined character, making no concessions to new fashions. Just as the Dada movement had based its ideas on the destruction of bourgeois civilization and values by the upheavals of 1914–18, so the new artists rejected a rationalism that had been discredited by the horrors of the war. They exploited unconventional models, such as children's art, which they saw as being uncorrupted by the academic, figurative spirit. Paul Klee and Joan Miró preceded them down this road and it was to the latter that they looked in particular for inspiration. Artists such as Dubuffet also drew on the art of the insane, on Surrealism, on Picasso's freedom of form and, of course, on naïve art in general. Leading exponents included Asger Jorn and Karel Appel. It was in this context that the international CoBrA movement was formed in 1949. It consisted of Danish, Belgian and Dutch artists, hence the name: "Co" for Copenhagen, "Br" for Brussels, and "A" for Amsterdam. The governing principle of this movement was the release and pleasure of pure painting. The Stedelijk Museum has a fine collection of CoBrA works.

Karel Appel ▲ *144 Men and Animals* of 1949 (below) is a typical example of the new style. Appel, born in Amsterdam in 1921, also made polychrome sculptures, often from plywood or expanded polystyrene ● 92.

CORNEILLE
Born in Liège in 1922, he painted *The Big Earth* (above) in 1958. Following the early, tumultuous years of CoBrA, he represents a more considered, less fiery mode of expression.

CONSTANT
Constant was born in Amsterdam in 1920 and he painted *Scorched Earth* (shown above) in 1951. Many years of his life were devoted to designing models of a Utopian city, a "New Babylon", before he returned to painting in the 1970's. CoBrA officially ceased to exist in November 1951.

An old poster advises visitors from the suburbs south of the park that they can quench their thirst at the *Schinkel* café.

BEHIND THE CONCERTGEBOUW. Here there is a residential area which also has a number of shops and restaurants. In the early 20th century this new district, which lay close to the concert hall and the Vondelpark, attracted very wealthy residents. Spacious houses line the streets, and there are little squares at the intersections. At no. 100 Van Breestraat there is a shop owned by a pharmacist whose ancestors left the Prinsengracht ninety years ago. The window displays many old postcards sent by servants to their families. Outside on the left there is an old plaque bearing the letter "T", which indicates that this establishment had a telephone. The shop also bears a sign with the emblem of the city's pharmacists: the bust of a black man (the "Gaper" ● *52*) sticking out his tongue to swallow a pill. Inside are piles of boxes for preserving medicinal herbs. A right-hand turn into Van Cornshuystraat leads to Willemsparkweg, with its luxury shops and residential villas. At no. 15 is the shop of the instrument-maker Max Möller, which has been established here since the early 20th century.

CAFÉ "WELLING"
This café at no. 2 Johannes Verhulstraat is the district's cultural meeting place.

VONDELPARK ★

Created in 1877, the Vondelpark was the second stage, after the Artis park of 1838 ▲ *268*, in a project to create a green belt around the city center. This fine garden stretches for more than a mile

Sign of the instrument maker Max Möller, at nº. 15 Willemsparkweg.

in length and measures over 300 yards at its widest point. The architect J.D. Zocher was responsible for transforming what had previously been marshland into a landscaped park, laying out alternative areas of lawns, trees and lakes on the damp, shifting ground. The park was originally frequented by rich local residents, but at the turn of the century it also began to attract the working classes from neighboring districts. At the end of the park near Constantijn Huygensstraat, there was a pretty glass and iron pavilion, which has now been converted into a CINEMA MUSEUM ★ with an old-style projection room that was brought here from Paris. There is also a tearoom and a statue of Vondel ● *109*, which stands close to the museum.

UNDESIRABLE "INHABITANTS". In the 1960's, the park lawns attracted all kinds of visitors: hippie craftspeople who were trying to sell their work, musicians, the unemployed and the homeless; after protests from local residents these "inhabitants" were dislodged. However, the Vondelpark is still invaded, particularly on Queen's Day (April 30) when trading restrictions are lifted. Anyone is allowed to sell anything, so Amsterdam is temporarily transformed into a giant flea market. The Vondelpark is reserved specifically for children, who can earn money by playing instruments and doing tricks, for example. The park's western exit leads to another residential district.

"VIENNESE" RIDING SCHOOL ★. This riding school at no. 140 Vondelstraat, the interior of which is pictured on the left, is the work of A.L. van Gendt. The ring, covered with a metal roof, was inspired by the one at the Spanish Riding School of Vienna. The school is still extremely active and it once had as many as 143 stalls ◆ *295*.

VONDELKERK ● *78*. The Vondelkerk, a former Roman Catholic church built around 1880, stands in a small square on Vondelstraat. It was designed by the architect P.J.Cuypers. The building fell into disuse and was bought in the 1980's for a symbolic florin. It has now been converted into a glass-fronted office block. Side by side on Roemer Visscherstraat, from nos. 22 to 30, stand five amusing houses, each of which represents a different country.

The notice (top) advertises the youth hostel ("Jeugdherberg") that stands on the edge of the park at no. 5 Zandpad (Sand Path). It used to house a domestic science school. Above, the Vondelpark pavilion, the Vondelkerk, a Roman Catholic church built around 1880, and the Spanish ("Spanje") façade in Moorish style of one of the five country houses on Roemer Visscherstraat. Left, detail of the mosaic that decorates no. 12 Hobbemastraat.

To each his own "museum"
Amsterdam is a city teeming with collectors and antique-dealers, particularly in the Nieuwe Spiegelstraat district.

There is the pale pink "ITALIE"; the pink and white "SPANJE" in Moorish style, grey "FRANKRIJK", "RUSLAND" with its onion-shaped dome, and "ENGLAND", now a hotel: they are designed to exhibit the characteristic style of each of the countries.

THE "VONDEL FREE STATE" ★ ▲ *127*

It was in this peaceful, aristocratic district that one of the most spectacular episodes in the history of the squatter movement unfolded. On February 23, 1980, a group of sixteen people moved in to squat at no. 72 Vondelstraat. The police arrived at night and violently removed the occupiers, who offered no resistance. Six days later the building was again taken over by an Amsterdam squatters' group. This time they were armed with helmets, iron bars, stink bombs and stones and they quickly erected defensive barricades around the house. Though many spectators came to stare or even briefly to join in, the "Vondel Free State" lasted for only three days. On the morning of March 3, 1,200 police backed up by six army tanks, a helicopter, marksmen, armored vehicles and water cannon cleared the site. The building was evacuated calmly and became the property of the city in 1982.

Three days of freedom!
In March 1980 no. 72 Vondelstraat became the home of the "Vondel Free State". However, it was not long before more than a thousand Amsterdam police attacked this "Utopia" within the city, and annexed the "state" by taking charge of the building.

PETER CORNELISZ HOOFTSTRAAT. This street is the oldest main thoroughfare in southern Amsterdam. Today it is lined with shops selling international brands of luxury ready-to-wear clothing. Almost all the buildings have balconies, and where the street crosses Vandeveldestraat the visitor can admire the magnificent verandas of two houses in particular. Nos. 22 and 32 Jan Luijkenstraat are striking Art Deco buildings with wooden balconies, stained-glass windows and sculptures.

ANTIQUE SHOPS AND ART GALLERIES ● *52, 54*

Starting from the Rijksmuseum and crossing the Singelgracht in the direction of the city center, you come to a district full of antique shops and art galleries. Amsterdam has always been a city of collectors. Some were simple middle-class people who bought pictures from famous painters, others were rich patricians who collected all kinds of objects ▲ *182*. In the early 18th century, for example, Jacob de Wilde set up a "museum" containing books, scientific instruments and exotic objects. The Amsterdam art market went through a slump in the 19th century, but then recovered, notably after the building of the three Museumplein museums and the establishment of various forms of state assistance for artists. In recent decades Nieuwe Spiegelstraat has become the main district for galleries and luxury antique shops. Most of these specialize in glassware, scientific instruments, watches, coins or maps.

This antique shop is located on the Nieuwe Spielelgracht, in the antique-collectors' district.

Jordaan

Noordermarkt, *239*
Noorderkerk, *239*
Hollands gin (Genever), *240*
The "Hofjes", *240*
Lindengracht, *242*
The Provos, *243*
Bloemgracht, *245*
"Our House", *247*
Lauriergracht, *248*
Elandsgracht, *248*

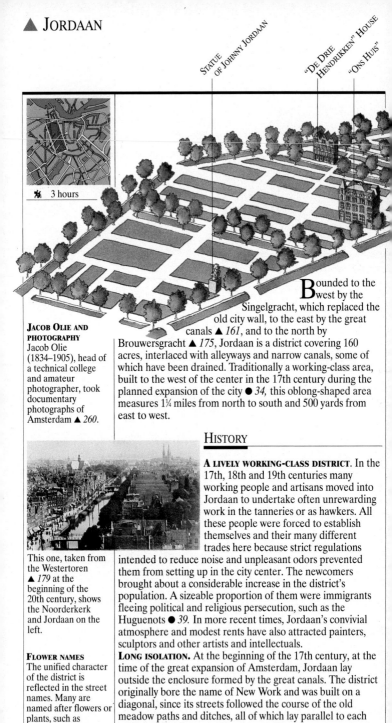

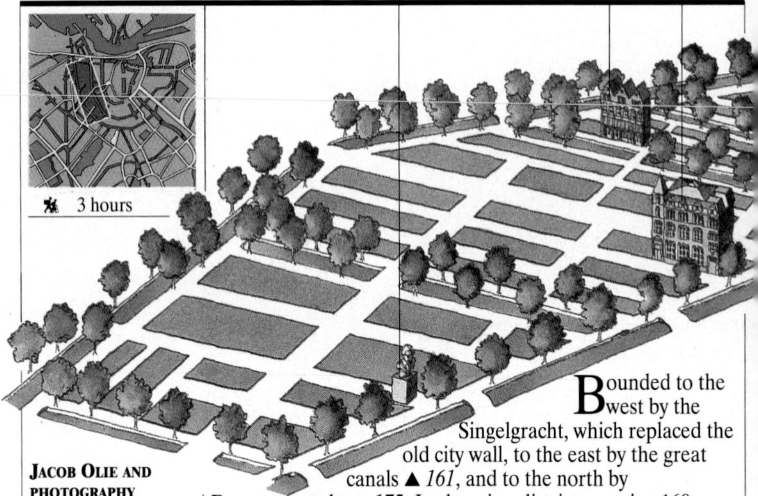

STATUE OF JOHNNY JORDAAN

"DE DRIE HENDRIKKEN" HOUSE

"ONS HUIS"

🚶 3 hours

Bounded to the west by the Singelgracht, which replaced the old city wall, to the east by the great canals ▲ *161*, and to the north by Brouwersgracht ▲ *175*, Jordaan is a district covering 160 acres, interlaced with alleyways and narrow canals, some of which have been drained. Traditionally a working-class area, built to the west of the center in the 17th century during the planned expansion of the city ● *34,* this oblong-shaped area measures 1¼ miles from north to south and 500 yards from east to west.

JACOB OLIE AND PHOTOGRAPHY
Jacob Olie (1834–1905), head of a technical college and amateur photographer, took documentary photographs of Amsterdam ▲ *260*.

This one, taken from the Westertoren ▲ *179* at the beginning of the 20th century, shows the Noorderkerk and Jordaan on the left.

HISTORY

A LIVELY WORKING-CLASS DISTRICT. In the 17th, 18th and 19th centuries many working people and artisans moved into Jordaan to undertake often unrewarding work in the tanneries or as hawkers. All these people were forced to establish themselves and their many different trades here because strict regulations intended to reduce noise and unpleasant odors prevented them from setting up in the city center. The newcomers brought about a considerable increase in the district's population. A sizeable proportion of them were immigrants fleeing political and religious persecution, such as the Huguenots ● *39.* In more recent times, Jordaan's convivial atmosphere and modest rents have also attracted painters, sculptors and other artists and intellectuals.

LONG ISOLATION. At the beginning of the 17th century, at the time of the great expansion of Amsterdam, Jordaan lay outside the enclosure formed by the great canals. The district originally bore the name of New Work and was built on a diagonal, since its streets followed the course of the old meadow paths and ditches, all of which lay parallel to each other running from southwest to northeast.
Even after 1860, when new districts were built up on the other side of the ramparts to the west, Jordaan remained comparatively cut off, since the main thoroughfares

FLOWER NAMES
The unified character of the district is reflected in the street names. Many are named after flowers or plants, such as Egelantier (Dog Rose), Anjelier (Carnation), Akelei (Columbine), Laurier (Laurel), Roos (Rose), Palm, Goudsbloem (Marigold) and so on.

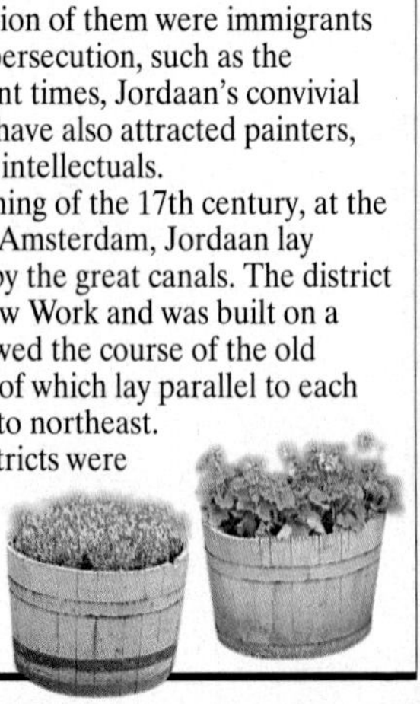

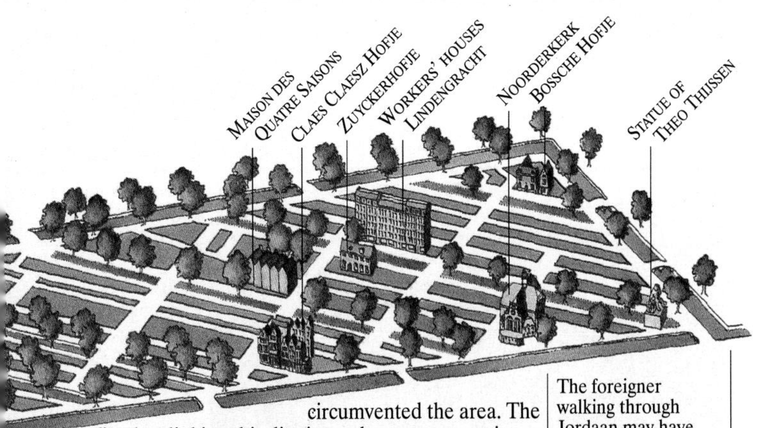

circumvented the area. The first bus linking this district to the center came in 1908, but after a few months the service had to be stopped: the citizens who lived along the route were well known for their plain speaking, and they complained vociferously that the exhaust fumes were dirtying the washing they put out to dry. It was not until 1924 that a regular link by electrified tramway was established with the town center.

Diminishing population. Following the demolition of some residential buildings and the conversion of housing into workshops, the number of apartments has shrunk considerably. It fell from around 16,000 at the beginning of the century down to 8,000 and has now gone back up to 11,500 following the implementation of a program of urban renewal. In 1900 the district still had about 77,000 inhabitants and one Amsterdammer in seven lived here, but today there are only 20,000 left.

Historical remains. No matter how proud the inhabitants of Jordaan may be of the district's 350 years of history, there are few 17th-century buildings to be found here. Only 1 percent of apartment blocks have a façade from that period, 20 percent date from the 18th century, and even more boast 19th-century façades. Today more than eight hundred of the district's residential blocks are classified as historical monuments. In the 19th century Jordaan suffered from a growing demand for housing linked to industrialization: backyards were gradually developed, and whole families piled into one room, while others moved into basements. Around 1850 the first measures were taken to curb this sometimes tragic state of affairs, and the first blocks of workers' housing were built.

The foreigner walking through Jordaan may have difficulty remembering the street names ◆ *286*.

A friendly district
Because Jordaan was originally, and still is, a working-class district, visitors wandering through it find a pleasant, relaxed and friendly atmosphere. It has flowers blooming everywhere, shops both modern and original, and cafés, including *t'Smalle*, a tiny and welcoming brown café ● *50*. Its interior, with the characteristic stained-glass windows, dates from 1780. In summer it has tables outside looking over the narrow Egelantiersgracht.

Cartouche on the façade of no. 53 Lindengracht.

THE NOORDERMARKT
This market for secondhand clothes and furniture is held every Monday.

MYSTERIOUS ETYMOLOGY. Much has been written about the origins of the word Jordaan. According to the best-known explanation, Jordaan is derived from the French "jardin" or garden ● *44*. In a poem of the early 18th century, *In praise of gin*, the drinker and poet Robert Hennebo describes Prinsengracht and Jordaan as looking out over fields. In reality Jordaan has never been remotely like a garden, despite its windowsills laden with geraniums, the pots full of flowers and tubs planted with bushes that can be seen throughout the district. Scholars have a very different version: according to them, the district's name is inspired by the Jordan, the river that flows through the Holy Land. This biblical title is said to have been bestowed on the area by the people living on the banks of the Prinsengracht, between Brouwersgracht to the north of Jordaan and Passeerdersgracht to the south. The historian Kannegieter suggests the most unusual hypothesis: he believes the word comes from the Jordanne, a river in the Auvergne, which French immigrants to the district in the 17th century, Huguenots from the Auvergne ● *31, 39*, compared to the Prinsengracht because of its pollution level. The traditional image of these immigrants also suits the current inhabitants of the district, who are said to be pigeon-fanciers and anglers, lovers of sentimental songs and dancing to barrel organ music.

NOORDERKERK STRAAT CENTRUM

A STORY OF REFLECTIONS
This cartouche at nos. 55 and 57 Lindengracht, decorated with fish floating in a tree, echoes the reflection of the houses in the canal waters, as do the street name and date which are engraved backwards. Every Saturday morning there is a lively market on Lindengracht.

THE BLOODY TROUBLES OF 1934 ● *32***.** At the end of June 1934, when the worldwide economic crisis forced the government to adopt an austerity program, it was decided to reduce the already inadequate allowances paid to the unemployed by 10 percent. This drastic reduction infuriated the population, and the situation was not helped by a spell of exceptionally high temperatures. The summer was to be long and hot. Trouble broke out in various working-class districts of the city. In July 1934 a protest march was organized in Jordaan which subsequently degenerated into a riot. The police were confronted with barricades built of paving stones, wooden beams, crates and assorted items of furniture. At night the streets remained in darkness because the inhabitants had smashed the streetlights. After a few days the authorities decided to send in the military police and army units in tanks. Jordaan was truly in a state of war. Raised bridges were also used as fortifications, if we are to believe the writer Theun de Vries, who recounts the events of that summer in his novel *The*

The violent riots of summer 1934.

Militiaman: "During this period, the police were constantly charging, and the lurking armored monsters encircled besieged Jordaan, bristling with muzzles at the ready. Payments to the rebels had been suspended. The armed men surrounding the fortress looked vicious. Behind the bridges and the barricades, hunger began to come to their aid."

A HEAVY TOLL. These riots ended on July 9, 1934, with six people dead, more than thirty injured and a large number placed under arrest. The situation had been far more serious than in 1917, despite the shortage of food at the end of the Great War, and also more alarming than the sinister riot of 1886, when the city authorities had banned a cruel public entertainment which consisted of tearing the head off a live eel hung from a line on Lindengracht (which had not been filled in by then). For a long time after the 1934 troubles, the district's inhabitants remained resentful about a government that had done very little to reduce unemployment.

THIJSSEN
The socialist writer Theo Thijssen (1879–1943), a pioneer in the educational field, recounted his youth in Jordaan in *Kees de Jongen*. The schoolboy Kees is represented with his creator on the statue sculpted by Hans Bayens in 1979 and erected in front of the Thijssen café.

NOORDERMARKT AND NOORDERKERK ★ ● *78*

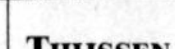

Fairs have been held on the Noordermarkt (Northern Market) square since 1627. Today there is a very lively flea market where excellent bargains can be obtained, and on Saturday mornings there are stalls selling small birds and organic produce grown by smallholders. The square was built between 1620 and 1623 by Hendrik Staets ▲ *163*, city architect; on it stands the Noorderkerk (Northern Church), created for the new northern area of Amsterdam. The original project had been initiated by Hendrick de Keyser ▲ *156*, but he died in 1621 before he could complete it. A great number of Protestant churches were built on this model, which is extremely simple: the base is in the shape of a broad Greek cross, with three triangular additions at the transept crossing. A cartouche over one of the central doors states that the foundation stone was laid on June 15, 1620, and the first mass was heard there on Easter day 1623.

Pierre Fouquet (1729–1800), a seller of drawings, prints and paintings of Walloon origin, did this drawing of the Noorderkerk, which stands on the bank of Prinsengracht.

HOLLANDS GIN (GENEVER)

● 64

The triangle formed by Brouwersgracht, Lijnbaansgracht and Palmgracht, known as Driehoekstraat, used to be a marsh, but it was drained in 1650 during the expansion of Amsterdam.

THE MANUFACTURE OF HOLLANDS GIN. The unusual taste of this powerful alcoholic drink, of around 70 degrees proof, is due to the malt that is its main ingredient. Commercial travelers, whose work brought them to Amsterdam in large numbers, had a great fondness for it. They would often take a glass just before embarking on a sea voyage to stave off seasickness. Today the production of hollands gin (genever or geneva) is highly developed. However, some of the old distilleries have preserved the traditional techniques: one of these is Van Wees, at no. 14 Driehoekstraat.

SPIRITS
Hollands gin or Genever, a spirit obtained by distilling fermented cereal pulp, was originally distilled over juniper berries. These pea-sized berries are blue or blackish in color and can be found in mountain woodland. This was the world's first gin, invented in

the Netherlands at the beginning of the 17th century. A plaque at the entrance to the very old Kees van Wees distillery (above) represents a boiler in a still (top). Hollands is one of the Amsterdammers' favorite drinks and it is drunk primarily in institutions called *proeflokalen* ● 50, ◆ 296, cafés specializing in strong liquors. Bols is one of the chief producers of hollands.

THE "HOFJES"★

AN ANCIENT TRADITION. In the Middle Ages Amsterdam was a pioneering city as far as help for the elderly was concerned, as there were special hostels where people could go to alleviate the poverty and worries of old age. The first *hofjes* (almshouses) date from the 17th century and were usually founded by rich citizens. These almshouses, of which there are many in Jordaan, also provided shelter for widows and

other needy people at a time when there was no form of state welfare provision. The city seems to have been a welcoming place for older people in all sorts of ways. Indeed, the philosopher René Descartes ▲ *179*, who stayed here in 1631, advised one of his French friends in a letter to choose Amsterdam for his retirement ● *99*.

COMMEMORATIVE INSCRIPTIONS. Despite the fact that they are located in the heart of the city, these *hofjes* occupy a fair amount of land. They often consist of several small houses built round an inner courtyard or in front of a small garden. Affixed to many of their façades are commemorative plaques in memory of the founders. For the seventh centenary of Amsterdam in 1975 the tourist board published a booklet listing the addresses of all the *hofjes*, but it had to be withdrawn from sale after their occupants complained that they were being disturbed too often by visitors.

A WALK ROUND THE "HOFJES". Those almshouses that bear the letter "L" on the bottom right of their doors (L for *Lid*: member) belonged to members of the Calvinist Reformed church, who made gifts to the diaconate. This letter acted as a marker for deacons coming to collect alms. After the Beguine convent ▲ *122*, LINDEN HOFJE at nos. 94 to 112 Lindengracht is the oldest almshouse in Amsterdam: it dates from 1616. SUYCKERHOFJE at nos. 149 to 163 Lindengracht, founded in 1667 by Pieter Jansz Suyckerhof, took in forsaken Protestant women. In 1650 on the site of a Carthusian monastery in Karthuizerstraat the architect Daniel Stalpaert ● *36* built the HUYS ZITTEN WEDUWEN HOFJE retirement home. ANSLO HOFJE at no. 50 Egelantierstraat, a delightful and intimate space threatened with destruction by the forces of nature, was saved by an association known as the Friends of Old Amsterdam. CLAES CLAESZ HOFJE, located on the corner of Egelantiersstraat and 1st Egelantierdwarsstraat (entrance via no. 3 of the latter street) today provides homes for music students around a small courtyard with a fountain. Some of these *hofjes*, which are increasingly being protected from the public, are real treasures. This is especially true of 'T VENETIAE HOFJE (nos. 104 to 142 Elandstraat), which has a particularly pretty garden. Do not hesitate to push open the doors in order to see their charm for yourself.

DIMINISHING NUMBER OF ALMSHOUSES
There used to be nearly a hundred almshouses in

Jordaan. Today only around seventy-five *hofjes* remain in all of Amsterdam, many of them still located in Jordaan.

From top to bottom: the cartouche on Anslo's *hofje;* detail from the Bossche *hofje;* view of the garden of 't Venetiae *hofje;* fountain in the courtyard of Claes Claesz *hofje,* and cartouche on Bossche *hofje.* The last of these, at nos. 22 to 26 Palmgracht, is the work of Arent Dirxen Bosch, a Baptist merchant, and gives the date of construction.

TOWN PLANNING

The Dutch love lace curtains of every kind and style. In this district they demonstrate the pride of members of a working-class community who like their homes to look smart, while also serving the practical purpose of allowing the curious to look out without being seen by passers-by.

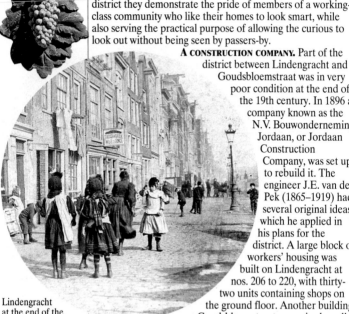

Lindengracht at the end of the 19th century.

A CONSTRUCTION COMPANY. Part of the district between Lindengracht and Goudsbloemstraat was in very poor condition at the end of the 19th century. In 1896 a company known as the N.V. Bouwonderneming Jordaan, or Jordaan Construction Company, was set up to rebuild it. The engineer J.E. van der Pek (1865–1919) had several original ideas which he applied in his plans for the district. A large block of workers' housing was built on Lindengracht at nos. 206 to 220, with thirty-two units containing shops on the ground floor. Another building on Goudsbloemstraat comprised small, inexpensive studio apartments. The Jordaan Construction Company went into liquidation in 1971, however, and the two blocks were sold to a private individual.

A REBELLIOUS POPULATION. In 1969 Amsterdam city council had drawn up a plan to renovate Jordaan. The town planners considered the district's old housing to be in a badly decayed state and consequently they decided to demolish it completely, and rehouse the existing occupants in tall tower blocks. However, the rents would have been much higher, and the new blocks would have stripped Jordaan of its identity. After protests by the inhabitants, their plan had to be abandoned. In 1973 there was a consensus in favor of a new plan for renovation, which involved a smaller number of demolitions and the spacing out of new buildings. Today Jordaan has retained its special charm. The cartouches, such as the black horse that can be admired at no. 241 Lindengracht, still form a link with the past, in spite of the newly established art galleries and expensive shops.

QUIET CHARM. The café De Gijs is situated on the corner of Lijnbaansgracht, one of the canals that encloses the district, together with Brouwersgracht and Prinsengracht. Further down, the Hotel Acacia and a number of small gardens planted along the canalside lend an atmosphere of

THE NAMES OF TRADES
On the façades of the workers' housing at nos. 206 to 220 Lindengracht the following inscriptions can be read: *In den Steenhouwer* (To the stone-breaker), *In den Grondwerker* (To the roadworker), *In den Loodjieter* (To the plumber), *In den Smit* (to the smith), and *In den Metselaar* (To the mason).

CARTOUCHES:
"At the fat pig", the sign of the old butcher's at no. 26 Goudsbloemdwars-straat; and the black horse at no. 241 Lindengracht.

TYPICAL DÉCOR The curtains at Jordaan's windows are one of the district's distinctive features.

tranquillity. At right angles to Gietersstraat, a street whose name commemorates an old foundry where bells and cannon parts were produced (*gieten* means "to cast"), runs Tichelstraat, which bears the name of an old brickworks making tiles and majolica, a form of Italian Renaissance pottery. Here a Roman Catholic church was built dedicated to St Anthony of Padua. The entrance is at no. 47 Lijnbaansgracht.

A shop on the corner of Tichelstraat and Karthuizerstraat, and houses along the Lijnbaansgracht, on the western edge of Jordaan.

THE PROVOS ● 33

Not so long ago no. 14 Karthuizerstraat, where the remains of basement apartments can be seen, was the headquarters of the Provo movement, the first radical movement in Dutch society, founded in the 1960's.

MODERN AGITATORS. As the name suggests, the Provo movement consisted of "provocative" agitators, young protesters who had decided to take on the establishment as represented by the police, politicians and civil servants. They skillfully exploited the interest the movement generated, particularly in the press, and became known for their "happenings". During the summer of 1964 the movement's creator, Robert Jasper Grootveld, decided to gather its sympathizers around the Lieverdje, a bronze statue on Spui Square representing a street urchin. This statue, donated by a local cigarette manufacturer, became a regular Saturday evening rallying-point for an anti-tobacco campaign that was humorous in tone ▲ *123*.

AGAINST POLLUTION. The non-violent activists of this movement were against the use of the atomic bomb and American intervention in Vietnam. They were green before their time, drawing up bold plans to make their city, which they decreed the "magical center" of the world, a healthier place to be. For example, they recommended the use of

"Jordaan, a large working-class area to the west of the Dam, with flowers in its streets, inhabited cellars, steps flanked by benches, and houses leaning forward, backward or sideways, displays its lack of privacy, its linen, fuschias and kids."

Maurice Gauchez, *Le Charme de la Hollande*

This watercolor portrays Goudsbloemgracht in the 17th century, shortly after Jordaan was established.

A street in Jordaan: 2nd Tuindwarstraat.

THE SALE OF HOT WATER
This stone sign, carved in 1726, decorates a dwelling in Boomstraat (nos. 24 to 28) where hot water and fire-lighters were once sold. Before 1905, when Jordaan was connected to the gas supply, there were shops where people could buy hot water and a burning hot brick, used as a foot-warmer. During the Second World War furnaces were once more used to provide such forms of heating.

bicycles painted white ● *58*, the color of innocence and purity, and launched a "white cars" plan with the support of the city council. An electric car designed by a Provo engineer was gradually to replace traditional vehicles as a means of urban transport. The aim of the operation was to turn public opinion against the car, polluting symbol of the consumer society.

INTOLERANCE THRESHOLD. The first issue of *Provo* magazine, which came out on July 12, 1965, promoted the movement's ideas. This manifesto had been written by a philosophy student who was not afraid to criticize the Provos as a "lazy bunch"; they were too laid-back for his taste, and he hoped they would one day become true revolutionaries. On March 10, 1966, the reputation of the group, which consisted of about thirty active members, crossed the Dutch borders. It was on that day in Amsterdam that the heir to the throne, Princess Beatrix, married a German, Claus von Amsberg. The Provos could not accept this marriage to a citizen of the country that had been responsible for so much misery and they set off stink bombs near the bridal coach as the procession left the church ▲ *128.* Confrontation between police and demonstrators lasted well into the night. From that moment the young members of the Provo group revised their policy of non-violent action and further demonstrations degenerated into pitched battles. The sympathy and admiration with which these anarchists had previously been regarded now changed to a sense of irritation, and even fury. The natural tolerance of the people of Amsterdam was stretched to its limits. The movement finally faded out after a split between those in favor of political action and those against.

THE GREEN GNOMES. After 1967 the Kabouters (Sprites or Gnomes) continued the Provo movement. They favored a

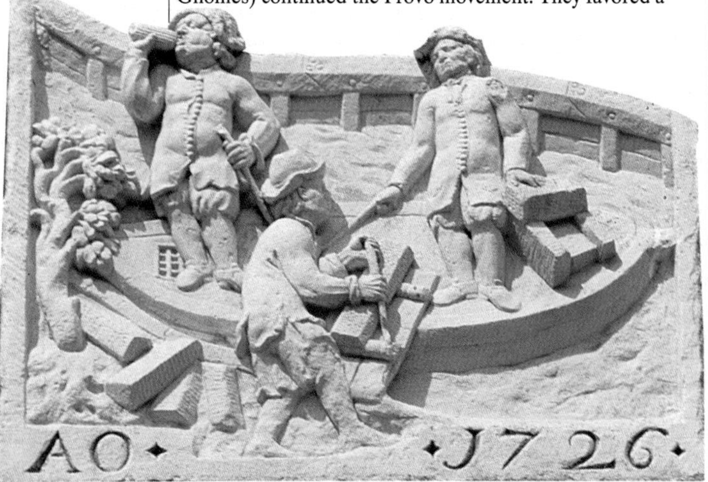

JORDAAN WAS BRIEFLY THE PRESERVE OF THE PROVOS. TODAY THE INHABITANTS OF THE DISTRICT, THE PAINTERS, SCULPTORS AND STUDENTS, ARE THEIR PEACEFUL DESCENDANTS.

BASEMENTS
As this 19th-century painting shows, entire families lived in gloomy basement apartments. Some good examples can still be found in Karthuizerstraat, not far from the headquarters of the Provo movement, which was at no. 14. The police often raided the place looking for subversive writings.

complete ban on cars within the city center and a return to self-sufficiency through city-based farms.They also wanted windmills to be used to generate electricity and combat pollution. They were far more politically active than the Provos had ever been. Their constructive and imaginative ideas gave rise to plans for new ministries. One of these would oversee the banning of cars, while another would be responsible for helping the elderly. Such ideas were not so farfetched, and were eventually put into practice in various ways, in the Netherlands as elsewhere.

AN AUTHENTIC DISTRICT

In some of the transverse streets, such as Tuindwarsstraat and 2nd Egelantierdwarsstraat, shops offer surprising and unusual objects for sale. The doll shop, its shelves lined with countless heads, is just one example. And everywhere the typical net curtains demonstrate the importance to the inhabitants of their homes.

BLOEMGRACHT ★. Bloemgracht (Flower Canal) with its residential atmosphere, enjoys a degree of prestige in this working-class district. It is wryly nicknamed the "Jordaan Herengracht". Here stand eighty-five apartment blocks built around 1800, which are carefully preserved, since they have been declared historic monuments. In the 16th and 17th centuries three generations of the Blaeu family, who were famous printers and mapmakers, lived at nos. 74 and 76 and also had their shop here ● *41, 54*. Jan Blaeu's atlases now sell for $40,000 each, when they are in very good condition. The cartouches at nos. 19, 23 and 77 show a pelican, a lion and a sower, respectively. In this respect Bloemgracht is no exception to the general rule in Jordaan: its houses are frequently decorated with cartouches and stone signs.

STONE SIGNS. The tradition of decorating façades with *gevelstenen,* as they are called, goes back to 1452, the tragic date of a huge fire following which it was hard for the inhabitants to recognize their homes and shops because of the extent of the damage. After this, rectangular plaques with bright colors were affixed all over the district. They bore a

Endless old steps are tucked away in Jordaaan and stairways decked with flowers lend the alleyways a joyful air.

"Herengracht, the Gentlemen's Canal, came first to confirm the power of the merchants. Keizersgracht and Prinsengracht came later. Then came the others, the little transverse canals named for trees and flowers, the Lily, the Dog Rose, the Rose and the Laurel, between which the people lived, in the district called Jordaan: the shipwrights, porters and sailors, men with loud voices who brought the atmosphere of the open sea into the narrow alleys."
Cees Nooteboom, *Beneath the water sign*

JORDAAN HOMES
An old scene in a Bloemgracht house (below). This canal, which inhabitants jokingly compare to the prestigious Herengracht, is a pleasant place to walk (center). Its banks are lined with 17th-century houses like "De Drie Hendricken" (below right).

AN ENVIRONMENT IN PROGRESS
Today the redeveloped Jordaan has far fewer unplanned buildings and hovels than it used to have. Nevertheless dwellings remain that are far from models of their kind. There are still some very badly designed blocks at the corner of Lijnbaansgracht and Marnixstraat. Below, a modern, low-rent apartment on 2nd Bloemdwarsstraat.

relief showing a scene or emblem symbolizing the occupant's profession and were placed above the entrance or on the gable. These façade stones fell into disuse, however, in the 18th century, when the French introduced a numbering system ▲ *185*.

THE DE KEYSER ASSOCIATION. At nos. 87 to 91 Bloemgracht, three façades surmounted by step gables dating from 1642 have been renovated. Known as "DE DRIE HENDRICKEN" (the Three Hendricks) ★, these houses have belonged since 1929 to the Hendrick de Keyser Association, as has the Bartolotti House on the Herengracht ▲ *170*. Since it was set up in 1918, this association has sought to buy historic apartment blocks in order to ensure they are preserved and maintained in good repair. The activities of the association, which bears the name of the famous architect who died in 1621 ▲ *156*, cover the whole of the Netherlands: it is currently responsible for 280 apartment blocks, of which 82 are in Amsterdam.

THE FESTIVE TRADITION ▲ *46***.** "Throughout history music has always been a passion of the Dutch people, indeed one of their most burning passions. There are therefore numerous concerts in Amsterdam. Concerts in the open air in summer, in comfortable halls in winter." (Henry Havard, *Holland as the crow flies*). Every year the Jordaan festival enlivens the district for part of September, ending with a cycle race organized on a Sunday. This Amsterdam music festival, during which the beer and nostalgia flow freely, restores the true atmosphere of Jordaan: the Jordaan of lively slang, of language full of colorful imagery, the Jordaan of paradoxical politics, whose inhabitants traditionally declare themselves to be monarchists while lining up beneath the Socialist and Communist banners when it comes to voting. Here, too, is the Jordaan of traditional Dutch dress: jumpers, velvet trousers and black wool caps for the men, skirts, jackets and leather sandals for the women, clogs for the children. Lastly, this is the Jordaan of the barrel organ, an instrument as characteristic of the city as the gables in its architecture ▲ *48*. This lively festival draws Amsterdammers from every corner of the city, particularly former inhabitants of Jordaan who have moved elsewhere. Throughout the rest of the year, the cafés organize public dances, a practice which is unique to this district. Jordaan likes to be different – always has and always will. And if a fight breaks out during festivities the inhabitants prefer not to call the police, keeping their troubles to themselves.

THE SOUTH OF JORDAAN

The Rozengracht cuts Jordaan into two parts, north and south. The northern part, the true heart of Jordaan, has remained authentic, while the smaller southern part, home of small businesses and craft workers, has changed over time.

"OUR HOUSE". Ons Huis at nos. 6 to 32 Rozenstraat is a cultural center which was established on the initiative of welfare pioneer Hélène Mercier (1839–1910). An admirer of the work of English woman Octavia Hill in London, she co-founded various social institutions in Amsterdam. Together with Alette Jacobs, the first woman doctor in the Netherlands, she carried out home visits in Jordaan and gave advice on, among other things, effective hygiene, good nutrition and the management of personal finances. Having visited them, Hélène Mercier was able to describe the unhealthy homes of Jordaan families and the pitiful conditions in which they lived in a number of articles. In 1887 she opened the first soup kitchen in Amsterdam and in 1892 she founded Ons Huis, which was used as a venue for debates, conferences and concerts for workers.

ON THE TRAIL OF CELEBRITIES. The Bols Taveerne at no. 106 Rozengracht stands next to an old distillery (nos. 99 to 105) which is now transformed into shops, studios and small

BLOEMGRACHT DÉCOR
Cartouches of the pelican (no. 19) and the unicorn (no. 23), and a window of the house on the corner of 2nd Bloemdwars-straat.

OPERETTA
De Jordaanprinses (*The Prince of Jordaan*) by Max Gabriel illustrates the celebratory and working-class aspects of the district, where a festival is held every September. In Jordaan music used to reign all year round: barrel-organ players filled its streets. While one musician turned the handle, two of his friends went round with a hat ● *48*.

This photograph of Bloemstraat, taken by Jacob Olie ▲ *260* at the beginning of the 20th century, shows the Westertoren ▲ *179* in the distance. The tower dominates the district.

HIS PSEUDONYM WAS JOHNNY JORDAAN
Singer of lively and sentimental songs, Johnny Jordaan first gained fame during the district's festival in 1950. His statue stands on the corner of Elandsgracht and Prinsengracht and fans called the spot Johnny Jordaanplein. Prinsengracht ▲ *176*, the eastern boundary of Jordaan, is represented in the watercolor above right.

apartments. Favored by artists, the district used to be home to several famous painters. Rembrandt ▲ *156, 179, 218* lived at no. 184 Rozengracht from 1660; this was to be his last home in Amsterdam, and he died there. George Hendrich Breitner ● *88* ▲ *258*, the Amsterdam Impressionist, lived along Lauriergracht, further to the south. In the 17th century the painter Govert Flinck, an admirer and follower of Rembrandt, and the philosopher Amos Comenius (1592–1670), the Czech humanist who was a pioneer of active education, also lived on Lauriergracht. Comenius, who was buried in the Walloon Church of Naarden, adored Amsterdam, calling it "cherished among cities, jewel of the Netherlands, Europe's cry of joy".

LITERARY HERO. At no. 37 Lauriergracht there is a recently built block that appears at first glance to have nothing particularly significant about it. However, this was the home of M. Droogstoppel, hero of the famous novel *Max Havelaar* by Multatuli (1820–87), whose real name was Eduard Douwes Dekker ▲ *166*. Droogstoppel, a literary character so famous that his name has now passed into everyday speech in the Netherlands, is a Protestant coffee salesman. Stubborn and self-righteous, he claims to be in love with truth and common sense, both qualities with which he is not abundantly gifted. *Max Havelaar* was a work that violently attacked the colonial policy of the time and it was also enormously influential in the Dutch literary revival of 1880. The hero's address is given in the first line of the novel, which reads: "I am a coffee broker and I live at no. 37, Lauriergracht. I am not accustomed to the writing of novels or any other similar occupation, so it has taken me a long time to decide to order a few extra reams of paper and to begin [this] work...".

THE JORDAAN SINGING STAR. At the corner of Elandsgracht and Prinsengracht stands a statue of Johnny Jordaan, whose real name was Jan van Musscher. He was a popular singer who came from the district and who was well known throughout the Netherlands. Discovered during the Jordaan festival of 1950, where he was the first prizewinner, he often worked with another musician, Tante Leen, who came second in the same festival.

Food distribution during the Liberation on Elandsgracht. Only Jodenbuurt, a district to the east of the center, rivalled Jordaan in its poverty ▲ *158*.

Old Port West

Herenmarkt, *250*
Haarlemmerbuurt, *251*
Dutch West India Company, *252*
Nassauplein, *254*
Spaarndammerbuurt, *254*
Spaarndammerplantsoen, *256*
The "Ship", *256*
Zaanhof, *257*
Prinseneiland, *258*
Realeneiland, *259*
Bickerseiland, *260*
Crossing the IJ, *261*
North Amsterdam, *261*

▲ OLD PORT WEST

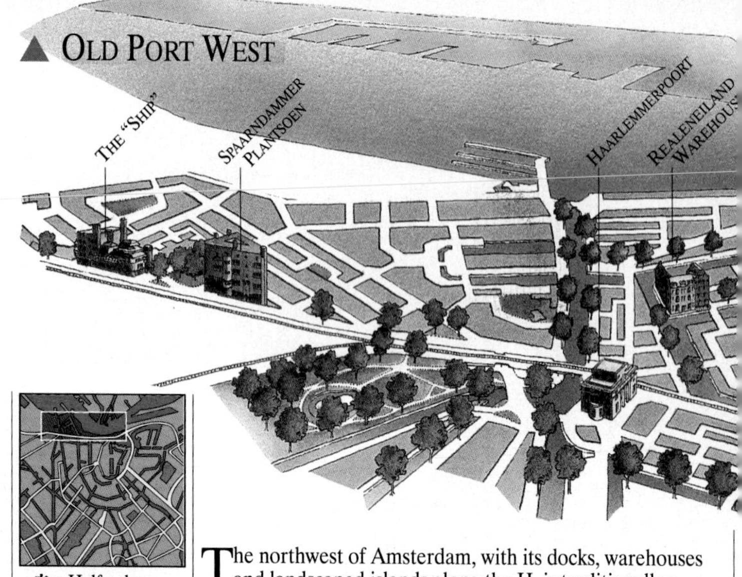

Half a day

Haarlemmerstraat and Haarlemmerdijk have been shopping streets for a long time, as this old shoe advertisement shows.

Koop PAANAKKER's
SCHOENWERK.
't Goedkoopst en sterkst in 't dragen.
Utrechtschestraat 123.
Haarlemmerstraat 93.
Leidschestraat 61.

The area is still bustling today.

The northwest of Amsterdam, with its docks, warehouses and landscaped islands along the IJ, is traditionally a working-class area not unlike Jordaan ▲ *235*. But in contrast to Jordaan, there is no historical or architectural unity between the Haarlem district (Haarlemmerbuurt), the western islands and the Spaarndam district (Spaarndammerbuurt), despite their geographical proximity. Nevertheless these districts are important in the history of Amsterdam and have not lost their charm.

HERENMARKT

During the third expansion of the city in 1612 ● *34*, the Haarlemmerpoort (Haarlem Gate) that stood here was replaced by a pig market. At this time the Herenmarkt (Lords' Market) was sometimes jokingly called "Hoerenmarkt" (Prostitutes' Market). In 1635 it was given a special superintendant whose role it was to "purge the district of thieves, whores and other riff-raff". The West India Company building is situated at no. 75 on nearby Haarlemmerstraat ▲ *252*.

THE SOUP KITCHEN RIOTS ("SOEPLOODSOPROER"). In 1833 a law was passed making landlords responsible for the tax payments of those tenants whose rent was less than 80 florins. The "small" landlords felt this was unacceptable and refused to pay. They banded together to form a landlords' committee chaired by Johannes Blokhoff, a hardware dealer and owner of more than 170 blocks of flats, whom the authorities decided to prosecute. On July 2, 1835, his furniture was seized for auction and taken to the Herenmarkt "soup kitchen", so-called because it was the place where soup was distributed to the poor in winter. The auction proved unsuccessful: people in the crowd began to throw stones, after which nobody wanted or dared to make a bid, and the sale was put off until a later date. That evening a crowd armed with wooden staves rampaged through the district, smashing windows at the home of a tax collector who lived on the Keizersgracht. When they reached the soup kitchen, the rioters smashed its windows and looted the goods inside. The revolt came to an end with the burning of the wooden building. A short time later the tax measure was suspended.

Coffee, tea and cocoa cartouches on the façade of no. 60 Haarlemmerstraat (above). A very old tea shop sign at no. 45 Haarlemmerdijk (opposite, center).

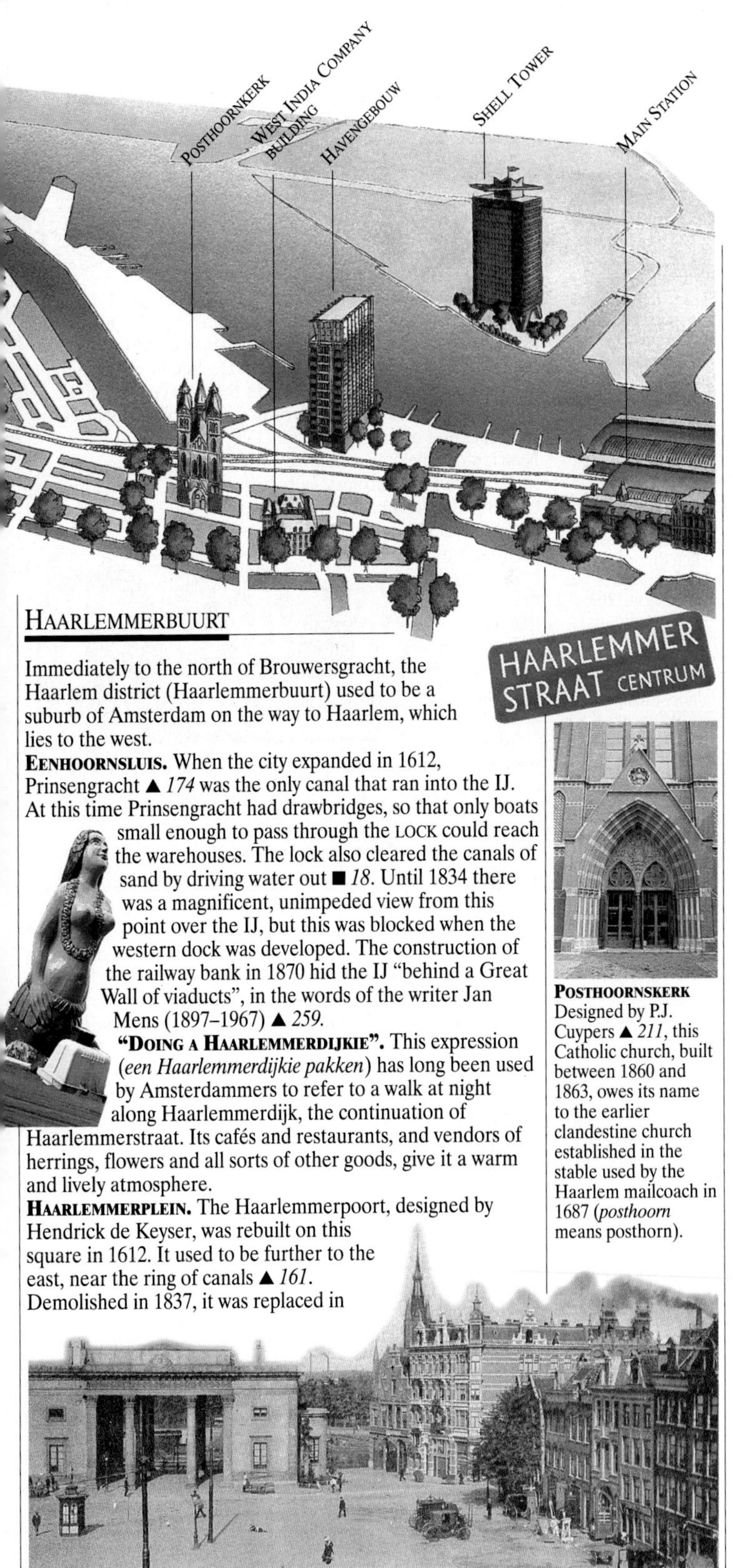

HAARLEMMERBUURT

Immediately to the north of Brouwersgracht, the Haarlem district (Haarlemmerbuurt) used to be a suburb of Amsterdam on the way to Haarlem, which lies to the west.

EENHOORNSLUIS. When the city expanded in 1612, Prinsengracht ▲ *174* was the only canal that ran into the IJ. At this time Prinsengracht had drawbridges, so that only boats small enough to pass through the LOCK could reach the warehouses. The lock also cleared the canals of sand by driving water out ■ *18*. Until 1834 there was a magnificent, unimpeded view from this point over the IJ, but this was blocked when the western dock was developed. The construction of the railway bank in 1870 hid the IJ "behind a Great Wall of viaducts", in the words of the writer Jan Mens (1897–1967) ▲ *259*.

"DOING A HAARLEMMERDIJKIE". This expression (*een Haarlemmerdijkie pakken*) has long been used by Amsterdammers to refer to a walk at night along Haarlemmerdijk, the continuation of Haarlemmerstraat. Its cafés and restaurants, and vendors of herrings, flowers and all sorts of other goods, give it a warm and lively atmosphere.

HAARLEMMERPLEIN. The Haarlemmerpoort, designed by Hendrick de Keyser, was rebuilt on this square in 1612. It used to be further to the east, near the ring of canals ▲ *161*. Demolished in 1837, it was replaced in

POSTHOORNSKERK
Designed by P.J. Cuypers ▲ *211*, this Catholic church, built between 1860 and 1863, owes its name to the earlier clandestine church established in the stable used by the Haarlem mailcoach in 1687 (*posthoorn* means posthorn).

Canal to Haarlem
In 1632 a canal was dug linking Amsterdam to Haarlem. Passenger transportation by horse-drawn barge was an immediate success. The first boat sailed when the city gate opened in the morning, after which there was a sailing every hour. In the 17th century 250,000 passengers a year used the service. When the Haarlemmerweg was improved in 1762, land transport presented serious competition for the barges, and the railway finally finished them off. On September 20, 1839, the first train departed, parallel to the canal, heading for Haarlem. Between 1843 and 1878 the main station of the Dutch railway company was located at the entrance to the Westerpark.

1840 by the Willemspoort, which is still there today (below, in 1903). Amsterdammers continue to call it Haarlemmerpoort out of habit. The name Willemspoort (William's Gate) commemorates the unveiling of the monument by the sovereign William II when he entered the city in the year of his coronation. In the 19th century, until 1864, the gate was used not for the defence of the city but for the collection of municipal taxes. Originally, Haarlemmerplein was the place where stagecoaches and farmers' carts were parked but later the neighboring stables were demolished or converted into garages. After the road was built alongside the railway line, the buildings on the north side disappeared. Today traffic no longer passes through the gate: a bridge has been built next to it over the Westerkanaal.

The Dutch West India Company

From Nieuw Amsterdam to New York. In the courtyard of the Dutch West India building ▲ *250*, there is a statue of Pieter Stuyvesant, governor of New Netherland from 1647 to 1664. It was donated by the cigarette manufacturers of the same name. The statuette and the wall plaque to the right of the entrance commemorate the fact that it was here in 1625 that the West India Company (*West-Indisch Compagnie*: WIC) took the decision to establish a fortress and a colony (Nieuw Amsterdam and Nieuw Nederland) on the southernmost point of the island of Manhattan in the River Hudson, which the Englishman Henry Hudson had discovered while in the service of the great Amsterdam merchants. In 1664 the English occupation put an end to the Dutch colony: Nieuw Amsterdam became New York ● *30*.

A cartouche with a picture of a porpoise at no. 45 Haarlemmerdijk (above). In the center (above), the first seat of the West India Company in 1623. Its Haarlemmerstraat façade, remodeled in 1825, bears the image of a swan, the symbol of Dutch Lutheranism.

Conquest of the "Silver fleet". In 1621 the WIC, sister organization to the East India Company (VOC) ▲ *146*, was granted a monopoly on trade and navigation for America and West Africa by the Dutch parliament. This trade, coupled with piracy during the Eighty Years' War against Spain, guaranteed profits, and the merchants' money was used to fund war on the high seas and in the richest colonies of Spain. At first this aggression was rewarded: Portuguese and Spanish ships loaded with rich cargo were captured. In 1628 Admiral Piet Heyn defeated the Spanish "silver fleet", the *Zilvervloot*. This exploit is commemorated in a song popular in the 19th century, entitled *de Zilvervloot*: *Piet Heyn zijn naam is klein, z'n dade benne groot: hij heeft gewonne de Zilvervloot* ("Piet Heyn, his name is small, but his exploits are great, he defeated the Silver fleet"). This song was not only performed at the

Nieuw Amsterdam in 1656.

opening of the Colonial Institute in 1926 (today the Tropen Institut, or Royal Institute of the Tropics ▲ *274*), but can still be heard today in football stadia. The plunder, worth around 11½ million florins at the time, was stored in the cellars of the West India Company building. The riches secured by the capture of the Silver fleet made it possible to pay the shareholders a dividend for the first time – of 75 percent! The share price rose by over 200 percent. The crews of the privateer fleet were promised seventeen months' extra pay. When this payment was slow in coming, between forty and fifty sailors advanced on the West India Company building on February 12, 1629, "beating drums and armed with a cannon, in a drunken state". As the sailors had no powder at their disposal, the cannon was not fired. The town militia was able, without violence, to prevent another conquest of the Silver fleet.

The Company's failures. Despite this considerable plunder, the WIC was never as successful as the VOC. The WIC's expeditions generally cost more than they made in profits. For example, in the period between 1623 and 1636 it cost 46 million florins to arm eight hundred ships, but these brought in only 40 million in booty. Lack of money forced the directors of the WIC to leave the Herenmarkt building in 1647. They set themselves up in the Rapenburg warehouses, which were completed in 1642, close to the Oude Schans and the Montelbaanstoren ▲ *154*. Once peace was signed with Spain in 1648 ● *30*, further plundering was out of the question, and the conquest of part of Brazil was insufficient financial compensation for the loss. A revolt by the Portuguese in that colony led to the loss of the territory in 1654, and this costly war took the WIC to the brink of bankruptcy. It was due chiefly to trade in gold and slaves in West Africa that it survived until 1674, in which year it collapsed. The Company was finally dissolved in 1791.The

Pieter Stuyvesant

New premises
In 1647 the WIC moved to quayside premises in the port (the Rapenburg warehouses).

MYTHOLOGICAL SYMBOL
On the base of Domela's statue is an image of Prometheus, who stole fire from the gods and gave it to humans. To punish him, Zeus chained him to a rock. In 1887 Domela was also given a prison sentence, for treason.

CANALS AND INDUSTRIES
The opening of the North Sea canal in 1876 ● *37* ▲ *262*, shown below, and the construction of the Western Canal (Westerkanaal) made this area attractive to industries and port-related activities.

Haarlemmerstraat building was at first used to house guests of the city, then between 1825 and 1952 it served as a Lutheran home for orphans and old people.

NASSAUPLEIN

STATUE OF FERDINAND DOMELA NIEUWENHUIS. "This monument was unveiled in 1931 in memory of the founder of libertarian socialism in the Netherlands, Ferdinand Domela Nieuwenhuis (1846–1919), whose powerful slogan – Justice for all – called on the oppressed to fight for their rights." So reads the inscription at the foot of the statue, unveiled in the presence of thousands of Amsterdammers. "From Christian to anarchist" was the phrase used by Domela Nieuwenhuis to describe his life: he became a priest in 1869 and converted to anarchism in 1897 after some time as a socialist. His Frisian friends gave him the messianic title "Our Savior" ● *32*.

SPAARNDAMMERBUURT ★

The Spaarndam district (Spaarndammerbuurt) is chiefly known to tourists for its pre-war architecture in the style of the Amsterdam School ● *84*. However, its more distant past as a working-class district has left its mark on the history of the city. The construction around 1870 of the dike with its railway line and the Western Canal (Westerkanaal) cut Spaarndammerbuurt off from the rest of the city.

SPAARNDAMMERSTRAAT AND SPAARNDAMMERDIJK. The Spaarndam road and dike were the first part of the district to be built. Designed by monks in the 12th century, the Spaarndammerdijk follows the right bank of the IJ and ends to the north of Haarlem. Until 1834, when the Westerdijk, known today as Tasmanstraat, was built, the Spaarndammerdijk held back the waters of the IJ. Between the dike and the water there was nothing but reed-covered marshes, which became flooded at high tide. After the construction of the Westerdoksdijk closer to the center, Spaarndammerstraat was built over the top of the dike.

The Western Sugar Refinery. What is now Sugar Square (Suikerplein) was once land belonging to the Western Sugar Refinery, established in 1882 beside the Van Noordtgracht. In the 1980's inexpensive housing was built on this site as part of the process of urban renewal.

The Western Sugar Refinery
The Refinery, which employed seven hundred people, closed down in 1965.

A working-class district. In Assendelftstraat as in Spaarndammerstraat, Houtrijkstraat and Polanenstraat, the first working-class housing was built around 1880. These so-called "revolutionary" constructions had alcoves in which bunk beds were stacked up, to be reached by ladders. In the 1930's this area became the "poor people's district", mostly inhabited by dockers and laborers. During the Jordaan revolt of 1934 shops were looted here too ▲ *238*. In 1969 the city council launched a program aimed at improving life in Spaarndammerbuurt and Zeeheldenbuurt. The demolition of the "alcove" housing set the seal on this process. Following a dispute with the authorities, the 11,000 remaining inhabitants were granted among other concessions the building of two retirement homes.

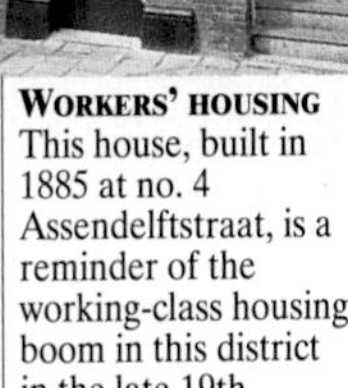

Workers' housing
This house, built in 1885 at no. 4 Assendelftstraat, is a reminder of the working-class housing boom in this district in the late 19th century.

Municipal baths. Located in Polanenstraat, the baths first opened their doors in 1916 with the motto: "A good bath every week!" The city council wanted to extend "water education" to include the working-class districts. The bathhouse, refitted with individual facilities, finally closed in 1984 after a long period of use.

Building by housing associations. Philanthropists and housing associations have ensured that this district has been well endowed with low-cost rented accommodation. In Polanenstraat the houses between nos. 54 and 60 were built in 1902 by P.W. Jansen, a rich industrialist who planned them to occupy a

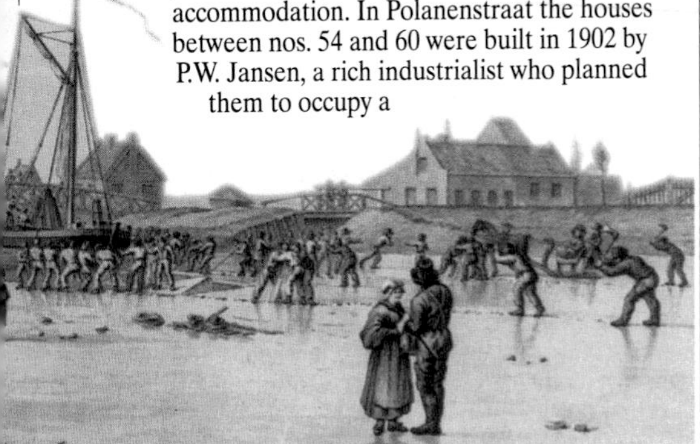

Morality and hygiene
One of the founders of the Delie food products company, P.W. Jansen, hoped to inspire the underprivileged classes for whom he built his housing with ideas of improved morality and hygiene. Families with children of both sexes were not permitted to rent his one-room studio apartments, because of the lack of "decency"!

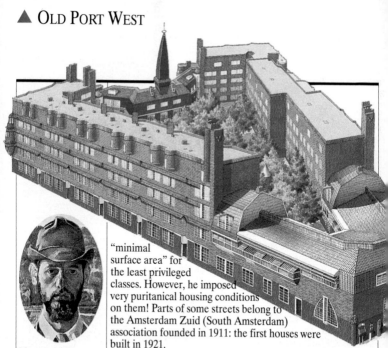

MICHEL DE KLERK
Brilliant architect of the "Ship", De Klerk (1884–1923) also designed, among other things, the series of amusing houses in Ronnerplein and Schwartzeplein ▲ *278*.

Just next to "The Ship's" post office, in the street, the blue giro, the red fire point and the city electricity board's green meter were all designed according to the tenets of the Amsterdam School.

"minimal surface area" for the least privileged classes. However, he imposed very puritanical housing conditions on them! Parts of some streets belong to the Amsterdam Zuid (South Amsterdam) association founded in 1911: the first houses were built in 1921.

SPAARNDAMMERPLANTSOEN ★. Along a little square at the corner of Zaanstraat and Spaarndammerplantsoen stands the earlier of the two major works of the Amsterdam School in this district ● *84*. Between 1913 and 1915 Michel de Klerk built this block as part of what was originally a large project for three housing blocks. The second block is on the other side of the gardens. The building planned for Wormerveerstraat never came into being. Soaring prices during the First World War forced architect and entrepreneur Kees Hille, who was working with De Klerk, to abandon his project. It was taken over by the Eigen Haard (Own Home) house-building association, founded in 1911 by employees of the Netherlands railway and tramway company. The Spaarndammerplantsoen block bears the name of Eigen Haard.

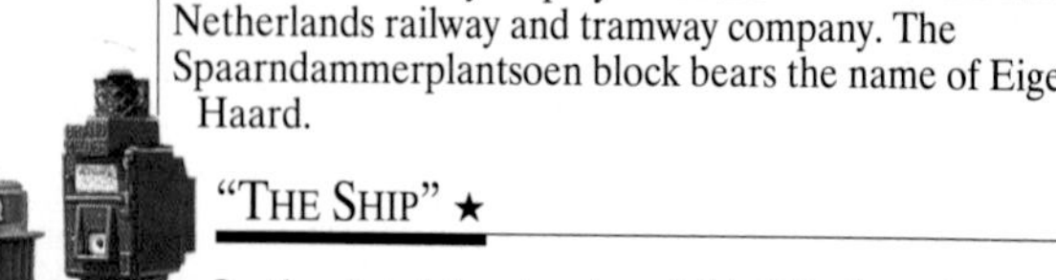

"THE SHIP" ★

On the site of the abandoned third block on Oostzaanstraat ● *84*, Michel de Klerk designed a building constructed in 1921 and called the "Ship" (*Het Schip*). As early as the 1920's the city council would take its official visitors to see this supreme example of Amsterdam School architecture, an unusual collection of dwellings in the shape of a triangle looking on to both Zaanstraat and Hembrugstraat. The architecture of the "Ship" was criticized for its complexity; it proved time-consuming and costly to build. However, for its first tenants, who had until then been used to nothing but alcove housing, hovels and slums, these dwellings were

"a dream in brick". One added, "for me, it was a jubilation. I thought that in the future everyone would be housed in this way. It was a bit like living in Paradise." Or, as a worker's wife put it at the funeral of De Klerk in 1923, "Spaarndammerplein is like a fairytale we dreamed of as children, because it's something that did not exist before for our children." The main emphasis was on the exterior of the building, and the living space itself tended to receive less attention. The windows have a rather unusual form, and each one is divided into many small panes, so that a two-room apartment, for example, has no fewer than eighty-one of these panes, which the Amsterdam School architects chose to place high up. According to them, the windows were made small and positioned high up to encourage the worker to turn his attention to the interior of his new apartment and enjoy concentrating on his own living space. Only the oldest of the blocks (Eigen Haard, dating from 1915) had its original windows replaced when the apartments were renovated between 1977 and 1980. The Historical Monuments Fund, which paid for this work, refused to grant permission for it to be carried out in the other buildings, although it did accept the raising of the floors by 7 inches.

AVANT-GARDE DECORATION
The "Ship's stern", characterized by the famous small, pointed tower, can be seen in Hembrugstraat.

POST OFFICE ★. This little post office at the end of the "Ship" on the Spaarndammerplantsoen side also bears the hallmark of the Amsterdam School, from the turret at the top to the original interior decoration, which has been maintained in good condition.

ZAANHOF. On the other side of the street there is a porch leading to Zaanhof, a small garden surrounded by residential buildings. Zaanhof was created by two housing associations, Het Westen (The West) and Patrimonium (Patrimony). The siting of green spaces next to this combination of towers and low buildings owes much to the English concept of "garden cities". Zaanhof was built during the First World War, when the Netherlands remained neutral. This fact is commemorated by a few lines of poetry engraved in stone above nos. 88 and 98. Similarly, over nos. 112 to 114, at the same level as the porch, the following words can be read: "Clothes make the honor, dignity and grace of man. The well-built house is the clothing of life. Praise be to God by whose will the city council gave the people festive clothes to wear, in joy and ceremony." In this way the whole philosophy behind the

Next to this, on the corner of Zaanstraat, a modern-day watchtower similarly demonstrates the lighter side of this whimsical architecture.

This church used to stand in Zaanstraat, but was demolished during the building work carried out at the beginning of the 20th century.

provision of low-rent working-class housing is summed up on the walls of the Zaanhof block, which is so different in appearance from the "Ship".

PRINSENEILAND ★ ● 76

On the western islands (Prinseneiland, Bickerseiland and Realeneiland) between Spaarndammerbuurt ▲ *254* to the west and Westerdok and the IJ to the east, there were once shipyards, tar distilleries, fish-salting and -smoking houses and large warehouses. The first of the islands, Prinseneiland (Prince's Island), can be reached from Haarlemmerplein ▲ *251* by passing under the railway. After going down Sloterdijkstraat and crossing Nieuwe Teertuinen, the visitor takes the little bridge over Prinseneilandsgracht and arrives on the island.

AN OLD INDUSTRIAL DISTRICT. The western islands were created during the first phase of urban expansion in 1612 ● *34* by piling earth on sandy spits of land. Here, far from the chic canal district ▲ *161*, shipyards, forges, timber stores, tar distilleries and rope factories were set up. The street names commemorate these past activities. In 1644 the storage and processing of tar and pitch were transferred to Nieuwe Teertuinen (New Tar Fields). These highly inflammable materials were used to seal joints on wooden ships. The wood and barrels were stored on the quaysides, where building was forbidden. Indeed, there are still no permanent buildings on most of the quays. The first building sites on Prinseneiland were sold publicly in 1623. In the 18th century there was almost nothing but warehouses on the island. To the right of the Prinseneilandsgracht bridge, near the old shipyard tar works of Ouwerkerk, the last capstan in Amsterdam can be seen. It was used to load and unload barrels of tar, grease and oil.

THE PRINSENEILAND MIRACLE. In the 17th century Jetske Klaes had been suffering from paralysis of the legs for fourteen years. On the night of October 13, 1676, an angel appeared at her bedside and she was able to walk again. It was said that the angel visited her several times. The news spread through the city like wildfire. Among the many people who came to see what had happened was the artist Jan Luycken, who wrote the story down. After that people talked of the "miraculous houses" on Prinseneiland, until they were demolished in 1733 to make way for more warehouses.

GALLOWS ROAD. Galgenstraat and Galgenbrug (Gallows Road and Bridge), which lead to Bickerseiland, refer to the view of the other side of the IJ where, until 1795, the bodies of Amsterdam's condemned criminals were left exposed, at the mercy of the birds, on gallows, stakes and wheels ▲ 262.

GEORGE HENDRICK BREITNER
Breitner (1857–1923), a painter and photographer ● *87*, often captured life and work in Amsterdam on canvas or film. His studio and home were located at no. 24b Prinseneiland. In 1898 the entrepreneur C.J. Maks offered him the use of these rooms in exchange for painting lessons for his son.

Above right: the Prinseneiland bridge.

The shipyard at Prinseneiland, painted by Breitner in 1902.

The quays and warehouses of Prinseneiland in 1896 (above). The Duba shipyard at no. 34 Prinseneiland is one of the last still working (left).

REALENEILAND ★ ●76

This island is reached by Drieharingenbrug (Three Herrings Bridge), which replaced an earlier floating wooden bridge. The name Realeneiland comes from Laurens Jacobszoon Reaal (1588–1648), who bought some land here at the beginning of the 17th century. The "restored" warehouses from no. 160 to no. 178 on the Realengracht quay have been entirely rebuilt and do not date from the 17th century, unlike the double warehouse at nos.13 to 14, which is more authentic. The steel ring at the foot of this warehouse, which can be found at the corner of Taandwarsstraat, is extremely rare. It was used to facilitate the hauling of merchandise during loading and unloading.

Red fox cartouche at no. 24 Nieuwe Teertuinen, and the three herrings (*drie haringen*) in Vierwindenstraat, opposite the bridge from Prinseneiland to Realeneiland. Three Herrings House is surmounted by three chimneys.

ZANDHOEK ★. This quay is reached by passing beneath the small houses on the little Jan Mens Square, which commemorates the fact that Jan Mensplein(1897–1967), the author of the novel *The Golden Real* (1940), rescued this district of dockers and the unemployed from oblivion. Thanks to him, houses destined for demolition were preserved and restored. The main character in his novel, *Griet Manshande*, was landlord of De Gouden Reaal café, located at no. 14 Zandhoek. Zandhoek (Sand Corner) owes its name to the sand market that was established here in 1634 by municipal decrees. Sand was in great demand for urban expansion and also for weighting ships. The concentration of the sand trade in this one place and the appointment of a supervisor, who had his office in the building opposite no. 10 Zandhoek, was intended to put an end "to the numerous frauds which happen every day in the sale of sand". The house at no. 10 Zandhoek is notable for being the birthplace of the photographer Jacob Olie (1834) ▲ *236, 260*.

Nos. 9 to 12 Realengracht on Realeneiland once housed a freight company and its warehouse. It carried goods from Amsterdam to Rotterdam and Roosendaal.

The Port of Amsterdam Seen from the IJ by Ludolf Backhuyzen (1631–1708) ● *88*. Commercial traffic on the IJ was intense during the Golden Century. Today the river has regained a more peaceful aspect. Rotterdam has become far more important, and activity in the port of Amsterdam has moved west.

HISTORIC WHEAT SILO
On Barentszplein to the north of Zandhoek there is a majestic wheat silo built in 1895 on the banks of the IJ, convenient for unloading ships. There are plans to renovate this building, currently occupied by squatters, which is classified as a historic monument.

BICKERSEILAND ★ ● *76*

The Bickers were among Amsterdam's most powerful merchant and governing families in the 17th century. In 1631 Jan Bicker (1591–1653), one of the Bicker brothers, bought the island that was to bear his name. On it he built shipyards and houses. He moved from Keizersgracht into a three-story house at the corner of Grote Bickerstraat and Minnemoersstraat. The house, demolished around 1700, had a tower named "Bicker's Tower", which enabled its owner to see the entire island as well as the IJ. In 1890 the last new ship left the eleven shipyards along the banks of the IJ and in the 1960's the city council decided to develop the island into an office complex. In 1963 the first of the old shipyards was demolished. Only the sign was preserved: it now decorates the entrance to an office block. In 1970 the inhabitants founded the Western Islands Action Committee in order to preserve the island as a residential area. In 1973 "De Narwal", the second office block of the series, was completed, but the demolition ended there. The Action Committee succeeded in maintaining the rest of the island as a residential zone. The west side of the island is destined for the building of low-rent housing. The name Keerpunt (Turning Point), a road located between Touwslagerstraat (Rope Factory Street) and Zeilmakerstraat (Sailmaker

Jacob Olie took his first photographs around 1860, with a camera he had made himself. The theme of these pictures was the western islands. At first Olie used collodion wet plates, so for his first portraits of family and neighbors, his subjects had to stay completely still for about twenty minutes.

«AT DUSK, INVITE THE CITIZENS TO LOOK OVER TO THE OTHER SIDE OF THE IJ, SO REFRESHING IS THE MAGNIFICENT SIGHT OF HOW AMSTERDAM, AS BOLD AS IT IS BEAUTIFUL, REIGNS OVER THE OCEANS.» E. J. POTGIETER (1808-1875)

Andries Bicker (1586–1652) by B. van der Helst (1613–70) ▲ *224*. Brother of Jan Bicker, he was mayor of Amsterdam and traded a great deal with Russia.

❝The shipyard built a fleet for the admirals to sail.
And Bicker's island creates islands that set out
Following all the directions of the compass, to contain the great sea
By means of cannons from one anchorage to the next.❞
Joost van den Vondel.

Street), marks the change of policy forced on the city council concerning urban renewal. Grote Bickerstraat, Touwslagerstraat and Hollandse Tuin (Dutch Garden) along the water's edge lead to Korte Prinsengracht. This in turn leads to the quays behind the Central Station▲ *138*, from where ferries cross the IJ.

CROSSING THE IJ ★ ■ *16*

As early as 1340 there was a ferry to Volewijck (Bird District) on the other side of the IJ, but the first regular crossings were started much later. After 1660 the inhabitants of Volewijck built a canal to take barges to Purmerend, north of Amsterdam ■ *20*. On the north bank of the IJ a superintendent's house was transformed into a tollhouse (Tolhuis) in 1663. Around 1835 a ferry was put into service for a short period. Seven years later the first steamer was launched, and after 1897 the municipal ferry made regular crossings to Tolhuis. Since 1912 passage has been free of charge. A new working-class district grew up in north Amsterdam around 1920, and the flow of traffic into the city increased. Since the opening of the tunnel under the IJ in 1968, motor vehicles are no longer allowed on the ferry.

The son of Andries Bicker, Gerard (1622–66) by B. van der Helst.

NORTH AMSTERDAM ★ ■ *16*

Volewijck, once a sandy spit in the IJ, came under the jurisdiction of Amsterdam in the 14th century. The present-day site of the Shell laboratories, dominated by a tower built in 1971, is the place where condemned criminals

The panoramic view of Amsterdam from the districts to the north of the IJ attracts many visitors, particularly on Sundays. The Tolhuis, surrounded by a large sports field and a park with a dance floor, used to be one of Amsterdam's greatest attractions.

were once executed. Until 1795 bodies were hanged from gallows there "as an example to all". The last person to be condemned to death in Amsterdam was executed in 1854 ▲ *258*.

THE NORTH HOLLAND CANAL. At the beginning of the 19th century silting of the IJ estuary was preventing the passage of ships, so a 50-mile long canal was built. Opening in 1824, it functioned as a navigable route between Amsterdam and the sea for half a century. Starting just opposite today's Central Station, it soon became impractical, however. Its many bridges and locks led to stoppages and extra costs, and ships grew increasingly larger. In 1876 its role was taken over by the shorter and wider North Sea Canal ● *32, 37* ▲ *254*.

MEEUWENLAAN. After the opening of the North Sea Canal, Amsterdam's economic boom also encouraged the industrial development of North Amsterdam. Oil storage depots, shipyards and refitting businesses were established to the south of Meeuwenlaan. At the same time workers' housing was being built, often by housing associations. Following the completion of the tunnel under the IJ, part of the industrial zone was abandoned.

Market day on Westerdokskade on the banks of the IJ, at the beginning of the 20th century.

STARLING PARK. Lijsterweg leads to Spreeuwenpark (Starling Park). Building first took place here between 1911 and 1915, following a plan drawn up by H.P. Berlage ▲ *279*, J.C. van Epen and J.H. Rijna. Urban renewal has not spared these buildings.

MOTORWAL. These shops with apartments on the upper floors were designed in 1982 by the architect Rem Koolhaas. Koolhaas, who was appointed to supervise the development of plans for the IJ, was responsible for the new buildings on this former site of shipyards and factories.

IJPLEIN. On this square, which you cross on leaving Meeuwenlaan, a sober plaque from the old factory of *Hollandia Kattenburg & Co* commemorates the round-up of November 11, 1942. On that day the Germans, with the help of some Dutch accomplices, encircled the Hollandia factory and arrested and deported 359 Jewish staff members ● *33* ▲ *180*.

THE TOLLHOUSE
The Tolhuis gave its name to a street and to the small district that surrounds it in north Amsterdam. Built in the 17th century, it was situated at the end of a land spit in the middle of the IJ.

Plantage

Hortus Botanicus, *264*
Union of Diamond Workers, *266*
Moederhuis, *267*
Hollandse Schouwburg, *267*
Artis, *268*
Entrepotdok, *269*
Maritime Museum, *269*
Eastern islands, *272*
De Gooier windmill, *273*
Oranje-Nassau barracks, *273*
Muiderpoort, *274*
Tropen museum, *274*

▲ PLANTAGE

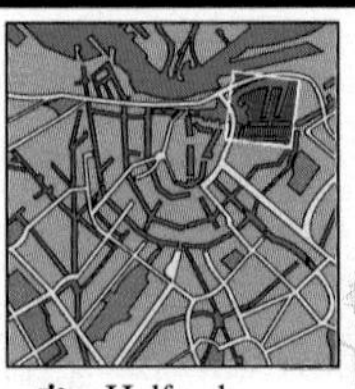

Half a day

AMSTERDAM'S PALM TREES
The greenhouse in the Botanical Gardens contains an extensive palm tree collection, including the oldest plant in the garden, the cycas, a palm several hundred years old which is also the world's oldest potted plant.

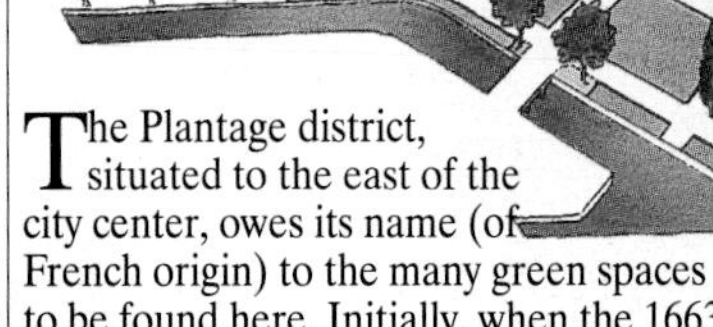

The Plantage district, situated to the east of the city center, owes its name (of French origin) to the many green spaces to be found here. Initially, when the 1663 city wall was completed ● *34*, the land was simply banked up and divided into lots. The original pattern of perpendicular paths still characterizes its layout today. Plantage became the district of gaming houses and prostitution, but was rehabilitated in the mid 19th century by the city council, which located a zoo here, among other attractions.

In the 17th century burgomaster Pancras chose a potted coffee tree from the Botanical Gardens as a gift to Louis XIV of France. The Sun King sent this plant to be cultivated in his American colonies, where it became the ancestor of the American coffee plant. Similarly, the production of palm oil, today a major activity in Indonesia, is due to plants from the Hortus Botanicus that were replanted in Java in the days of the Dutch East India Company.

HORTUS BOTANICUS ★

The Hortus Botanicus (Botanical Gardens) at no. 2 Plantage Middenlaan was founded in the 17th century, when economic prosperity enabled the wealthy merchants to become patrons. After the closure of the convents on the edge of the city during the religious conflicts ● *29*, their gardens of medicinal herbs had been neglected. However, in 1618 the magistrature granted the permission sought by the doctors and pharmacists of the city to set up a medicinal garden. This was first located on the banks of the Amstel, on Vlooienburg Square, the site of the present-day Muziek Theater, or "Stopera" ● *33* ▲ *160*. The expansion of the city caused it to be moved several times, until in 1682 it was finally established in Plantage with the dual function of being a botanical garden (planted for the doctors and pharmacists) and a pleasure park for Amsterdammers. In 1877 the Hortus Botanicus became part of the Amsterdam city university, and the great botanist Hugo de Vries (1848–1935) became its director in 1886 ▲ *267*. Sadly the university had to reduce its support for the garden due to lack of funds but today the Friends of the Amsterdam Plantage Hortus carry out a great deal of work on conserving

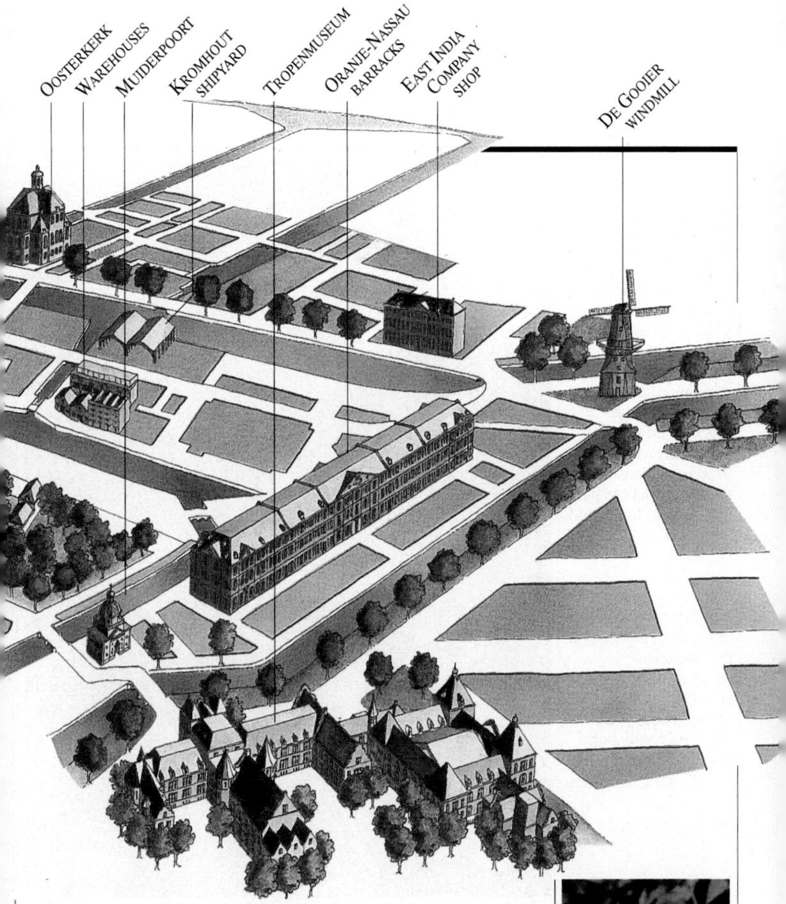

Oosterkerk
Warehouses
Muiderpoort
Kromhout shipyard
Tropenmuseum
Oranje-Nassau barracks
East India Company shop
De Gooier windmill

and renovating it. An administrative body of more than eight thousand members, including representatives from both the university and the city council, organizes activities and conferences for volunteers aimed at encouraging public support for the preservation of the Botanical Gardens. Its importance is not only aesthetic but also historical. In the 16th and 17th centuries ships of the Dutch East India Company brought back all kinds of exotic plants, which were transported in glass cases. From them, many new and useful plants were cultivated in the Botanical Gardens and then disseminated throughout the whole of Europe.

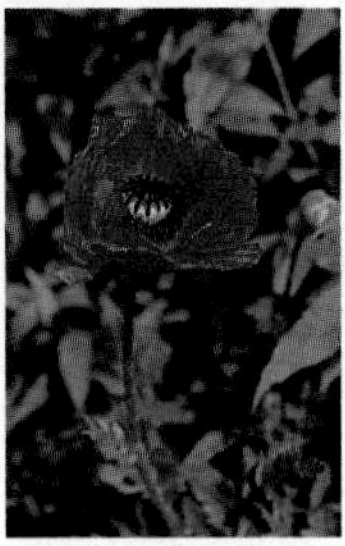

Poppy flower
A species grown in the Hortus Botanicus.

H E T Y.
Open Haven Front
Dijk Gracht
Westelijk Dok
Oostelijk Dok
Nieuwe Vaart

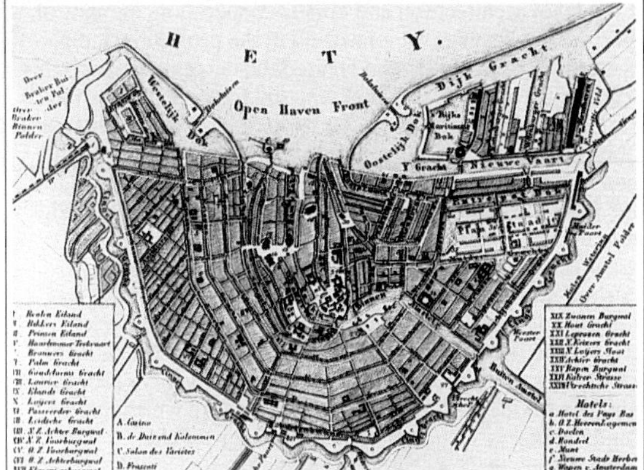

"Plantaadje"
This 18th-century map shows the Plantage district (here called Plantaadje) as a large open space to the east of the heart of Amsterdam. To its north lies the Nieuwe Vaart, a canal giving access to the eastern islands, where there was a port protected by a dyke ● *34*.

THE "BERLAGE FORTRESS"
The ANDB at no. 9 Henri Polaklaan was one of the first important designs by Berlage, an architect who greatly influenced urban planning in Amsterdam. He designed the new Stock Exchange ▲ *133* at about the same time and also produced plans for whole districts as part of a project to expand the city ▲ *278*.

"Brick is the material that gives Amsterdam its uniquely recognizable face. All H.P. Berlage's architectural work relies on brick, both inside and out."
Max Van Rooy

THE MOTHERS' HOUSE
Based in the house shown above, the Moederhuis was built in the late 19th century. The left-hand part is new, and the whole building is decorated with panels and stripes in blue, green and purple.

GENERAL UNION OF DIAMOND WORKERS ● *80*

In 1894, following a successful strike by diamond workers seeking better pay and working conditions, the General Union of Diamond Workers (*Algemene Nederlandse Diamantbewerkersbond*: ANDB) was founded by Henri Polak and Jan van Zutphen. This association gave a tremendous boost to the modern Dutch trade union movement. In 1899 the great architect Hendrik Petrus Berlage (1856–1934) ▲ *279* designed the organization's headquarters, creating what has been called the Burcht van Berlage (Berlage Fortress). It was a model of architectural and artistic cooperation, as many of Berlage's colleagues were involved in the project, including Richard Roland Holst, who created the decorative panels; his wife Henriette van der Schalk who did the ceramics for the various poetical maxims on display extolling the socialist spirit of brotherhood; Jac. van den Bosch, who did the panelling; and Lambertus Zijl, who made a bas-relief. The pinnacle (in the form of a diamond) and exterior galleries incorporated into the main façade reflect Berlage's interest in the architecture of the Italian *palazzo*. The stairway inside, decorated with colored bricks and small carved details, was intended to symbolize the progress of the working class toward the light. Today this building houses the MUSEUM OF DUTCH TRADE UNIONS, which retraces the history of socialism and of working-class political activity, both of which had a fundamental influence on the development of the Netherlands ● *32* ▲ *254*.

THE PLANTAGE DISTRICT LONG COMBINED GREEN SPACES AND THEATERS. THE THEATER HAS GONE, BUT THE ZOO IS STILL HERE TO ENTERTAIN VISITORS.

MOEDERHUIS

In the late 1970s Aldo van Eyck, an architect born in 1918, completed his project for a Moederhuis (Mothers' House) at no. 33 Plantage Middenlaan, which would be surrounded by houses built in the 19th century. The aim of this brightly colored house (pictured opposite, below), which belongs to the Hubertus Foundation, is to offer accommodation to very young single pregnant women, so that they can embark upon motherhood in relatively comfortable circumstances. Van Eyck undeniably represents the conscience of post-war Dutch architecture. Of particular note among this important architect's other buildings and designs is his "small town" idea, a city-run orphanage in the southwest of Amsterdam, completed in 1960 and composed of eight pavilions with dome-covered inner courtyards. This group of buildings, nicknamed the "kasbah", was later renovated and converted to house the Berlage Institute, an international center for the training of architects.

HUGO DE VRIES
Physiologist and director of the Hortus Botanicus, De Vries developed a widely accepted theory of mutations. He lived at 9 Plantage Parklaan.

HOLLANDSE SCHOUWBURG

The Dutch Theater (Hollandse Schouwburg), located at no. 24 Plantage Middenlaan, was founded under the name of the Artis Theater in 1893, and remained the center of theatrical life in the Netherlands until 1914. The building was requisitioned by the Germans during the Occupation and given an unfortunate role as the gathering point where the city's Jews were brought before being deported to the camp of Westerbork (Drenthe province) and on to the extermination camps. The building has now been converted to commemorate these tragic years, in homage to those deported ▲ *180*. Only the façade and walls of the theater auditorium still stand. The present monument is in stark contrast with the many variety theaters that once stood here, and which made 19th-century Plantage an elegant place of leisure for the bourgeoisie. There was a close bond between the local residents and the theater, thanks to Herman Heijermans, writer and artistic director, who moved here with his theatrical group at the end of the 19th century. The list of classics that ran triumphantly for several months in this district includes *Ghetto* (1899); *Op Hoop van Zegen (By the Grace of God, a Sea Play*, 1900), the story of a fishing boat whose owner knows it is no longer seaworthy and which indeed goes down with all hands ("We pay dearly for fish" says one of the protagonists); *Schakels* (*Shackles,* 1903); *Uitkomst* (*Solution*, 1907); and above all *De Wijzer Kater* (*The Wise Tomcat*), which was translated into many different languages and staged abroad.

WERTHEIMPARK
This little park opposite the Hortus Botanicus was created in 1895. In 1905 the local inhabitants held celebrations to mark the tenth anniversary of its opening. In 1992 the Auschwitz monument was unveiled here.

THE HOLLANDSE SCHOUWBURG

The Amsterdam zoological gardens date from the 19th century.

ARTIS

With the foundation in 1838 of the Artis park in Plantage Kerklaan by Doctor G.F. Westerman, president of the Natura Artis Magistra (Nature as Teacher of Art) Association, Amsterdam gained a zoological garden where a great number of eminent biologists have since worked. One of these was Max Weber, the first professor of biology at the University of Amsterdam. Since the 19th century schoolchildren, families and tourists have flocked to this park which, besides the zoo, contains a planetarium, an ENTOMOLOGICAL MUSEUM (reached through no. 64 Plantage Middenlaan) and an aquarium. The zoo has the usual classic displays: big cats in cages, elephants, giraffes and hippopotamuses in enclosures, a pool for pelicans and flamingos, one for sealions and one for polar bears, a penguin island, an aviary, an aquarium, and so on. The ZOOLOGICAL MUSEUM contains the Heimans-diorama (slides showing plant and bird life in a landscape of dunes), named in memory of Eli Heimans (1861–1914), a schoolteacher who founded the journal *Levende Natuur* (*Living Nature*) with his colleague Jac. P. Thijsse. They were both instrumental in establishing protected sites in the Netherlands by founding the Association for the Preservation of Natural Monuments in 1905. The presence of the zoo, the Hortus Botanicus and the small Wertheimpark – which takes its name from the banker and patron Abraham Carel Wertheim (1832–97), who supported the economic and social development of Amsterdam during the second half of the 19th century – means that Plantage is regarded as the city's "green lung".

An old mongoose cage at the zoo.

REHABILITATION OF 1858. Around the point where Plantage Middenlaan crosses Plantage Kerklaan stand houses that date from the rehabilitation of the district undertaken by the city council in 1858. Here whitewashed façades and small cast-iron balconies represent a style that was dominant during the first phase of reconstruction. Toward the end of the century the styles became more mixed.

VIEW OF THE ENTREPOTDOK IN 1833
The warehouses lining the dock had just been built at this date. All kinds of goods were unloaded here, including barrels of wine and oil (opposite, top).

ENTREPOTDOK ■ *18* ● *76*

After crossing Plantage Doklaan, a long road that runs along the north side of Artis park, you come to the Entrepotdok canal, which is lined with warehouses. About 500 yards of the canal's quayside is entirely taken up by a row of eighty-two former maritime warehouses, each bearing the name of a town in the kingdom of the Netherlands. This impressive complex was built between 1827 and 1840 as a general national storage depot and as a warehouse for duty-free goods that were not checked by customs. There was an entrance under constant surveillance in Kadijksplein, at the western end of the warehouses, the point where the canal led into the port. Following the construction of a larger warehouse close to the new dockside installations, these buildings lost their original function and became storehouses for a variety of goods until the Second World War. After this they were abandoned and gradually fell into ruin. In the early 1980s work was started to restore the warehouses and to build social welfare housing, under the supervision of the architect Jop van Stigt. To make the buildings more accessible, Van Stigt created internal streets by cutting out the center of the warehouse complex. This housing complex is a fine example of Amsterdam's urban renewal program.

MARITIME MUSEUM ★

This museum (Scheepvaartmuseum), on the banks of Oosterdok and with its entrance on Kattenburgerstraat, occupies a 17th-century building that was for a long time the main Admiralty shop, linked to the VOC ▲ *146*. The building then became the naval arsenal, finally being converted into a museum when the arsenal was restructured and moved to ports closer to the sea. Remarkably well laid out, it reconstructs the history of the Dutch navy ▲ *270*.

THE OLD PORT
A figurehead decorates the façade of no. 46 Entrepotdok. Nos. 50 to 60 ("Middelburg") and 64 (Entrepotje café) have passages that lead through the warehouses to Laagte Kadijk (an old dyke protecting the alluvial land beyond Saint Anthony dyke along the IJ, depicted left when it was breached in 1651). Near the lock on Hoogte Kadijk is an iron bascule bridge that has replaced the former swing bridge. To the left on the other side of the bridge is the entrance to the former Kromhout shipyard, now home to an organization and museum displaying techniques for building and repairing ships (Werfmuseum 't Kromhout). Beyond this, at the far end, lies Kadijksplein, a small square with the Koffiehuis van den Volksbond (coffeehouse for dockers belonging to the Union of the People) at no. 2. No. 4 marks the entrance to the docks, leading to the quayside, while no. 18 is the Zeemanshuis (Seamen's Mission).

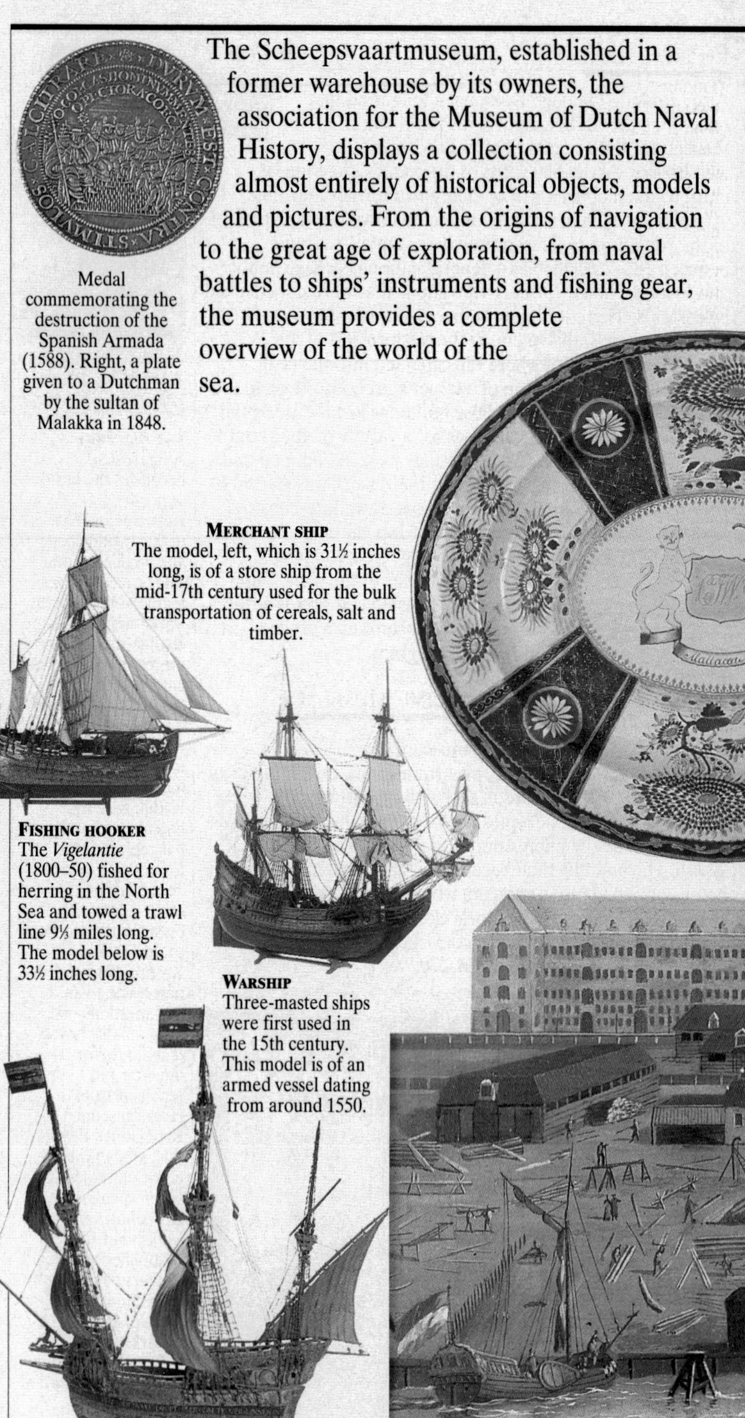

The Scheepsvaartmuseum, established in a former warehouse by its owners, the association for the Museum of Dutch Naval History, displays a collection consisting almost entirely of historical objects, models and pictures. From the origins of navigation to the great age of exploration, from naval battles to ships' instruments and fishing gear, the museum provides a complete overview of the world of the sea.

Medal commemorating the destruction of the Spanish Armada (1588). Right, a plate given to a Dutchman by the sultan of Malakka in 1848.

MERCHANT SHIP
The model, left, which is 31½ inches long, is of a store ship from the mid-17th century used for the bulk transportation of cereals, salt and timber.

FISHING HOOKER
The *Vigelantie* (1800–50) fished for herring in the North Sea and towed a trawl line 9⅓ miles long. The model below is 33½ inches long.

WARSHIP
Three-masted ships were first used in the 15th century. This model is of an armed vessel dating from around 1550.

The Admiralty warehouse
Built in 1656 by Daniel Stalpaert, this building was used for storing the shipbuilding materials used by the neighboring yard. It now houses the Maritime Museum ● *76*.

M.H. Tromp
A Dutch admiral (1598–1653) who died during a battle against the English ▲ *146*.

Helm heads
These heads of carved and painted wood were decorations for helms and date from the early 19th century. Left, bust of an oriental woman; right, the head of a Moor.

Dutch East India Company shipyards
This shipyard was located right beside the great warehouse. The company had several yards, of which this was the largest. It had three dry docks, an anchor forge and a cannon foundry (painting by J. Mulder, around 1690) ▲ *146*.

J.E.J. Capitein
The African-born pastor of the fort of Saint George of Elmina in West Africa (1656).

Launching a ship built on the island of Wittenburg in the 19th century.

EASTERN ISLANDS ■ *18*

PETER THE GREAT'S VOYAGE
As a youth the future Tsar Peter the Great (1672–1725) was strongly influenced by the commander of his guards, Colonel François Lefort, a Swiss officer who had spent many years in the Netherlands, spoke Dutch and enjoyed sea travel. Around 1684 Lefort invited shipbuilders to come to Russia to build a frigate for his royal pupil. The young Tsar Peter thus learned both how to speak Dutch and how to sail. In 1697 Russia sent a diplomatic mission to Holland led by Lefort. The Tsar, who was traveling with him incognito, arrived on August 17, set up house in Zaandam, north of Amsterdam, and stayed in the Netherlands until January 15, 1698, learning a great deal about shipbuilding. A plaque on the wall of the Werkspoor Museum commemorates these events ● *31*.

Kattenburg, Wittenburg and Oostenburg, the three eastern islands, were artificially created in the IJ by means of earth embankments during the expansion of the city in 1658 ● *34*. Today they still jut out into the IJ and are separated from the other districts by the NIEUWE VAART, a canal running parallel to Entrepotdok. They are linked to the rest of the city by two bridges situated at either end of the Nieuwe Vaart.

WITTENBURG. The OOSTERKERK (Eastern Church) was built on the banks of the Nieuwe Vaart in 1671. Pierre Hémony ▲ *128* cast the bell weighing 1.7 tons which still sounds the hour today. The church was built by the architect Daniel Stalpaert ● *36*. It stands on more than 1,800 piles, and the dampness of the ground, combined with the earthquakes of 1755 and 1756, has caused many cracks to appear in the walls. Buttresses have been erected to protect the building. The church, which was closed in 1962, has been restored and now has a new role as the socio-cultural center of the district.

OOSTENBURG. For nearly three centuries this third island was the scene of intense industrial activity. From 1666 to 1822 almost its entire area was covered with the rope factories and workshops of the Dutch East India Company ▲ *146*. Around 2,000 men were employed on the island. However, in 1796 the Company went bankrupt and was dissolved by the revolutionary authority set up by the French. New businesses were located on the former Company's land, including, in 1827, Paul van Vlissingen and A.E. Dudok van Heel's factory making steam-powered machinery and other equipment. The company became the Netherlands' largest employer, with more than 1,600 workers in 1856. Competition got the better of it, sadly, and the factory closed in 1891. The site was sold to the Dutch Shipbuilding Company. The equipment was bought by the state railway and the Dutch Railway Company, and the business was reorganized under the name Werkspoor (Shipyard Railway). Close links between the Dutch Shipbuilding Company and Werkspoor led to a great number of orders for the navy and for the construction of large bridges and Diesel machines. The history of this industrial past has been put on display in the WERKSPOOR MUSEUM, located in the former VOC rope factory on Oostenburgergracht, at the corner with Conradstraat. Today the island is devoted mainly to housing, most of which is recent, shops, a sports center and a park.

The Oranje-Nassau barracks in the 19th century.

De Gooier windmill ★ ● 68

On Funenkade (Funen Quay) stands the last windmill from Amsterdam's city wall, built in 1658 during the expansion of the city ● *34*. During the Second World War the 17th-century De Gooier windmill, with its mechanical millstones, was often used because of a shortage of fuel. Next to it the Funenkade public baths have been converted into a brewery with old tiled floors, known as 't IJ. Since the closure of the Heineken brewery ▲ *276* on Stadhouderskade, this is the only brewery left in Amsterdam. It produces a strong beer that is 18 degrees proof, brewed with Amsterdam's fresh running water and called Colombus, after the legend of Columbus' egg, making a pun on "egg" (*ei* in Dutch) and IJ, the port's river. As well as Columbus, they brew Struis, Natte, Zatte and some other beers. The Y-bier bar is only open after 4p.m.

Oranje-Nassau barracks

The very impressive façade on Sarphatistraat, Amsterdam's longest, belongs to the Oranje-Nassau barracks. They were built during the French occupation, when the Netherlands were part of the Napoleonic Empire ● *32* , and financed by the city of Amsterdam. They were originally called Saint-Charles' Quarter, in homage to Marshal Charles Oudinot, who laid the foundation stone on November 17, 1810. The project, conceived by Picot de Moras, was completed by the Amsterdam architect Abraham van der Hart (1747–1820). It was four years before the first soldiers could move in, and by then the French had already left, the year before. The course of history can be read on the pediments: three bear the French arms from which the French eagle has been removed to make way for the Dutch lion. Most remarkable is

Dr Samuel Sarphati (1813–66), above, played a major role in the life of the city in the 19th century ▲ *277*.

The Pioneers
The streets built behind the Oranje-Nassau barracks during the renovation of the area and the apartment blocks along the canal took their names from 19th- and early 20th-century women social pioneers and housing inspectors, such as Johanna Ter Meulen (1867–1937), above. The engineer Jacoba Mulder (1860–88), known as Kootje Mulder, had a great influence on the later organization of the 1934 expansion plan ● *36*.

THE FIRST MUIDEN GATE
The gate was built in the early 18th century and extensively reworked by Rauws in 1770. In this painting of 1756 by J. Ten Compe (1713–61), Singelgracht, the canal running along Amsterdam's city wall, can be seen with its row of windmills. The canal is still there, but the only remaining windmill is the De Gooier mill ▲ *273*.

MAURITSKADE
This quay along Singelgracht became the site of several factories in the 19th and 20th centuries.

The original aim of the Royal Institute of the Tropics was to study the Dutch colonies: the Dutch East Indies (now Indonesia), Surinam and the Antilles. The museum's theater-restaurant stages shows and films from developing countries, as well as offering exotic meals.

the central tympan, in which Napoleon's arms have been replaced by the personal arms of William I of Orange, first king of the Netherlands. The barracks were returned to the city by the Ministry of Defence and converted into apartments and offices.

MUIDERPOORT

The Muiden Gate is a building in the classical style designed by Cornelis Rauws between 1769 and 1771. It is one of the last of the old city gates still in existence. It was here in 1811 that Napoleon made his entry into the capital of Holland. Legend has it that only the first few hundred of his troops were properly clothed and equipped. Behind these came the soldiers of Napoleon's real old guard, who were all in tatters and had to be housed, clothed and fed by the Amsterdammers. The building is now a tax information office.

TROPENMUSEUM

The Royal Institute of the Tropics was established in 1910, and in 1926 Queen Wilhelmina opened this large complex, the style of which was inspired by the Rijksmuseum ▲ *212*. Today the Institute is concerned with collecting information on developing countries. Its departments of agronomics and tropical hygiene play an important part in ecological and medical research, particularly into yellow fever and malaria, and in work on nutrition and eating habits. The museum, which shares the same building, is devoted to tropical countries and their customs. The displays on the top floor showing Bedouin tents and Indian bazaars are particularly popular with children.

De Pijp and the South

Heineken Brewery, *276*
Development of a district, *277*
Albert Cuypstraat market, *277*
Sarphatipark, *277*
The southern project, *278*
Henriette Ronnerplein, *280*
Thérèse Schwartzeplein, *280*
Cooperatiehof, *280*
«Skyscraper», *280*

▲ De Pijp and the South

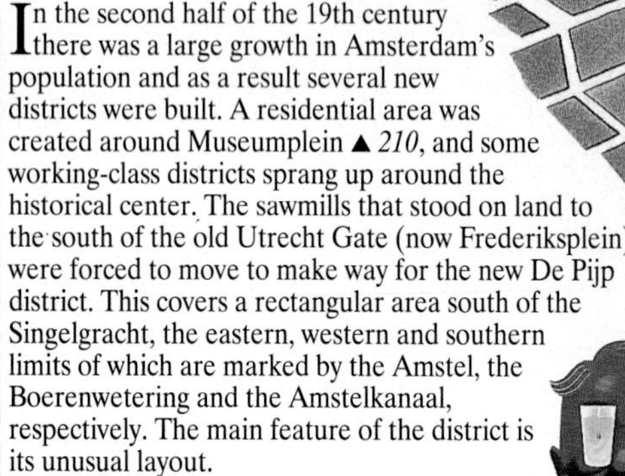

🚶 Half a day

The history of beer
The Heineken museum uses old and modern equipment to trace the history of the beer's production. Brewery buildings in the 19th century (bottom).

In the second half of the 19th century there was a large growth in Amsterdam's population and as a result several new districts were built. A residential area was created around Museumplein ▲ *210*, and some working-class districts sprang up around the historical center. The sawmills that stood on land to the south of the old Utrecht Gate (now Frederiksplein) were forced to move to make way for the new De Pijp district. This covers a rectangular area south of the Singelgracht, the eastern, western and southern limits of which are marked by the Amstel, the Boerenwetering and the Amstelkanaal, respectively. The main feature of the district is its unusual layout.

Heineken Brewery

The imposing brick edifice of the former brewery on Stadhouderskade has now been turned into a museum describing how the beer is made and documenting the history of Heineken. Some years ago the company moved production to more modern, better designed factories in the provinces ▲ *273*, but this place preserves the history of the company. The first brewery was established here at the end of the 16th century and was bought by Adriaan Heineken in 1864. The business proved so successful that its products have long been exported throughout the world. It is certainly the world's best-known brand of Dutch beer. It owes much of its success to a secret ingredient called fermenting agent "A", which was developed by one of Louis Pasteur's students. The façade on Stadhouderskade, behind which lies the museum, is all that is left of the original building, which was designed by the architects B.J. and W.B. Ouerdag in 1932–4. The rest of the site is being totally transformed and developed around a new square along Quellijnstraat on the corner of Ferdinand Bolstraat.

Origin of the district's name
One explanation is that the long narrow ditches that had been filled in were said to look like pipes (*Pijp*). Another is that the chimneys of the De Hooiberg brewery (Heineken's predecessor) were reminiscent of pipes. This was also one of the first districts outside the center to be supplied with gas, provided by the Pijpgascompagnie.

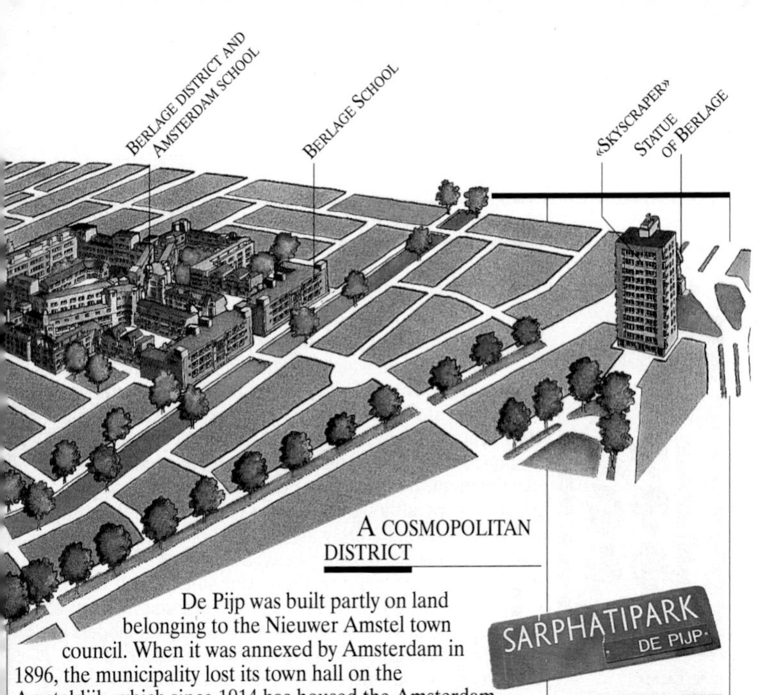

A COSMOPOLITAN DISTRICT

De Pijp was built partly on land belonging to the Nieuwer Amstel town council. When it was annexed by Amsterdam in 1896, the municipality lost its town hall on the Amsteldijk, which since 1914 has housed the Amsterdam city archives (Gemeentearchief); these are open to the public. The De Pijp district in fact consists of two parts. The first, built between 1860 and 1890, is characterized by the standardized appearance of its buildings. These dwellings were designed to take up as little land as possible. Ditches were filled in and paved over to make streets, which, according to the directives, had to be 50 feet wide; all the buildings had to be four stories high. Most of the districts built in the 19th century around the old city reveal a similar lack of originality and style. However, the second part of the district, built between 1900 and 1930 to the south of Ceintuurbaan and the SARPHATIPARK, is in the style of the Amsterdam School. Today the old district has a very mixed ethnic population. Out of a total of about 40,000 inhabitants around 3,000 are Moroccans, about 2,500 are from Surinam and over 1,500 are Turkish. Many students also live in the district, for although some of the buildings have now been renovated, the older, cheaper housing has not disappeared and remains an attractive prospect for students and immigrants alike. There are opportunities for the Turks and Moroccans to set up small businesses and shops here, although they meet with fierce competition from the Dutch stallholders. All in all, De Pijp is a cosmopolitan area where trade flourishes.

ALBERT CUYPSTRAAT MARKET ★
Amsterdam's largest market, held in this street, has a lively, bustling atmosphere.

SARPHATIPARK
This park, established in the late 19th century, contains the Sarphati monument (above) dedicated to Dr Samuel Sarphati (1813–66), who founded a bank to finance his plans for a business school, a cleaning service and local housing ▲ *273*.

The southern project ● 36

Designed by H.P. Berlage (1856–1934), the southern project is now considered a model of its kind. Many town planners regard it as the finest 20th-century housing project in the Netherlands. The overall layout, in which, to quote one poet, "clear lines reign and the avenues bite into the horizon", was drawn up with great care by Berlage and accepted by the city council in 1917. The project was planned in further detail when the city, crammed inside its old walls, was in urgent need of new development. It is without a doubt the architect and planner's greatest work, although he did not design any of the district's individual buildings. Only the bridge over the Amstel at the end of Vrijheidslaan, which bears his name ● *66*, is by his hand. The arrangement of alternating squares and streets, broad avenues and quiet thoroughfares, monumental public buildings and apartment blocks, decorated with modest but magnificent designs, has made southern Amsterdam deservedly famous throughout the world. The canal linking the Amstel in the east to the Schinkel in the west is a crucial element in the project. The Amstelkanaal, as it is called, splits into two branches near its intersection with the Boerenwetering, where the Apollohal (sports hall) stands. These two branches, the North and South Amstelkanaal, join up again behind the Olympic Stadium ● *60*, and the canal then continues down to the Schinkel. The entire district was designed around this waterway. Although Berlage is its spiritual father, the southern project would not have been such a great success without the collaboration of other architects.

Three classes of housing. The building of an apartment block in Amsterdam was always entrusted either to a housing association (these were subsidized under the 1901 housing law) or to an individual. The builder would then invite an architect to come up with a plan that met the requirements of a supervisory committee, which was answerable to the city housing inspectorate. This demanding and tenacious committee took an interest in every detail. The expansion project committee required the provision of blocks of second- and third-class housing (housing for the middle and working classes) and of first-class housing (larger buildings and semi-detached houses). It also specified the height of buildings and provided a list of public monuments to be included. The building of the southern project was largely overseen by a group of architects who were most active between 1920 and 1930.

The Amsterdam School ● *84*. The influence of the Amsterdam School is obvious: the designers made great use of brick, wood and dressed stone – "decent and honest" materials, according to Berlage. As far as possible each street

A.S. Talma (1864–1916)
One of the leaders of the *Christelijk Werklieden Verbond* (Christian Workers' Association), founded in 1877 by orthodox Protestant workers. Bosses and employers were permitted to be associate members. Among its many activities, the association was involved in the building of "Patrimonium" social housing, a major program throughout the city after 1914. A street leading off Cooperatiehof in the De Pijp district bears the name of Talma.

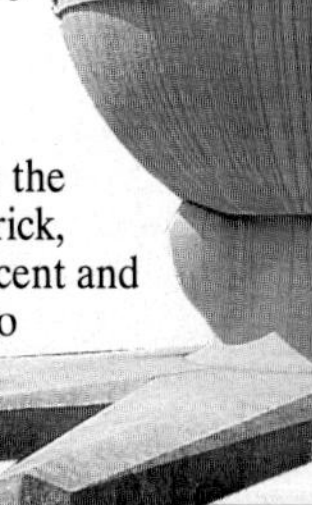

In memory of the pioneers
This monument pays homage to the pioneering associations that built the district in the early 20th century. It stands in the Cooperatiehof garden.

«LOOK AT THE DOORS, THE LETTERBOXES, THE ENTRANCES AND ABOVE ALL THE THEATRICALITY OF THE TILED ROOFS: THE DESIGNER LEFT NOTHING TO CHANCE.»

MAX VAN ROOY

HENDRIK PETRUS BERLAGE

The builder of the Stock Exchange ▲ *133* exerted a great influence on architecture and planning in Amsterdam during the late 19th and

early 20th centuries. His first building in the city was the Focke & Meltzer shop at the corner of Kalverstraat and the Spui ▲ *122*, which is now an English bookshop (W.H. Smith). He was originally influenced by Italian Renaissance architecture, but his style changed around 1890 with the building of the Bols 't Lootsje genever factory on the Rozengracht (1892) ▲ *247*. The Stock Exchange on the Damrak, his major work (completed in 1903), caused a sensation. After this, his main contributions to Amsterdam were the Mercatorplein, in the western expansion plan, and the southern expansion plan, the limit of which is marked by the bridge over the Amstel that bears his name (1932). Berlage also designed the municipal museum of The Hague. On the left are details of the façades of several buildings in the southern plan, including some on Tellegenstraat ● *84*.

THE "SKYSCRAPER"
In 1931 the architect J.F. Staal (1879–1940), who knew nothing of the Amsterdam School and was a supporter of the New Building (*'t Nieuwe Bouwen*) movement, built a large apartment block on a major site, located on a main intersection (Victorieplein). It was 130 feet high with twelve stories (this is exceptional in Amsterdam) and soon became known as the "skyscraper" (*Wolkenkrabber*). Inside are twenty-four apartments. Its highly modern appearance remains largely unchanged.

was to be treated as a single unit, and efforts were made systematically to create a coherent work of art. The architects wanted to differentiate the new districts from those outlying areas which had been built in the late 19th century. They succeeded in creating a distinctive style by giving the buildings some unique elements: for example, every now and then the usual method of laying bricks horizontally on the row beneath gives way to vertical brickwork. The rounded forms of the buildings, the irregular line of the façades, the corbelled balconies (bow windows) and corner turrets show how the architects gave their imagination free rein.

ATTENTION TO DETAIL. In this district you will find a number of houses and apartment blocks with porches, windowframes, numbers and letterboxes that display enormous attention to detail: they are decorated with wrought ironwork, carved stone and stained glass. Around forty architects collaborated in the realization of the project, some of them contributing more than others. Two of the main participants, Michel de Klerk (1884–1923) ▲ *256* and Pieter Lodewijk Kramer (1881–1961), helped to write the Amsterdam School's first manifestos through an association called De Dageraad (The Dawn – i.e. of socialist tendencies). Their major works include the HENRIETTE RONNERPLEIN and THÉRESE SCHWARTZEPLEIN ★; this symmetrical group of identical houses is famous for its extraordinary forms. It is reached via the COOPERATIEHOF ★, which lies at the center of an entirely geometric little district. TELLEGENSTRAAT, the street encircling Cooperatiehof, also contains some interesting examples of this distinctive architecture.

VICTORIEPLEIN
RIVIERENBUURT

STATUE OF BERLAGE. Berlage chose squares and crossroads as the sites for monumental buildings, and he preferred them to have a specific function in the community. Few of his projects actually came to fruition, however. The sculptor Hildo Krop (1884–1970) contributed some important additions to the southern project. Krop's statue of Berlage stands on the Victorieplein. The architect is shown holding a compass and pencil as he looks out over the Amstel. Behind him the Staal "SKYSCRAPER" hides Merwedeplein, where the upper floor of no. 37 houses the former apartment of the Frank family. They had to leave it on July 6, 1942, to go into hiding at no. 263 Prinsengracht ▲ *180*.

USEFUL INFORMATION

TRAVELING TO AMSTERDAM, *282*
GETTING AROUND IN AMSTERDAM, *284*
FINDING YOUR WAY, *286*
PROFILE OF THE CITY, *287*
LIVING IN AMSTERDAM, *288*
AMSTERDAM IN A DAY, *292*
AMSTERDAM IN TWO DAYS, *293*
AMSTERDAM FOR FREE, *294*
CAFÉS OLD AND NEW, *296*
AMSTERDAM BY NIGHT, *298*
UNUSUAL AMSTERDAM, *300*
PRE-WAR AMSTERDAM, *301*
EN ROUTE FOR AMSTERDAM, *302*
HAARLEM CITY AND REGION, *304*
THE WATERLANDS AND POLDERS, *306*
THE VECHT VALLEY, UTRECHT AND AMERSFOORT, *308*
USEFUL WORDS AND PHRASES, *310*

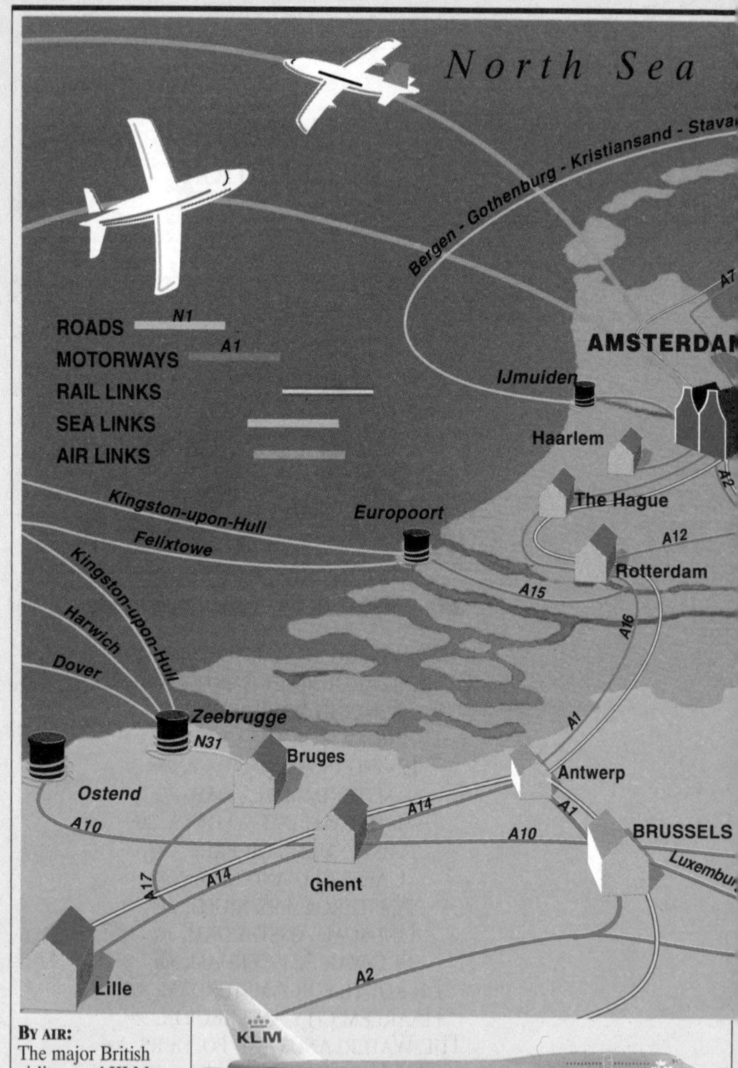

By air:
The major British airlines and KLM together provide an almost hourly daytime service from London Heathrow, and there are around eleven services a day from Gatwick. Many other important cities in the UK are also directly linked with Amsterdam. There are several direct flights to Amsterdam from JFK, New York, Chicago, Los Angeles and San Francisco. All flights arrive at Schiphol international airport, about 9 miles from Amsterdam, which is linked by rail with Central Station. Trains run every 15 mins and a single journey costs 5.25 Fl. There is also a KLM bus service, for the use of airport passengers, which costs 15 Fl. It stops at all the main Amsterdam hotels. But be careful because there are two different routes. A taxi will take you to the city center for around 50 Fl. For further information contact British Airways, British Caledonian, British Midland, KLM or Transania.

By train:
There are day- and night-time services from London Liverpool St and Manchester City to Amsterdam via Hoek van Holland. The crossing takes about 7 hrs. For a shorter Channel crossing, travel from London Victoria, via Dover to Ostend.

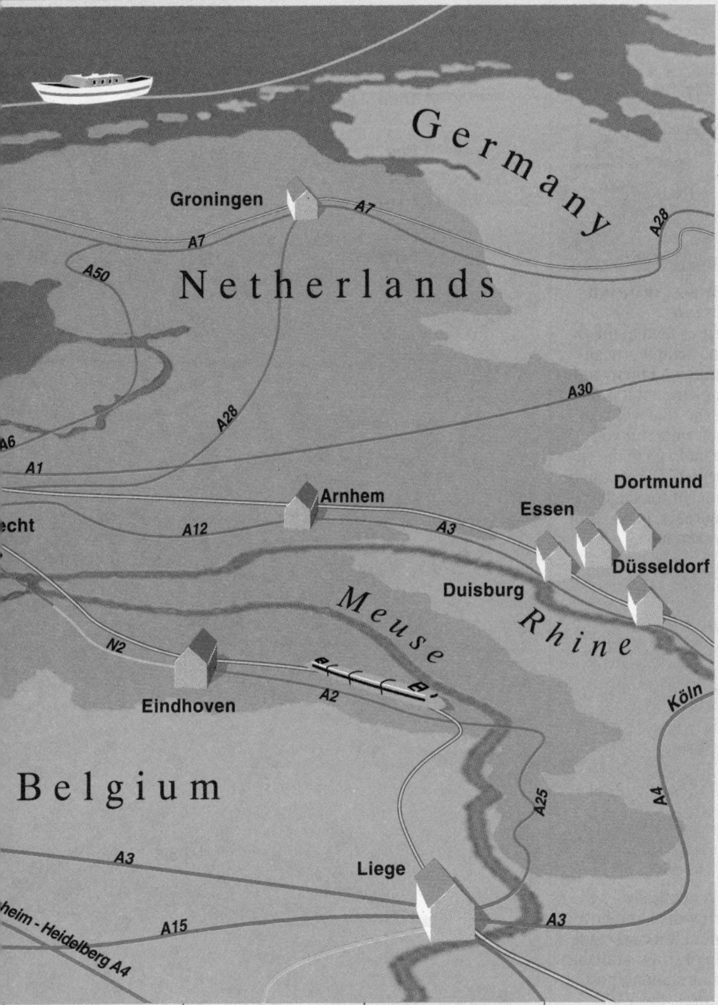

Germany
Groningen
A7
A28
A50
Netherlands
A30
A28
A6
A1
Arnhem
Dortmund
Essen
echt
A12
A3
Düsseldorf
Duisburg
Meuse
Rhine
N2
Eindhoven
A2
Köln
Belgium
A25
A4
A3
Liege
A15
A3
heim - Heidelberg A4

By coach:
The Hoverspeed City Sprint, daily from London's Victoria Coach Station, takes only 10 hours.

By car:
The quickest option is probably to take the jetfoil from Dover to Ostend, or the ferry from Dover to Zeebrugge, and then drive up through Antwerp, Breda and Utrecht. Sealink operate two services a day between Harwich and Hoek van Holland (daytime crossing just under 7 hrs). Journey time from the Hoek to Amsterdam is about 3½ hrs. The Olau Line also offers two sailings a day (7 hrs) between Sheerness and Vlissingen. Once in Amsterdam, there is hardly anywhere to park and cars are frequently clamped or towed away. It is advisable to leave cars outside the city center and use public transport.

By Channel Tunnel:
London Waterloo to Brussels takes 3¼ hours. Take a car – return fare from £130 to £220 – or travel on the Eurostar train – return fare from £85 apex to £195 first class.
Tel: 01233 617 575

BY BUS, TRAM AND METRO
Buses tend to follow the main thoroughfares, and there is also a metro but it is the trams that will take you wherever you want to go in the city center. Tickets can be bought for single journeys, in books or – even more

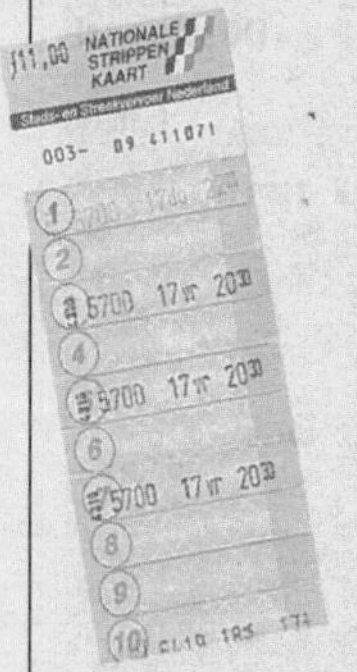

economically – as a *strippenkaart* (above), literally a card made up of strips, available from stations, post offices, the VVV office and some newsagents. The city is divided into transport zones, and one strip per zone plus one per fare is required. In general this means using two strips in the city center, which is a single zone.
Alternatively, you can buy a *dagkaart*, an unlimited travel card that is valid for one or for several days. These tickets and cards can be used on any of Amsterdam's public transport networks, but must be stamped in the correct way, as inspections are frequent and fines are heavy. They can be bought from the transport office (GVB) at the Central Station, in post offices and newsagents.

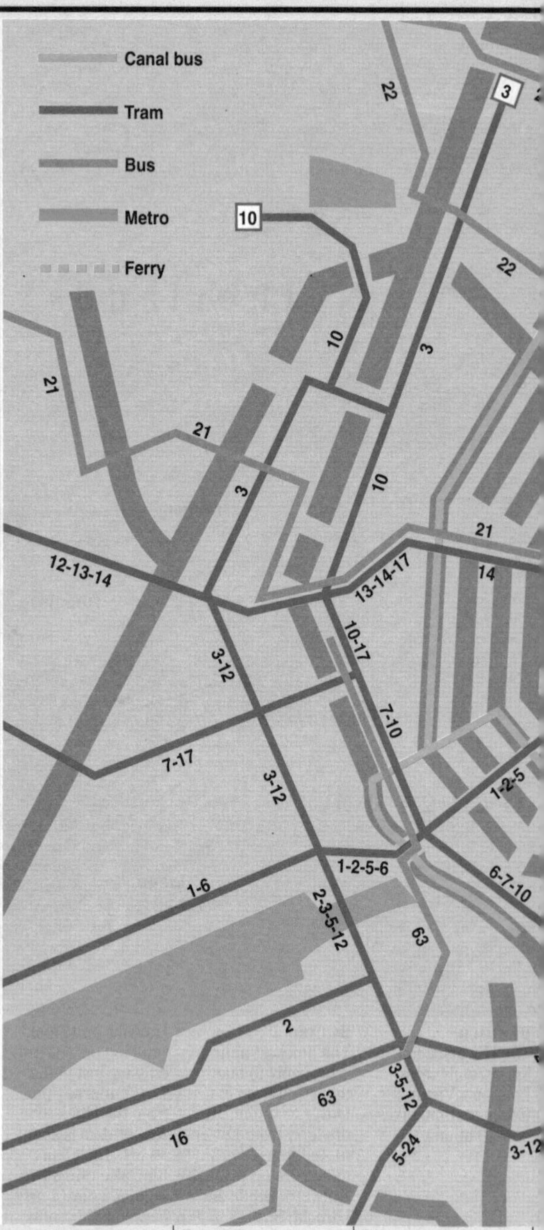

BY TAXI
Taxis are relatively expensive but very comfortable. It is best to telephone the booking office (6 77 77 77) or find a taxi rank, although some can be hailed in the street.

BY BICYCLE
Bicycles are the most romantic, the quietest and most practical means of transport once you have mastered the back-pedalling coaster-brake system used on many Dutch

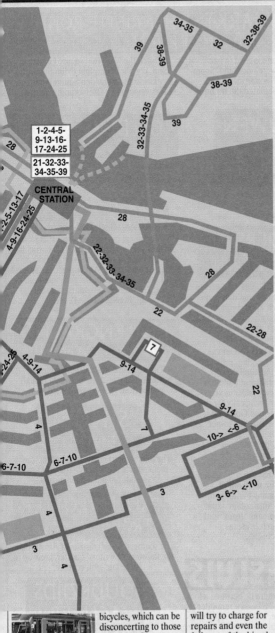

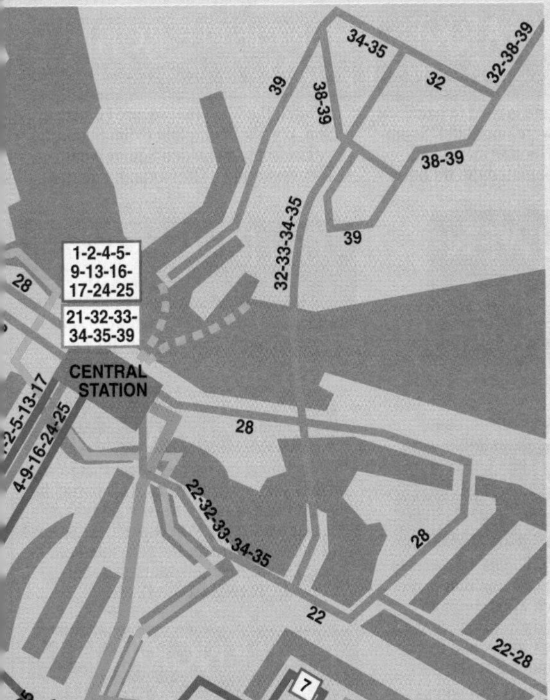

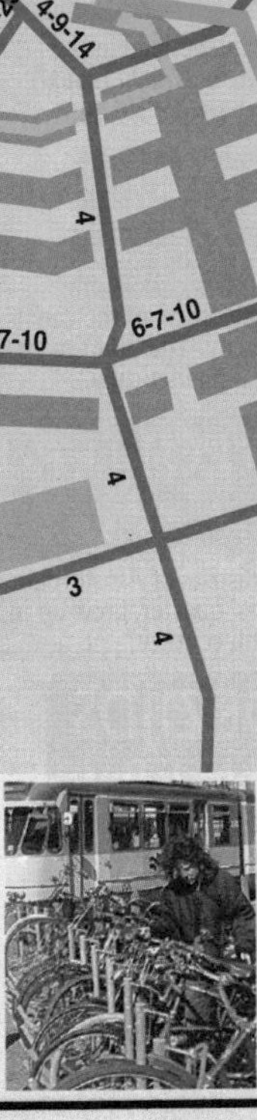

bicycles, which can be disconcerting to those accustomed to handbrakes. They are easy to park and can go anywhere (there is almost no one-way system for bicycles). Beware of the rental companies, as some will try to charge for repairs and even the full cost of the bicycle if it is lost or stolen. This practice is in fact illegal, so refuse to pay and, if necessary, call the police. The De Beurs company in the Dam is recommended as it repairs minor damage free of charge.

– De Beurs
No. 62a Damrak,
Tel. 6 22 32 07.

– Rent-a-Bike
Pieter Jacobsz. dwarsstraat 11,
Tel. 6 25 50 29.

By canal

A regular public service, the Canal Bus, links the Central Station and the

Rijksmuseum with three stops en route, while the Museum Service, which also leaves from Central Station, calls at all Amsterdam's main museums. Tickets are on sale at the tourist office (VVV) ◆ *288, 316*. There are also private companies that operate boat trips on the canals, and their landing stages are mostly to be found opposite the station or near the Rijksmuseum. Pedalos can also be hired near the Rijksmuseum. Children love them.

By ferry:

There is a free ferry service that runs every eight minutes between Central Station and North Amsterdam. It does not take cars, only bicycles and buses.

Cycle routes in the country near Amsterdam are indicated with signs like this.

WESTERMARKT
CENTRUM

Markt means "market" and is used in names of places where markets were once held. Some places, such as the Noordermarkt and Nieuwmarkt, have perpetuated the tradition.

NIEUWEN
DIJK
CENTRUM

Names can sometimes be misleading. The Nieuwendijk (New Dyke) is in fact the oldest dyke in Amsterdam.

ANJELIERS
STRAAT CENTRUM

Carnation Street (*straat*). The narrow streets of the Jordaan district (a name that may come from the French word *jardin*, or garden) are often named after flowers, e.g. the Rosengracht (Rose Canal), and trees, Lindenstraat (Linden Street).

7f
7e
VOOR
7d
ACHTER
7c
VOOR
7b
ACHTER

STREET NUMBERS
This plaque giving the numbers of different buildings may make us yearn nostalgically for the Dutch Golden Age, when each owner had a "personalized" stone sign: the famous cartouches that can still be seen on the front of many buildings in Amsterdam. *Voor* means "front" and *achter* means "back".

BERENSLUIS

What connection can there be between a lock (*sluis*) and bears (*beren*)? *Sluis* is a reminder that the water in Amsterdam's canals is replenished every evening, but what about *beren?* Some things about the city remain a mystery.

HILLETJESBRUG

Hilletjes Bridge (*brug*). There are around one thousand bridges in Amsterdam, many more than in Venice.

HENRIETTE RONNER
PLEIN
DE PIJP

In Dutch the word for "square" is usually *plein*, e.g. the Muntplein (Mint Square), Leidseplein (Leiden Square) and Rembrandtplein (Rembrandt Square).

GELDERSEKADE
CENTRUM

Gelderland quay. The Dutch word *kade* is often pronounced and spelt *kaai.*

EERSTE ANJELIERS
DWARSSTRAAT CENTRUM

A *dwarsstraat* is a narrow street that joins a main street at right-angles. This particular dwarsstraat runs into Anjeliersstraat (Carnation Street). Where there are several of these side streets, they are numbered, e.g. Eerste Anjeliersdwarsstraat (first), Tweede (second), etc.

REALENGRACHT
CENTRUM

This is a canal in Realeneiland in the northwest of Amsterdam. *Gracht* (canal) comes from the verb *graven* (to dig).

SINGEL
(CENTRUM)

The Singel (belt) is the oldest of the canals that encircle the old city. The other main canals fan out alphabetically.

PAULUS POTTER
STRAAT ZUID

The southern (*Zuid*) district of Amsterdam, the fashionable writers' quarter, grew up in the late 19th century.

OUDEZIJDS
ACHTER
BURGWAL
CENTRUM

The *burgwallen* were the first fortifications of Amsterdam. *Oudezijds* means "old district".

Amsterdam is an agglomeration of villages, which now constitute eighteen separate districts, including Jordaan, Nieuwmarkt, Pijp, Bos en Lommer, Osdorp and Geuzenveld. As a result of structured urban planning ● *36*, these districts can be further subdivided into social categories, from working-class districts to more residential garden suburbs. And yet the city has maintained a measure of unity by managing to avoid both over-expansion and over-crowding. With 714,000 inhabitants and a surface area of just under 50,000 acres, there is an average of only 2.1 people per house even though there are two-and-a-half times more single people than families.

THE WIND IN HER SAILS
Amsterdam is a flourishing city. The birth rate is higher than the death rate, more people move into Amsterdam than leave it, and there is more construction than demolition. There is always some renovation or building work going on, wherever you go in the city.

ECONOMY
Amsterdam has gradually become de-industrialized. The metallurgical, ship-building, engineering and manufacturing industries disappeared in the 1960's, and since then Amsterdam has established a reputation as an important business center. The total amount of office space has increased from 873,000 square yards in 1980 to 1,734,200 square yards in 1990.

SOCIAL SYSTEM
Neither wealth nor poverty is excessively obvious in Amsterdam. The city's housing policy (half the accommodation is rented by cooperatives) and the social security system are important contributory factors in this levelling process. However, the number of inhabitants relying on a benefit allowance (currently 10 percent of the population) is continuing to increase. There is 9 percent unemployment, which is twice the national average.

A YOUNG, COSMOPOLITAN CITY
Amsterdam is both a young (half the inhabitants are aged between twenty and twenty-five) and a cosmopolitan city (129 different nationalities live within the city limits). One in every five Amsterdammers is of other than Dutch origin ● *40*.
For example, there are 60,000 Surinamese, 39,000 Moroccans and 28,000 Turks. In Amsterdam's primary schools more than half the children are often from ethnic groups. The city's future will, of necessity, be multicultural ▲ *277*.

A FINANCIAL CAPITAL
Amsterdam is the financial center of the Netherlands. The port of Amsterdam is still extremely active, and in 1992 a total of 4,800 merchant ships docked there to unload grain, ore, hydrocarbons and cars. The main product handled by the port is cocoa, with one-fifth of the world's cocoa production passing through Amsterdam: a reminder of the days of the East India Company ● *30*.

THE CITY'S COAT OF ARMS
The three crosses of St Andrew, the patron saint of fishermen, took on a new meaning after the Second World War when Queen Wilhelmina declared them to be symbols of the city's resolve (*Vastberaden*), heroism (*Heldhaftig*) and mercy (*Barmhartig*). The lions symbolize courage, and the imperial crown was awarded to Amsterdam by the Emperor Maximilian ● *28*.

Amsterdam's long-standing reputation for tolerance is a tradition that is still very much in evidence today. Amsterdammers speak several languages, extend a warm welcome to visitors and are among the most peaceable citizens of Europe. Visitors could not find a better or more pleasant environment in which to walk, visit places of interest, and enjoy the sights and sounds of the city... All you have to do to blend in with the local population is to be relaxed. And tolerance does not just mean access to drugs and prostitution – issues that are all too familiar in the Dutch capital – but the freedom to behave as you please in an atmosphere of mutual respect.

TOURIST INFORMATION
The VVV, or Dutch tourist board, near the station (above) is always busy, whatever the time of day. It is an extremely efficient organization which will even book a hotel room for you. There is a smaller VVV office at Leidsestraat 106. If you want to go to the theater or a concert you will find all the cultural information you need at the AUB Uitburo, a central booking office in the Leidseplein. Magazines such as *What's On, Time Out* and *Uitkrant* ◆ *299* (free) provide information on cinemas, concerts, plays, exhibitions and museums.

DRUGS
Soft drugs such as cannabis are sold in some of Amsterdam's coffeeshops.

PROSTITUTION
The prostitutes in Amsterdam's redlight district, known as the *walletjes,* do not solicit in the street. They sit in windows, lowering the blind when they have a customer. They work in teams to provide a round-the-clock service.

Festivals and processions

	J	F	M	A	M	J	J	A	S	O	N	D
• Commemoration of the dockers' strike against the deportation of the Jews		25										
• Carnival		●										
• Procession of the miracle of the Host			●									
• Blues festival			●									
• Antiques fair			●									
• World Press Photo				●								
• National museum weekend (Reduced or free admission)				●								
• Queen's Day (National holiday)				31								
• Liberation Day					5							
• Kunst Rai (art fair : paintings, sculpture, photographs)					●	●						
• Holland Festival (music, dance, theater)						●						
• Amsterdam marathon (date varies)												
• Concerts on the Prinsengracht								●				
• Uitmark (preview of shows for the coming season)								●				
• Jazz festival								●	●			
• Jordaan festival									●			
• Flower festival									●			
• National Monument Day									●			
• St Nicholas												●

Public holidays:
New Year's Day, Easter Monday, April 30 (Queen's Day, a national holiday), Ascension Day, Whit Monday, Christmas Day, December 26.

Temperature and rainfall

Seasonal variations

There is no ideal time of year to visit Amsterdam. The city is beautiful all year round for different reasons. The mild temperatures and the warm glow of September evenings are particularly pleasant, but there is also something special about the beginning of December, with its invigorating cold and the festive atmosphere of St Nicholas ● *46*.

The main tourist season lasts from April to September with another peak period during the week of Christmas and New Year.

Many exhibitions and tourist attractions are free ◆ *294*, but the cost of visiting Amsterdam can be high, if you stay in one of the luxury hotels. Some restaurants can be expensive but in general they offer excellent quality for the money. Prices are lower in the Indonesian and other "ethnic" restaurants, snack bars and cafés. As far as shopping is concerned, remember that the Dutch have a flair for business and are persuasive salesmen.

CHANGING CURRENCY
This is no problem in Amsterdam, but it is worth checking the exchange rate, as some Bureaux de Change charge extremely high commission. Avoid changing money in hotels, where rates are exorbitant.

THE EXCHANGE RATE
The exchange rate is around 2.50 Fl to the £ sterling and 1.50 Fl to the $ US.

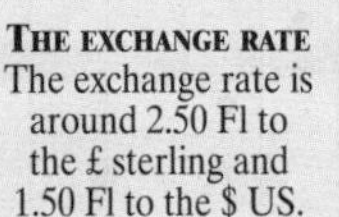

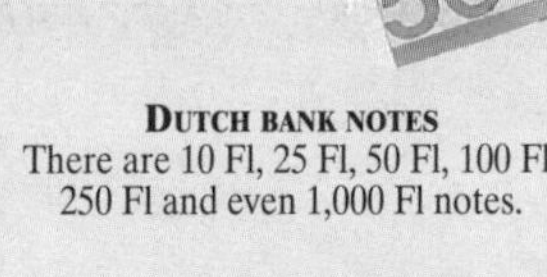

DUTCH BANK NOTES
There are 10 Fl, 25 Fl, 50 Fl, 100 Fl, 250 Fl and even 1,000 Fl notes.

POSTAL SERVICE
The main Amsterdam post office is located at nos. 250–6 Singel. A stamp for EC countries costs 1 Fl. For the US it costs 1 Fl.

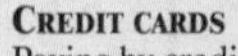

CREDIT CARDS
Paying by credit card gives a better exchange rate, as you do not have to pay commission. Cards can also be used in the automatic cash machines installed in most banks, although the exchange rate is not as favorable. Most hotels and restaurants take credit cards but not all, so do check first.

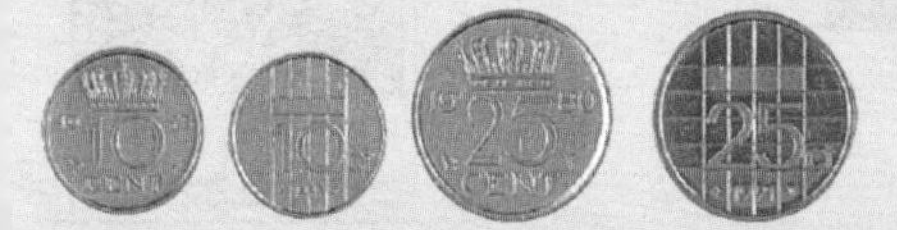

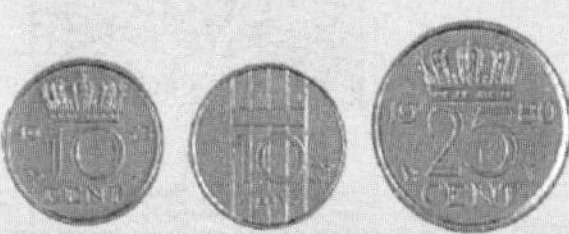

Coins
There are 100 cents to a *gulden* (guilder or florin). Coins come in values of 5, 10 and 25 cents and 1, 2.5 and 5 guilders.

THE COST OF A TELEPHONE CALL
from AMSTERDAM to
England
1.10 Fl/min.
USA
1.70 Fl/min.
Germany
90c./min.
Italy
1.45 Fl/min.
Japan
3.5 Fl/min.
Spain
1.45 Fl/min.
Local calls : 0,25 Guilders/ 5 min.

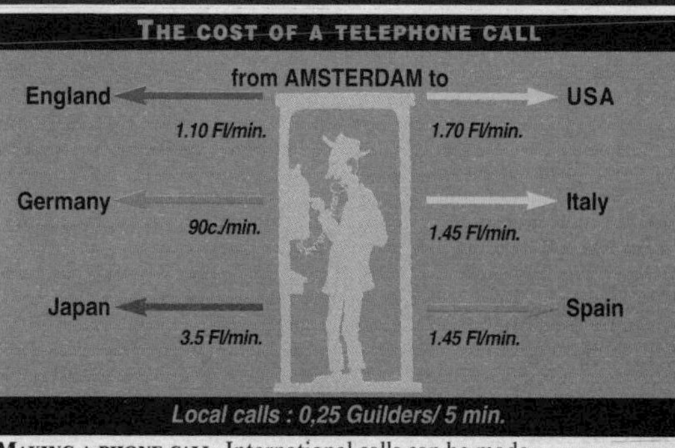

Telephones
Central Amsterdam telephone boxes are almost all for cards, which can be bought from post offices, the Central Station, the VVV and some shops. To make a phone call with coins, go to cafés. There is a telephone center – the Tele Talk Center – at no. 101 Leidsestraat which offers a fax service.

Making a phone call. International calls can be made direct from a telephone box or post office. There is also an operator service (06-0410), particularly for collect charge calls. Calls made from hotels are relatively expensive. To telephone Amsterdam from England, dial 00 + 31 20, followed by the number of the person you are calling. To telephone England from Amsterdam, dial 00 + 44, followed by the number of the person you are calling. From the US to Amsterdam, dial 011 + 31 20 and from Amsterdam to the US dial 00 + 1.

250

ptt telecom
ptt telecom

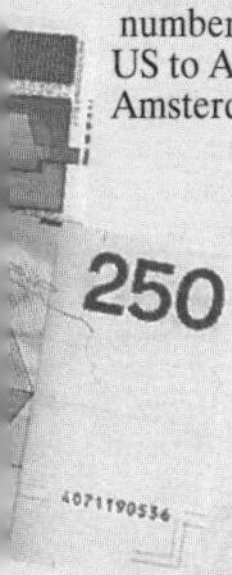

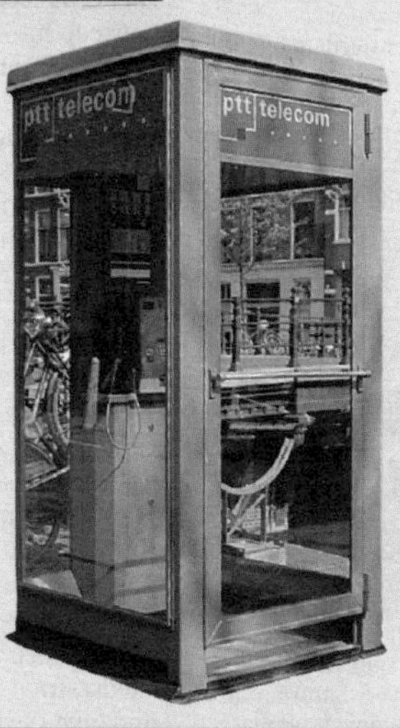

Opening and closing times
Shops in the tourist center of Amsterdam may now be open all day (7am–10pm) including Sunday. Otherwise they open at around 9am (11am on Mondays) and close at around 6pm (5pm on Saturdays). They stay open late on Thursdays and are closed all day Sunday. Restaurants are often closed at lunchtime. Go to cafés for good light lunches. Restaurants serve dinner from around 5pm until 11pm, and tend to close on a Sunday or Monday.

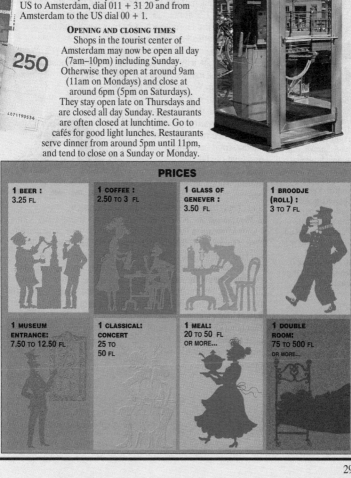

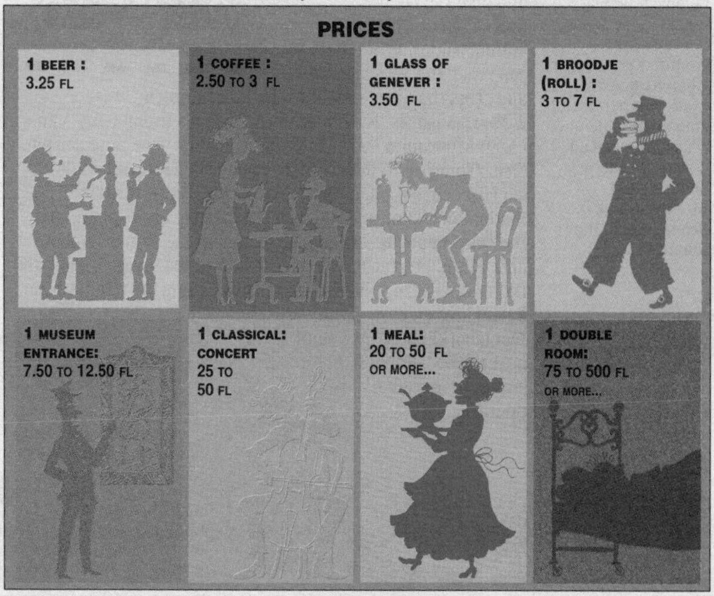

PRICES
1 BEER : 3.25 FL
1 COFFEE : 2.50 TO 3 FL
1 GLASS OF GENEVER : 3.50 FL
1 BROODJE (ROLL) : 3 TO 7 FL
1 MUSEUM ENTRANCE: 7.50 TO 12.50 FL
1 CLASSICAL: CONCERT 25 TO 50 FL
1 MEAL: 20 TO 50 FL OR MORE...
1 DOUBLE ROOM: 75 TO 500 FL OR MORE...

ON THE CANALS:
Why not see Amsterdam by the Canal Bus? You can break the 1½-hour sightseeing trip at any one of the three stopping-off points.

HEALTH-FOOD MARKET:
Every Saturday an organic food market is held in the square in front of the Noorderkerk (North Church) ◆ *325* Musicians perform among the stalls which are weighed down with cheeses and fruit. On Mondays there is a flea market in the square.

WHERE THE TWO CANALS MEET:
The Brouwersgracht (Brewers' canal) ▲ *175*, bordered by warehouses and lined by houseboats ▲ *176*, meets the Prinsengracht (Prince's Canal) ▲ *176* opposite the Noorderkerk.

DAY ONE. 9AM. As you leave Central Station, you can choose between hiring a bicycle or walking. Start your day by visiting the Singel canal★ and the Lutheran Church ▲ *165*. Then retrace your steps and make your way toward the Brouwersgracht, which joins the Prinsengracht in front of the Noorderkerk (North Church) ▲ *239*.

10AM. Why not treat yourself to an apple tart and coffee at the Twee Prinsen on the corner of Prinsenstraat? You are now within easy reach of the Keizersgracht and the "House of Heads" ★ ▲ *173* at no. 123. By walking along the Leliegracht, you can join the Herengracht, where you will find the Bartolotti House ★ ▲ *170* at nos. 170–2.

12 NOON. As you hear the carillon of the Westerkerk (West Church) ▲ *179*, why not visit the Anne Frank House at no. 263 Prinsengracht, followed by lunch at the Het Land van Walem café at no. 449 Keizersgracht ◆ *322* ?

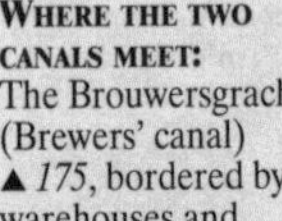

2PM. Back on the Herengracht, make your way toward the Golden Bend ★ ▲ *198* which runs between Leidsestraat and Vijzelstraat and take the Nieuwe Spiegelstraat with its many antique shops. From there you can reach the Weteringschans and cross the Singelgracht to the Museumplein.

2.30PM. Visit the Rijksmuseum▲ *212* and the nearby Van Gogh Museum ▲ *214*. Museums in Amsterdam close at 5pm.

5PM. Going up to the northern end of the Hobbemakade via Hobbemastraat, cross the Wetering Bridge from the Stadhouderskade and discover the evening atmosphere of the Prinsengracht. At the intersection of the Prinsengracht and Reguliersgracht, you have a view of the seven bridges and the wooden Amstelkerk; enjoy a stroll along the river Amstel.

8PM. Have an early dinner at Café Dantzig (kitchen open until 10pm) next to the "Stopera" before going there for ballet or opera.

DAY TWO. Modern art enthusiasts who ran out of time on their first day can take the opportunity to visit the Stedelijk Museum ★ ▲ *214*, ◆ *323* (open from 11am to 5pm).

9AM. Why not start this second day with a trip to the Singel flower market ▲ *187*. Then make your way along the Singel to the lively Spui Square,with its cafés and bookshops ▲ *122,* and from there to the peace and quiet of the Begijnhof ★ ▲ *122*. Leaving the Begijnhof via the Gedempte Begijnensloot, you can visit the "Gallery of the Civic Guard" and the Historical Museum ★ ▲ *123*.

12.30PM. Cross the Kalverstraat and the Rokin and take the next street on the left, the quiet Nes, to the Dam ★, the Royal Palace and the Nieuwekerk (New Church) ▲ *128*. Then follow Raadhuisstraat, crossing the four canals (the Singel, Herengracht, Keizersgracht and Prinsengracht) into the Jordaan district ▲ *235*. Make your way through to the Brouwersgracht, then cross into the Binnenoranjestraat. Bickerseiland is just across the main road.

2PM. Here you can visit the former shipyards and impressive warehouses of the western islands and wander via Prinseneiland and Realeneiland, ending at Zandhoek on the Westerdok ★ ▲ *116*.

3PM. Return via Bickerseiland to the Central Station where a number 22 bus will take you to the Maritime Museum ★ ▲ *270*. Near the station you can see the Schreierstoren (Weepers' Tower) and Sint Nicolaaskerk on Prins Hendrikkade and, further to the east, the strange outline of the Art Deco Scheepvaarthuis ▲ *154*. Follow the Oudezijds Voorburgwal canal to the Amstelkring Museum, with its "clandestine" church ▲ *137*, or, further on, the Oudekerk (Old Church) ▲ *134*, which is famous for its carillon and organ. From there you can return to the Nieuwmarkt ▲ *152* .

4 PM. Visit the Rembrandthuis Museum ★ ▲ *156* in Jodenbreestraat or the Jewish Historical Museum, housed in two former synagogues (the entrance is at no. 3 Nieuwe Amstelstraat) ▲ *158*. After that, take a break at the nearby De Jaren café (formerly a savings bank) in Nieuwe Doelenstraat. In the evening you have a choice between baroque music at the historic English Reformed Church in the Begijnhof, modern jazz at the Bimhuis (no. 73 Oudeschans) or African music at the Melkweg.

THE GALLERY OF THE CIVIC GUARD
This covered alleyway with its collection of paintings of Amsterdam's 17th-century militia, is part of the Historical Museum ▲ *123*. There is a pleasant café where tables are set out in the courtyard in summer.

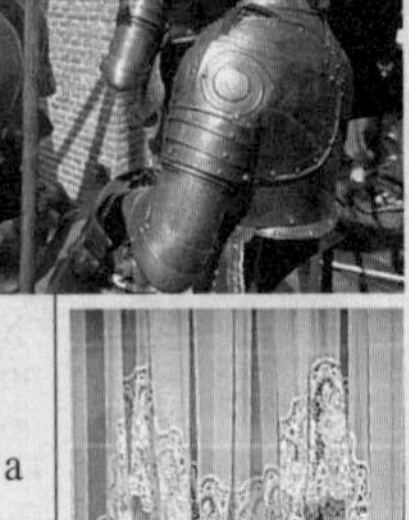

JORDAAN
The Jordaan district is a fascinating maze of narrow streets and canals bordered by shops, houses with attractive net curtains and brown cafés.

Leaving aside its rather expensive hotels, Amsterdam's reputation as one of the least expensive tourist capitals in Europe is well deserved. It goes to such lengths in offering free attractions that tourists can wander through much of the city center without having to pay for anything.

CARILLONS. Regardless of the level of cloud cover over Amsterdam, the pure sound of the city's nine carillons can always be heard loud and clear. The number is a world record, for which the city is indebted to the Hémony brothers, who settled in the Netherlands in 1655 and cast large numbers of bells ▲ *128*. These bells have survived the ravages of time and still strike the hour, as well as fulfilling their primary purpose as musical instruments. Carillon concerts are held at the Westertoren (Westerkerk, on Tuesdays from noon to 1pm) ▲ *179*, the Zuidertoren (Zuiderkerk, on Thursdays from 10 to 11am) ▲ *156*, the Munttoren (on Fridays from noon to 1pm) ▲ *120* and the Oudekerkstoren (on Saturdays from 4 to 5pm) ▲ *134*. The master bell-ringers, who are not without a sense of humor, often play adaptations of the latest popular hits!

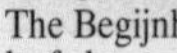

BEGIJNHOF
The Begijnhof is a leafy haven of tranquillity in the old center of Amsterdam. It has been magnificently restored and planted with very old trees. History does not record whether or not the modern inhabitants of this women's retreat are as pious as their predecessors, but the same meditative atmosphere prevails.

FROM HOUSE TO HOUSE. The oldest house in Amsterdam, dating from 1475, is to be found in the BEGIJNHOF (entrance from the Spui). The "NARROWEST HOUSE IN THE WORLD" is not, as proudly stated by the canal-boat guides, the one at no. 7 Singel. Only a yard or so wide when viewed from the canal, this is in fact only the rear entrance to a house which, seen from the front, is of much more ordinary dimensions. By contrast, the house with a bell gable at no. 22 Oude Hoogstraat (between the Dam and Nieuwmarkt) really is tiny, measuring 2½ yards wide by 6½ yards long! Only a stone's throw away, at no. 29 Kloveniersburgwal, is the impressive Trippenhuis ▲ *151*, built in 1660 by two wealthy merchant brothers. It has the longest façade (24 yards) in Amsterdam. It is best seen from the opposite side of the Kloveniersburgwal.

A MUSICAL INTERLUDE. There is a free lunchtime concert every Tuesday at the "Stopera" ▲ *160* (Boekmanzaal), from 12.30 to 1pm, performed by full-time musicians of the Muziektheater (the Netherlands Philharmonic Orchestra and the orchestra of the Netherlands National Ballet). At the same time on Wednesdays (except during the summer), the Concertgebouw opens its luxurious concert rooms to give public rehearsals ▲ *216*. Gregorian vespers are heard at Sint Nicolaaskerk at 5pm on Sundays.

Gardens. Take an after-lunch stroll and explore the garden of the Rijksmuseum at no. 42 Stadhouderskade (open from Tuesdays to Saturdays, 10am to 5pm) and the nearby VONDELPARK (Stadhouderskade). The Vondelpark (named after the Netherlands' most famous poet ▲ *109)* bears some resemblance to New York's Central Park. Its designer, Jan David Zocher, wanted to break with the formal tradition of French gardens by creating large expanses of lawn, broken up by apparently natural clumps of trees and lakes. In the age of the hippies the park became a notorious "campsite", and thirty years later the Vondelpark is still a popular venue, particularly in summer, for open-air concerts and performances.

Unexpected discoveries. Turn right out of the Vondelpark, past the back of the Filmmuseum, and you will find yourself in Vondelstraat. Cross the paved porchway of no. 140 and push open the heavy door. You are now in one of Amsterdam's most underrated and unexpected attractions: the HOLLANDSCHE MANEGE (the Dutch riding school) ▲ *233*, a magnificent building dating from the late 19th century and still in use today. Twenty minutes' walk away you will come across a spectacular example of "street art" and modern museum ideology. Fifteen huge paintings of Amsterdam's 17th-century civic guard hang in a narrow, covered street that runs between the Historical Museum ▲ *123* (at no. 92 Kalverstraat) and the Begijnhof, illustrating at a glance the history of the city's regents and corporations. Although *The Night Watch* is part of the same series, it has been separated from its fellows and is exhibited independently at the Rijksmuseum ▲ *212*.

The garden of the Rijksmuseum: As well as a collection of garden statues, the garden of the Rijksmuseum also contains stone ruins from all over the Netherlands. Collected almost haphazardly since the end of the last century, today they present an overview of almost five centuries of Dutch history.

The Hollandsche Manege: This magnificent example of an urban equestrian center – along the lines of the Spanish Riding School in Vienna – was built in 1882 and is still in use today.

GAMES
If you are a serious chess player, go to the chess café Het Hok (1 Leidsedwarsstraat 134); other chess cafés, some of which also have backgammon, are: De Tuin ◆ *325*, De Jaren ◆ *318*, 't Loosje (Niewmarkt 32), Schutter (Voetboogstraat 13), De Doelen (Kloveniersburgwal 125), De Gaeper (Staalstraat 4), and De Falck (Falckstraat 3). For pool: Dulac ◆ *297*, *317* and 't Loosje.

If we are to believe the doubtful authenticity of popular tradition, the first two inhabitants of Amsterdam in the 13th century could find nothing better to do than to open a café ● *28*. Reliable historical records inform us that the Dutch of the Golden Age were enthusiastic drinkers and committed smokers. They have left their descendants a legacy of "brown" cafés, so called because of the color of their walls, darkened by age and nicotine and further enhanced by the dark wood of the fittings. In these cafés customers can read the newspapers (English ones are widely available) cocooned in comfort, joke with their friends while discussing the issues of the day, or play games (see left). Brown cafés are an ideal place for visitors to meet local inhabitants and experience a typical slice of Amsterdam life in an atmosphere that can only be described as *gezellig*. Since the adjective is virtually impossible to translate, visitors would be best advised to find out for themselves what it means by visiting one of the establishments listed below ● *50*.

BROWN CAFÉS

CAFÉ "HOPPE"(above left)**.** This is the best known and one of the most popular of Amsterdam's brown cafés. So much so that at peak times customers will drink outside on the pavement if necessary (nos 18–20 Spui). ▲ *122*, ◆ *318*.

"CHRIS". The oldest brown café in Amsterdam. Beware if you go to the toilet: the flush is behind the seat (no. 42 Bloemstraat).

"DE DRIE FLESCHJES". Known as a *proeflokaal* (tasting house) ● *50*, where the specialty is hollands gin (juniper flavored gin) drawn from these large old casks (left). It dates from 1650 and has a very warm and friendly atmosphere (no. 18 Gravenstraat) ● *28* ▲ *130* ◆ *318*.

"DE KARPERSHOEK". A "maritime" atmosphere in what must surely once have been a sailors' bar. However, the sand on the floor is definitely a modern addition (no. 2 Martelaarsgracht).

"PAPENEILAND". Formerly part of a coffin-maker's establishment, the café still gives customers the impression that they have stepped out of their previous life and into an animated Dutch painting (no. 2 Prinsengracht) ▲ *176*.

"Wijnand Fockink". The barman will obligingly tell visitors how to drink liqueur from their brimming glasses. And as they lift their heads, they can admire the collection of painted bottles representing Amsterdam's mayors since 1591 (no. 31 Pijlsteeg).

"In de Wildeman". This café seems to have resulted from the unlikely combination of a medieval tavern and a pharmacy. And there are some very good remedies, including 150 different sorts of beer (no. 5 Niewezijds Kolk).

The "new cafés"

In contrast to the cosy warmth of the brown cafés, Amsterdam has recently seen the introduction of cafés with a metallic, high-tech décor. Their interior design is not their only attraction; they also offer a selection of buffets and meals that no one would refuse.

"De Jaren". Famous for its two terraces overlooking the Amstel... as well as for its chocolate cake, sandwiches and salads (nos. 20–2 Nieuwe Doelenstraat) ▲ *160*, ◆ *318*. This building was once a savings bank and latterly offices. Traces of three canal houses can still be discerned here – Rembrandt is said to have lived at the back of one of them.

"Dantzig". Also has a terrace overlooking the Amstel, and boasts the unusual feature of being located directly beneath the committee room of the Amsterdam city council. It is in a modern building that houses both the City Hall and the "Stopera" (opera house). A very chic venue on opening nights (no. 15 Zwanenburgwal) ▲ *160*, ◆ *318*.

"Dulac". This café ◆ *317*, inspired by and named after the French illustrator of the *Arabian Nights*, Edmond du Lac, was formerly a bank and the vault has been converted into a beer cellar with a good pool table (no. 118 Haarlemmerstraat).

"Luxembourg". This is a large café with a rather artificial "Latin Quarter" atmosphere and 1930's-style decoration; it never seems to go out of fashion (nos. 22–4 Spui) ▲ *122*. Customers tend to be young with a large contingent of students and a smattering of publishers.

Bar talk

Café regulars have developed a coded language of which it is essential to have a basic understanding. Beer served (frequently) on draught is (always) served with a head. The depth of the head should be equal to the combined width of the index and middle fingers. Customers who want a small glass of beer should ask for a *kleintje pils* (a little beer). True Amsterdammers rarely drink beer on its own but with a glass of hollands gin, a combination which is either referred to as a *kopstoot* (a blow to the head) or a *stelletje* (duo) ● *64*. Hollands gin (which has several pseudonyms) is served in a glass filled to the brim and it is the customer's lips that must go to the glass and not vice versa. The Dutch equivalent of "cheers" is *proost* ◆ *310*.

THE LEIDSEPLEIN
When night falls, this square, with its neon lights, bars and many outdoor tables, is one of the liveliest in the city.

Amsterdammers tend to eat their evening meals early, at around 6pm. After dinner, the city has a wide range of entertainments on offer to suit everyone, from those interested in intellectual pursuits, music, dance and theater, to those who enjoy gambling, nightclubs and socializing in cafés. The Rembrandtplein ▲ *207* is one of the main centers for the latter kind of nightlife and the café tables around the edge of this square are very popular. The Leidseplein is also popular and some nightclubs are still buzzing as the dawn breaks at 5am.

THEATER. If you love watching the red curtain rise after the lights have gone down, do not assume instantly that the language barrier will prevent you from going to some of the fifty or so theatres and cabaret venues, for they sometimes stage productions in foreign languages.Theater listings can be found posted up in cafés.

CINEMA. Similarly, do not hesitate to go to the movies: films are never dubbed. The three most famous cinemas showing art movies and experimental work are Desmet (no. 4a Plantage Middenlaan), Kriterion (170 Roetersstraat) and Rialto (340 Ceintuurbaan). The Movies (Haarlemmerdijk 161) ◆ *316* and Cinecenter (off Leidseplein) are good for British and American films and the Tuschinski ◆ *321* also shows some of the more popular current movies. The latter is, with the Movies and Desmet, an Art Deco gem worth seeing.The national film archive is housed in the Filmmuseum, in a building at the city center end of the Vondelpark that looks as though it belongs in a seaside resort ▲ *233*. Film listings can be found posted up in cafés and on the outside of the cinemas.

CLASSICAL MUSIC. Does your soul yearn for the classics? Then sink into the velvet seats of the Concertgebouw (no. 98 Van Baerlestraat) ▲ *216*, ◆ *323*; for contemporary music fans, the place to go is De IJsbreker (no. 23 Weesperzijde).

GAMBLING. For those who like to test their luck, or, alternatively, those who feel they have cash to spare, the Casino (no. 64 Max Euweplein), a bright and modern establishment, will prove a popular attraction. It has a total of twenty-five gambling tables, where you can play your choice of French roulette, American roulette, Black Jack, Punto Banco and the Big Wheel (a local specialty), amongst others.

NIGHT-TIME MUSIC
The Concertgebouw is famous for the marvelous accoustics of its main concert hall and for its orchestra. Less well known are the delightful chamber music concerts held in its smaller hall ▲ *216* ◆ *294*. You also have a choice at the Muziektheater (Waterlooplein), where ballets alternate with operas, performed either by the famous resident companies (the Netherlands Opera Company and the Dutch National Ballet) or by guest companies ▲ *160* ◆ *294*.

The Amsterdam Muziektheater
Better known by its nickname the "Stopera", this is a grand modern opera house, built on the banks of the Amstel and opened in 1987.

Cafés-concert. There are innumerable cafés where live music is played to suit every kind of taste. Decibel-lovers can drink their fill in the hard rock enclave formed by the group of cafés on Voorburgwal, near the Dam Nieuwezijds; but many more bars regularly have blues and jazz bands of a wide variety of styles. The main jazz cafés are the Alto (no. 115 Korte Leidsedwarsstraat), Bimhuis (no. 73 Oudeschans), Odeon (no. 460 Singel) ◆ *321*, De Melkweg (no. 234 Lijnbaansgracht), the Bamboobar (no. 115 Lange Leidsedwarsstraat), Het Heerenhuys (no. 114 Herengracht), De Heeren van Aemstel (no. 5 Thorbeckeplein) and De Engelbewaarder (no. 59 Kloveniersburgwal, Sunday 4–7pm only). Fans of the samba, Brazilian music and other Latin American rhythms can have the time of their lives at the Canacao Rio (no. 86 Lange Leidsedwarstraat) or at the Rum Runners (no. 277 Prinsengracht, Sunday afternoons). For a younger audience, the West Pacific Club (Westergasfabriek Westerpark) is a popular bar with loud music and dancing. The Schuim (Spuistraat 189) is young and buzzing as is Seymour Likely (N.Z. Voorburgwal 250).

Discotheques. As in every capital city, it is when the cafés close (1am on weekdays, 2am at weekends) that the discos begin to hot up, throbbing into the small hours of the following morning. The most fashionable and therefore difficult to get into are the notorious IT (Amstelstraat 24) ◆*323* and Roxy (465 Singel) ◆ *321*, Escape (11–15 Rembrandtplein) ◆ *323* and Richter (36 Reguliersdwarsstraat). Its name ("36 on the Richter scale") reflects its décor and the wild and chaotic atmosphere. Try also Odeon (a beautiful patrician house at 460 Singel), Tempel (Herengracht 114) or Mazzo (Rozengracht 114), all of which are popular and good.

Going out
If you want to see a show you need to know what is on, so consult *Uitkrant* (monthly), available free in hotels and cafés. It will tell you what there is to do, and you can then book your ticket at the AUB Ticketshop office on the ground floor of the Stadsschouwburg on the Leidseplein. The office is open from Monday to Saturday 10am to 6pm (tel. 6 21 12 11). *Time Out*, on sale at newsagents, is also very useful.

WATERLOOPLEIN FLEAMARKET
Every weekday you will find a large fleamarket on the Waterlooplein. Clothes, shoes and other secondhand goods are on sale there, including books, records, stamps, furniture and, as is only right in such a place, plenty of charming bric-à-brac. This junk-dealer's paradise is also a haunt of pickpockets. Tourists beware!

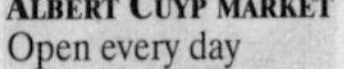

ALBERT CUYP MARKET
Open every day except Sunday, the Albert Cuypmarkt with its 350 multi-colored stalls is like a bazaar and market combined; here you will find literally everything, both good and bad.

You could, as Gabriel Garcia Marquez did, regard Amsterdam as a South American metropolis; but it is not necessary to have the rich imagination of a novelist to set off on an escapist journey through its streets.

SHOPS. The transports of love are catered for at one of the world's few "condom specialists", Het Gulden Vlies (Warmoesstaat). For men and women, scented and fragrance-free, colored or colorless, plain or patterned: did you have any idea that the world of contraceptives was so rich and varied? This unusual shop is almost like any other: it offers a gift-wrapping service, but you cannot try on or exchange the goods. The historic shop of Jacob Hooij ◆ *326* near the Nieuwmarkt (Kloveniersburgwal 12) is the place to go for herb teas and natural remedies. They are sold from ancient jars and drawers. The smell is wonderful.

MUSEUM. The Tropen Museum (no. 2 Linnaeusstraat) ◆ *326* is most illuminating. Housed next door to the Tropical Institute, it is one of the few museums in the developed world to concentrate entirely on developing countries. Particularly interesting are the reconstructed streets of various distant countries, through which the visitor can wander. In the basement the Soeterijn presents theatrical, musical and cinematographic productions from all over the world ▲ *274*.

MARKETS. The enormous and eclectic Albert Cuyp market (Albert Cuypstraat) is open every day except Sunday. The city's oldest flea market (see also the Noordermarkt ▲ *239*, ◆ *292*) is held every day on the Waterlooplein near the "Stopera" ▲ *160*. There is also an art market in 't Spui on Sundays, also in the Thorbeckeplein.

RESTAURANTS... OR SPOILT FOR CHOICE?
Cosmopolitan Amsterdam is varied in its culinary tastes: you can eat here in any language. But why not try Dutch cuisine? It does exist! You will find it at its best at Hollands Glorie (no. 220–1 Kerkstraat) ◆ *322*, De Roode Leeuw (nos. 93–4 Damrak) ◆ *318*, which serves marrowfat peas and champagne, or, better still, at Dorrius (Nieuwezijds Voorburgwal 5) ◆ *316* where you will be served the sort of filling food that Dutch mothers cook. *Eet smakelijk!* (Enjoy your meal!)

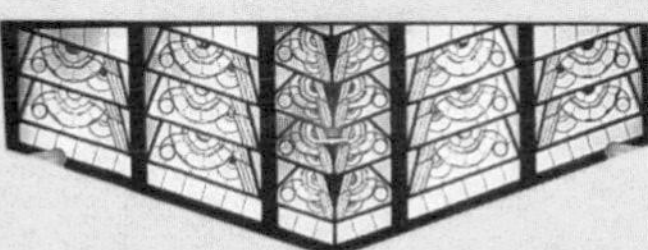

ART DECO SAUNA
Most of its decorative elements used to belong to the large Parisian store Le Bon Marché.

One of the charms of Amsterdam in our own "fin-de-siècle", is that it offers a chance to travel back in time to the early years of the 20th century. Here are some good places for lovers of Art Deco and Art Nouveau to visit.

"AMERICAN" HOTEL. Go straight to the café-restaurant of this establishment. In the company of a budding novelist, a group of earnest young women discussing how to set the world to rights, students and a ballerina, you can eat or just have a drink in an environment with "Jugendstil" stained glass, furniture and sculptures (Leidseplein) ▲ *191,* ◆ *324*.

ATHENEUM BOEKHANDEL & NIEUWSCENTRUM. Explore Amsterdam's main bookshop, which has, among its many other riches, a wide choice of foreign-language books. Its extraordinary newspaper stands are stocked with publications from all over the world. Once you have bought your reading matter, take time to study the splendid Art Nouveau façade, dating from 1904 (nos. 14–16 Spui) ● *54* ▲ *122*.

BARBER SHOP. This superb barber's salon was established in 1934, in what used to be a post office, to the left of the entrance to the Stock Exchange (no. 5 Beursplein).

SAUNA. If you want to sweat it out, why not do it in company and in unusual surroundings? The spirit of the 1920's haunts this sauna, which, unlike its guests, is dressed up to the nines. From the stairway to the wall lamps, the bathrooms to the paneling, and from the tiled floors to the stained glass, "turn of the century" steaming is guaranteed (no. 115 Herengracht).

HAJENIUS. This "smoker's house" has become a proper institution. With its collection of a thousand pipes and cigars from Sumatra, it is known to connoisseurs throughout the world. But it is also a luxurious interior, where the visitor can experience 1,400 square feet of wonderful, guaranteed original Art Deco, from the marbled walls and oak shelves to the bronze light fittings. What is more, even non-smokers will receive the most courteous reception (no. 92 Rokin) ▲ *141*.

TUSCHINSKI. They don't build Art Deco cinemas like this any more (no. 26 Reguliersbreestraat) ▲ *208,* ◆ *321*. Opulent and luxurious, its atmosphere is unique. The Movies and Desmet are also Art Deco gems.

BARBER SHOP
This elaborate barber's salon receives its clients beneath brick arches, designed by Berlage, in a setting worthy of Rudolph Valentino: porcelain and exotic woods, stained-glass windows and seats by Thonel.

TUSCHINSKI
A cinema built in 1921, carpeted from top to bottom, with balconies and the kind of lighting the Great Gatsby or a Hollywood film star might expect to greet his entrance. The perfect setting for a chic "last night" in the city.

THE LANDSCAPE OF HOLLAND
You will see canals, cows, windmills and bright green grass when you visit this part of the Netherlands.

If you come from Ostend or Zeebrugge by car, via Antwerp, you can explore many places of interest on your journey through the Netherlands to Amsterdam. We suggest the following itinerary, with various stops to choose from en route.

"What there is to see in Delft is the loveliest light in all Holland... This clear, moist atmosphere is pure Vermeer."
Paul Claudel

BREDA

HAVERMARKT. The Havermarkt (Hay Market) in the town center has a number of brasseries where you can try a Dutch breakfast consisting of a *broodje* (a soft roll) with a cup of coffee, or an *uitsmijter* (a substantial meal of ham and egg on toast), named after the waiter whose job it is to eject drunks from cafés.
SPANJAARDSGAT. You can walk from the Havermarkt to the SPANJAARDSGAT (Spaniards' Breach), a remnant of the old fortifications. The CASTLE, hidden behind two large towers, was the favorite retreat of William the Silent ● *30*. You can sit in the castle's former grounds, now called the VALKENBERG PARK, and contemplate its BEGIJN convent. The last Begijn in the Netherlands still lives there ▲ *122*.

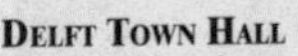

DELFT TOWN HALL
This building dates from 1620 and was designed by Hendrick de Keyser, the famous Amsterdam architect. His style is a mixture of the Baroque and the Renaissance.

NORTH OF DORDRECHT

KINDERDIJK WINDMILLS ★. These windmills are named after the "child's dyke", where in the great flood of 1421, the sea washed up a cradle containing a crying child and a cat. Nineteen windmills can be seen here ● *68*.
ALBLASSERWAARD. To the north of Dordrecht near the Lek, a tributary of the Rhine and a thoroughfare used by barges, lies the Alblasserwaard (*waard*: lowland surrounded by rivers), now enclosed by dykes and transformed into a polder.

ROTTERDAM

The world's largest port, shelled by the Germans in 1940, has today become a city of the future and the gateway to Europe, with its tunnels, motorways and the famous KLEINPOLDERPLEIN INTERCHANGE. In the center, near the STADHUIS (City Hall) and in front of the De Bijenkorf (Beehive) department store further down Coolsingel Canal, you can see Naum Gabo's enormous metal sculpture (1957). At the far end of Leuvehaven stands yet another reminder of the city's martyrdom: Zadkine's monument "To a devastated city" commemorates the horrors of May 14, 1940. But this is a major city: to see all of it properly would require a great deal of time.

BREDA'S MONUMENTS
The Church of Our Lady dates from the 15th century and the town hall was built in the 18th century. Its entrance hall houses a reproduction of *Las Lanzas* (*The Surrender of Breda*, 1635–6) by Velazquez, depicting the war between the Dutch and the Spanish ● *30*.

)utch, The Hague, seat of government, of Parliament and of the monarch's court, is ed 's Gravenhage, often abbreviated to ı Haag. It is a diplomatic center close to sea: a quiet, pleasant, residential city , ted with palaces, parks and squares.

ELFT ★

ırn inland from the Zeeland coast and the vast earthworks the Rhine delta, symbol of mastery over the water, where e anti-storm barrier was opened in 1986, and head for Delft. hy not take a canal trip here? Boats leave from the ijnhaven pier (departures 10.30am to 6pm). Before driving , do a bit of window shopping and have a look at the onderful Delftware, decorated in a range of blues on a white ckground.

HE HAGUE

ou can have tea or dine at the luxury Hôtel des Indes (no. 56 ange Voorhout). You could also eat at SCHEVENINGEN, the ach of The Hague, at the Kurhaus, a magnificent building ting from 1885. Or you may prefer to go on to the pier; e Lobster Pot is at no. 23 Dr Lelykade.

AURITSHUIS ★. The royal picture gallery at no. 8 Korte jverberg, one of the world's most prestigious museums ncluding works by the Flemish School, Rubens, Rembrandt d Vermeer), is housed in a 17th-century residence (open am to 5pm, 11am to 5pm on Sundays and public holidays, osed Mondays and January 1).

UITENHOF. At no. 8 on this square stands the Binnenhof (see low), today used by the parliament.

EIDEN ★

nis town is home to the country's oldest university, where any foreign thinkers studied. Leiden was also a place of fuge for the Huguenots and was the home for many years of e main group of Pilgrims before they sailed to America. ollow the RAPENBERG, the prettiest canal in Leiden: the core the university is in the former church of the Convent of hite Nuns. Not far from there you can visit the glasshouses d Orangery of the botanical gardens.

NDEGEEST CASTLE. Descartes retired to the seclusion of this stately home outside Leiden for a prolonged period.

ROTTERDAM MUSEUM
Of particular interest is the Boyumans-Van Beuningen Museum at nos. 18–20 Museumpark, with its collections of Dutch, Italian and other paintings, from the primitives to contemporary art (including eleven Kandinskys) (open 10am to 5pm, closed Mondays, January 1 and April 30).

The library of Leiden University.

BINNENHOF
In the courtyard of the former palace of the Stadholders and the Estates General at The Hague stands the Knights' Hall (13th century), which looks like a church.

FRANS HALS MUSEUM Since 1913 the works of Frans Hals have been displayed in a former old people's home built in 1608 by the architect Lieven de Key. Its façade consists of a series of low houses surmounted by windows set in step gables. It is typical of the Dutch houses whose images have been passed down to us by Vermeer and de Hooch ▲ *225*. The floor of black and white marble flags, the mullioned windows, the pewter and silverware give the interior a particular charm.

Haarlem is about 12½ miles west of Amsterdam on the river Spaarne, close to the North Sea. The city was founded in the 10th century and grew very prosperous in the 15th to 17th centuries due to the manufacture of linen and the cultivation of flowers from bulbs ■ *24*.

GETTING TO HAARLEM FROM AMSTERDAM

Leave Amsterdam by the Haarlem Gate (Haarlemmerpoort) ▲ *251* and take the Haarlemmerweg (Haarlem Road). Or take one of the very frequent trains; the journey lasts about ten minutes.

HALFWEG. This point halfway between the two cities is the site of the locks separating the polders of the former Haarlem lake from the North Sea Canal.

HAARLEM ★

AMSTERDAM GATE. This 15th-century building has pepper-pot towers and a massive keep. Start your walk through the city at the station, a monument to the Art Nouveau style.

FRANS HALS MUSEUM ★. Haarlem was the meeting-place for artists such as Jacob van Ruysdael ▲ *222*, Pieter Saenredam ▲ *129* and Frans Hals ▲ *224*. The work of Frans Hals, the 17th-century master of Dutch painting, remains vibrant, as you can see from his eight paintings of the civic guards and regents. The entire collection is remarkable (no. 62 Groot Heiliglang, open 11am to 5pm, 1 to 5pm Sundays and public holidays, closed January 1 and December 25).

GROTE MARKT ★. On the Great Market square, an excellent place to stop and eat, stands the STATUE OF LAURENS COSTER (15th century), regarded in the Netherlands as the inventor of printing, ten years before Gutenberg. Also worth seeing are the 14th-century STADHUIS (City Hall) and the VLEESHAL (Meat Market), an example of Dutch Renaissance architecture built by Lieven de Key (17th century).

TEYLER MUSEUM ★. Not far away, at no. 16 Spaarne, the Teyler Museum, the oldest in the Netherlands (1778), is devoted to the arts and sciences (open 10am to 5pm, 1 to 5pm Sundays and public holidays, closed January 1 and December 25). Here you can see many old machines, including one of the first to run on electricity. Try not to miss it. The WAAG (Public Weighing House) at the corner of Damstraat, built in 1598, is worth a detour.

THE GREAT CHURCH Saint Bavo's (15th century) on the square of the Great Market is the jewel of Haarlem: it is said that both Handel and Mozart played its famous organs, built in 1738 by Christian Müller and decorated by Daniel Marot.

Right, statue of Laurens Coster.

AROUND HAARLEM

TULIP-MANIA. The 17th century witnessed great prosperity in Haarlem as a result of the cultivation of flowering plants from bulbs: the tulip was brought from Asia Minor and became an object of financial speculation, contributing to the enrichment of the entire region ■ *24* ▲ *187*. The road to Hillegom,

These two cartouches decorate the façade of the house at no. 63 Jansenstraat.

20 September
1839
1939
Aangeboden door den Bond van Gepensioneerden bij de Ned. Spoor-en Tramwegen.
Tergelegenheid van het 100 Jarig bestaan der Spoorwegen.
Zenith Gouda

en the road to Lisse, will take you to the TULIPSHOW north Vogelenzang (open Good Friday to end May, 8am to 6pm, d from July to September, 9am to 5pm), and then to the EUKENHOF gardens ★, home of bulbs (open from end March end May, 8am to 6.30pm).

RUQUIUS MUSEUM ★. On the way back to Haarlem you can sit this museum established in 1849 on the edge of the rmer Haarlem lake in the first pumphouse used to ain the lake in the early 19th century. This useum documents the development of technology r controlling water, including the creation of the olders, barriers and dykes, and has a moving model pen 10am to 5pm high season, 11am to 5pm ındays and public holidays, 10am to 4pm low ason, 11am to 4pm Sundays and public holidays).

PAARNDAM. You can try the taste of smoked eel washed down ith good beer in this picturesque village, surrounded by a ke in which several locks are set. Don't miss the statue of ANS BRINKER: this little boy is said to have saved the town om flooding by spending an entire night plugging a crack at had appeared in the dyke with his finger!

HE NORTH SEA

ANDVOORT. This seaside resort is very popular, particularly ith Amsterdammers ■ *22*. The village is rather dull but the ach is wide and very good for walks. Until 1985 the etherlands Formula One Grand Prix was held here; the rcuit in the dunes can be seen from the beach.

LOEMENDAAL. The dunes road leads to this village, where u can go for a long walk in the national park, De ennemerduinen, open from sunrise to sunset.

MUIDEN. This town at the end of the North Sea Canal ▲ *254* famous for its three locks, the most recent of which is over 300 feet long and over 130 feet wide. IJmuiden is Western urope's largest fishing port: take advantage of the fact and ve a fish dinner in one of the quayside restaurants before turning to Amsterdam, 12½ miles away.

HAARLEM STATION
Whether waiting for a train, or just for the sheer pleasure of it, stay long enough in this station to look at, among other things, the superb First,

Second and Third Class waiting rooms and the tobacconists', all in the Art Nouveau style.

THE TSAR'S CABIN
Peter the Great stayed at Zaandam in 1697. His wooden house is at no. 23 Krimp (open 10am to 5pm, 1 to 5pm Saturdays and Sundays, closed January 1, December 25 and 26).

To the north of Amsterdam lies North Holland ▲ *12*, a strip of land bounded to the west by the North Sea and to the east by the former Zuiderzee, which became the IJsselmeer when it was enclosed by a dyke.

ZAAN REGION ● 6

ZAANDAM. On the central square you can see the statue of PETER THE GREAT ▲ *272*, opposite the Apollo Theater.
KOOG AAN DE ZAAN. There is a Windmill Museum at no. 18 Museumlaan (open 10am to 5pm, 2 to 5pm Saturdays, Sundays and public holidays, closed Mondays, January 1 and December 25) ● *68*.
ZAANDIJK. Here you will find the Zaan region's museum of antiquities (open 10am to noon and 2 to 4pm, closed Saturdays and Sunday mornings, Mondays, January 1, Easter Sunday and December 25). To the south is De Dood (Death), a 17th-century flour mill that can be visited on the third Saturday of the month in summer from 2 to 5pm.

ZAANSE SCHANS ★. Zaanse Schans (the Zaan Fortifications) is a kind of ecological museum on the Kalverringdijk. It is an inhabited village with working windmills. The 17th- and 18th-century houses, all from the local area, were restored on site around 1950. There are many shops and windmills to visit, although their opening times have unfortunately not been standardize (most are open between 9am and 5pm). They include a clog factory (*klompenmakerij*) ● *64*, a bakery museum (*bakkerijmuseum*), the Catharina Hobve cheese factory (*kaasmakerij*), tea house (*theekoepel*), clock museum (*uurwerkenmuseum*), the Albert Heijn grocery (Kruidenierswinkel), the North House (Het Noorderhuis), a windmill for grinding pigments called De Kat (The Cat), a windmill for grinding all kinds of grain called De Zoeker (Th Seeker) and, south of the village, an oil-pressing windmill called De Ooievaar (The Stork). The first windmill, a sawmi was built on the magnificent Kalverringdijk (boat trips 10am to 5pm in summer) in 1592 by Cornelis Corneliszoon. The mills soon multiplied, until there were more than five hundred in the region.

MARKEN
It is best to view this town, which has retained its original character, by walking through it.

FROM MONNICKENDAM TO ENKHUIZEN

MONNICKENDAM. The town center is dominated by the SPEELTOREN, tower of the former town hall bui in 1591. It has a chiming clock with moving figures.
MARKEN ★. Until 1957 Marken was an island, and before the Zuiderzee was enclosed with a dyke in the 1930's, it was often battered by storms. Fishermen sailed from the island out to the North Atlantic. Today it is linked the Waterland by a dyke.
VOLENDAM ★. This is one of the most popular of the old

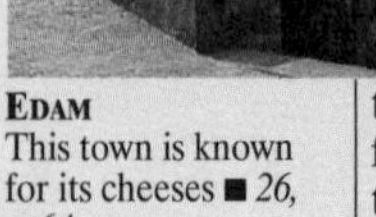

EDAM
This town is known for its cheeses ■ *26*, ● *64*.

HUIZEN. There are boat trips from this ner major fishing port to Urk, Stavoren Medemblik. Tickets can be obtained 1 Rederij Naco, at no. 9 Tramplein. On quayside of the old port, called the Dijk, can read the words: "Happiness is better 1 wealth". At the entrance to the port stands the Drommedaris, an enormous 16th-century tower with a splendid set of chimes. The terrace is open to visitors (10am to midnight in the high season, noon to midnight low season), as is the weapons museum (open 2 to 5pm in summer, closed Saturdays).

iiderzee ports. Here, as at Marken, traditional dress is still rn.

AM ★. In the center of Edam is the TOWN SQUARE with its bled houses and a small MUSEUM at no. 8 Damplein (open 10am to 4.30pm high season, 2 to 4.30pm on Sundays). Also worth seeing are the KAASMARKT (the old Cheese Market) and the 15th-century SAINT NICHOLAS'S CHURCH (open 2 to 4.30pm).

HOORN. The tourist train that runs between Hoorn and Medemblik is a kind of museum on wheels (two departures per day from May to mid-September, except Mondays).

ENKHUIZEN. The wonderful ZUIDERZEE MUSEUM ★ at no. 18 Wierdijk can be reached by ferry from the station. A living iseum in the form of a large village, it traces the history of e area. There are houses to visit, gardens to explore, and monstrations of traditional skills such as fish-smoking and pe-making. Children can spend the day wearing Dutch stume (open 10am to 5pm high season).

EW POLDERS ★

e Houtribdijk dyke provides access to Lelystad, which is in e IJsselmeer.

LYSTAD. Lelystad is a new town and the capital of evoland, a brand new province created entirely on three cently constructed polders. East Flevoland was surrounded a dyke and drained between 1950 and 1957. Since 1960 the wns of Lelystad, Dronten, Swifterbat and Biddinghuizen ve sprung up from the ground on stilts. Lelystad kes its name from the engineer Lely, who drew up e plan for draining the Zuiderzee ▲ *192*. Here u can see the MUSEUM, which tells the epic story the polders (open 10am to 5pm high ason, 1 to 5pm low season, Sundays and blic holidays, closed Saturdays, January 1 and ecember 25) and, to the south of the town, the *ehond* (Seal), a wrecked boat over 75 feet ng, dating from 1878.

OSTVAARDERSPLASSEN NATURE RESERVE. eading toward Amsterdam from Lelystad, u will cross this reserve, which ovides sanctuary for many kinds of rds ■ *20*.

MERE. The architecture of this town the Gooimeer lake is modern and usual. To return to Holland you must oss the HOLLANDSEBRUG (Holland idge). Of the five polders planned the IJsselmeer development, four ve already been established, mprising over 555,000 acres of ained land.

The arms of Edam. A canal with boats at Monnickendam (left).

HOORN STORIES
It was at Hoorn that the first herring net was woven and Cape Horn owes its name to the sailor Schouten (1580–1625), born in this town, who was the first to round the Cape with J. Lemaire (1585–1616). In Hoorn you can visit the Museum of West Fries (Westfries museum) at no. 1 Rodę Steen (open 11am to 5pm, 2 to 5pm Saturdays, Sundays and public holidays, closed January 1 and December 25) and the Waag (public weighhouse), a magnificent building in blue stone dating from1609.

ZAANSE SCHANS
Several perfectly maintained windmills are open to the public.

THE VECHT VALLEY
The Vecht river used to be an important shipping route. Since 1952 this role has been taken over by the Amsterdam-Rijnkanaal (canal from the Rhine to Amsterdam). A road runs alongside this now peaceful, winding river, which is lined with opulent villas and small country residences surrounded by magnificent grounds. Fine properties ★ overlooking the river can be seen all along the Vecht. Many of these country houses were built in the Golden Age of the 17th century for Amsterdam's rich merchants, who went there to get away from it all. The most beautiful section of the river must be that between Loenen and Breukelen, the town that gave its name to the New York district of Brooklyn. After Breukelen there are three interesting stately homes: Nijenrode, Haar and Zuylen.

NIJENRODE CASTLE
A 17th-century building now converted into a college for business studies.

HAAR CASTLE
This mansion was built at Haarzuilens in the 14th century (open March 1 to August 15, and October 15 to November 15, 11am to 4pm, 1 to 4pm Sundays).

You can explore the area southeast of Amsterdam with thi itinerary. Leave the capital by the road to Diemen and continue to Muiden, a port on the edge of the new polders.

MUIDEN

The CASTLE (Muiderslot) is an old brick fortress (no. 1 Heren gracht, open 10am to 4pm high season, 1 to 4pm Sundays and public holidays, 10am to 3pm low season, closed Saturdays, January 1 and December 25 and 26) built in 1205 to defend the Vecht estuary. Count Floris V of Holland was murdered there in 1296 because his policies were unpopular. In the 17th century the castle housed the Muider-kring, a group of scientists led by P.C. Hooft ▲ *186*, and was visited by Vondel ● *109* and Constantijn Huygens.

THE VECHT VALLEY ● 6

LOENEN. As you arrive, you will glimpse a tall windmill with a balustrade called De Hoop (Hope) ● *68*. The pretty houses are covered with flowers, and you ca have a good *koffie* (coffee) with *spritsen* (shortbread) or *poffertjes* (like tiny, light doughnuts).
LOOSDRECHT MERES ★. Next you will see the Loosdrecht meres, which cover about 6,000 acres of old peat bog. There are several yachting marinas in the meres, which are a paradise for watersports fans. You can also visit Nieuw-Loosdrec with its CASTLE, now converted into a museum, and Oud-Loosdrecht, the region's main tourist center.

UTRECHT ★

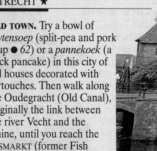

OLD TOWN. Try a bowl of *erwtensoep* (split-pea and pork soup ● *62*) or a *pannekoek* (a thick pancake) in this city of old houses decorated with cartouches. Then walk along the Oudegracht (Old Canal), originally the link between the river Vecht and the Rhine, until you reach the VISMARKT (former Fish Market). From here you can see the 17th-century

UYLEN CASTLE ★ Slot Zuylen was the residence of elle van Zuylen, alias Isabelle de Charrière 740–1805), a well-known writer who was a friend of adame de Staël, Benjamin Constant and James oswell. (Guided tours at 10am, 11am, 2pm, 3pm d 4pm. Low season, Saturdays and Sundays at m, 2pm and 3pm)

omtoren, or Cathedral Tower (open 10am to 5pm high eason, noon to 5pm low season, Saturdays, Sundays and ublic holidays), and the Domkerk (former cathedral). etween 8.30am and 5pm visit the 19th-century IJKSUNIVERSITEIT (university), with its cloister, and the ational Museum "From Musical Clock to Street Organ" o. 10 Buukerkhof, open 10am to 5pm, 1 to 5pm on Sundays, osed Mondays and public holidays). Walk along the ieuwegracht with its elegant houses to the 11th-century aint Peter's Church, the Janskerkhof (Gothic church of Saint ohn) and Pieter d'Hont's statue of Anne Frank ▲ *180*.

USEUMS. Choose between the CENTRAL MUSEUM (no. 1 gnietenstraat, open 10am to 5pm, 2 to 5pm Sundays and ublic holidays, closed Mondays, January 1 and December 5), HET CATHARIJNECONVENT MUSEUM (no. 63 ieuwegracht, open 10am to 5pm, 11am to 5pm Saturdays, undays and public holidays, closed Mondays and January 1), nd the University Museum (no. 166 Bilstraat, open 10am to om, 1 to 5pm Sundays, closed Mondays and public holidays).

MERSFOORT ★

his medieval city east of Utrecht is the birthplace of Johan an Oldenbarnevelt (1547–1619), founder of the Dutch East ndia Company in 1602 ▲ *150*, and of the painter Piet Mondriaan (1872–1944) ▲ *228*.

N THE WAY BACK TO AMSTERDAM

AREN. The Singer Museum at no. 1 Oude Drift houses 19th-entury paintings and sculptures (including works by Courbet, antin-Latour and Rodin), and a collection of Chinese art open 11am to 5pm, noon to 5pm Sundays, closed public olidays).

AARDEN ★. This town was covered by floodwater in the 12th entury. You can see its complex system of fortifications in e shape of a twelve-pointed star with six bastions, built in e 17th century and surrounded y marshes.

AMERSFOORT
Amersfoort, with its many monuments, is surrounded by ramparts into which *Muurhuizen* (wall houses) are set. A surprising feature is De Amersfoortse Kei, a boulder weighing nine tons standing upright on one of the lawns. The Onze Lieve Vrouwe Toren (Our Lady

Tower) dates from the 15th century. The Sint-Joriskerk (Saint George's Church) is in the Romanesque style. Groenmarkt and the Koppelpoort, with a fortified bridge and grinding mill, date from the Middle Ages.

◆ Useful words and phrases

A few hints on pronunciation:

aa, oo, uu, ee: long vowels, e.g. zee (as in gate), jaar (as in cart)
oe: always pronounced as in "soon", e.g. toerist (tourist)
ij, ei: as in "fine", e.g. dijk (dyke)
ou, au: as in "how", e.g. oud pronounced "out"
ui: pronounced "ow"
ie: "i" is always long, e.g. vier pronounced "fear"
j: pronounced "y", e.g. jaar (yar)
g: in the throat like the Scottish "ch" in loch, e.g. goed (ghoot)
ch: also hard, in the throat, e.g. Maastricht
w: pronounced "v"
v: pronounced "f"

For practical reasons, the order of the words and phrases below(English–Dutch) is reversed when you are more likely to come across the word in writing.

Common phrases

YES: ja
NO: nee
PLEASE: alstublieft
A.u.b.: PLEASE
THANK YOU: dank u
EXCUSE ME: pardon
GOOD MORNING: goedemorgen
GOOD EVENING: goedenavond
GOODBYE: dag
TODAY: vandaag
TOMORROW: morgen
YESTERDAY: gisteren
verboden: FORBIDDEN
gevaar: DANGER
I AM ENGLISH/ AMERICAN: ik ben engels/americaans
I DON'T UNDERSTAND: ik versta u niet
DO YOU SPEAK ENGLISH? Spreekt u engels?
CAN YOU HELP ME? kunt u me helpen?
Inlichting: INFORMATION

The days of the week

maandag: MONDAY
dinsdag: TUESDAY
woensdag: WEDNESDAY
donderdag: THURSDAY
vrijdag: FRIDAY
zaterdag: SATURDAY
zondag: SUNDAY

Numbers

ONE: een
TWO: twee
THREE: drie
FOUR: vier
FIVE: vijf
SIX: zes
SEVEN: zeven
EIGHT: acht
NINE: negen
TEN: tien

Hotels, cafés, restaurants

HOTEL: hotel
RESTAURANT: restaurant, eethuisje
CAFÉ/BAR: koffeehuis
BROWN CAFÉ (BAR): kroeg, bruincafé
Coffeeshop: CAFÉ/SNACK BAR. NO ALCOHOLIC DRINKS. SOFT DRUGS SOMETIMES AUTHORIZED
ROOM: kamer
KEY: sleutel
SHEET: laken
BLANKET: deken
BATHROOM: badkamer
WC: toilet
BREAKFAST: ontbijt
LUNCH: lunch
DINNER: diner
MENU: menu, kaart
BREAD: brood
ROLL: broodje
Uitsmijter: HAM AND EGGS ON BREAD (SUBSTANTIAL)
Dagschotel: DISH OF THE DAY
HERRING: haring
MUSSEL: mossel
CHEESE: kaas
SALAD: sla
VEGETABLE: groente
FRUIT: fruit
Appelgeback: APPLE TART
Pannekoek: PANCAKE
ICE CREAM: ijs
Rijsttafel:SPECIALTY OF INDONESIA
WATER: water
HOT CHOCOLATE: warme chocolade
COFFEE: koffie
TEA: thee
WITH/WITHOUT MILK/SUGAR: met/zonder melk/suiker
LAGER: pilsje
ALE: (donker) bier
WINE: wijn
RED WINE: rode wijn
ROSE WINE: rosé wijn
WHITE WINE: witte wijn
GIN: jenever
GLASS: glas
CARAFE: karaf
BOTTLE: fles
WAITER: ober
MAY I HAVE THE BILL PLEASE? Mag ik de rekening, alstublieft?
BILL: rekening
THE TOILETS? het toilet?

Getting around

WHERE IS...? waar is...?
IS IT NEAR? is het dichtbij?
IS IT FAR? is het ver weg?
LEFT: links
RIGHT: rechts
TURN LEFT/RIGHT: liksaf/rechtsaf
STRAIGHT ON: rechtdoor
SOUTH: zuid
NORTH: nord
WEST: west
EAST: oost

Travel

Vertrek: DEPARTURE
Aankomst: ARRIVAL
Vertraging: DELAY
TRAVEL AGENT: Reisbureau
PLANE: vliegtuig
AIRPORT: luchthaven
BOAT: schip
PORT: haven
Rederij: SHIPPING COMPANY
TRAIN: trein
STATION: station
Perron: PLATFORM
Spoor: PLATFORM
LEFT LUGGAGE: bagagedepot
PETROL/GAS STATION: benzinestation

Visiting the city

BOAT TRIP: rondvaart
VISIT: bezoek
OPEN: open
CLOSED: gesloten
Ingang: ENTRANCE
Uit(gang): EXIT
TICKET OFFICE: loke
TICKET: kaartje
TOWN: stad
DISTRICT: stadswijk
HOUSE: huis
GARDEN: tuin
ZOO: dierentuin
WINDMILL: molen
CHURCH: kerk
WAREHOUSE: pakhu
THEATER: schouwburg
CINEMA/MOVIE THEATER: bioscoop
MUSEUM: museum
EXHIBITION: tentoonstelling
ART GALLERY: kunstgalerij
TOURIST OFFICE: V.V.V.
CUSTOMS OFFICE: douanekantoor
POLICE: politie
POST OFFICE: postkantoor
POSTAGE STAMP: postzegel
HOSPITAL: ziekenhui

Shopping

BUREAU DE CHANGE wisselkantoor
FOR HIRE: te huur
FOR SALE: te koop
GULDEN: florin/guilder
PRICE: prijs
HOW MUCH IS IT? wat kost dit?
EXPENSIVE: duur
CHEAP: goedkoop
Uitverkoop: SALE
MARKET: markt
BAKER: bakker
PATISSERIE: banketbakkerij
GROCER: kruidenier
BUTCHER: slager
DELICATESSEN: delicatessenzaak
CHEMIST: apotheek
FLORIST: bloemist
FILM PROCESSING: fotozaak
TOBACCONIST: tabakswinkel
NEWSPAPER KIOSK: krantenkiosk
NEWSPAPER: krant
BOOKSHOP: boekhandel
ANTIQUE DEALER: antiekzaak
JEWELER: juwelier

USEFUL ADDRESSES

- VIEWPOINT
- ISOLATED
- LUXURY RESTAURANT
- MODERATE RESTAURANT
- BUDGET RESTAURANT
- LUXURY HOTEL
- MODERATE HOTEL
- BUDGET HOTEL
- CAR PARK
- SUPERVISED GARAGE
- TELEVISION
- QUIET
- SWIMMING POOL
- CREDIT CARDS
- REDUCTION FOR CHILDREN
- NO ANIMALS
- MUSIC
- LIVE BAND

NOTE:
MANY HOTELS IN AMSTERDAM ARE THREE OR FOUR STORIES TALL AND MOST DO NOT HAVE ELEVATORS. ENQUIRE IN ADVANCE IF THIS IS A PROBLEM.

◆ Budget
◆◆ Typical
◆◆◆ Luxury

	PAGE	WITH CAFÉ	VIEW	GARDEN - TERRACE	PRIVATE DINING ROOM	BREAKFAST	CREDIT CARDS	OPEN AFTER 11PM	SPECIALTIES	PRICES
CITY CENTER WEST										
CAFÉ ESPRIT	316	●	●	●			●		M	◆◆
CAFÉ LUXEMBOURG	316	●	●				●		M	◆◆
CRIGNON CULINAIRE	316				●				FR	◆◆
D'VIJFF VLIEGEN	316		●	●	●		●		M	◆◆◆
DE KEUKEN VAN 1870	316						●		N	◆
DE SILVEREN SPIEGEL	316		●		●				N FR	◆
DORRIUS	317						●		N	◆◆◆
DULAC	317	●							M	◆◆
KANTJIL	317		●	●			●		F-E	◆◆
1E KLAS	317	●	●		●	●	●		M	◆◆
LE PETIT LAPIN	317						●		FR	◆◆
LIEVE	317				●				M	◆
LUCIUS	317						●		F	◆
LUDEN	317		●	●			●	●	FR	◆◆
MARAKECH	317		●				●		M	◆
THE ASIAN CARIBBEAN	317		●				●		F-E	◆◆
VASSO	317		●	●			●		I	◆◆
CITY CENTER EAST										
ATRIUM	318		●	●	●				M	◆
CAFÉ BERN	318	●						●	M	◆
CAFÉ DE JAREN	318	●	●	●		●			M	◆◆
DANTZIG	318	●	●	●					M	◆◆
DE SLUYSWACHT	319	●	●	●	●		●		M	◆◆
EXCELSIOR	319		●	●	●		●		FR	◆◆
FRASCATI	319	●							M	◆
KAPITEIN ZEPPOS	319			●			●		M	◆
ORIENTAL CITY	319		●				●		F-E	◆◆
NORTHERN CANALS										
LE TOUT COURT	320						●	●	FR	◆◆
CAFÉ DE PRINS	320	●	●						FR	◆
CHRISTOPHE'	320		●				●		FR	◆◆
D'THEEBOOM	320						●		FR	◆◆
DE GOUDSBLOEM	320			●			●		FR	◆◆
MR. PANCAKE	320		●						FR	◆◆
RUM RUNNERS	320			●						◆◆
ZUID ZEELAND	320		●	●			●		M	◆◆
SOUTHERN CANALS										
CAFÉ HET MOLENPAD	321	●	●	●					M	◆◆
CALZONE	321		●	●	●		●	●	I	◆
DYNASTY	322			●	●				F-E	◆◆

: Fish N: National
-E: Far Eastern M: Modern
R: French T: Tourist
Italian V: Vegetarian
: Local Y: Young

	PAGE	ALSO CAFÉ	VIEW	GARDEN - TERRACE	PRIVATE DINING ROOM	BREAKFAST	CREDIT CARDS	OPEN AFTER 11PM	SPECIALTIES	PRICES
RROLTRUMPIE	322								N	◆
ET TUYNHUYS	322			●			●		M	◆◆◆
OLLANDS GLORIE	322						●		N	◆
ORT	322		●	●			●	●	M	◆◆◆
ETZ	322	●	●				●		M	◆◆
RINSENKELDER	322			●	●		●	●	I FR	◆◆◆
OSES'S CANTINA	322			●	●		●	●		◆◆
LUIZER	322				●		●		F	◆◆
AN PUFFELEN	322	●	●	●	●		●		FR	◆◆
ALLEN	322	●	●	●	●	●	●		M	◆◆
USEUMS										
ARTHOLDY	323		●	●	●		●		M	◆◆◆
ODEGA DE KEYZER	323	●	●	●	●		●	●	FR	◆◆◆
RASSERIE LA TOSCA	323			●			●		I	◆
RASSERIE MAXIE'S	323	●		●			●		M	◆
E BLAUWE HOLLANDER	323								N	◆
E KNIJP	324						●	●		◆◆
E OESTERBAR	324						●		F	◆◆
E SMOESHAAN	324	●		●			●		M	◆◆
ANGERIE	324				●		●		FR	◆◆◆
IRAFIORI	324		●				●		I	◆◆◆
AMA SEBO	324						●		F-E	◆
ORDAAN										
OLHOED	325			●	●				V	◆◆
AFÉ DE TUIN	325			●		●	●			◆
E GROENE LANTAARN	325						●		FR	◆◆
E KIKKER	325			●	●	●	●		FR	◆◆◆
ET STUIVERTJE	325			●	●		●		FR	◆◆
OTELSCHOOL AMST.	325						●		FR	◆
ORREINEN	325			●	●		●		FR	◆
ANGO BAY	325								F-E	◆◆
PECIAAL	325						●		V F-E	◆◆
OSCANINI	326								I	◆◆
LD PORT WEST										
GOUDEN REAEL	326		●	●			●		FR	◆◆
LANTAGE										
E IJSBREKER	326	●	●	●					M	◆◆
AMAN SARI	326								F-E	◆◆

◆ CHOOSING A HOTEL

◆ < 150 Fl
◆◆ 160 to 265 Fl
◆◆◆ > 275 Fl

	PAGE	GARDEN - TERRACE	TV IN BEDROOM	SEMINAR ROOMS	QUIET	VIEW	RESTAURANT	24-HOUR SERVICE	NO. OF ROO	PRI
CITY CENTER WEST										
AMSTERDAM RENAISSANCE	317		●	●	●		●	●	425	◆◆◆
AVENUE HOTEL	318		●					●	50	◆◆
DE ROODE LEEUW	318	●	●	●	●	●	●		80	◆◆
GRAND HOTEL KRASNAPOLSKY	318								420	◆◆◆
HOTEL DIE PORT VAN CLEVE	318		●	●	●		●	●	99	◆◆◆
HOTEL SOFITEL	318		●	●	●		●	●	150	◆◆◆
NOVA HOTEL	318		●		●				58	◆◆
VICTORIA HOTEL	318		●	●	●		●		305	◆◆◆
CITY CENTER EAST										
DOELEN KARENA HOTEL	319		●	●	●	●	●		85	◆◆◆
HOTEL EUREKA	319		●		●	●			16	◆
HOTEL DE L'EUROPE	319	●	●	●	●	●	●	●	100	◆◆◆
HOTEL THE GRAND	319	●	●	●	●	●	●	●	166	◆◆◆
RHO HOTEL	319								130	◆◆
NORTHERN CANALS										
AGORA	320	●	●		●	●			15	◆◆
AMBASSADE	320		●		●	●		●	52	◆◆
HET CANAL HOUSE	320				●	●			26	◆◆
HOTEL ESTHEREA	320		●		●	●			75	◆◆
HOTEL HEGRA	320					●			11	◆
HOTEL HOKSBERGEN	320		●		●	●			14	◆
HOTEL PULITZER	320	●	●	●	●	●	●	●	230	◆◆◆
TOREN	321		●		●	●			43	◆◆
WATERFRONT HOTEL	321		●		●	●		●	12	◆◆
SOUTHERN CANALS										
AMSTEL HOTEL	322	●	●	●	●	●	●	●	79	◆◆◆
AMSTERDAM WIECHMANN HOTEL	322		●	●	●	●			36	◆◆
BRIDGE HOTEL	322				●	●		●	27	◆◆
CITY HOTEL	322		●						13	◆
DE LANTAERNE	322		●			●			24	◆
DIKKER & THIJS	322		●	●	●	●	●	●	25	◆◆◆
HANS BRINKER	322								30	◆

	Page	Garden - Terrace	TV in Bedroom	Seminar Room	Quiet	View	Restaurant	24-Hour Service	No. of Rooms	Price
Hotel de Munck	*322*	●	●		●	●			12	♦
Hotel de la Poste	*323*				●	●			15	♦♦
Hotel Prisenhof	*323*				●	●			10	♦
Hotel van Haalen	*323*				●	●			20	♦
Schiller Karena	*323*		●		●	●	●		95	♦♦
The Seven Bridges	*323*	●	●		●	●			11	♦♦
MUSEUMS										
Acca International	*324*		●	●	●				35	♦♦
American Hotel	*324*	●	●	●	●	●	●	●	188	♦♦♦
AMS Hotel Holland	*324*		●		●				62	♦♦
AMS Hotel Terdam	*324*		●						95	♦♦
Amstel Botel	*324*		●		●	●			55	♦
Amsterdam Hilton	*324*	●	●	●	●	●	●	●	279	♦♦♦
Cok Business Hotel	*324*	●	●	●	●	●	●		30	♦♦♦
Cok Superior Tourist Class	*324*	●	●	●	●	●	●		50	♦♦♦
Cok Tourist Class	*324*	●	●	●	●	●	●		80	♦♦
Garden Hotel	*324*	●	●	●	●		●	●	98	♦♦♦
Hotel Acro	*324*		●		●				51	♦
Hotel De Filosoof	*324*	●	●	●	●	●			25	♦♦
Hotel Fita	*324*		●		●				16	♦
Hotel Maas	*324*		●		●	●			28	♦♦
Hotel Museumzicht	*325*				●	●			14	♦
Hotel Trianon	*325*	●	●	●	●			●	52	♦♦
Hotel Van Gogh	*325*	●			●			●	18	♦
Hotel Verdi	*325*	●	●		●				12	♦
Jan Luyken	*325*		●	●	●			●	62	♦♦♦
Jolly Hotel Carlton	*325*		●	●	●	●	●	●	219	♦♦♦
Marriott	*325*	●	●	●	●	●	●		392	♦♦♦
Prinsen Hotel	*325*	●	●		●			●	41	♦♦
Quentin	*325*	●	●		●	●			16	♦
JORDAAN										
Acacia	*326*		●		●	●		●	14	♦
Belga	*326*		●		●				10	♦

GENERAL

EMERGENCY SERVICES
(police, fire brigade, ambulance)
Tel. 06 11.

POLICE
Elandsgracht 117
Tel. 5 59 91 11.

HOSPITALS
– Onze Lieve Vrouw Gasthuis
1e Oosterparkstraat 279
Tel. 5 99 91 11
– Prinsengracht Ziekenhuis
Prinsengracht 769
Tel. 5 50 32 00

CENTRAL POST OFFICE
Singel 250–6
Tel. 5 56 33 11.

VVV TOURIST OFFICE
Stationsplein 10
Tel. 06 34 03 40 66.
Opposite the station. Information on cultural activities, museum opening and closing times, map of the city, and also a hotel booking service.
Another office at:
Leidsestraat 1
Tel. 06 34 03 40 66

INTERCITY ROOM SERVICE
Van Ostadestraat 348
Tel. 6 75 00 64.
Open 10am–5pm
Closed Sat. and Sun.
Apartments available on a weekly or monthly basis.
800 Fl–1,500 Fl.

AMSTERDAM HOUSE
Amstel 176a
Tel. 626 25 77
Fax 626 29 87
Houseboats and apartments available on a nightly or weekly basis – or more.
From175 Fl a night to 1,175 Fl a week.

CITY CENTER WEST

CULTURE

AMSTELKRING MUSEUM (ONZE LIEVE HEER OP ZOLDER/OUR LORD IN THE ATTIC)
Oudezijds Voorburgwal 40
Tel. 6 24 66 04
Open 10am–5pm, Sun. and public hols 1–5pm.

AMSTERDAM HISTORICAL MUSEUM (AMSTERDAMS HISTORISCH MUSEUM)
Kalverstraat 92
Tel. 5 23 18 22
Open 10–5pm. Sat. and Sun 11am–5pm.

BEGIJNHOF
15th-century English Reformed Church.
English Sunday service 10.30am (Catholic mass in church opposite at 12.15pm). Concerts – mostly Baroque – most Thurs., Fri., and Sat. evenings in season, and Sun. afternoons.

BERLAGE EXCHANGE
Damrak 277
Tel. 6 27 04 66
Open 9am–5pm.
Closed Sat., Sun. and public hol.
Lecture theaters and concert halls. Superb décor.

MADAME TUSSAUD SCENERAMA
P & C Building Dam 20
Tel. 6 22 99 49
Open 10am–5.30pm.
Waxworks museum.

NEW CHURCH (NIEUWEKERK)
Dam
Tel. 6 26 81 68
Open 11am–6pm.
Often stages interesting exhibitions.

OLD CHURCH (OUDEKERK)
Oude Kerkplein 23
Tel. 6 24 91 83
Open 11am–5pm, low season 11am–3pm.
The oldest church in Amsterdam. Organ recitals.

ROYAL PALACE (KONINKLIJK PALEIS)
Dam
Tel. 6 24 86 98
Open 12.30–4pm.
Closed Tues., Wed., and Thurs. in May.

ST NICOLAS CHURCH (SINT NICOLAASKERK)
Prins Hendrikkade 76
Open 11am–4pm Mon. and Sun., and low season 1–4pm.

THE MOVIES
Haarlemmerdijk 161
Tel 6 24 57 90
Small, delightful Art Deco cinema-cum-café, showing the best English-language films.

WEEPERS' TOWER (SCHREIERSTOREN)
At the corner of Prins Hendrikkade and Geldersekade.
16th-century tower.

RESTAURANTS

CAFÉ ESPRIT
Spui 10a
Tel. 6 22 19 67
Open 10am–6pm, Thurs. 10am–10pm.
Designer café, lovely terrace facing the Spui and the University. A popular tourist haunt. Specialties: salads, snacks, Californian dishes.
10 Fl–20 Fl.

CAFÉ LUXEMBOURG
Spui 22–4
Tel. 6 20 62 64
Open 10am–1am, Fri. and Sat. 10am–2am.
Specialties: club sandwiches, salads (Japanese), Dutch cuisine. No dinners.
10 Fl–25 Fl.

CRIGNON CULINAIRE
Gravenstraat 28
Tel. 6 24 64 28
Open 6–9.30pm.
Closed Sun. and Mon.
Behind the Nieuwekerk, in a quaint, narrow street, famed for its selection of cheeses. Specialties: fondues.
20 Fl–35 Fl.

D'VIJFF VLIEGEN
Spuistraat 294–302
Tel. 6 24 83 69
Open 5.30–10.30pm.
In a row of 18th-century houses, with chandeliers, copper, dark wood, old paintings and good food. Specialties: modern cuisine, gastronomy.
60 Fl–90 Fl.

DE KEUKEN VAN 1870
Spuistraat 4
Tel. 6 24 89 65
Open 11.30am–8pm, Sat. and Sun. 4–9pm
Legacy of the workers' (and charity) movements of the 19th century, this very simple but excellent restaurant attracts the poor and executives alike with its genuine Dutch cuisine at minimal prices.
10 Fl–15 Fl.

DE SILVEREN SPIEGEL
Kattengat 4–6
Tel. 6 24 65 89
Open noon–2pm, 6–10pm. Closed Sun.
In two lovely black houses with leaning façades, a popular restaurant, gastronomy and Davidoff.
50 Fl–90 Fl.

◆ HOTEL KRASNAPOLSKY ◆

"A gorgeous café in the center of town [...] an immense place with a lofty, gilt ceiling." This is how the writer Joseph Conrad described the café-restaurant of the Hotel Krasnapolsky, with its great glass roof.

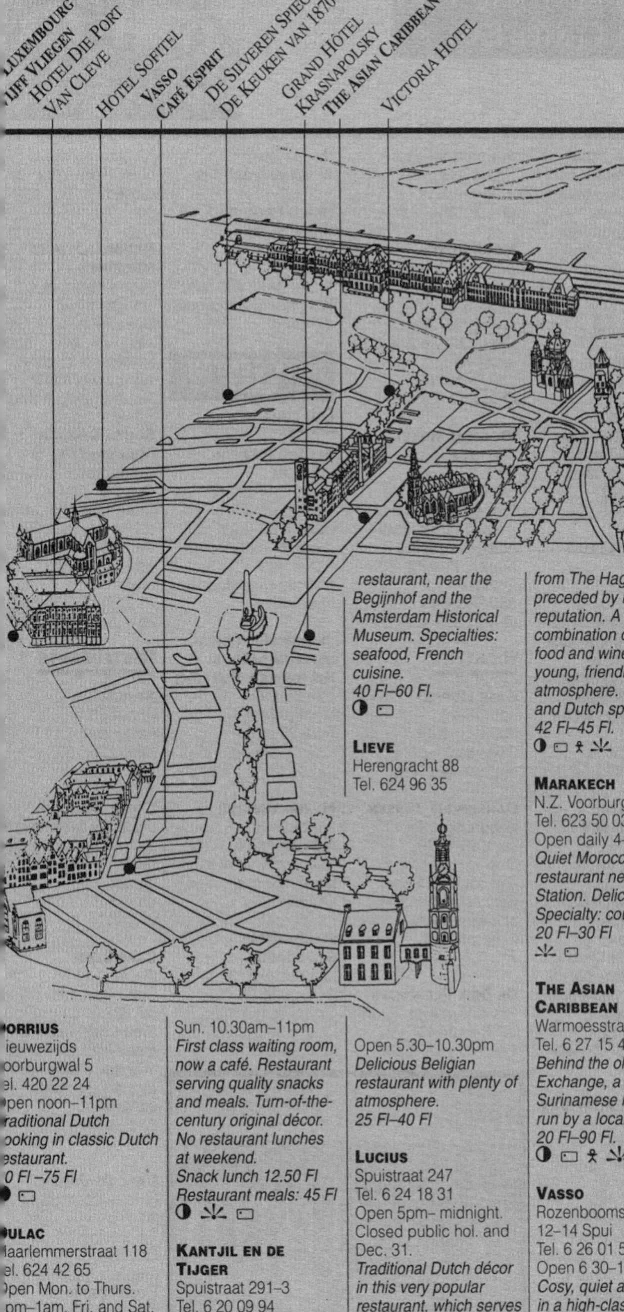

restaurant, near the Begijnhof and the Amsterdam Historical Museum. Specialties: seafood, French cuisine.
40 Fl–60 Fl.
◑ ▭

LIEVE
Herengracht 88
Tel. 624 96 35

from The Hague, preceded by its reputation. A tasteful combination of Dutch food and wine and a young, friendly atmosphere. French and Dutch specialties.
42 Fl–45 Fl.
◑ ▭ 🚶 ☀

MARAKECH
N.Z. Voorburgwal 134
Tel. 623 50 03
Open daily 4–10.30pm
Quiet Moroccan restaurant near the Station. Delicious food. Specialty: couscous.
20 Fl–30 Fl
☀ ▭

THE ASIAN CARIBBEAN
Warmoesstraat 170
Tel. 6 27 15 45
Behind the old Berlage Exchange, a spacious Surinamese restaurant, run by a local celebrity.
20 Fl–90 Fl.
◑ ▭ 🚶 ☀ P

ORRIUS
ieuwezijds
oorburgwal 5
el. 420 22 24
pen noon–11pm
raditional Dutch ooking in classic Dutch estaurant.
0 Fl –75 Fl
● ▭

ULAC
aarlemmerstraat 118
el. 624 42 65
pen Mon. to Thurs. pm–1am, Fri. and Sat. pm–2am, Sun. pm–1am
rt Deco café. Good, imple meals. 7–foot nd 9-foot pool tables.
5 Fl–30 Fl
●

E KLAS
entral Station, latform 2B
el. 624 42 65
pen 9.30am–11pm,

Sun. 10.30am–11pm
First class waiting room, now a café. Restaurant serving quality snacks and meals. Turn-of-the-century original décor. No restaurant lunches at weekend.
Snack lunch 12.50 Fl
Restaurant meals: 45 Fl
◑ ☀ ▭

KANTJIL EN DE TIJGER
Spuistraat 291–3
Tel. 6 20 09 94
Open 4.30–11pm.
Fashionable Indonesian restaurant with modern décor and spicy cuisine.
20 Fl–50 Fl.
◑ ▭ 🚶 ☀ ✈

LE PETIT LAPIN
Nieuwezijds
Voorburgwal 306
Tel. 6 24 94 25
Open 6–10.30pm.
Very pleasant

Open 5.30–10.30pm
Delicious Beligian restaurant with plenty of atmosphere.
25 Fl–40 Fl

LUCIUS
Spuistraat 247
Tel. 6 24 18 31
Open 5pm- midnight. Closed public hol. and Dec. 31.
Traditional Dutch décor in this very popular restaurant, which serves simple fish dishes from the North Sea and elsewhere.
35 Fl–70 Fl.
○ ▭ ✈

LUDEN
Spuistraat 306
Tel. 6 22 89 79
Open noon–1am, Sat. and Sun. noon–1.30am.
A restaurant that has moved to the capital

VASSO
Rozenboomsteeg
12–14 Spui
Tel. 6 26 01 58
Open 6 30–11pm.
Cosy, quiet atmosphere in a high-class Italian restaurant. Beautiful décor. A stone's throw from the Begijnhof.
55 Fl–80 Fl.
◍ ▭ ☀ ✈

ACCOMMODATION

AMSTERDAM RENAISSANCE
Kattegat 1
Tel. 6 21 22 23
Fax 6 27 52 45

Large international modern hotel but individualistic and with helpful service. Swimming-pool and sauna, own garage, suites with private terrace.
395 Fl–425 Fl

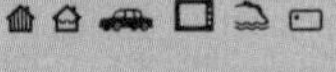

AVENUE HOTEL
N.Z. Voorburgwal 27
Tel: 623 83 07
Fax 638 39 46
Converted East India Company warehouse in the center of town.
150 Fl–210 Fl

DE ROODE LEEUW
Damrak 93
Tel. 555 06 66
Fax 620 47 16
A Best Western hotel. Functional décor but it is in the heart of Amsterdam near the Dam and its restaurant specializes in Dutch food.
199 Fl–295 Fl

GRAND HOTEL KRASNAPOLSKY
Dam 9
Tel. 5 54 91 11
Fax 6 22 86 07.
Luxury hotel on Dam Square. Huge, unprepossessing building (apart from its winter garden), but the most comfortable hotel in the city center.
350 Fl–465 Fl.

HOTEL DIE PORT VAN CLEVE
Nieuwezijds Voorburgwal 178–180
Tel. 6 24 48 60
Fax 6 22 02 40.
An institution in the heart of Amsterdam, it has attracted visitors for more than a century. Restaurant renowned for its traditional Dutch cooking. Large numbers of groups
195Fl–276 Fl.

HOTEL SOFITEL
Nieuwezijds Voorburgwal 67
Tel. 6 27 59 00
Fax 6 23 89 32.
Functional, comfortable rooms but overlooking a noisy main road.
International class. Sauna and gym. Around 350 Fl.

NOVA HOTEL
N.Z. Voorburgwal 276–280
Tel. 623 00 66
Fax 627 20 26
Old house, central, family-run.
150 Fl–195 Fl

VICTORIA HOTEL
Damrak 1–6
Tel. 6 23 42 55
Fax 6 25 29 97.
Well-equipped rooms in a turn-of-the-century hotel opposite the Station. Bustling location.
350 Fl–395 Fl.

NIGHTLIFE

CAFÉ HOPPE
Spui 18–20
Tel. 6 23 78 49
Open 8am–1am, Fri. and Sat. 8am–2am.

DANSEN BIJ JANSEN
Handboogstraat 11
Tel. 6 20 17 79
Open 11pm–4am, Fri. and Sat. 11pm–5am.
Club popular among students. Lively atmosphere.

DE DRIE FLESCHJES
Gravenstraat 18
Tel. 6 24 84 43
Open noon–8.15pm.
Closed Sun.
Attractive brown café.

HENRI PROUVIN
Gravenstraat 20
Tel. 6 23 93 33
Open 4–11.30pm.
Closed Mon. and Sun.
Wine tasting throughout the day.

CITY CENTER EAST

CULTURE

ALLARD PIERSON MUSEUM
Oude Turfmarkt 127
Tel. 5 25 25 56
Open 10am–5pm, Sat. and Sun. 10am–1pm.
Closed Mon.
Famous archeological museum.

JEWISH HISTORICAL MUSEUM (JOODS HISTORISCH MUSEUM)
Jonas Daniël Meyerplein 2–4
Tel. 6 26 99 45
Open 11am–5pm.
Closed for Yom Kippur.

MUZIEKTHEATER
Amstel 3.
Nicknamed the "Stopera", built at the same time as the new City Hall.

PORTUGUESE SYNAGOGUE
Mr Visserplein 3
Tel. 6 25 35 09
Open 10am–4pm
Closed Sat., public holidays and Yom Kippur. Low season open 10am–2pm. Closed Fri., Sat. and Sun.

REMBRANDTHUIS MUSEUM
Jodenbreestraat 4–6
Tel. 6 24 94 86
Open 10am–5pm, Sun and public hol. 1–5pm
Rembrandt's house, with a collection of etchings and paintings

SOUTH CHURCH (ZUIDERKERK)
Zandstraat
Open 12.30–4.30pm.
Closed Sat., Sun. and public hol. Late night Thurs. 6–9pm. Belfry visits in the high season: Wed. 2–5pm, Thur. and Fri. 11am–2pm, Sat. 11am–4pm.

RESTAURANTS

ATRIUM
Oudezijds Achterburgwal 237
Tel. 5 25 39 99
Open noon–2pm, 5–7pm.
Cheap, utilitarian university canteen in the Binnengasthuis, in the heart of the canal district.
From 5 Fl.

CAFÉ BERN
Nieuwmarkt 9
Open 4pm–1am
Tel. 622 00 34
Brown café, open for meals in the evenings. Informal. Specialties: fondues. Booking essential.
25 Fl–40 Fl

CAFÉ DE JAREN
Nieuwe Doelenstraat 20–2
Tel. 6 25 57 71
Open 10am–1am, Fri. and Sat. 10am–2am.
Good fresh food. Kitchen closes at 10pm for dinners. Chess boards available.
15 Fl–35 Fl.

DANTZIG
Zwanenburgwal 15
Tel. 6 20 90 39
Open 10am–1am, Fri. and Sat. 10am–2am.
Specialties: salads, omelettes, modern continental cuisine.

◆ CAFÉ DE JAREN ◆

Typical of a new kind of Amsterdam establishment, this vast, ultra-modern café on the banks of the Amstel is famous for its two spacious terraces and its excellent sandwiches.

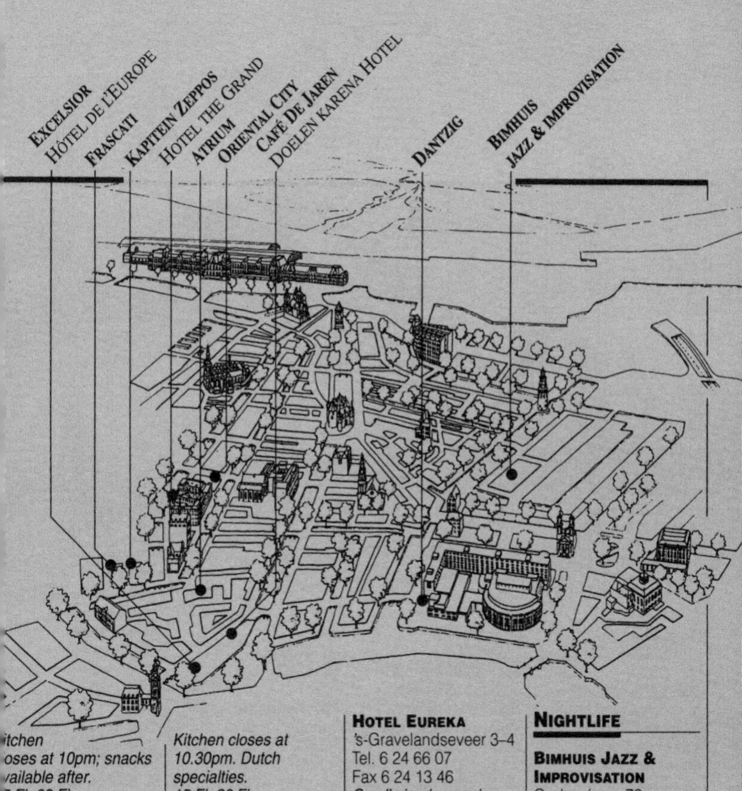

itchen
oses at 10pm; snacks
vailable after.
5 Fl–60 Fl.

E SLUYSWACHT
odenbreestraat 1
el. 6 25 76 11
pen 11am–1am
695 lock-keeper's
ouse, now a café with
rivate dining rooms
ostairs for dinners.
Vonderful small terrace
n canal, opposite
embrandthuis.
5 Fl–40 Fl

XCELSIOR
ieuwe Doelenstraat
-8
el. 6 23 48 36
pen 12.30–2.30pm,
–10.30pm.
enowned restaurant of
e Hotel de l'Europe.
elightful terrace on the
anks of the Amstel.
pecialties: game, wine,
rench cuisine.
0 Fl–200 Fl.

RASCATI
es 59
el. 6 24 13 24
pen 4pm–1am, Fri.
nd Sat. 1.30pm–2am.
djoining a theater,
ose to Dam Square,
is café, which is
rowded before and
fter performances,
ttracts a very lively,
ultured clientèle.

Kitchen closes at 10.30pm. Dutch specialties.
15 Fl–26 Fl.

KAPITEIN ZEPPOS
Gebed Zonder End 5
Tel. 6 24 20 57
Open 11am–1am, Sat. and Sun. 4pm–3am.
Near the university, a friendly bar-restaurant with live music. Very pleasant terrace. Specialties: salads, snacks, French cuisine.
25 Fl–40 Fl.

ORIENTAL CITY
Oudezijds Voorburgwal 177–9
Tel. 6 26 83 52
Open 11.30am–11pm.
A high-class Chinese restaurant frequented by the Asian community. Wide choice of Chinese and Indonesian dishes.
30 Fl–60 Fl.

ACCOMMODATION

DOELEN KARENA HOTEL
Nieuwe Doelenstraat 24
Tel. 6 22 07 22
Fax 6 22 10 84.
This famous and spacious hotel on the banks of the Amstel once housed Rembrandt's studio.
335 Fl.

HOTEL EUREKA
's-Gravelandseveer 3–4
Tel. 6 24 66 07
Fax 6 24 13 46
Small simple canal-house hotel right in the center and on the water, yet very quiet.
100 Fl–200 Fl

HOTEL DE L'EUROPE
Nieuwe Doelenstraat 2–8
Tel. 6 23 48 36
Fax 6 24 29 62.
Prestigious hotel on the banks of the Amstel. Very luxurious with an outstanding restaurant, the Excelsior.
495 Fl–555 Fl.

HOTEL THE GRAND
Oudezijds Voorburgwal 197
Tel. 5 55 31 11
Splendid, prestigious hotel in the former City Hall. Grand French cooking. Luxury suites. Swimming-pool and sauna.
545 FL–2,500 FL

RHO HOTEL
Nes 5–23
Tel. 6 20 73 71
Fax 6 20 78 26.
Close to Dam Square and very near to the center. Friendly, with basic accommodation.
135Fl–195 Fl.

NIGHTLIFE

BIMHUIS JAZZ & IMPROVISATION
Oudeschans 73
Tel. 6 23 33 73.
On the quayside, in industrial surroundings; welcomes the "switched on" young for concerts and improvisations.

NORTHERN CANALS

CULTURE

ANNE FRANK'S HOUSE
Prinsengracht 263
Tel. 5 56 71 00
Open 9am–5pm, June to August 9am–7pm. Closed for Yom Kippur.

DE RODE HOED
Keizersgracht 102
Tel. 6 25 73 68
Open 9am–5pm
Closed Sun. and Mon.
Former Remonstrant church, used for theater and concerts of early music. Tel. 6 34 09 21 for details.

MULTATULI MUSEUM
Korsjespoortsteeg 20
Tel. 6 38 19 38
Open Tues. only 10am–5pm.
Telephone for appointment.

NEDERLANDS THEATER INSTITUUT
Herengracht 168
Tel. 6 23 51 04

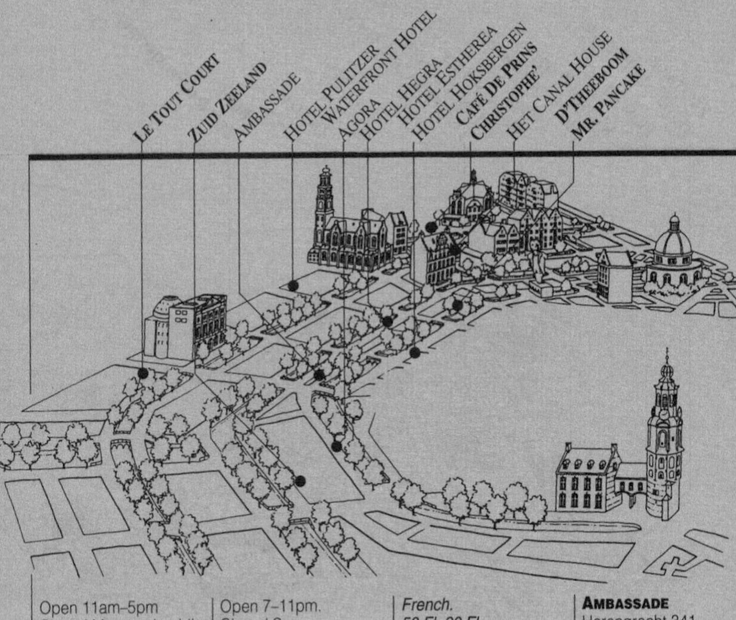

Open 11am–5pm
Closed Mon. and public hol.
Mime, theater and dance museum.

THEATER FELIX MERITIS
Keizersgracht 324
Tel. 6 23 13 11
Open 10am–8.30pm, Sat. 3–8.30pm.
Home of the Shaffy experimental theater.

VAN BRIENEN HOFJE
89–133 Prinsengracht.
Former almshouse.
Open all day.
Just push open the door

WEST CHURCH (WESTERKERK)
Westerkerk
Prinsengracht – Westermarkt.
Belfry visits Apr. to Sept., Mon.–Sat. 10am–4pm. Cantata services once a month Sept. to May on Sun. 10.30am.

RESTAURANTS

CAFÉ DE PRINS
Prinsengracht 124
Tel. 6 24 93 82
Open 10.30am–10pm, Fri. and Sat. 10am–2am
Opposite Anne Frank's House, a cosy, friendly café for a cultured clientèle. Exhibitions of photographs and paintings. Specialties: fondue savoyarde.
10Fl–25 Fl.

CHRISTOPHE'
Leliegracht 46
Tel. 6 25 08 07
Open 7–11pm.
Closed Sun.
Quality cuisine in a post-modern décor. Specialties: terrine de foie gras au jurançon, baked lobster.
80 Fl–130 Fl.

D'THEEBOOM
Singel 210
Tel. 6 23 84 20
Open 11am–3pm, 6–10.30pm.
A converted warehouse. Excellent French cuisine and trendy clientèle. Generous servings and good value for money. Book for the evening.
42 Fl.

DE GOUDSBLOEM
Reestraat 8
Tel. 5 23 52 83
Open 6–10.30pm.
The upmarket restaurant of the Pulitzer is located in a converted warehouse, very close to the Westerkerk. Excellent wine cellar. Specialties: French and Batavian, eel ravioli with sautéed oysters.
50 Fl–100 Fl.

LE TOUT COURT
Runstraat 13
Tel. 6 25 86 37
Open noon–1am, Sat. and Sun. 6pm–1am.
One of the best restaurants in the city. The chef is very affable and the service excellent. Booking essential. Specialties: French.
50 Fl–90 Fl.

MR. PANCAKE
Raadhuisstraat 6
Tel. 6 27 85 00
Open 10am–8pm, Sun. 11am–8pm.
Hollywood-style décor. A spacious crêperie, generally a mixed clientèle.
10 Fl–35 Fl.

RUM RUNNERS
Prinsengracht 277
Tel. 6 27 40 79
Open 4pm–1am, Sat. 2pm–2am, Sun. 2pm–1am.
Tropical restaurant. Good cocktails but touristy and noisy.
30 Fl–50 Fl.

ZUID ZEELAND
Herengracht 413
Tel. 6 24 31 54
Open noon–2.30pm, 6.30–11pm, Sat. and Sun. 6–11.30pm.
Situated on the canalside. Cool garden, high-class cuisine.
30 Fl–60 Fl.

ACCOMMODATION

AGORA
Singel 462
Tel. 6 27 22 00
Fax 6 27 22 02.
High-class hotel, near the flower market. Very clean. Good value for money. Excellent breakfast included.
145 Fl–190 Fl.

AMBASSADE
Herengracht 341
Tel. 6 26 23 33
Fax 6 24 53 21.
Lovely hotel beside the most exclusive canal. Impeccable service.
250 Fl–265 Fl.

HET CANAL HOUSE
Keizersgracht 148
Tel. 6 22 51 82
Fax 6 24 13 17.
Superb little hotel, quie and opulent. The best i its class. Ideal location.
195 Fl–240 Fl.

HOTEL ESTHEREA
Singel 303–9
Tel. 6 24 51 46
Fax 6 23 90 01.
Friendly, superbly located canalside hotel
175 Fl–325 Fl.

HOTEL HEGRA
Herengracht 269
Tel. 6 23 78 77
Fax 6 23 81 59.
Closed Jan. 15–Feb. 1
Small, inexpensive hotel beside a canal. Friendly service.
Around 125 Fl.

HOTEL HOKSBERGEN
Singel 301
Tel. 6 26 60 43
Fax 6 38 34 79.
Small, clean, traditiona canal-house hotel. Excellent location.
130 Fl–145 Fl.

HOTEL PULITZER
Prinsengracht 315–31
Tel. 5 23 52 35

Fax 6 27 67 53.
Undoubtedly one of the best hotels in Amsterdam. Made up of twenty-four old houses overlooking two canals. Prestige and tradition.
800 Fl–4,000 Fl.

TOREN
Keizersgracht 164
Tel. 6 22 60 33
Fax 6 26 97 05.
Picturesque canalside hotel. Good value.
165 Fl–275 Fl.

WATERFRONT HOTEL
Singel 458
Tel. 6 23 97 75
Fax 6 20 74 91.
Charming and central. Excellent service.
120 Fl–195 Fl.

NIGHTLIFE

ODEON JAZZ & CLUB
Singel 460
Tel. 6 20 97 22
Open 11pm–5am.
Three floors of music in beautiful house. Caters for all tastes. Disco in the cellar, jazz upstairs.

ROXY
Singel 465–7
Tel. 6 20 03 54
Open 11pm–4am Fri. and Sat. 11pm–5am.
A popular disco which attracts young people, trendies, executives, famous DJs.

SOUTHERN CANALS

CULTURE

BIJBELS MUSEUM
Herengracht 366
Tel. 6 24 24 36
Open 10am–5pm, Sun. and public hol. 1–5pm. Closed Mon.

CAT MUSEUM (KATTENKABINET)
Herengracht 468
Tel. 6 26 53 78
Open 11am–5pm. Closed Mon.

JAN SIX COLLECTION
Amstel 218.
Apply to the Rijksmuseum for permission to visit. (Tel. 6 73 21 21).

STADSSCHOUWBURG
Leidseplein 26
Tel. 6 24 23 11.
Amsterdam municipal theater showing a range of productions.

TUSCHINSKI CINEMA
Reguliersbreestraat 26
Tel. 6 26 26 33
Open 12.15–10pm. Guided tours July–Aug., Sun. and Mon. at 10.30am.
The famous cinema, built in 1921, with original Art Deco fittings.

VAN LOON MUSEUM
Keizersgracht 672
Tel. 6 24 52 55
Open 10am–5pm, Mon. and Sun. 1–5pm.
Opulent family house designed by Adriaan Dortsman.

WILLET–HOLTHUYSEN
Herengracht 605
Open 11am–5pm.
17th-century patrician house.

RESTAURANTS

CAFÉ HET MOLENPAD
Prinsengracht 653
Tel. 6 25 96 80
Open noon–1am, Fri. and Sat. noon–2am.
Old brown café frequented by the litterati. Exhibitions of paintings. Terrace. Specialties: salads.
20 Fl–30 Fl.

CALZONE
Reguliersdwarsstraat 57
Tel. 627 3833
Open noon till midnight
Behind Singel flower market, large terrace. Young and friendly. Pizzas and salads
20 Fl–40 Fl

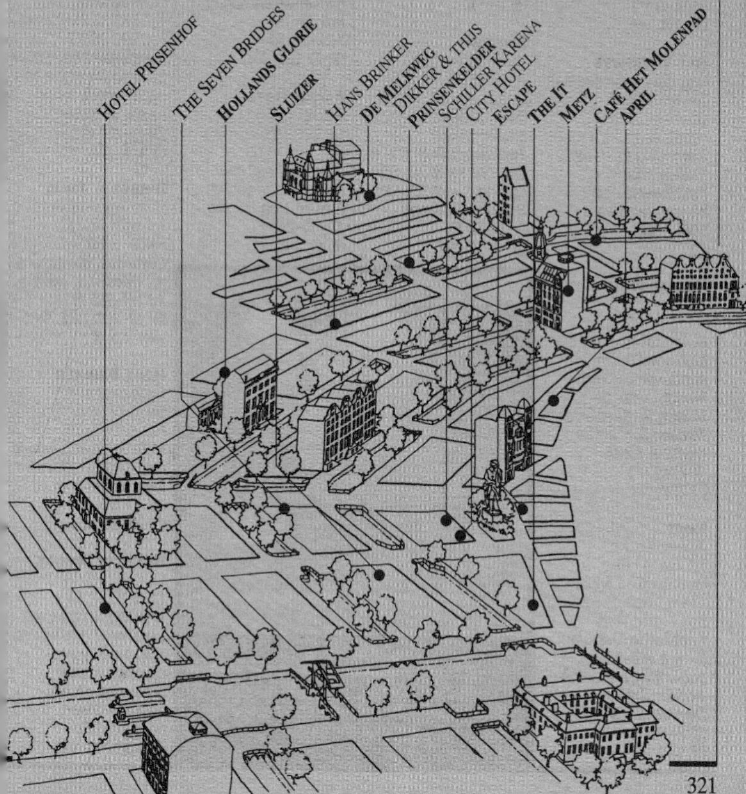

Hotel Prisenhof
The Seven Bridges
Hollands Glorie
Sluizer
Hans Brinker
De Melkweg
Dikker & Thijs
Prinsenkelder
Schiller Karena
City Hotel
Escape
The It
Metz
Café Het Molenpad
April

HOTEL DE FILOSOOF

DYNASTY
Reguliersdwarsstraat 30
Tel. 6 26 84 00
Open 5.30–11pm
Closed Tues.
1994 Restaurant of the Year. Smart Chinese and Thai restaurant. Pleasant surroundings. Booking essential.
50 Fl–80 Fl.

ERROL TRUMPIE
Leidsestraat 46
Tel. 6 24 02 33
Open 9am–6pm.
Tea room–patisserie serving cakes, rolls, snacks, Flemish tarts and Dutch pancakes.
10 Fl–15 Fl.

HET LAND VAN WALEM
Keizersgracht 449
Tel. 6 25 35 44
Open Mon. to Thurs. 9am–1am, Fri. and Sat. 9am–2am, Sun. 9.30am–1am.
Grand café; breakfasts, snacks and meals. Terrace at canal side and garden at the back.
15FL–30FL

HET TUYNHUYS
Reguliersdwarsstraat 28
Tel. 6 27 66 03
Open Mon. to Fri. noon–3pm, 6–11pm
Interesting food with French accent. Fashionable and elegant restaurant
50FL–70FL

HOLLANDS GLORIE
Kerkstraat 220–2
Tel. 6 24 47 64.
Dutch cooking and old-fashioned Dutch surroundings. Very friendly; near the Muntplein. Specialties: smoked fish, grilled mussels, steak.
30 Fl–50 Fl.

KORT
Amstelved 12
Tel. 626 11 99
Open Sun. to Thurs 11am–10pm, Fri. and Sat. 11am–11pm.
Enchanting restaurant terrace in summer, under the trees at the wooden Amstel church. Dinners and snacks.
50 Fl–75 Fl

METZ
Keizersgracht 453
Tel. 6 24 88 10
Open Mon. 11am–5pm, Tues.–Sat. 9.30am–5pm, Thurs. 9.30am–8pm. Closed Sun.
Modern restaurant on the top floor of the Metz & Co. department store. Lovely view over the town. Specialties: smoked salmon, salads, brunch, teas.
15 Fl–30 Fl.

PRINSENKELDER
Prinsengracht 438
Tel. 4 22 27 77
Open 6–1am
17th-century warehouse beautifully renovated. French-Italian cooking. Very friendly; warmly recommended.
25 Fl–30 Fl.

ROSE'S CANTINA
Reguliersdwarsstraat 38
Tel. 6 25 97 97
Open 5–11pm.
Mexican specialties.
15 Fl–30 Fl.

SLUIZER
Utrechtsestraat 43–5
Tel. 6 22 63 76
Open noon–midnight, Sat. and Sun. 6pm–midnight.
Two restaurants: one for fish, one for meat. Soft lighting, simple décor. Booking essential.
30 Fl–65 Fl.

VAN PUFFELEN
Prinsengracht 377
Tel. 624 6270
Open Mon. to Fri. 3pm–1am, Sat. noon–2am, Sun. noon–1am.
Brown café plus restaurant with plenty of atmosphere. Tapas are served in the café side Popular with the locals . Kitchen closes at 11pm.
15FL–40FL

ACCOMMODATION

AMSTEL HOTEL
Prof. Tulpplein 1
Tel. 6 22 60 60
Fax 622 58 08
The most prestigious luxury hotel in the city, dating back to 1867. On the banks of the Amstel.
825 Fl–4,500 Fl.

AMSTERDAM WIECHMANN HOTEL
Prinsengracht 328
Tel. 626 33 21
Fax 626 89 62
Three converted canal houses at junction of two canals.
150 Fl–250 Fl

BRIDGE HOTEL
Amstel 107–111
Tel: 623 70 68
Fax: 624 15 65
Pleasant hotel near Magere Brug on the Amstel. Good rooms.
130 Fl–250 Fl

◆ THE IT ◆

This late-night discotheque in the city center close to the Amstel is very popular with trendies and gays.

CITY HOTEL
Utrechtsestraat 2
Tel. 6 27 23 23.
Small, very clean hotel on the Rembrandtplein. Excellent value for money. 5% surcharge when paying with credit cards.
95 Fl–125 Fl.

DE LANTAERNE
Leidsegracht 111
Tel. 623 22 21
Fax 623 26 83
Inexpensive hotel near Leidseplein where two canals meet. 3-bed rooms available.
70 Fl–125 Fl

DIKKER & THIJS
Prinsengracht 444
Tel. 6 26 77 21
Fax 6 25 89 86.
Luxurious, comfortable, Art Deco style hotel
280 Fl–365 Fl

HANS BRINKER
Kerkstraat 136
Tel. 6 22 06 87
Fax 6 38 20 60.
Hotel for young people, clean and well located Dormitories from 40 Fl.
76 Fl–118 Fl.

HOTEL DE MUNCK
Achtergracht 3
Tel. 6 23 62 83
Well located on small canal near Amstel river. 18th-century sea-captain's house, renovated. Quiet. Recommended.
85FL–160-FL

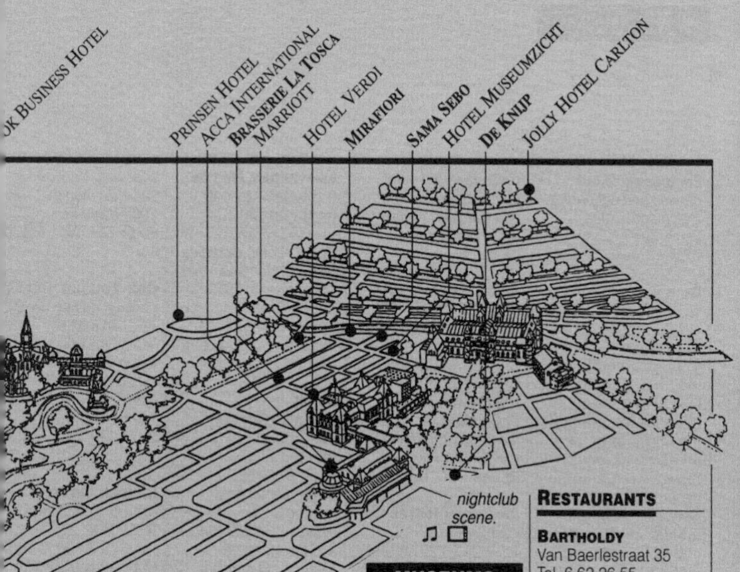

OTEL DE LA POSTE
eguliersgracht 3-5
el. 6 23 71 05.
amily hotel; a museum iece near the embrandtplein. leally located at the tersection of two anals, but expensive. round 200 Fl.

OTEL PRINSENHOF
rinsengracht 810
el. 6 23 17 72
ax 6 38 33 68
harming, tastefully ecorated hotel. ood value for money. 20 Fl–160 FL

OTEL VAN HAALEN
rinsengracht 520
el. 6 26 43 34
ccentrically old-ashioned hotel in a anal-house. Some ooms without bathroom 5 Fl–150 Fl

CHILLER KARENA
embrandtplein 26–36
el. 6 23 16 60
ax 6 24 00 98.
uperb location.Cool, errace for summer. omfortable rooms. round 315 Fl.

HE SEVEN BRIDGES
eguliersgracht 31
el. 6 23 13 29.
mall, inexpensive otel, with clean, leasant rooms. enerous breakfasts erved in the room. 25 Fl–200 Fl.

NIGHTLIFE

APRIL
Reguliersdwarsstraat 37
Tel. 6 25 95 72
Open 2pm–1am.
Gay bar-restaurant, on the "grungy" side

DE MELKWEG
Lijnbaansgracht 234
Tel. 6 24 84 92
Open 7.30pm–5am
Closed Sun.
Concert hall in the evening, disco at night. "The Milky Way" is very impressive and very touristy; it will also make anyone over 35 feel old.

ESCAPE
Rembrandtplein 11–15
Tel. 6 22 35 42
Open 10pm–4am ,Fri. and Sat. 10pm–5am.
Immense disco with all the latest equipment, packed with hundreds of teenagers.

HAVANA DANSCAFÉ
Reguliersdwarsstraat 17–19
Tel. 6 20 67 88
Open 4pm–1am, Fri. and Sat. 2pm–2am.
Pleasant bar-disco where gays and trendies congregate after dinner.

THE IT
Amstelstraat 24
Tel. 6 25 01 11
Open 11pm–4am.
Closed Sun. to Wed.
Gay disco, very popular with the young and trendy. Mecca of the

MUSEUMS

CULTURE

CONCERTGEBOUW
Concertgebouwplein 2–6
Tel. 6 71 83 45.
Concert hall for classical music.

HEINEKEN BREWERY (HEINEKEN BROUWERIJ)
Stadhouderskade 78
Closed Sun. and public hol.
Guided tours 9.30am and 11am, and all the beer you can drink at the end.

NETHERLANDS FILM MUSEUM (NEDERLANDS FILMMUSEUM)
Vondelpark 3
Tel. 5 89 14 00
Open 10am–9.30pm; Sat. 6–9.30pm, Sun. noon–9.30pm,

RESISTANCE MUSEUM (VERZETSMUSEUM)
Lekstraat 63
Tel. 6 44 97 97
Open 10am–5pm, Sun. and public hol. 1–5pm
Closed Mon. and May 4

RIJKSMUSEUM
Stadhouderskade 42
Tel. 6 73 21 21
Open 10am–5pm, Sun. and public hol.1–5pm.

STEDELIJK MUSEUM
Paulus Potterstraat 13
Tel. 5 73 29 11
Open 11am–5pm.

VAN GOGH MUSEUM
Paulus Potterstraat 7
Tel. 5 70 52 00
Open 10am–5pm

RESTAURANTS

BARTHOLDY
Van Baerlestraat 35
Tel. 6 62 26 55
Open noon–2.30pm, 5.30–11pm; Sat and Sun 5.30–11pm only
Chic restaurant opposite Concertgebouw on edge of Museumplein. Mediterranean cuisine. 35 Fl–50 Fl

BODEGA DE KEYZER
Van Baelestraat 96
Tel. 6 71 14 81
Open 9am–11.30pm (kitchen open noon–11.30pm). Closed Sun.
Old fashioned café restaurant with atmosphere, opposite Concertgebouw. 40 Fl–60 Fl

BRASSERIE LA TOSCA
P.C. Hooftstraat 128
Tel. 6 73 55 95
Open 9am–10pm, Sun. noon–10pm.
Smart clientèle. Opera music in the evenings. Friendly service. Specialties: Italian, salads, fresh pasta. 20 Fl–35 Fl.

BRASSERIE MAXIE'S
P.C. Hooststraat 100
Tel. 6 79 20 04
Open 11am–11pm (kitchen closes 9.30pm)
Quiet, modern and pleasant, with garden at the back. 20 Fl–30 Fl

DE BLAUWE HOLLANDER
Leidsekruisstraat 28
Tel. 6 23 30 14
Open 5–10pm.
Near the Leidseplein.

For those who like crowds and big parties. Dutch specialties.
20 Fl–30 Fl.

DE KNIJP
Van Baerlestraat 134
Tel. 6 71 42 48
Open noon–3pm, 5.30pm–12.30am, Sat., Sun. and public hol. 5.30pm–12.30am.
Near the Stedelijk and the Concertgebouw, a very popular, friendly restaurant. Turn-of-the century décor. Specialties: Zeeland oysters, Mediterranean cuisine, wines.
30 Fl–50 Fl.

DE SMOESHAAN THEATER CAFÉ
Leidsekade 90
Tel. 6 27 69 66
Open 11am–1am (kitchen open Tues.-Sat. 5.30–9.30pm)
A lively complex, with a young, cultured clientèle. Booking essential. Specialties: salads, pasta, French-Italian cuisine.
25 Fl–50 Fl.

MANGERIE
Garden Hotel
Dijsselhofplantsoen 7
Tel. 6 64 21 21
Open 6–11pm.
Closed Sun.
Revamped in 1994, it is now less formal. One of the culinary highlights of Amsterdam. Booking essential. Specialties: French cuisine.
50 Fl–120 Fl.

MIRAFIORI
Hobbemastraat 2
Tel. 6 62 30 13
Open noon–3pm, 5pm–midnight (kitchen closes at 10.30pm).
Closed Tues.
Possibly the best, and certainly the oldest Italian restaurant in Amsterdam.
45 Fl–55 Fl.

SAMA SEBO
P.C. Hooftstraat 27
Tel. 6 62 81 46
Open noon–2pm, 6–10pm. Closed Sun.
Close to the museums. An Indonesian restaurant that boldly combines exotic charm and Batavian tradition.
30 Fl–50 Fl.

ACCOMMODATION

ACCA INTERNATIONAL
Van de Veldestraat 3a
Tel. 6 62 52 62
Fax 6 76 27 62.
Not far from the Van Gogh Museum. Quiet, friendly, comfortable.
175 Fl–250 Fl.

AMERICAN HOTEL
Leidsekade 97
Tel. 6 24 53 22
Fax 6 25 32 36
Majestic Art Deco hotel located near the canals and the museums. Small rooms. Sauna.
400 Fl–460 Fl.

AMS HOTEL HOLLAND
P.C. Hooftstraat
Tel. 6 83 18 11
Fax 6 76 59 56
A quiet hotel just off the Vondel Park in museums area.
130 Fl–180 Fl

AMS HOTEL TERDAM
Tesselschadestraat 23
Tel. 6 83 18 11
Fax 6 83 83 13
Near Vondel Park and Leidseplein, formerly 19th-century houses.
180 Fl–260 Fl

AMSTERDAM HILTON
Apollolaan 138–140
Tel. 6 78 07 80
Fax 6 62 66 88
Out of center. Contains John Lennon and Yoko Ono's historic 1969 "Bed-in" suite.
Around 550 Fl.

BOTEL (AMSTEL BOTEL)
Oosterdokskade 2–4
Tel. 6 26 42 47
Fax 6 39 19 52
Modern hotel boat moored on the river between Central Station and the Maritime Museum. Functional rooms. Ask for one on the river side.
109 Fl–148 Fl

COK BUSINESS HOTEL
Koninginneweg 34–6
Tel. 6 64 61 11
Fax 6 64 53 04
Very close to the Vondelpark and the museums, a complex of hotels in three different categories. Spacious, modern rooms in the top category.
220 Fl–260 Fl.

COK SUPERIOR TOURIST CLASS
Koninginneweg 34–6
Tel. 6 64 61 11
Fax 6 64 53 04
Still very pleasant rooms, but less spacious. Very good value for money.
200 Fl–240 Fl.

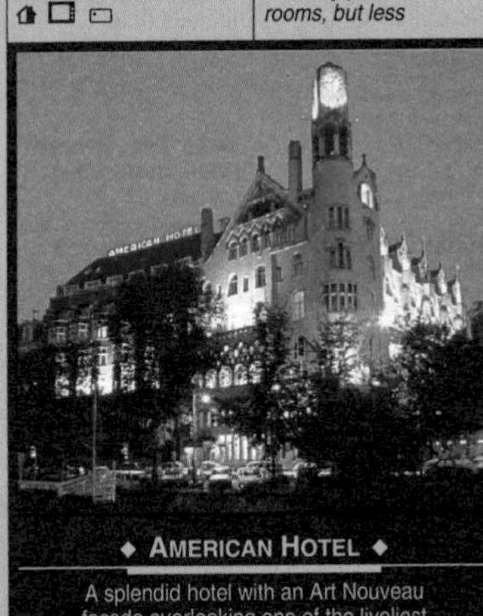

◆ AMERICAN HOTEL ◆

A splendid hotel with an Art Nouveau façade overlooking one of the liveliest squares in Amsterdam. It is especially famous for its stunning 1930's bar, a favorite haunt of artists.

COK TOURIST CLASS
Koninginneweg 34–6
Tel. 6 64 61 11
Fax 6 64 53 04
Again, this hotel gives excellent value for money.
180 Fl–210 Fl.

GARDEN HOTEL
Dijsselhofplantsoen 7
Tel. 6 64 21 21
Fax 6 79 93 56
Out of center. One of the most renowned hotels in Amsterdam. Luxury rooms with jacuzzi. Good value for money. Excellent restaurant.
420 Fl–445 Fl.

HOTEL ACRO
Jan Luykenstraat 44
Tel. 6 62 05 26
Fax 6 75 08 11
A stone's throw from the museums, a modern hotel, spick and span and functional.
125 Fl–140 Fl.

HOTEL DE FILOSOOF
Anna van de Vondelstraat 6
Tel. 6 83 30 13
Fax 6 85 37 50
Near the Vondelpark and the museums, an odd hotel associated with a group of philosophers.
145 Fl–175 Fl.

HOTEL FITA
Jan Luykenstraat 37
Tel. 6 79 09 76
Near the Van Gogh Museum. Spacious rooms. Good value for money.
120 FL–175 Fl.

HOTEL MAAS
Leidsekade 91
Tel. 6 23 38 68
Fax 6 22 26 13
A reasonable hotel between the museums and the Leidseplein, with a personal touch.
125 FL–325 Fl.

otel
useumzicht
ın Luykenstraat 22
·l. 6 71 52 24
ny hotel overlooking e Rijksmuseum, ·eap and very well run ·a charming owner.
; Fl–135 Fl.

otel Trianon
·W. Brouwersstraat 3–7
·l. 6 73 20 73
·x 6 73 88 68.
art of the AMS chain, ·mfortable but lacking character. Adjoining e Concertgebouw.
30 Fl–244 Fl.

otel Van Gogh
ın de Veldestraat 5
·l. 6 62 52 62
nall hotel lacking in ·arm, but as near as ·u can get to the Van ·ogh Museum.
) Fl–75 Fl.

otel Verdi
anningstraat 9
·l. 6 76 00 73
·x 6 73 90 70
amily-run hotel near e museums. Small, ·mfortable rooms, ·cently refurbished.
0FL–150 Fl.

an Luyken
ın Luykenstraat 58
·l. 5 73 07 30
·x 6 76 38 41
arge, quiet, secluded ·tel close to the ·useums. Good value ·r money.
·ound 280 Fl.

olly Hotel Carlton
jzelstraat 4
·l. 6 22 22 66
·x 6 26 61 83
entral, comfortable, ·ut overlooking a main ·oroughfare.
·ound 460 Fl.

arriott
·adhouderskade 21
·l. 6 07 55 55
·x 6 07 55 11.
odern, friendly hotel, ·ose to the canals and e museums.
10 Fl–460 Fl.

Prinsen Hotel
Vondelstraat 38
Tel. 6 16 23 23
Fax 6 16 61 12.
Delightful hotel near the Vondelpark.
150 Fl–195 Fl.

Quentin
Leidsekade 89
Tel. 6 26 21 87
Fax 6 22 01 21
Charming hotel, near the Leidseplein.
68 FL–145 Fl.

Nightlife

Bourbonstreet Live Blues Jazz
Leidsekruisstraat 8
Tel. 6 23 34 40
Open 10pm–4am, Fri. and Sat. 10pm–5am.
Friendly atmosphere, but quality varies depending on the night and the band (blues or jazz).

Jazz Café Alto
Korte Leidsedwarsstraat 115
Tel. 6 26 32 49
Open 8pm–2am, Fri. and Sat. 8pm–3am.
Next to the Leidseplein there is a very lively jazz café that attracts bands from all over the world.

Jordaan

Culture

North Church (Noorderkerk)
Noordermarkt.
Flea market on Mon., Organic markets on Sat.

Restaurants

Bolhoed
Prinsengracht 60
Tel. 6 26 18 03
Open noon–10pm.
Vegetarian restaurant. A little terrace for use in the summer. Cheap.

Café De Tuin
2nd Tuindwarstraat 13
Tel. 6 24 45 59
Open 10am–1am , Fri. and Sat. 10am–2am.
Jazz café decorated entirely in wood, smelling of beer and tobacco. Specialties: brunches. No dinners. Backgammon and chess boards available.
6 Fl–20 Fl.

De Groene Lantaarn
Bloemgracht 47
Tel. 6 20 20 88
Open 6–9pm.
Friendly restaurant in an old house built in 1628. Especially pleasant in winter. Specialties: fondues.
30 Fl–50 Fl.

De Kikker
Egelantiersstraat 128–30
Tel. 6 27 91 98
Marble façade overgrown with ivy. One of today's most fashionable restaurants. Booking essential. Specialties: French.
60 Fl–90 Fl.

Hegeraad
Noordermarkt 34
Tel: 6 24 55 65
Many say this is the most beautiful "brown café" in Amsterdam.

Het Stuivertje
Hazenstraat 58
Tel. 6 23 13 49
Open 5.30–10.30pm. Closed Mon.
Very famous restaurant, delicious cuisine. Booking absolutely essential. Specialties: French, fish, vegetarian.
40 Fl–50 Fl.

Hotelschool Amsterdam
Elandsgracht 70
Tel. 6 23 84 28
Open noon–2pm, 5.30–8.30pm. Closed Sat., Sun. and from mid-July to mid-Aug.
A hotel school that offers quality cuisine at inexpensive prices. Set menu. Specialties: French.
22 Fl–30 Fl.

Lorreinen
Noordermarkt 42
Tel. 6 24 36 89
Open 6–10.30pm
Closed Tues.
Situated near the Noorderkerk. Excellent French specialties.
40 Fl–50 Fl.

Mango Bay
Westerstraat 91
Tel. 6 38 10 39
Open 5.30–11pm.
Specialties: exotic.

Speciaal
Nieuwe Leliestraat 142
Tel. 6 24 97 06
Open 5.30–11pm.
Closed public hol.
Indonesian restaurant reputed for its quality cuisine. Specialties: vegetarian dishes.
30 Fl–50 Fl.

◆ Flea Market ◆

The popular Noordermarkt flea market contributes to the cheerful, relaxed atmosphere of Jordaan. It takes place every Monday in front of the Noorderkerk.

THIJSSEN
Brouwersgracht 107–9
Tel. 6 23 89 94
Brown café. Young clientèle and pleasant atmosphere.

TOSCANINI
Lindengracht 75
Tel: 6 23 28 13
Open from 6pm
Bustling Italian restaurant. Book. Around 50 FL.

ACCOMMODATION

ACACIA
Lindengracht 251
Tel. 6 22 14 60
Fax 6 38 07 48
Family-run hotel on the canal. The rooms smell pleasantly of wood. Around 125 Fl.

BELGA
Hartenstraat 8
Tel. 6 24 90 80
Fax 6 23 68 62.
Charming small hotel in the heart of the canal district. Rooms with all "mod cons". 125 Fl–145 Fl.

NIGHTLIFE

DE REIGER
Nieuwe Leliestraat 34
Tel. 6 24 74 36
Open 11am–1am, Fri. and Sat. 11am–2am.
Very lively bar where locals gather.

MAZZO
Rozengracht 114
Tel. 6 26 75 00
Open 11pm–5am.
A very trendy disco.

'T SMALLE
Egelantiersgracht 12
Tel. 6 23 96 17
Open 11am–1am, Fri. and Sat. 11am–2am.
Delightful café overlooking a quiet canal. Lovely terrace.

OLD PORT WEST

RESTAURANTS

DE GOUDEN REAEL
Zandhoek 14
Tel. 6 23 38 83
Open noon–10.30pm, Sat. and Sun. 6.30–10.30pm.
Located in a charming little port. Specialties: French regional dishes. 50 Fl–80 Fl.

PLANTAGE

CULTURE

DESMET CINEMA
Plantage Middenlaan 4a
Tel. 6 27 34 34
Open 6.30–10.30pm.
Art Deco cinema-cum-café, with English-language films. Gay nights at the weekend.

DUTCH MARITIME MUSEUM
Kattenburgerplein 1
Tel. 5 23 22 22
Open 10am–5pm, Sun. 1–5pm. Closed Mon.

KROMHOUT MUSEUM NAVAL SHIPYARD
Hoogte Kadijk 147.
Near the Maritime Museum.

NATURA ARTIS MAGISTRA ZOO
Plantage Kerklaan 40
Tel. 5 23 34 00
Open 9am–5pm. Closed Mon.
Zoo and zoological museum, geological museum, planetarium and aquarium.

TROPEN MUSEUM
Linnaeusstraat 2
Tel. 5 68 82 95
Open 10am–5pm, Sat., Sun. and public hol. noon–5pm.

RESTAURANTS

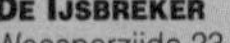

DE IJSBREKER
Weesperzijde 23
Tel. 6 68 18 05
Open 10am–1am, Fri. and Sat. 10am–2am.
A delightful café on the banks of the Amstel. Specialties: brunches, wines, vinho verde. 10 Fl–30 Fl.

TAMAN SARI
Plantage Kerklaan 32
Tel. 6 23 71 30
Open 5–11pm
Good Indonesian restaurant close to Artis Zoo. Quiet. 25 FL–40 FL.

SHOPPING

ALBERT CUYP MARKET
Albert Cuypstraat
Open 9am–5pm
Closed Sun.
The biggest market in Amsterdam. You can find virtually anything here.

ANTIQUARIAAT STAAL
Staalstraat 11
Tel. 6 23 18 05
Open11am–6pm.
Closed Sun.
Vast selection of old books.

ANTIQUE BOOKS MARKET
t'Spui and Oudemanhuispoort
Open 10am–4pm every Friday.
Plenty of books, especially from the 18th century.

CONDOMERIE HET GULDEN VLIES
Warmoesstraat 141
Tel. 6 27 41 74
Open 1–6pm, Sat. noon–5pm. Closed Sun and Feb.

DE WATERWINKEL
Roelof Hartstraat 10
Tel. 6 75 59 32
Open 9am–6pm, Sat. 9am–5pm Closed Sun.
Devoted purely to mineral water of all sorts, some of which are highly unusual.

DE WITTE TANDEN WINKEL
Runstraat 5
Tel. 6 23 34 43
Open 10am–6pm, Sat. 10am–5pm. Closed Sun
Everything to do with toothbrushes!

FLEA MARKET
In the square in front of the Noorderkerk every Monday and on the Waterlooplein from Mon to Sat.

GEELS & CO.
Warmoesstraat 67
Tel. 6 24 06 83
Open 9am–6pm.
Closed Sun.
Amsterdam's oldest "coffee-shop". Museum open Tues., Thur. and Sat.

KEIJZER
Prinsengracht 180
Tel. 6 24 08 23
Open 9am–5.30pm, Sat. 9am–5pm. Closed Sun.
Specialists since 1839, in coffee and tea. Friendly, original décor.

MIGNON
Vijzelstraat 125
Tel.4 20 26 87
Open 5pm–1am.
This is one of the so-called "Avondwinkels", grocery shops that open when the other ones close.

JACOB HOOIJ
Kloveniersburgwal 12
Open Mon. noon-6pm, Tues. to Fri. 8.15am–6pm, Sat. 8.15am–5pm
Near the Nieuwmarkt. Herbalists since 1734. Herbs, teas and natural remedies.

◆ KEIJZER ◆

On the edge of Jordaan, this very old tea and coffee merchant's concocts "house" mixtures appreciated by connoisseurs for generations.

APPENDICES

BIBLIOGRAPHY, *328*
LIST OF ILLUSTRATIONS, *330*

Essential reading

◆ *Amsterdam, Blue Guide*, ed. Charles Ford, Norton, New York, and A&C Black, London, 5th ed. 1993.
◆ Hopkins (A.): *Holland*, Faber & Faber, London, 1988.
◆ Lambert (A.M.): *The Making of the Dutch Landscape*, 2nd ed., 1985.
◆ Rosenberg (J.) et al.: *Dutch Art and Architecture 1600–1800*, Penguin, London, rev. ed. 1988.
◆ Schama (S.): *The Embarrassment of Riches. An Interpretation of Dutch Culture in the Golden Age*, Collins, London, 1987.
◆ Wilson (C.H.): *The Dutch Republic and the Civilization of the 17th Century*, Weidenfeld & Nicolson, London, 1968.

General

◆ Blaeu (W.) and Blaeu J.): *Grand Atlas of the 17th-century World*, ed. J. Goss and P. Clark, Studio Editions, London, 1990.
◆ Elias (E.) et Van Wijk (E.): *Holland. Wonderland out of the Water*, Batsford, London, 1956.
◆ Haley (K.D.H.): *The British and the Dutch*, George Philip, London, 1988.
◆ Havard (H.): *The Heart of Holland*, transl. C. Hoey, Bentley & Son, London, 1880.
◆ Hollander (F.): *Houseboats in Amsterdam*, Bauverlag, Wiesbaden, 1983.
◆ Kistenmaker (R.), Van Gelder (R.): *Amsterdam: The Golden Age (1275–1795)*, Abbeville Press, New York, 1983.
◆ Meijer (E.): *The Rijksmuseum*, Scala, London, 1985.
◆ Nieuwhoff (C.), Diepraam (W.), Oorthuys (C.): *The Costumes of Holland*, Elsevier, Amsterdam and Brussels, 1985.
◆ Olie (J.): *Photographer of 19th-century Amsterdam*, Van Gennep, Amsterdam, 1981.
◆ Regin (D.): *Traders, Artists, Burghers*, Van Gorcum, Amsterdam, 1976.
◆ Schama (S.): *The Embarrassment of Riches. An Interpretation of Dutch Culture in the Golden Age*, Collins, London, 1987.
◆ Spies (P.), Kleijn (K.), Smit (J.) and Kurpershoek (E.), photographs Van Oord-de Peel (A.): *The Canals of Amsterdam*, D'ARTS, Amsterdam, 1991.
◆ Vanderheiden (A.): *The Story of Amsterdam*, Rootveldt Boeken, Amsterdam, 1987.
◆ Wilson (C. H.): *Holland and Britain*, Collins, London, 1946.

History

◆ Boxer (C.R.): *The Dutch Seaborne Empire 1600–1800*, 1965.
◆ Carasso (D.): *A Short History of Amsterdam*, Amsterdam Historical Museum, 1985.
◆ Cotterell (G.): *Amsterdam*, 1972.
◆ Geyl (P.): *The Revolt of the Netherlands 1555–1609*, Cassell, London, 1988; *The Netherlands in the 17th Century 1609–48*, Cassell, London, 1989.
◆ Grimal (H.): *Decolonization: The British, French, Dutch and Belgian Empires 1919–63*, 1978.
◆ Huizinga (J.): *Dutch Civilization in the 17th Century and Other Essays*, compiled P. Geyl and F.W.N. Hugenholtz, 1968.
◆ Israel (J.I.): *The Dutch Republic and the Hispanic World 1606-61*, Clarendon Press, Oxford, 1982.
◆ Parker (G.): *The Dutch Revolt*, Penguin, Harmondsworth, rev. ed. 1988; *Spain and the Netherlands 1559–1659*, Fontana, London, 1990.
◆ Prevenier (W.) and Blockmans (W.): *The Burgundian Netherlands*, 1986.
◆ Rowen (H.H.): *The Princes of Orange*, 1988.
◆ Wilson (C.H.): *The Dutch Republic and the Civilization of the 17th Century*, Weidenfeld & Nicolson, London, 1968.

Society

◆ Colijn (H.): *Of Dutch Ways*, Dillon Press Inc., Minneapolis, Minnesota, 1980.
◆ Goudsblom (J.): *Dutch Society*, Random House, New York, 1968.
◆ Griffiths (R.T.): *The Economy and Politics of the Netherlands since 1945*, 1980.
◆ Lijphart (A.): *The Politics of Accommodation: Pluralism and Democracy in the Netherlands*, 2nd ed. rev. 1975.
◆ Newton (G.): *The Netherlands: An Historical and Cultural Survey 1795–1977*, 1978.
◆ Shetter (W.Z.): *The Netherlands in Perspective: The Organizations of Society and Environment*, 1987.
◆ Van Amersfoort (H.): *Immigration and the Formation of Minority Groups: The Dutch Experience 1945–75*, 1982.
◆ Zumthor (P.): *Daily Life in Rembrandt's Holland*, transl. S.W. Taylor, Weidenfeld & Nicolson, London, 1942.

Geography

◆ Lambert (A.M.): *The Making of the Dutch Landscape*, 2nd ed., 1985.
◆ Meijer (H.): *Compact Geography of the Netherlands*, 5th rev. ed., 1985.

Literature

◆ Baudelaire (C.): *Paris Spleen*, transl. L. Varäse, Peter Owen, London, 1947.
◆ Camus (A.): *The Fall*, transl. Justin O'Brien, Hamish Hamilton, London, 1957.
◆ Conrad (J.): *The Mirror of the Sea*, J.M. Dent & Sons Ltd, London, 1906.
◆ Descartes (R.): *Correspondence*, 1631
◆ Diderot (D.): *Voyage en Hollande*, Maspéro, Paris, 1982
◆ Frank (A.): *The Diary of Anne Frank*, trans. B.M. Mooyaart-Doubleday, Pan Books, London, 1954.
◆ Freeling (N.): *Love in Amsterdam*, Penguin, Harmondsworth, 1975; *A City Solitary*, Heinemann, London, 1985; Cold Iron, Deutsch, London, 1986.
◆ Hillesum (E.): *Etty, A Diary 1941-3*, transl. A.J. Pomerans, Cape, London, 1983.
◆ Meijer (R.P.): *Literature of the Low Countries*, 1978.
◆ Mulisch (H.): *The Assault*, transl. C.N. White, Penguin, Harmondsworth, 1986
◆ Multatuli: *Max Havelaar, or the Coffe[e] Auctions of the Dutch Trading Company*.
◆ Nooteboom (C.): *Rituals*, transl. A. Dixo[n], Penguin, Harmondsworth, 1992
◆ Weevers (T.): *Poetry of the Netherlands in [i]ts European Context 1170–1930*, 1960.
◆ Van de Wetering (J.) *Hard Rain*, Gollancz, London, 1987.
◆ Wolkers (J.): *Turkish Delight*, transl. G. Kilburn, Futura Publications, London, 1975.

Painting

◆ Alpers (S.): *The Art [of] Describing*, John Murray, London, 1983
◆ Descargues (P.): *Dutch Painting*, Thame[s] and Hudson, London, 1959.
◆ Fromentin (E.): *The Masters of Past Time: Dutch and Flemish Painting from Van Eyc[k] to Rembrandt*, ed. H. Gerson, Phaidon, Oxford, 1981.
◆ Fuchs (R.H.): *Dutch Painting*, Thames and Hudson, London, 197[8]
◆ Genaille (R.): *Flemis[h] Painting from Van Eyc[k] to Bruegel*, transl. L. Schenk, Zwemmer, London, 1956.
◆ Jaffé (H.L.C.): *De Stijl: Visions of Utopia*.
◆ Lambert (J.-C.): *Kare[l] Appel*, Abbeville Press, New York, 1980.
◆ Luttervelt (R. van): *Dutch Museums*, Thames and Hudson, London, 1960.
◆ Meijer (E.R.): *Dutch Painting: 17th Century*, McGraw-Hill, New Yor[k], 1963.
◆ Overy (P.): *De Stijl*, Thames and Hudson, London, 1991.
◆ Rosenberg (J.) et al. *Dutch Art and Architecture 1600–1800*, Penguin, London, rev. ed. 1988.
◆ Stechow (W.): *Dutch Landscape Painting o[f] the 17th Century*
◆ Van der Endt (N.): *Amsterdam naief. Amsterdam naive*, Cantecleer, De Bilt, 1987 (in Dutch and English).

◆ **HALS** ◆

BAARD (H.P.): *Frans als*, Thames and udson, London, 1981.
DESCARGUES (P.): *Hals: ographical and ritical Study*, 1968.
KÜHLER (N.), LEVY-VAN ALM (K.): *Frans Hals: ilitia Pieces*, Gary chwartz/SDU, The ague, 1990.
SLIVE (S.): *Frans Hals, vols.*, 1971.

◆ **MONDRIAAN** ◆

GAY (P.): *Art and Act*, arper and Row, New ork and London, 1976.
JAFFÉ (H.L.C.): *Piet ondriaan*, Thames nd Hudson, London, 970.
SEUPHOR (M.): *Piet ondriaan: Life and ork*, Thames and udson, London, 1957.

◆ **REMBRANDT** ◆

ALPERS (S.): *embrandt's Enterprise*, hames and Hudson, ondon, 1988.
BENESCH (O.): *The rawings of embrandt, 6 vols.*, 973.
BONNIER (H.): *embrandt, transl. V. enedict*, Pall Mall ress, London, 1970.
BREDIUS (A.): *The omplete Edition of the aintings of Rembrandt*, v. by H. Gerson, 1969.
FUCHS (R.): *embrandt in msterdam*, New York, 969.
GERSON (H.): *embrandt Paintings*, ew York and London, 968.
HAAK (B.): *embrandt: His Life, is Work, His Time*, 969.
KITSON (M.): *embrandt*, Oxford, 982.
SLIVE (S.): *Rembrandt nd his Critics 630–1730*, The Hague, 953.
STRAUSS (W.) AND VAN ER MEULEN (M.): *The embrandt Documents*, ew York, 1979.
WHITE (C.): *embrandt as an tcher*, 2 vols., 1969; *embrandt*, Thames nd Hudson, London nd New York, 1984.

◆ **VAN GOGH** ◆

BONAFOUX (P.): *Van ogh*, 1990.
◆ CABANNE (P.): *Van Gogh*, transl. M. Martin, 1963.
◆ *The Complete Letters of Vincent van Gogh*, intro. by V.W. van Gogh, 3 vols., 1958.
◆ HULSKER (J.): *The Complete Van Gogh: Paintings, Drawings, Sketches*, 1980.
◆ MCQUILLAN (M.): *Van Gogh*, 1989.
◆ SCHAPIRO (M.): *Van Gogh*, 1988.
◆ STEIN (S.A.): *Van Gogh. A Retrospective*, 1986.

◆ **VERMEER** ◆

◆ BLOCH (V.): *All the Paintings of Jan Vermeer*, London, 1963.
◆ SNOW (E.A.): *A Study of Vermeer*, University of California Press, Berkeley and London, 1979.
◆ *Vermeer of Delft*, Phaidon, Oxford, 1978.
◆ WHEELOCK (A.K.): *Jan Vermeer*, Thames and Hudson, London, 1981.

◆ **ARCHITECTURE** ◆

◆ BROERS (P.), KEMME (G.), KIERS (J.), MATTIE (E.), VAN DER WERF (J.), VAN KLINKEN (M.), VAN LEEUWEN (W.), PHOTOGRAPHS DERWIG (J.): *Amsterdam Architecture. A Guide*, ed. G. Kemme, Thoth, Amsterdam, 1992.
◆ HUET (B.), BOHIGAS (O.), KRIER (R.), OTIS (L.), JAHN (H.): *Amsterdam. An Architectural Lesson*, Thoth, Amsterdam, 1988.
◆ KUYPER (W.): *Dutch Classicist Architecture*, Delft, 1980.
◆ MATTIE (E.), photographs DERWIG (E.): *Amsterdam School*, Architectura & Natura, Amsterdam, 1991.
◆ ROSENBERG (J.) et al.: *Dutch Art and Architecture 1600–1800*, Penguin, London, rev ed. 1988.
◆ THORNTON (P.): *Seventeenth-century Interior Decoration in England, France and Holland*, 1978.

◆ **GUIDES** ◆

◆ *Amsterdam, Blue Guide*, ed. Charles Ford, Norton, New York, and A&C Black, London, 5th ed. 1993.
◆ ATTWELL (B.): *Amsterdam*, 1968.
◆ *Baedecker's Amsterdam*, rev. ed. 1991.
◆ *Holland, Belgium and Luxembourg, Rough Guide*, ed. M. Dunford and J. Holland, 1990.
◆ KNAP (G.H.): *The Port of Amsterdam*, 1970.
◆ LEITCH (M.): *Slow Walks in Amsterdam*, Hodder and Stoughton, London, 1990.
◆ MURRAY (J.J.): *Amsterdam in the Age of Rembrandt*, 1967.
◆ *Netherlands, Insight Guides*, ed. C. Catling, APA Publishing Ltd, London, 1992.
◆ *The Penguin Guide to Amsterdam*, ed. V. Westzaan, transl. P. Vincent, Harmondsworth, 1990.
◆ REINEWALD (C.): *Amsterdam Arts Guide*, Art Guide, London, 1985.
◆ STOUTENBEEK (J.) AND VIGEVENO (P.): *A Guide to Jewish Amsterdam*, Jewish Historical Museum, Amsterdam, 1985.
◆ VAN DER HEYDEN (A.) AND KROON (B.): *The Glory of Amsterdam: An Explorer's Guide*, 1975.

ACKNOWLEDGMENTS

We would like to thank the following publishers or copyright-holders for permission to reproduce the quotations on pages 98–112.

◆ ALFRED A. KNOPF, INC.: Excerpt from *The Fall*, by Albert Camus, translated by Justin O'Brien (Alfred A. Knopf, Inc. 1957). Reprinted by permission. (Reprinted in the UK by permission of Hamish Hamilton).

◆ ALFRED A. KNOPF, INC.: Excerpt from *The Embarrassment of Riches*, by Simon Schama, copyright © 1987 by Simon Schama. Reprinted by permission. (Reprinted in the UK by permission of HarperCollins Publishers).

◆ DOUBLEDAY and VALENTINE MITCHELL PUBLISHERS: Excerpt from *Anne Frank: The Diary of a Young Girl*, by Anne Frank, copyright © by Otto Frank. Rights outside the US controlled by Valentine Mitchell Publishers, London. Reprinted by permission of Doubleday, a division of Bantam Doubleday Dell Publishing Group, Inc. and Valentine Mitchell Publishers.

◆ FABER & FABER LIMITED: Excerpt from *Holland*, by Adam Hopkins, copyright © Adam Hopkins. Reprinted by permission of the author.

◆ FARRAR STRAUS & GIROUX, INC.: Poem "Rembrandt" from *Notebook 1967–8*, by Robert Lowell, copyright © 1969 by Robert Lowell. Reprinted by permission. (Reprinted in the UK by permission of Faber & Faber Limited)

◆ NEW DIRECTIONS PUBLISHING CORPORATION: Excerpt from *Paris Spleen*, by Charles Baudelaire, translated by Louise Varese, copyright © 1970 by New Directions Publishing Corp. Reprinted by permission. (Reprinted in the UK by permission of Peter Owen Ltd.)

Cover : Tourist poster © Musée de la Publicité, Paris.
1 Nieuwmarkt. 19-27, negative Jacob Olie © GAA.
2/3 *Waalseilandsgracht,* photo Jacob Olie © GAA. *Ships in the Houthaven,* negative G. Breitner © RKD.
4/5 *Woman on the Lindengracht,* negative G. Breitner © RKD. Amsterdam. *Teertuinen Prinseneiland,* negative G. Breitner © RKD.
6/7 *Damrak between Vrouwensteeg, Baafjessteeg and Zoutsteeg,* April 30, 1897, negative Jacob Olie © GAA. *On the Rokin,* negative G. Breitner © RKD.
9 *The Zuiderkerk Seen from Groenburgwal,* 1873–4, oil on canvas, Claude Monet © Philadelphia Museum of Art, Wilstach Coll.
16 Photo © P. van Dijk/Gallimard.
18 Photo of heron © P. van Dijk/Gallimard.
19 Photo of canal © Hollandse Hoogte, P. van Riel. Photo of lock © P. van Dijk/Gallimard.
21 Painting (top of page) © Rijksmuseum Zuiderzeemuseum, Enkhuizen.
23 Photos © Frits van Daalen.
24–5 Photos © International Center for Flowering Bulbs, Hillegom.
26 Painting © Frans-Hals Museum, Haarlem. Photos © Dutch Office for Dairy Produce.
27 Coat of arms of the city of Amsterdam © Privatecoll.
28 Parchment and seal dated October 27, 1275 © GAA. Oudekerk and canal, 1891 © Explorer.
29 *Charles V aged about 16,* oil on canvas, B. van Orley, Louvre © R.M.N. *Battle between the Spanish and the Dutch,* May 1573, oil on canvas, H.C. Vroom © Rijksmuseum, Amsterdam. Prince of Orange sign © GAA.
30/31 Panorama, etching © GAA.
30 *Marie de' Medici's Arrival in Amsterdam in 1638* © Gallimard Archives. *Portrait of Pieter Stuyvesant* (c. 1610–82) © Iconographisch Bureau. Naval battle © National Maritime Museum, Antwerp.
31 *Portrait of Johan de Witt,* 1672, etching © Bibl. Nat., Paris/Viollet. *The States General of the Netherlands Meeting at The Hague,* 1651 © Viollet Coll. *The Prussian Army Entering Amsterdam,* 1800, oil on canvas, anonymous © AHM.
32 *The Lutheran Church on Fire* © GAA. *Napoleon in Amsterdam,* October 8, 1811, etching © GAA. *Port of Amsterdam,* oil on canvas, Nicolaas Baur (1767–1820) © AHM. Portrait of F. Domela Nieuwenhuis © GAA.
33 The Allied forces entering Amsterdam, May 1945 © Kryn Taconis/Magnum. Flood © Fotoarchief Spaarnestad. Demonstration in Amsterdam © Leonard Freed/Magnum. Queen Beatrix © Geeraerts/Gamma.
34 Plan of Amsterdam in 1655, 1795 © Privatecoll. Plan, 1866 © GAA.
34/35 Map Amsterdam (1674) by Visscher, Kog Coll. © Rijksmuseum Foundation, Amsterdam.
35 *Amsterdam's new canal* © GAA. Plan of the Amsterdam region © Private coll.
36 *Map of Amsterdam,* 1560, by Jacob van Deventer © Rijksarchief in Noord-Holland, Haarlem. Plan of Amsterdam, 1612 © Private coll.
36/37 Map engraved by Cornelis Anthonisz. Kog Coll. © Rijksmuseum, Amsterdam.
37 Watercolor map © Universiteitsbibliotheek, Amsterdam.
38 *Portrait of Francis Gomar* (Gomarus), etching © Bibl. Nat. *Portrait of Pierre Bayle* (1647–1706), pencil © Iconographisch Bureau. *Portrait of Baruch Spinoza* (1632–77), etching © Roger-Viollet. Studying Jewish literature © Private coll.
38/39 *Fishers of Souls,* oil on wood, A.P. van de Venne © Rijksmuseum, Amsterdam.
39 *Allegory on the quarrels between Remonstrants in 1618* (1721), oil on wood, A. van der Eyck © Musée des Beaux-Arts de Lyon. Public Catholic service (1892) © GAA.
40 Sextant and page from Geographia Blaviana, Joan Blaeu Atlas, vol. I 1661 © Bibl. Nat. Squat on Spuistraat © P. van Dijk/Gallimard. Chinese travelling salesman © Fotoarchief Spaarnestad *De groene griet,* 1986, oil on wood, Lotte Funke © Hamer Gallery, Amsterdam.
40/41 Map of Europe, Joan Blaeu Atlas © Bibl. Nat.
41 Coffeeshop © List/Sipa/Image. Portrait of Descartes after Frans Hals, Louvre © RMN. Southeast Asians and Africans © Fotoarchief Spaarnestad.
42 Cartouche of a writer © P. van Dijk/Gallimard. Costumes © H. Cassiers. Volendam © Olaf Klyn Productions. Men © Georges Viollon/Rapho.
42/43 Classroom © Private coll.
43 Men seated (top of page) © Rapho. Old-style script © GAA.
44 St Antonia School sign © P. van Dijk/Gallimard. Portrait C. Nooteboom © C. Sarramon. Old lettering, etching © GAA. Fisherman's wife, Volendam, negative H. Berssenbrugge, 1920 © Rijksmuseum Zuiderzee, Enkhuizen.
45 *Fish with Lemon,* oil on wood, Pieter Claesz © Rijksmuseum, Amsterdam.
46 St Nicholas © Broquet/Explorer. Sailors poster © Nederlands Theater Instituut.
47 *Marie de' Medici in Amsterdam in 1638,* etching, S. Savrij © AHM. *The Queen Mother's Birthday,* oil on canvas Zelko Premerl © Hame Gallery. The Queen Mother's birthday © P. van Dijk/Gallimard. *Traveling fair,* lithograp by Graeyvanger © GAA.
48 Double bass © Ja Bogaerts/HH. Accordion © Wallrafen/HH. Brass band © Van der Noort/HH. Barrel organ © Bogaerts/HH. Street musicians © NBT. Concertgebouw orchestra © NBT.
49 *The Letter,* oil on canvas, J. Vermeer © Rijksmuseum, Amsterdam. *Old musical instruments,* oil on wood, Westerkerk interior, Gérard de Lairesse (1641–1711) Private coll.
50/51 All photos © Christian Sarramon, except *Eerste Klas, Hooghoudt, De Zeilvaart, De Jaren,* a *De Drie Fleschjes* © Christian Sarramon/Flammarion Café de Kroon, 1906, gouache, Leo Gestel GAA.
52 Stained-glass window © Mazin/Top. Shop window © Van d Hilts. Details of window displays © C. Sarramon.
53 Hairdresser's salo and coffee © C. Sarramon. "Gaper" sign Partoguiste Coll. © P. van Dijk/Gallimard. *Old Apothecary's, Sho* pen and ink (1877) © GAA.
54 Cover of *Marie de Medici's Arrival in Amsterdam,* Caspar Barlaeus © Koniklijke Bibliotheek, The Hagu *Portrait of Hugo Groti* etching © Bibl. Nat. Children's book (1759 Amsterdam © Universiteitsbibliothee *Amsterdam. Gaming House on Kalverstraa* oils, I. Ouwater © Rijksmuseum, Amsterdam.
55 I. Elzevier's signature © Explorer/Archives. Title page of Blaeu's Geography © Bibl. N

itle page of Houwlijck, y Jacob Cats, ordrecht (1655) © tlas Van Stolk.
ijksmuseum Library terior © C. Sarramon.
6 *Shade lamp* © Rob ckhardt 1992.
urniture, Delft tiles and upboards, ijksmuseum interior © . Sarramon.
7 *Chairs* by G. ietveld © tedelijkmuseum, msterdam.
urr eats/Jurr drinks © ob Eckhardt 1990.
Upside-down" lamp © ob Eckhardt 1992.
leo-Gothic De Stijl rmchair © C. arramon.
msterdam School upboard © C. arramon.
kind of Hugo © Rob ckhardt 1989.
8 Flower-stall bicycle) P. van Dijk/Gallimard.
implex poster, 910–20 © Nederlands eclammuseum Coll.
8/59 Miscellaneous icycles © P. van ijk/Gallimard.
aricature, colored tching © Private coll.
9 Advertisement howing woman on icycle © Musée de la ublicité, Paris.
olding bike, etching, rivate coll.
0 Rowing © H. Vallrafen/HH.
jax 1904 © Ajax Club rchives.
owing, 1913, negative . van Elfrinkhoff © tichting Nederlands oto/Haarlem.
0/61 *Skating Scene,* il on wood, Adam van reen (1599/1665), ouvre © RMN.
1 Skaters (top of age) © M. Hers/NBT.
9th-century leisure ursuits, etching © AA.
lympic Games poster, 928 © Musée de affiche, Paris.
kating on the canal © . de Kam/HH.
4 Van Nelle ackaging, 1930 © aags emeentemuseum oll., Amsterdam.
ther illustrations © allimard.
7 *Dam Square by light,* oil on canvas, .H. Breitner 1857–1923) © Van oorst van Beest

Gallery, The Hague.
88/89 *The Port of Amsterdam* (1674), oil on canvas, Ludolf Backhuizen, Kunsthistorisches Museum, Vienna © E. Lessing/Magnum.
View of Amsterdam from the IJ, 1671-80, pen and watercolor by Doumer © GAA.
89 *View of Amsterdam* (1641), pen and ink, Rembrandt © Archives/Gallimard.
90 *View of the Herengracht, Amsterdam,* oil on canvas, Jan Wijnants (1630–1684) © The Cleveland Museum of Art.
90/91 *Annual lepers' procession,* 1633, oil on canvas, A.V. Nieulandt © AHM.
91 *The Flower Market,* 1670–5, oil on canvas, Gerrit Berckheyde © AHM.
92 *The Port of Amsterdam,* oil on canvas, Willem van de Velde II the Younger (1663–1707), held by the Rijksmuseum, Amsterdam © Explorer/Archives.
92/93 *View of the IJ, Amsterdam,* oil on canvas, Karel Appel © Property of Christie's.
93 *Haringpakkerstoren* (detail), by A. Stork, B. de Geus van der Heuvel Coll. © Giraudon.
94/95 *The Zuiderkerk seen from Groenburgwal* 1873–4, oil on canvas, Claude Monet © Philadelphia Museum of Art, Wilstach Coll.
96 *The Vegetable Market in Amsterdam,* oil on canvas, Gabriel Metsu (1629–67), Louvre © RMN.
97 *Abraham Visited by an Angel,* ink sketch by Rembrandt, Bibl. Nat. Print Coll. © E. Lessing, Magnum.
98 Village near Zaandam © P. Berger/Rapho.
99 *The Leidsegracht in Autumn,* 1983, oil on canvas, Zeljko Premerl, Meijer Coll. © Hamer Gallery, Amsterdam.
100 *Swan House on the Singel,* pencil © GAA.
101 *Boats on a Canal,* etching © Bibl. Nat. Paris

102 *Shop Window,* oil on canvas Isaac Israels © Rijksmuseum, Amsterdam.
102/103 Panorama © GAA.
104 Demonstration on the Dam © Leonard Freed/Magnum.
105 *Barrel Organ,* acrylic, Aad Groenendijk © Hamer Gallery.
106 Etching of a canal © Private coll.
107 Etchings of household scenes © Van Stolk Atlas.
108 No. 375 Herengracht, gouache © GAA.
110/111 *Panorama,* etching © GAA.
112 *Plan and view of the IJ,* 1857, watercolor and pen, J. Galman © GAA
113 Photo of façade © H. Lozès.
114/115 Houses and bikes © C. Sarramon.
Red light district © J.P. Porcher/Explorer.
116/117 Photos © H. Lozès (top) © C. Sarramon (boats).
118 © C. Sarramon.
119 *The Dam with Amsterdam's new City Hall,* 1688, oil on canvas, Jan van der Heyden (1637–1712), Louvre © RMN.
120 Head sign © P. van Dijk/Gallimard.
121 Cartouche © P. van Dijk/Gallimard.
The Singel in Winter, etching by Fouquet © Private coll.
122 Cartouche and Begijnhof house© P. van Dijk/Gallimard.
Begijnhof, 1986, oil on wood, Lotte Funke © Hamer Gallery, Amsterdam.
122/123 Begijnhof, etching © GAA.
123 All negatives © P. van Dijk/Gallimard.
124 *Silver funeral medal,* by J. Grill © AHM.
Noorderkerk , c. 1664, oil on canvas, A. Beerstraten © AHM.
Wooden statue of a woman, gravenbeeld, vroom © AHM.
Goudsbloemstraat, pen and ink, W. Hekking © AHM.
Paul and Barnabas at Lystra, Pieter Lastman © AHM.
Cartouches museum interior © P. van Dijk/Gallimard.
Merry tavern, A. van Ostade © AHM.
125 *Adoration of the Magi* (details), oil, Pieter Aertsz © AHM.
Lame man, 1610, etching, J.G. van der Vliet © AHM.
Goliath, c. 1650, by Albert Jansz © P. van Dijk/Gallimard.
126 Squat in Spuistraat © P. van Dijk/Gallimard.
Bridge, watercolor © GAA.
Squat © H. Peretz.
127 *Rokin,* oil on canvas, G. Breitner © Van Voorst van Beest, Gallery, The Hague.
Etching of Rokin © GAA.
128 Royal Palace © P. van Dijk/Gallimard.
128/129 *The Dam,* 1656, colored etching by Ligelbach © GAA.
129 *Old Amsterdam City Hall,* 1651, oil on canvas, P.J. Saenredam © Rijksmuseum, Amsterdam.
Photo of the Dam © Yo Trung Dung/Cosmos.
130 Café cartouche © P. van Dijk/Gallimard.
Church and old post office © P. van Dijk/Gallimard.
Florist, 1917, colored pencil, M. Monnickendam © GAA.
130/131 *The Damrak,* watercolor © P. van Dijk/Gallimard.
131 *Portrait of the Cartographer Johanes Blaeu,* oil on canvas © Vereeniging Nederlands Historisch Scheepvaart Museum.
Street sign and houses © P. van Dijk/Gallimard.
132 *The Exchange,* etching © Private coll.
The Amsterdam Exchange, 1668, oils, Job Berckheyde © AHM.
The Exchange, etching © KB.
133 Façade, Berlage's Exchange © P. van Dijk/Gallimard.
Portrait of H.P. Berlage 1916, etching by J. Toorop © Iconographisch Bureau.
Interior of Berlage's Exchange © C. Sarramon.
134 Interior of the Oudekerk © A. Lorgnier.
134/135 Drawing of the Oudekerk © M. Pommier/Gallimard.

135 Oudekerk organ © J.J. Schroevers.
136 Back street © P. van Dijk/Gallimard.
Shop in the red light district © C. Sarramon.
The Old Quarter, 18th-century, colored etching © Archives/Explorer.
137 Cartouches, street sign, house façade © P. van Dijk/Gallimard.
Interior of the Amstelkring © C. Sarramon.
Couple, gouache © GAA.
138 Central Station (top of page) © Private coll.
Street sign, façade and canal © P. van Dijk/Gallimard.
Port, watercolor © Private coll.
139 *Nieuwmarkt*, 1756, colored etching © GAA.
140 Portrait of Allard Pierson, Private coll. © GAA.
House on the Rokin © P. van Dijk/Gallimard.
141 Etruscan sarcophagus © Allard Pierson Museum.
Boats on the Rokin, etching © Bibl. Nat.
142 *Church door on Oudezijds Voorburgwal*, etching © GAA.
Carriage entrance and street sign © P. van Dijk/Gallimard.
Canal, watercolor © GAA.
143 Cartouches, shop, window decorations © P. van Dijk/Gallimard.
Oudezijds Achterburgwal, early 20th century © Private coll.
144 *Admiralty House*, 1764, etching © GAA.
Art Deco hotel The Grand © P. van Dijk/Gallimard.
Gathering of the Burgomasters, 1597, etching © GAA.
Children Questioning, 1949, soluble glass and paint on a mixture of cement and sand, by Karel Appel © Private coll.
145 Street sign, shop and church sign © P. van Dijk/Gallimard.
Old Walloon Church, 18th century, colored etching © Explorer.
146 *VOC Ship*, 1647, etching, W. Hollar © Nederlands Historisch Scheepvaart Museum.
VOC plate, blue and white china, 17th century © Scheepvaart Museum.
Portrait assumed to be of Admiral Cornelis Tromp, mid–17th century, Dutch school, Louvre © RMN.
VOC Headquarters, etching © Gallimard Archives.
146/147 *Return from the Second Voyage to the Indies*, 1599, oils, H.C. Vroom © AHM.
147 *Relations between the Japanese and the Dutch*, 1680, anonymous © Scheepvaart Museum, Amsterdam.
The Batavia Market, 1658, oils, A. Beeckman © Scheepvaart Museum, Amsterdam.
Shells, vol. III of the book by F. Valentijn © AHM.
Plant drawing, H. d'Acquet Coll. (1632–1706) © Library of the. Landbouwuniversiteit, Wageningen.
Ceylonese script © Universiteitsbibliotheek, Amsterdam.
VOC Factory at Houghly in Bengal, 1665, oil on canvas, H. van Schuylenburg © Scheepvaart Museum, Amsterdam.
148 *Portrait of M.A. de Ruyter*, oil on canvas, F. Bol © Scheepvaart Museum, Amsterdam.
Saltcellar from China, 1635–45 © Groningen Museum.
148/149 *VOC Factory in Bengal*, oil on canvas, H. V. Schuylenburg © Rijksmuseum, Amsterdam.
149 View of the Maritime Museum © A.J. Hilgersom.
Passion flower drawing, H. d'Acquet © Universiteitsbibliotheek, Amsterdam.
Erythrina Orientalis, gouache, N. Witsen Voll. (1641–1717) © Teyler Museum, Haarlem.
Dutch Squadron of the East India Company, oils, Ludolf Backhuysen (1631–1708), Louvre © RMN.
Grapefruit, H. d'Acquet Coll.© Universiteitsbibliotheek, Amsterdam.
150 Dutch East India Company building © P. van Dijk/Gallimard.
Canal, 1879, colored etching © GAA.
151 Kloveniersburgwal, Trippenhuis © GAA.
Cartouche and sign © P. van Dijk/Gallimard.
Herbalist's, interior © C. Sarramon.
152 *St Anthony's Gate*, 19th century, etching © Bibl. Nat.
House on the water © P. van Dijk/Gallimard.
152/153 *Nieuwmarkt*, 1765, oils, Isaak Ouwater © AHM.
153 Skating poster © GAA.
154 Cartouche and exterior, Scheepvaarthuis © P. van Dijk/Gallimard.
Interior of the Scheepvaarthuis © C. Sarramon.
Montelbaanstoren, 1544, etching © GAA.
154/155 Etching of canal and Montelbaanstoren © Bibl. Nat.
155 Street sign, cartouches and doorway © P. van Dijk/Gallimard.
Montelbaanstoren, 1986, oil on canvas, Jannie Kuiper © Hamer Gallery.
156 *Self-portrait*, Rembrandt, etching © Rembrandt Museum, Amsterdam.
Zuiderkerk © P. van Dijk/Gallimard.
H.C. de Keyser, 1621, etching © GAA.
St Antony's Church, watercolor © GAA.
157 *Diamond-cutting Works*, etching © DR.
Monument © P. van Dijk/Gallimard.
Rembrandt's House, watercolor © GAA.
158 Moses and Aaron Church © P. van Dijk/Gallimard.
Portrait of J.D. Meijer, oil on canvas, L. Morits (1773–1850) © Rijksmuseum, Amsterdam.
Façades of the Portuguese Synagogue, 1724, wash drawing, B. Picart © AHM.
159 *Interior of the of the Portuguese Synagogue*,1680, oils, E. de Witte © Rijksmuseum, Amsterdam.
Engraved medal, Portuguese Synagogue © GAA.
View of the Synagogue of the German Jews © DR.
160 *General view of Amsterdam*, colored etching, anonymous, Bibl. Marmottan, Paris © Explorer.
Interior of the "Stopera" © P. van Dijk/Gallimard.
Groenburgwal canal © DR.
161 Keizersgracht © H Lozès.
162 *Portrait of C.P. Hooft*, etching © GAA.
Map of Amsterdam 1612, Nic. Visscher © Rijksmuseum, Kog Coll
163 View of the Singel © P. van Dijk/Gallimard
164 Lutheran Church © P. van Dijk/Gallimard.
Street sign © P. van Dijk/Gallimard.
Round Luthersekerk, Singel, etching © GAA.
165 Cartouche at No. 74 Singel, cats' houseboat, House of the Swan © P. van Dijk/Gallimard.
166 Cartouche next to No. 8 Blauwburgwal, cartouche No. 188 Singel © P. van Dijk/Gallimard.
Torensluis, etching © GAA.
Gable with three heads at No. 116 Singel © P. van Dijk/Gallimard.
167 *Multatuli*, drawing © GAA.
View of the Singel, 166 (detail), oil on canvas, Abraham Stork © Rijksbureau voor Kunsthistorisch Documentatie.
168 Cartouche at No. 11 Stromarkt © P. van Dijk/Gallimard.
Venice of the North, 1990, negative by Bern F. Eilers © GAA.
Plan of Venice, 16th century, Giovan Battista Arzenti © CIGA Hotels Coll./Daniel Venetië Hotel.
168/169 Panorama © Private coll.
169 *Bacino di San Marco*, oils, Caspar van Wittel, Private coll., Florence © Scala.
View of Venice, in Civitates orbiterrarum by G. Braun and F. Mohenber (first half of 17th century), Bibl. Nat © J.L. Charmet/Gallimard.
Portrait of Canaletto, etching © Bibl. Nat.
Plan of Amsterdam, 1538, Cornelis Anthonisz, oils © AHM.
170 Shopping arcade,

ɔs. 2353
ɑadhuistraat,
romolithograph ©
ΑA.
ɔnstruction of a
opping Arcade, oil on
nvas, G. Breitner ©
ΗM.
reet sign, corner
ulpture,
ɑadhuistraat © P. van
k/Gallimard.
71 Cartouche at No.
8–70 Herengracht ©
van Dijk/Gallimard.
*uis Bouwmeester
842–1925) in
aemeren beelden,
koude harten*, 1862,
oto C. Marcussen ©
ederlands Theater
stituut, Coll.
nsterdam.
niature theater of
ron van Slingelandt,
'81 © Nederlands
eater Instituut Coll.,
nsterdam.
*e Herengracht in
nsterdam,*
637–1712), oil on
nvas, Jan van der
eyden, Louvre ©
ΛN.
72 Cartouche at No.
'2 Keizersgracht,
othecary's sign at No.
Herengstraat,
eenpeace House ©
van Dijk/Gallimard.
72/173 *Old Church
the Remonstrants* ,
30, etching © GAA.
73 Van Houten poster
Private coll.
legory of Fame, G. de
iresse, oil on canvas
Rijksmuseum
undation,
nsterdam. House of
eads, No. 172
eizersgracht © P. van
ijk/Gallimard. \
74 *Whaler from the
oyal Fleet Rreturning
Amsterdam*, c. 1700,
van Salm © AHM.
e intersection of
ouwersgracht and
eizersgracht © P. van
ijk/Gallimard.
utch fisherman,
ching from the Traité
énéral des pêches ©
onds Gallimard.
75 Metal sign at No.
52 Brouwersgracht,
ew of the
ouwersgracht,
artouche from Nos
16–18
ouwersgracht, and
roenland warehouses
P. van Dijk/Gallimard.
*olphins in the
rouwersgracht*, oil on
anvas, Zelko Premerl
Hamer Gallery,
Amsterdam.
176 Cartouches, street sign and Nos. 2-4 Prinsengracht © P. van Dijk/Gallimard.
Brown café © H. Lozès.
177 All illustrations © P. van Dijk/Gallimard.
178 Café sign, intersection of Prinsengracht and Egelantiersgracht, No. 213 Prinsengracht, No. 126 Prinsengracht © P. van Dijk/Gallimard.
179 Cartouche No. 226 Prinsengracht © P. van Dijk/Gallimard.
Plaque commemorating Rembrandt, Westerkerk © Private coll.
Steeple of the Westerkerk, 1640–50, pen and wash by Rembrandt © AHM.
180 Photos of the interior, Anne Frank's House, poster and portrait of Anne Frank © AFF/AFS, Amsterdam.
Text: foreword to Anne Frank's diary with her signature © AFF/AFS, Amsterdam.
181 Anne Frank's House and canal, statue of A. Frank, Westmarkt © P. van Dijk/Gallimard.
Three photos of the first round-ups of Jews 1941 in Amsterdam in February © RIOD-fotoreproduktie.
Mrs Frank and her daughters © AFF/AFS, Amsterdam.
182 *Queen of Sheba and Early Musical Instrument*, 1631, organ decoration, Gerard de Lairesse © Private coll.
White marble foot with sandal, 16th century, Gerard and Jan Reynst Coll. (1599–1646), photo: A. J. de Kemp © Rijksmuseum van Oudheden.
183 *The Anatomy Lesson of Dr Tulp*, 1632, oil on canvas, Rembrandt © Mauritshuis, The Hague.
"Groote Keijzer", 1980 © H.C. Bouton, Amsterdam.
184 Cartouche at No. 320 Keizersgracht, Felix Meritis façade © P. van Dijk/Gallimard.
Peter Romanov (1672–1725), 1839, by C. de Moor, oil on canvas, Private coll. © Iconographisch Bureau.
The Amsterdam Schouwburg Fire on May 11, 1772, Seen from the Keizersgracht, colored etching © Nederlands Theater Instituut Coll., Theater Museum, Amsterdam.
185 All cartouches © P. van Dijk/Gallimard.
186 Delftware tulip vase © C. Sarramon.
Flower Market, 1987, oil on canvas, Elisabeth Gevaert © Hamer Gallery, Amsterdam.
186/187 *The Amstel and the Mint*, drawing from a photograph, by H. Clerget © GAA.
187 Adam and Eve cartouche (No. 367 Singel), Odeon (No. 460 Singel) © P. van Dijk/Gallimard.
Prinsengracht © H. Peretz.
188 All illustrations © P. van Dijk/Gallimard.
189 *The Leidsegracht in Winter*, oil on canvas, Zeljko Premerl, C.G. Lampe Coll. © Hamer Gallery, Amsterdam.
190 Stadsschowburg, Leidseplein © P. van Dijk/Gallimard.
191 The, former Leidsepoort, 1860 © GAA.
American Hotel interior © C. Sarramon.
192 *Portrait of Cornelis Lely* (1854–1929), negative A. Zimmermans © Iconographisch Bureau, The Hague.
Cake-maker's, no 579 Prinsengracht, 1893–9, etching © GAA.
Leaving the Theater at the Leidseplein, pen and ink © GAA.
193 *Peter the Great's charter of 1700*, written on parchment © GAA.
Archangel warehouse © P. van Dijk/Gallimard.
194 Bible Museum, four horsemen cartouche and intersection of the Keizersgracht and the Leidsegracht © P. van Dijk/Gallimard.
195 Canal and bridge © P. van Dijk/Gallimard.
No. 395 Herengracht, etching © GAA.
196 Marseille cartouche No. 401 Keizersgracht © P. van Dijk/Gallimard.
The art dealer, Theo van Gogh © Stedelijk Museum, Amsterdam.
The Art Bookshop of Van Gogh's uncle, No. 453 Keizersgracht, 1882, etching © GAA.
197 Cartouche and façade detail No. 401 Keizersgracht, Metz department store a No. 455 Keizersgracht © P. van Dijk/Gallimard.
Portrait of Jacob van Lennep, secretary, writer in the Atheneum © GAA.
196/197 *No. 508 Keizersgracht*, etching © GAA.
198 Cornice, No. 487 Herengracht, cornice at No. 475 Herengracht © P. van Dijk/Gallimard.
198/199 *The bend in the Herengracht*, 1685, oil on canvas, G.A. Berckheyde © Rijksmuseum, Amsterdam.
199 Cartouche at No. 419 Herengracht © P. van Dijk/Gallimard.
Jan Gildemeester's Art Gallery, 1794–5, oil on canvas, A. de Lelie © Rijksmuseum, Amsterdam.
200 *Portrait of Jan Six II*, etching © GAA.
Cat Museum interior © C. Sarramon.
Gable, Nos. 504-10 Herengracht © P. van Dijk/Gallimard.
201 Architect's drawing of Nos. 502-12 Herengracht © GAA.
Moors' heads and gable © P. van Dijk/Gallimard.
202 Façade detail of Nos. 57–63 Reguliersgracht © P. van Dijk/Gallimard.
Reguliersgracht, 1983, oil on canvas, C. Dhanani, Private coll. © Hamer Gallery, Amsterdam. Garden and Louis XVI drawing room, Van Loon Museum © C. Sarramon.
203 *The Four Ages and the Five Senses*, 1630, oil on canvas, Jan Miense Molenaer © Van Loon Museum, Amsterdam.
Façade and detail Nos. 57–63 Reguliersgracht © P. van Dijk/Gallimard.
204 *View of the Amstelkerk on the Reguliersgracht*, late 18th-century etching © GAA.
Amstelplein and Amstelkerk statue © P. van Dijk/Gallimard.
204/205 *The Amstel near the Prinsengracht*, 1852–63, color pencil sketch, Johannes Hilverdink © GAA.

205 Views of the Amstelhof and the Square Theater © P. van Dijk/Gallimard. *The Little Bridge*, 1986, oil on canvas, Nadia Becker, coll of the artist. © Hamer Gallery, Amsterdam.
206 *Sketch for the ceiling of No. 586 Herengracht*, 1743, pen and brush, Jacob de Wit (1743) © GAA. 1870's drawing room overlooking the garden and 1850's bedchamber of the Willet-Holthuysen Museum © AHM.
207 Archangel Michael, at No. 579 Herengracht © P. van Dijk/Gallimard. *Charcoal sketch for the ceiling of No. 586 Herengracht*, 1742, Jacob de Wit © GAA. *Statue of Thorbecke*, 1876, etching © GAA.
208 Interiors, Tuschinski Cinema © Tuschinski Theater, Amsterdam. Dome of the Tuchinski Cinema © P. van Dijk/Gallimard. *Reguliersplein*, 1869, oil on canvas, Andries Scheerboom © AHM.
209 *Bridge on the Singel*, oil on canvas, G. Breitner © Rijksmuseum, Amsterdam.
210 Poster © Private coll.
211 Portrait of the Architect Petrus Josephus Cuypers, photo 1888–9 © GAA. IJsclubterrein, later Museumplein, April 13, 1895, photo: J. Olie © GAA. Ijsclubterrain, April 1897 © Stedelijk Museum, Amsterdam.
212 Pediment of the Rijksmuseum © P. van Dijk/Gallimard. Skating on the Museumplein in 1895 © GAA.
212/213 *View of the Rijksmuseum*, 1885, oil on canvas, J. Hilverdink © AHM.
213 Pediment of the Rijksmuseum © P. van Dijk/Gallimard. *Portrait of J.A. Thijm*, 19th-century etching © GAA.
214 *Van Gogh Museum*, statue of Van Gogh © P. van Dijk/Gallimard. Stedelijk Museum under construction, photo, 1894 © GAA.
215 19th-century Velox etching © Private coll. Fire brigade, Museumplein © Private coll. Fire station and Wildschut café © P. van Dijk/Gallimard.
216 Architect's drawing of the Concertgebouw,. 1883, A.L. van Gendt © GAA. A.L. van Gendt, photo © GAA. Pediment, street sign and Concertgebouw façade © P. van Dijk/Gallimard. Portrait of J. Cramer, pencil drawing by © GAA.
217 *Architect's drawing*,1883, A.L. van Gendt © GAA. Portrait of Willem Mengelberg 1919 © GAA. Present-day orchestra © Private coll. *Portrait of Henri Viotta*, pencil drawing © GAA.
218 *The Jewish Bride*, 1665, oil on canvas, Rembrandt, and *Captain Cocq's Company*, also known as *The Night Watch*, 1642, oil on canvas, Rembrandt © Rijksmuseum, Amsterdam.
219 *The Syndics of the Drapers' guilds*, 1662, oil on canvas, Rembrandt © Rijksmuseum, Amsterdam. *Self-portrait in a Fur Hat and Dressed in White*, 1630, etching, Rembrandt © Rembrandt Museum, Amsterdam.
220/221 *View of a River in Winter*, oil on canvas, A. V. D. Neer (1603/04–77). *The Worship of the Golden Calf*, oil on wood, Lucas van Leyden (1494–1533). *Winter Landscape with Boat*, 1665, oil on wood, Salomon J. van Ruysdael. All from the Rijksmuseum, Amsterdam.
222/223 *Horseriding along the Beach at Scheveningen*,1876, oil on canvas, Anton Mauve (1838–88), *Windmill at Wijk*,1370, oil on canvas, Jacob van Ruysdael (1628/29–82), *Boar Hunt in a River Landscape*, oil on wood, Joos de Momper (1564–1635). *Winter Landscape*, oil on wood, H. Avercamp (1585–1634). All from the Rijksmuseum, Amsterdam.
224 *The Jolly Toper*,, 1628/30, oil on canvas, Frans Hals © Rijksmuseum, Amsterdam. *The Anatomy Lesson*, 1619 (detail), oils, T. de Keyser (1596/97–1667) © AHM.
224/225 *The Messenger*, 1670, oil on canvas, by Pieter de Hooch (1629–1683) © Rijksmuseum, Amsterdam.
225 *Banquet of the Civic Guard Celebrating the Treaty of Münster of June 18*, 1648, B. van der Helst © Rijksmuseum, Amsterdam. *Distribution of Bread to the Poor* (detail), 1627, oil on canvas, W. van den Valckert © AHM. *Woman Reading a Letter* (c. 1885), oil on canvas, J. Vermeer © Rijksmuseum, Amsterdam.
226/227 *The Château at Auvers-sur-Oise*, 1890, oil on canvas de Van Gogh.
226 *The Yellow House at Arles*,1888, oil on canvas, Vincent van Gogh.
227 *Woman in the Café du Tambourin*, Paris, 1887, oil on canvas, Van Gogh. *Leaving the Church at Nuenen*, 1884, oil on canvas, Van Gogh. All from the Vincent Van Gogh Fondation/Van Gogh Museum, Amsterdam.
228 *Counter-composition V*, 1924, oil on canvas, Theo van Doesburg. *Untitled*, 1986, pastel on paper, Salvo. *An Englishman in Moscow*, 1913–14, oil on canvas, Kasimir Malevich. *Woman Singing*, 1966, oil on canvas, Willem de Kooning.
229 *Still Life with Jug and Bottle*, 1909, oil on canvas, Georges Braque. *Reclining Nude before a Garden*, 1956, oil on canvas, Pablo Picasso. *Composition in Red, Black, Blue, Yellow and Gray*, 1920 oil on canvas, Piet Mondriaan. All from the Stedelijk Museum, Amsterdam.
230 *Men and Animals* 1949, oil on canvas, Karel Appel.
231 *The Big Earth*, 1958, oil on canvas, Corneille. *Scorched Earth II*, 1951, oil on canvas, Constant. All from the Stedelijk Museum, Amsterdam.
232 Café poster © Private coll. Café Welling and workshop sign © P. va Dijk/Gallimard. *Little Girls Reading*, 1890, etching © GAA.
233 Photos © P. van Dijk/Gallimard. *Vondelstraat riding school*, 1874, pen drawing by A.L. van Gendt © Kunsthistorisch Institu University of Amsterdam.
234 Antique dealers' signs and shop © P. v Dijk/Gallimard. Vondel free state, 198 © Jan Vonk.
235 Eilandsgracht © GAA.
236 Aerial view © GA Plant tubs © P. van Dijk/Gallimard.
237 Street signs and toy shop © P. van Dijk/Gallimard. 'T Smalle interiors © H Lozes.
238 Cartouches, stre sign and Noordermark © P. van Dijk/Gallimar 1934 riots © GAA.
238/239 View of the Market and the Noorderkerk © DR.
239 Statue of Thijsse © P. van Dijk/Gallimar
240 Cartouches © P. van Dijk/Gallimard. Van Wees distillery © Sarramon. Lucas Bols poster © GAA.
241 All photos © P. va Dijk/Gallimard.
242 Bunch of grapes cartouches © P. van Dijk/Gallimard. *Little girls on the Lindengracht*, G. Breitner © GAA.
243 Windows, shop window and canal © P van Dijk/Gallimard. *Goudsbloemgracht*, 1853, watercolor © GAA.
244 All photos © P. va Dijk/Gallimard.
245 Houses on the

nbaansgracht ©
HM.
eps and doll maker's
erior © P. van
jk/Gallimard.
46 Cartouche, canal
d façades © P. van
jk/Gallimard.
omestic interior,
ching © GAA.
47 Cartouches and
ndow © P. van
jk/Gallimard.
rdaanprinses poster,
20 © Nederlands
eater Instituut Coll.,
nsterdam.
oemstraat, Olie ©
AA.
48 Street sign and
ist © P. van
jk/Gallimard.
insengracht,
atercolor © GAA.
andsgracht in 1945 ©
AA.
49 View of Zandhoek
P. van Dijk/Gallimard.
50 Cartouches © P.
n Dijk/Gallimard.
oeshop interior © DR.
51 Street sign,
osthoornkerk and
op sign © P. van
jk/Gallimard.
aarlemmerplein © DR.
52/253 View of
euw Amsterdam (top
page) © DR.
52 Dutch East India
ompany Building,
ching © GAA.
artouche © P. van
jk/Gallimard.
53 Statue of P.
uyvesant © P. van
jk/Gallimard.
utch East India
ompany House in
41 © Gallimard.
54 Statue of Domela
euwenhuis © P. van
jk/Gallimard.
54/255 *Noord Zee*
anaal, 1880, etching ©
AA.
55 Old photo of sugar
finery © GAA.
orkers' house © P.
n Dijk/Gallimard.
56 Amsterdam School
ntrance and street
opliances © P. van
jk/Gallimard.
ortrait of De Klerk, ©
ivate coll.
57 Amsterdam School
uildings © P. van
ijk/Gallimard.
aanstraat, former
hurch, photo © GAA.
58 Street sign, lock ©
van Dijk/Gallimard.
ortrait of G.H. Breitner,
awing, Willem Witsen
Rijksmuseum,
nsterdam.
rinseneiland Shipyard,
oil on canvas, by G.H.
Breitner © Stedelijk
Museum Amsterdam.
259 Prinseneiland
warehouses © GAA.
Cartouches and
shipyard © P. van
Dijk/Gallimard.
Label © GAA.
260/261 *The Port of Amsterdam Seen from the IJ*, oils, Ludolf
Backhuyzen
(1631–1708), Louvre ©
RMN.
260 Zoutkectsgracht ©
GAA.
View of Zandhoek © P.
van Dijk/Gallimard.
261 *Portrait of Andries Bicker*, oil on canvas, B.
van der Helst (1613–70)
© AHM.
Gerard Bicker, oil on
canvas, B. van der
Helst © Rijksmuseum,
Amsterdam.
262 View of the IJ © P.
van Dijk/Gallimard.
Crowded port © GAA.
Tolhuis, etching © GAA.
263 Ship, The
Amsterdam © P. van
Dijk/Gallimard.
264 Hortus Botanicus
© P. van Dijk/Gallimard.
Plantage, etching ©
GAA.
265 Poppy © P. van
Dijk/Gallimard.
Map of Amsterdam ©
GAA.
266 Interior by H.P.
Berlage © H. Lozes.
Façade © P. van
Dijk/Gallimard.
267 Portrait of Hugo de
Vries © GAA.
Wertheimpark, 1895,
pen © GAA.
Former Theater on Plantage Parklaan,
gouache © GAA.
Façade of the
Hollandse Schouwburg
© P. van Dijk/Gallimard.
268 Artis cover ©
Private coll.
Round Cage, watercolor
© GAA.
268/269 *Entrepotdok*,
etching © GAA.
269 *Entrepotdok*,
etching © GAA.
Street sign © P. van
Dijk/Gallimard.
St Antony's Dyke,
etching © GAA.
270 Medal to
commemorate the
destruction of the
Armada, 1588 ©
Nederlands
Scheepvaart Museum,
Amsterdam.
Model fishing boat:
Vigelantie, dated 1800
© Scheepvaart
Museum, Amsterdam.
Model of a merchant
ship, c. 1650 ©
Scheepvaart Museum,
Amsterdam.
Model of a three-master,
warship 1550–60 ©
Scheepvaart Museum,
Amsterdam.
270/271 Plate, gift
from the Sultan of
Malakka, 1848 ©
Nederlands
Scheepvaart Museum,
Amsterdam.
Dutch East India Company Shipyard,
etching,J. Mulder ©
Nederlands
Scheepvaart Museum,
Amsterdam.
271 *Kattenburgerplein*
1663–70, etching ©
GAA.
Carved heads,
Nederlands
Scheepvaart Museum,
Amsterdam.
Portrait of Tromp ©
Nederlands
Scheepvaart Museum,
Amsterdam.
Portrait of J.E.J. Capitein, etching ©
Nederlands
Scheepvaart Museum,
Amsterdam.
272 Street sign and
coat of arms of the
Oranje-Nassau
barracks © P. van
Dijk/Gallimard.
Launching a Ship,
watercolor © GAA.
Portrait of Tsar Peter the Great, 1637 © Private
coll.
273 *Oranje-Nassau Barracks No. 154*
Sarphatistraat, etching
© GAA.
Street sign © P. van
Dijk/Gallimard.
Portrait of Samuel Sarphati (1813–66),
lithograph © GAA.
Portrait of J.E. Ter
Meulen (1867–1937) ©
GAA.
Cocoa mill, J. Olie, 1890
© GAA.
274 *Muiderpoort*, oil on
canvas (1756) by J. ten
Compe © AHM.
Mauritskade, etching ©
GAA.
Mauritskade, etching ©
GAA.
275 Albert-Cuyp
market © P. van
Dijk/Gallimard.
276 Heineken advert,
1953 © Het Nederlands
Reclamuseum.
276/277 Singelgracht,
Heineken Brewery,
etching © GAA.
277 Street sign,
Sarphati monument and
market © P. van
Dijk/Gallimard.
278 Street sign and
numbers © P. van
Dijk/Gallimard.
279 *Portrait of H.P. Berlage* (1856–1934),
pencil © GAA.
All façades and details
© P. van Dijk/Gallimard.
280 J.F. Staal
(1879–1940) plaque ©
GAA.
The "Skyscraper" on
Victorieplein © P. van
Dijk/Gallimard.
282 KLM plane © KLM.
283 Schipol airport ©
Le Diascorn.
Air France plane © Air
France.
Central Station © P. Le
Floc'h, Explorer.
Eurolines coach ©
Eurolines.
284 Tram © Vo Trung
Dung/Cosmos.
Tram ticket © DR.
285 Cyclists © Emile
Luider/Rapho.
Tram © P.
Kohn/Cosmos.
Boats © R. van der
Hilst.
Ferry © P. van
Dijk/Gallimard.
Pedalo © M. Gotin.
Bikes © A. Lorgnier.
286 All photos © Paul
van Dijk/Gallimard.
287 Port of Amsterdam
© A. Lorgnier.
Young girls © R. van
der Hilst.
Antique toy © C.
Sarramon.
288 Tourist Office ©
Paul van Dijk/Gallimard.
Museum guide and
What's on © Private coll.
Red light district © R.
van der Hilst.
290 ABN Bank sign ©
Paul van Riel.
Post Office © Cosmos
cl. P. Kohn.
291 Phone booth © P.
van Dijk/Gallimard.
292 Intersection of the
Leliegracht and
Keizersgracht © Paul
van Dijk/Gallimard.
Health-food market,
Jordaan © R.
Mazin/Agence Top.
Intersection of the
Brouwersgracht and
Prinsengracht © Paul
van Dijk/Gallimard.
293 Lift-bridge © C.
Sarramon.
Suits of armor in the
Amsterdam Historical
Museum and Curtain ©
A. Lorgnier.
294 Begijnhof statue ©
Paul van Dijk/Gallimard.

Begijnhof © Paul van Dijk/Gallimard.
294/295 Westerkerk belfry © GAA.
295 Rijksmuseum © A. Lorgnier.
Orchestra © M. Gotin.
Riding school © Paul van Dijk/Gallimard.
296 De Drie Fleschjes barrel and Café Hoppe interior © C. Sarramon.
297 De Drie Fleschjes shelf, De Jaren terrace and bottles © C. Sarramon.
298 Café terrace on the Leidseplein © R. van der Hilst.
Concertgebouw auditorium © P. van Riel/Hollandse Hoogte.
299 "Stopera" © Emile Luider/Rapho.
Two bridges © A. Lorgnier.
Uitkrant © DR.
300 Waterlooplein flea market © R. van der Hilst.
Mannekins © S. Grandadam.
301 Sauna, hairdresser's and Tuschinski Cinema © C. Sarramon.
302 *Dutch Landscape*, watercolor © Private coll.
Delft city hall © Dutch Tourist Office.
303 Leiden University Library and the Binnenhof at The Hague © Dutch Tourist Office.
304 Meat market © Frans-Hals Museum.
St Bavon's Church, Haarlem, and statue of Coster © Paul van Dijk/Gallimard.
305 Cartouches of No. 63 Jansenstraat, Haarlem, and details from Haarlem Station © Paul van Dijk/Gallimard.
306 Cartouche from Speeltoren of the former city hall at Monnickendam, house at Zaanse Schans, view of Edam, Marken street, Peter the Great's house © Paul van Dijk/Gallimard.
Marken stamp © Private coll.
307 Cartouche of the Edam coat of arms, Monnickendam port, and Zaanse Schans windmill © Paul van Dijk/Gallimard.
308 House between Breukelen and Loenen © Paul van Dijk/Gallimard.
309 Amersfoort house and medieval gate at Amersfoort © Paul van Dijk/Gallimard.

GAA: Gemeentearchief, Amsterdam.
AHM: Amsterdam Historisch Museum.
RMN: Réunion des Musées nationaux.
RKD: Rijksbureau voor Kunsthistorisch Documentatie.

ILLUSTRATORS:

Maps:
Valérie Gevers.
Colorist: Malou Camolli Beauchesne.

Nature:
15: Jean Chevallier, François Desbordes, Claire Felloni, Pascal Robin.
16–17: Anne Bodin, Donald Grant, Gilbert Houbre, Pascal Robin, Frédérique Schwebel.
18–19: Anne Bodin, Jean Chevallier, Denis Clavreul, François Desbordes, Pascal Robin.
20-21: Jean Chevallier, Denis Clavreul, François Desbordes, Claire Felloni.
22-23: Jean Chevallier, Denis Clavreul, François Desbordes, Claire Felloni, Guy Michel.
24-25: François Place, Claire Felloni.

Architecture:
65: Maurice Pommier.
66-67: Maurice Pommier.
68-69: Maurice Pommier.
70-71: Maurice Pommier.
72-73: Fabrice Moireau.
74-75: Pierre Poulain.
76-77: Maurice Pommier.
78-79: Maurice Pommier.
80-81: Gabor Szitia.
82-83: Michel Aubois.
84-85: Michel Aubois.
86: Michel Sinier.

Itineraries:
134–135: Maurice Pommier.
164–167: Fabrice Moireau.
181: Annabelle Rebière.
192–195: Fabrice Moireau.
256: Michel Aubois.
276: Annabelle Rebière.

Coloring of some of the etchings in the itineraries section: Concetta Forgia.

Useful information and addresses:
281-337: Maurice Pommier.

Computer graphics:
Paul Coulbois, Emmanuel Calamy.

In some cases we have been unable to contact the heirs to certain documents, or their publishers; an account remains open for them at our offices.

INDEX

◆ A ◆

A.N.D.B., union 266
Aalsmeer 25
Aartman, Adriaan 61
ABN-AMRO bank 200
Acacia Hotel 242
Acquet, Hendrick d' 149
Adelaert 194
Adriaan 61
Aertsz, Pieter 124, 134
Aglionby, William 102
Agnieten Kapel (St Agnes Chapel) 142, 143
Ajax club 60
Albert Cuypstraat market 277, 300
Alblasserwaard 302
Alkmaar 26
Allard Pierson Museum 141
Almere 307
Alpers, Svetlana 207
American Hotel 82, 301
Amersfoort 309
Amsberg, Claus von 244
Amstel 142, 160, 163, 172, 176, 205
Amstel Bridge 278
Amstelhof, almshouse 205
Amstelkannal 278
Amstelkerk 204
Amstelkring Museum 137
Amstelledamme, village 28, 34
Amstelveld 204
Amsterdam Foundation 28
Amsterdam Gate 304
Amsterdam School 57, 84, 278
Andrianople 187
Andriessen, M. 181
Anthonisz, Cornelis 34, 169
Appel, Karel 93, 144, 145
Archangel warehouse 193
Armenian Church 155
Arminius 39, 170, 173
Artis park 232, 268
Arzenti, G.B. 169
Assendelftstraat 255
Atheneum (Illustrae) 143
Aymon 194

◆ B ◆

Backhuysen, Ludolf 88, 149, 260
Baerle, Gaspard van 130, 143
Barber shop 301
Bartolotti House 170, 171, 292
Baudelaire, Charles 105
Bayens, Hans 239
Bayle, Piere 38, 39
Bazel, K. de 82, 200
Beatrix, Queen 33, 47, 183, 244
Beckmann 215
Beeckman, Andries 147
Beerstraten, Abraham 124
Begijnhof 122, 123, 294
Beijer, Jan de 164
Belmonte, Baron de 206
Berckheyde, Gerrit Adriaensz, 90, 198
Berckheyde, Job 132, 133
Berenstraat 184, 188
Bergen warehouse 175
Berlage, H.P. 37, 56, 57, 82, 84, 133, 212, 262, 266, 278, 279
Berlage's Exchange 81, 133
Berlage's "Fortress" 266
Berlage Institute 267
Berlage, statue of 280
Berlagebrug 67
Bethaniënstraat 151
Beulingsloot 195
Beulingstraat 194
Bible Museum 194
Bicker, Andries 261
Bicker, Gerard 261
Bicker, Joan 260
Bickerseiland 260
"Big Keijser" 183
Bilhamer, Joost Jansz, 130, 135
Binnenhof 303
Bisschop, Rem Egbertsz 170
Blaauwe, C.J. 57
black charger 194
Blaeu, J. 41, 55, 131, 245
Blauwbrug 66
Blauwburgwal 166
Bleys, A.C. 137
Bloemendaal 305
Bloemgracht 245, 247
Bloemenmarkt 187
Blois 195
Blokhoff, Johannes 250
Blokhuis 204
Bol, Ferdinand 178, 202
Bolhoed restaurant 178
Bonifatius 28
Bonnard, Pierre 215
Boom, Cornelis Pieter 155
Bosch, Arent Dirxen 241
Boswell, James 108, 309
Botanical Gardens 264, 265
Both, Pieter 150
Bouvries, J. des 57
Brahms 184
Breda 302
Bredero, Gerbrand Adrianszoon 44, 153, 154
Breen, Adam van 61
Breitner, George 88, 127, 170, 248, 258
Breukelen 309
Brienen, Aernout Jan van 176
Brienen, Jan van 170
Brienen, W. Joseph van 170
Brinker, statue by Hans 305
Brouwersgracht 175, 236, 240, 292
Brouwersplein 210
Brouwhuis Maximiliaan, café 151
Bruggen, Frans 217
Bruyn, S.A. de 214
Buitenhof 303
Busbecq, ambassador 187

◆ C ◆

Calkoen, Nicolaas 206
Calvinism 193
Campen, Jacob van 74, 78, 124, 128, 129
Camus, Albert 103, 137, 188, 201
Canal Bus 292
Canaletto 169
Capek, Karel 107, 111
Carmiggelt, Simon 44
Cat Museum 200
Catharijneconvent Museum 309
Cats, Jacob 55
Central Museum 309
Central Station 80, 81, 138
Cézanne, Paul 215
Chagall, Marc 215
Chailly, Riccardo 48
Charlemagne 28, 194
Charles V 29
Charrière, Isabelle de 309
Chris, café 296
Civilis, Julius 28
Clerget, H. 186
CoBrA, movement 215, 230
Cocq, Frans Banningh 126, 167
Coen, Jan Pieterzoon 151
Comenius, Amos 248
Compe, J. Ten 274
Concertgebouw 80, 184, 211, 216, 295, 298
Conrad, Joseph 109
Constant, Benjamin 309
Cooperatiehof 278, 280
Coster, Laurens Janszoon 54, 304
Coster, Samuel 184, 186
Coulon, Jean 200
Counter-Remonstrants 37, 170
Court, Pieter de la 130
Cramer, Joe 216
Cromhout, Jacob 194
Cruijff, Johan 60
Cruys, C. 134
Cuypers, P.J. 79, 80, 138, 174, 211, 212, 213, 216, 233, 251

◆ D ◆

Daan, Karin 179
Dam 128
Damrak 131, 140
Dantzig café 297
David, King 179
De Cruquius Museum 305
De Drie Fleschjes café 130, 296
De Drie Hendricken 246
De Duif, church 205
De Gijs café 242
De Gooier, windmill 69, 273
De Jaren café 160, 293, 297
De Karpershoek café 296
De Pijp district 277
De Rode Hoed 173
De Spaanse Gevel café 165
De Twee Zwaantjes café 178
De Utrecht apartment block 82
De Vergulde Gaper café 178
De Vergulde Pot warehouse 121
De Zaaier building 174
Deaconesses' almshouse 205
Deenick, Z. 202, 20
Delft 303
Delft, city hall 302
Deli Maatschappij

195
Derkinderen, A. 201
Descartes' House 179
Descartes, René 39, 98, 179
Deutz van Assendelft, Jean 206
Deutz, banker 198
Deutz, Willem Gideon 206
Deventer, Jacob van 35
Dhanani, Christine 202
Diderot, Denis 197
Domela Nieuwenhuis, Ferdinand 32, 254
Doomer, Lambert 88
Dortsman, Adriaan 74, 165, 202, 206
Dou, Gerard 199
Douwes Dekker, Eduard 167
Driehoekstraat 240
Droogstoppel, Mr 248
Duba shipyard 259
Dubuffet, Jean 215
Dulac café 297
Dune Water Authority 197
Dutch East India Company 30, 145, 146, 149, 150, 202, 203, 265, 272
Dutch East India House 72, 146
Dutch Northern Company 174
Dutch riding school 295
Dutch West India Company 77, 252, 30, 171, 253
Duyn, Roel van 33
Duyschot, Johannes 179

◆ E ◆

Eckhardt, Rob 56, 57
Edam 64, 306, 307
Eenhoornsluis 251
Eeghen, van, family 200
Eigen Haard association 256
Eijkebom warehouse 197
Eijnde, H.A van den 155
Eilers, B. 169
Elandsgracht 248
Elzevier, Isaak 55
Endegeest castle 303
Enkhuizen 307
Entrepotdok 268, 269
Epen, J.C. van 262
Ernst 215
Esser, professor 153
Evelyn, John 99
Exchange 132, 245
Eyck, A. van der 39, 86, 267

◆ F ◆

Faculty of Arts 167
Fahrenheit, physicist 197
Felix Meritis Theater 184, 216
Flevoland 307
Flinck, Govert 207, 248
Flines, Philips de 172
Floris V 134, 308
Flower Market 187
Focke & Meltzer, shop 279
Fokkens, Melchior 182, 198
Fouquet, Pierre 121, 144, 239
Frank, Anne 33, 100, 103, 178, 180
Frank family 180, 280
Frans-Hals Museum 304
Frederick-William II 31
Funenkade 273
Funke, Lotte 122

◆ G ◆

Gabriel, Max 247
Gallery of the Civic Guard 293
Garcia Marquez, Gabriel 300
Gauchez, Maurice 242
Gauguin, Paul 214
Geer, Louis de 173
Geeraerd Vossius 143
Geertruida, Sandrina Luisa 206
Geldersekade 35, 152, 153
Geloof warehouse 178
Gendt, A.L. van 80, 138, 170, 200, 216, 233
Gevaert, E. 186
Giorgione 172
Glatt, Josef 157
Goethe Institute 200
Gogh, Theodore van 214
Gogh, Vincent van 108, 214
Golden Bend 198
Goliath, statue of 125
Gomarus, Franciscus 38
Gosschalk, T. 203
Goudsbloemgracht 243
Goudstikker, Jacques 199
Grand Army stables 178
The Grand Hotel 144, 145
Great Synagogue 158, 159
Greef 66
Greenpeace association 172
Grieg 184
Grimburgwal 142
Groenburgwal 160
Groenland warehouse 77, 175
Groot, Hugo de (Grotius) 54
Grootveld, Robert Jasper 243
Grote Markt 304
Guicciardini, Lodovico 168
Gustavus-Adolphus, King 173

◆ H ◆

Haar castle 308, 309
Haarlem 304
Haarlem canal 252
Haarlem lock 164
Haarlem station 305
Haarlemmerbuurt 251
Haarlemmerdijk 250
Haarlemmerplein 251, 252
Haarlemmerstraat 250, 253
Habsburg empire 187
The Hague 303
Hajenius, tobacco shop 141, 301
Halfweg 304
Hals, Frans 203, 224, 304
Hart, Abraham van der 273
Hartenstraat 188
Havermarkt 302
Heads, House of 73, 118, 173
Health food market 292
Heemskerck, J. van 134
Heijden, Jan van der 134,171,193, 194, 215
Heijerman, Herman 267
Heiligeweg 121
Heimans, Eli 268
Heineken, Adriaan 276
Heineken Brewery 276
Heineken Museum 276
Heisteeg 186
Hekking, Willem 124
Helst, B. van der 261
Hémony, brothers 120, 128, 294
Hémony, François 131, 135, 182
Hémony, Pierre 272
Hendriks, Jan 145
Hennebo, Robert 238
Herengracht 36, 163, 166, 170, 171, 179, 186, 187, 188, 194, 195,198, 199, 203, 206, 292
Herenmarkt 250
Herenstraat 172
Hertzberger, H. 86
Heuvel, van den 171
Heyn, Piet 252
Hille, Kees 256
Hillehuis 84
Hilverdink, Johannes 205, 213
Historical Museum (Historisch Museum) 123, 124
Hofje Brienen, institution 176
hofjes 240
Hogesluis 205
Hollander, Franklin 176
Hollandse Schouwburg 267
Holthuijsen, Pieter Gerard 206
Holzbauer, Wilhelm 160
Honthorstraat 215
Hooch, Pieter de 304
Hooft, Cornelis Pietersz 52, 130, 162, 163, 186, 308
Hooft, Isabella 206
Hooft, shop 196, 197
Hoofthuis, P.C 167
Hoogte Kadijk 269
Hoop warehouse 178
Hoop, A. van der 212
Hoorn 307
Hop, Jacob 206
Hope, House of 182
Hopkins, Adam 101
Hoppe café 122, 296
Hortus Botanicus 264, 265
House of Hope 182
Houten, Gasparus van 173
Houtrijkstraat 255
Hudde, J. 134
Hudson, Henry 30, 153, 252
Huese, D. 57
Huidenstraat 186, 188
Huygens, C. 213, 304, 308

◆ I ◆

Ignatiuszoon 171
IJ 17, 260, 261
IJmuiden 305
IJplein 262
IJsselmeer 20, 60
In de Wildeman café 297
Indie warehouse 197
Institute of Contemporary Art 234

◆ J ◆

Jacob Hooy, herbalist 52, 151
"Jacob's Ladder", mansion 74
Jacobs, Alette 247
Jager, Herbert de 149
James, Henry 110
Jan Beekhuizen, pewter shop 52
Jan de Groot, bookstore 54
Jan Luijkenstraat 234
Jan Six I 130, 206
Jan Six II 200
Jansen, P. J. hairdresser 53
Jansen, P. W. 255
Janz, W. 148
Jewish History Museum 159
Jewish memorial 157, 160
Jong, H.L. de 208
Jongkind 215
Jordaan 36, 32, 162, 172, 175, 236, 238, 239, 242, 246, 247, 293
Jordaan, festival 246
Jordaan, Johnny 248
Juliana, Queen 33

◆ K ◆

Kabouters 244
Kalff, director of public works 37
Kalverstraat 121
Kandinsky, Wassily 215
Kannegieter, historian 238
Keijzer, shop 178
Keizersgracht 36, 67, 170, 173, 174, 179, 183, 184, 188, 194, 196, 202
Keukenhof park 25, 305
Key, Lieven de 304
Keyms, Reyers 193
Keyser Association 163, 246
Keyser, Hendrik de 72, 78, 120, 121, 124, 132, 150, 152, 154, 156, 167, 170, 171, 173, 179, 186, 239, 251, 302
Keyser, Pieter de 73, 173
Kinderdijk windmills 302
Kinderen, A.J. der 133
Kinsbergen, Admiral van 130
Kistenmaker, Renée 203
Klaes, Jetske 258
Klee, Paul 215
Klein, Yves 215
Klerk, Michel de 84, 256, 257, 280
Kloveniersburgwal 151
Kneulman, Carel 123
Koekstraat 194
Kok, A.A. 143
Kokadorus, Professor 204
Koningsplein 121
Koog aan de Zaan 306
Koolhaas, Rem 262
Korsjespoortsteeg 166
Kort café 204
Kramer, P.L. 84, 280
Krijtberg Church 78
Krombommsloot 77, 155
Kromhout shipyard 269
Kromhout, W. 82
Krop, Hildo 280
Kropholler, A.J. 82
Kuiperssteeg 142, 143

◆ L ◆

Lairesse, Gerard de 49, 172, 179
Langebrugsteeg 142, 143
Laren 309
Lastage 155
Lastman, Pieter 124
Lauriergracht 248
Lebrun, general 178
Lee, Adriaan van 149
Leenhoff, F. 207
Leeuwen, L. van 48
Leiden 303
Leidsegracht 36, 162, 163, 170, 193, 194, 195, 197
Leidseplein 298
Lelie, Adriaen de 178, 199
Leliegracht 172, 292
Lely, Cornelis 192
Lelystad 192, 307
Lemaire, J. 307
Lennep, Jacob van 197
Leopard House 170
Leyster, Judith 203
Liefde warehouse 178
Lievens, Jan 130
Lievertje, statue 243
Lijnbaansgracht 240
Lindeboom 197
Lindengracht 238, 239, 242
Lingelbach, J. 129
Lisse 25
Lock-keeper's house 156
Loenen 308
Loon, van, family 202
Loon, van, Garden 202, 203
Loon, van, Museum 202
Loon, Geertruijd van 203
Loosdrecht, meres 308, 309
Lord Pumerland 167
Louis, king 129, 144, 201
Lowell, Robert 111
Lutheran Church 187, 292
Lutma, goldsmiths 134
Luxembourg café 122, 297

◆ M ◆

Magere Brug 66, 205
Malevich, Kasimir 215
Mander, C. van 134
Manet, Edouard 214
Margaret, Duchess of Parma 29
Marie de Medici 47
Maritime Museum 76, 149, 269
Marken 306, 307
Marot, Daniel 198, 304
Marvell, Andrew 104
Mary of Burgundy 28
Matisse, Henri 215
Maurice, stadholder 30
Mauritshuis 303
Mauritskade 274
Maximilian, Emperor 28, 135, 173, 179
Meeuwenlaan 262
Meijer, Jonas Daniël 158
Meijerplein, Jonas Daniël 157
Mendes da Costa, J. 82, 133, 201
Mengelberg, Willem 217
Mens, Jan 259
Mercier, Hélène 247
Messina 172
Metsu, Gabriel 96
Metz, department store 196, 197
Metz, M. 57
Meulen, Johanna Ter 273
Mey, Johan Melchior van der 67, 84, 154
Meyer, Jan de 142
Militias 126
Mirabeau 39
Moederhuis (Mothers' House) 267
Molenaar, Jan Miense 203
Molensteeg 188
Möller, Max 232
Mondriaan, Piet 57, 215, 309
Monet, Claude 95, 215
Monico café 208
Monnickendam 306, 307
Montelbaanstoren 154, 155
Monulphus 213
Monument to homosexual victims 179
Moses and Aaron Church 78, 158
Mothers' House (Moederhuis) 266
Motorwal 262
Moucheron 172
Mozes en Aaronkerk 159
Mozes en Aaronstraat 132
Muiden 308
Muiderpoort 274
Mulder, Jacoba 273
Müller, Christian 304
Multatuli 166, 167, 197, 248
Multatuli Museum 166
Mundy, Peter 104
Muntplein 120, 186
Munttoren 121, 186, 187
Museum of Antiquities (Zaandijk) 306
Museumplein 210, 211, 292
Muziektheater 48, 160, 298

◆ N ◆

N.M.B. bank 86
N.R.C. squat 127
Naarden 309
Nanky de Vreeze Gallery 293
Napoleon I 32, 201, 274
Narrow house 74
Nassau, Maurice of 39
National Monument 129
Neer, Aert van der 221

Nes 142, 153
New York 195
Nienhuuys, J. 195
Nieulandt, Adriaen van 90
Nieuw Amsterdam 253
Nieuwe Spiegelstraat 234
Nieuwe Vaart, canal 265, 272
Nieuwekerk 34, 78, 128, 130, 131, 135, 136
Nieuwendijk 34, 286
Nieuwenhuis, T.W. 56
Nieuwezijds 34
Nieuwezijds Huiszittenhuis 178
Nieuwezijds Voorburgwal 123, 127
Nieuwmarkt 152
Niftrik, J.V. van 36, 211
Nijenrode castle 308, 309
Noorderkerk 78, 124, 176, 178, 236, 239
Noordermarkt 238, 239
Nooteboom, Cees 44, 188, 198, 204, 245
North Holland Canal 262
Nuñes, Manuel Isaak 206

◆O◆

Odeon 187
Oldenbarnevelt, Johan van 150, 309
Olie, Jacob 211, 212, 214, 236, 247, 259, 260
Olienmolen windmill 68
Ons Huis 247
Oostenburg island 272
Oosterkerk 272
Oostvaarders-plassen nature reserve 307
Open Havenfront, canal 138
Oranje-Nassau Barracks 273
Ossepooksteeg 164
Ostade, Adriaen van 125
Oud, J.J.P. 129
Oude Luthersekerk 121
Oude Schans 35, 155
Oude Spiegelstraat 186
Oudekerk 28, 34, 120, 131, 134, 135, 136
Oudekerk Foundation 136
Oudemanhuispoort 142, 144
Oudezijds 34
Oudezijds Achterburgwal 142, 150
Oudezijds Kolk, canal 138
Oudezijds Voorburgwal 136, 142
Ouerdag, B.J. et W.B. 276
Ouwater, Isaac 54, 152
Overlander, mayor 167

◆P◆

Palmgracht 240
Paltrok, windmill 67
Papeneiland café 176, 296
Patrician houses 171
Paulus Potterkade 213
Pauw, Michiel 171
Pek, J.E. van der 242
Pels brothers 197
Peter Cornelisz Hooftstraat 234
Peter the Great 31, 184, 193, 201, 272, 306
Peters, C.H. 81
Philip I 179
Philip II of Spain 29
Philip the Good 28
Picasso, Pablo 215
Pierson, Allard 141
Pieters, Claesz 182
Pijpgascompagnie 276
Pillenbrug 145
Pissarro, Camille 91
Pisuisse, singer 208
Plantage district 264
Polak, Henri 266
Polanenstraat 255
Pompadour patisserie 188
poorhouse 178
Poortje Rasphuis 121
Posthoornskerk 251
Potgieter, E.J. 261
Poussin, Nicolas 172
Premerl, Zelijko 175
Prince Bernhard Foundation 200
Prinseneiland (Princes' Island) 258, 259
Prinsengracht 36, 170, 172, 175, 184, 186, 188, 202, 205, 232, 248, 292
Prinsenhof 144
Provo magazine 244
Provo movement 33, 243, 245
Pushkin Alexander 184

◆R◆

Raadhuisstraat 167, 170, 170
Raedecker, J. 129
Raey, J. van 202
Rasphuis 121
Reaal, Laurens Jacobszoon 259
Realeneiland 259
Red light district 136
Reestraat 184, 188
Reguliersgracht 67, 202, 203
Reguliersmarkt 207
Regulierspoort 120
Reid, Christopher 106
Reijnst, Gérard 182
Rembrandt van Rijn 156, 167, 179, 182, 183, 198, 200, 206, 207, 212, 248
Rembrandt, tomb of 179, 182
Rembrandthuis 156
Rembrandtplein 208
Remonstrants 170
Renout 194
Rensselaer, van 134
Rietveld, Dirk 162
Rietveld, Gerrit 57, 196, 214, 215
Rijksmuseum 55, 56, 80, 138, 172, 178, 210, 211, 212, 292
Rijksmuseum, garden 295
Rijna, J.H. 262
Rijwielschool Velox 215
Rising Sun, House of the 170
Ritsaert 194
Roemer Visscherstraat 233
Rokin 127, 140, 141
Roland Holst, R.N. 133
Rooy, Max van 278, 133, 208, 266
Rotterdam Museum 303
Roux café 145
Royal Palace 126, 128, 130
Royal Tropical Institute 274
Rozengracht 247, 279
Ruisdael, Jacob van 222, 304
Runstraat 188, 195
Rusland 144
Ruusschen, Willem 144
Ruysdael, Salomon van 221
Ruyter, Admiral M.A. 31, 131, 148

◆S◆

Sade, Marquis de 184
Saenredam, Pieter 129, 304
Saint Nicholas, festival of 46
Saint-Omer 206
Saint-Saëns 184
Saint-Servaas Basilica 213
Sandberg, William 214, 215
Sarphati, Samuel 36, 205, 273, 277
Sarphatipark 277
Sarphatistraat 205, 273
Schama, Simon 99, 133, 187
Scheepvaarthuis 84, 154
Scheerboom, Andries 208
Schiller café 208
Schimmelpenninck, R.J. 130
Schinkel café 232
Schippersgracht 66
Schouten, navigator 307
Schouwburg 186
Schreierstoren 153
Schuylenburg, H.V. 148
Sertorio, Jeronimo 193
Shaffy Theater 184
Sheba, Queen of 179
The "Ship" 84, 256
Singel 25, 35, 162, 164, 186, 286, 292
Singelgracht 236, 274
Sint Antonies-breestraat 156
Sint Antoniespoort 152
Sint Nicolaaskerk 79, 137
Sint Olofspoort 138
Sintluciensteeg 125
Sipek, B. 57
Sitwell, Sacheverell 107
Six dynasty 200
Slagthuis 175
Slingelandt, Baron van 171
Sloop 174
Sluyterman 57
Sohier, Nicolaas 173
Sophia Augusta Foundation 214
"soup kitchen riots" 250
Spaar 175
Spaarndam 305
Spaarndammerbuurt 254
Spaarndammerdijk 254

Spaarndammerplantsoen 84, 256
Spaarndammerstraat 254, 255
Spanjaardsgat 302
Speyk, J.C. Van 130
Spieghel, Hendrik Laurensz 167
Spinoza, Baruch 98
Spitzberg 174
Spreeuwenpark (Starling Park) 262
Springer 66
Spui 122, 186
squatter movement 127
Staal, J.F. 82, 86, 280
Stadsbank van Lening 144
Staël, Madame de 309
Staets, Hendrick 239
Stalpaert, Daniel 36, 76, 129, 159, 241, 272
Stamp Market 127
Statue of Queen Wilhelmina on horseback 140
Statue of woman 124
Stedelijk Museum 211, 214
Stigt, Jop van 269
"Stopera" 33, 160
Storck, Abraham 93, 167
Stromarkt 164,168
Stryker, Dirck 193
Stuyvesant, Pieter 30, 252, 253
Suasso, J.L. 214
Suyckerhof, Pieter Jansz 240
Suys, T.F. 78
Swan House 165
Sweelinck, J.P. 134
Synagogue of the German Jews 158
Synagogue of the Portuguese Jews 79, 158

◆ T ◆

Talma, A.S. 278
Tasman, Abel 30, 148
Tellegenstraat 279, 280
Temple, William 103
Teyler Museum 304
Theater Museum 170, 171
Theater of the Scientific and Cultural Academy 184
Thesingh, Egbert 193
Thijm, A.J.P. 212
Thijm, J.A. 213
Thijsse, Jac. P. 268
Thijssen café 239
Thijssen, Theo 239
Thorbecke, Johan 138, 207
Thorbeckeplein 207
Three Canals, House on the 72, 142
Three Herrings, bridge 259
Titian 172
Tolhuis 262
Toorop, Jan 133
Torensluis bridge 166
Toulouse-Lautrec, Henri de 214
Trades Unions, Museum of the Dutch 266
Trip brothers 151
Trippenhuis 74, 151, 212
Tromp, Cornelis 146
Tropics Museum of the (Tropenmuseum) 274
Troubles of 1934 238
T' Smalle café 237
Tulp, Dr Nicolaas 130, 182, 183, 206 213
Tulp, House of Nicolaas 182
Tuschinski, Abraham 208
Tuschinski cinema 82, 208, 301

◆ U ◆

Udemans, Godfried 53
University Museum 309
Urchin statue 123
Utrecht 308, 309
Utrecht, bishop 134
Utrecht, bishopric of 28
Uyttenbogaert, Johannes 157

◆ V ◆

Valentijn, François 147
Valéry, Paul 163
Van Breestraat 232
Van Brienen House 170
Van Cornshuytstraat 232
Van Gogh Museum 214
Van Loon Museum 202
Vanderbilt, W. Henry 195
Vanderbilt, William Kissam 195
Vanvitelli 169
Vecht valley 308
Velazquez 302
Van de Velde the Younger, Willem 93
Venice 168
Venne, A.P. van de 38
Vermeer, Johannes 49, 304
Verwey, Albert 133
Vijzelstraat 200
Vingboons, Justus 151
Vingboons, Philip 74, 134, 171, 184, 187, 194, 194, 198
Vinkeles, Reinier 130
Viotta, Henri 217
Visscher, Claes Jansz 162
Visscher, Nicolaas 36
Visscher, Roemer 134
Vliet, J.C. van der 125
Vogelstruijs 186
Volendam 307
Vondel, Frederick Hendryck, 213
Vondel, Joost van den 183, 186, 213, 261, 308
Vondel, statue of 233
Vondelkerk 79, 233
Vondelpark 37, 210, 213, 232, 295
Vondelstraat 233
Vries, Hugo de 264, 267
Vries, Theun de 239
Vroom, Hendrick Cornelis 146
Vuillard, Edouard 215

◆ W ◆

Waals Eilandsgracht 67, 154
Wagenaar, Jan 155, 187
Walenkerk 145
Wallen café 292
Waterland 20, 306
Waterlooplein 33, 160
Waterlooplein flea market 300
Weber, Max 268
Wees, Kees van 240
Weissman, A.W. 214
Welling café 232
Werkspoor Museum 272
Wertheim, Abraham Carel 268
Wertheimpark 267
West warehouse 86
Westerkerk 79, 179, 182
Westerman, Dr G.F. 268
Westermarkt 179
Western Islands Action Committee 260
Western Sugar Refinery 254, 255
Westertoren 179, 236
whale-hunting 174
Wijnand Waag café 136, 152
Wijs en Zonen, tea shop 53
Wilde, Jacob de 234
Wildschut café 215
Wilhelmina, Queen 32, 33, 140
Willemsparkweg 232
Willemspoort 252
Willet, Abraham 206, 207
Willet Garden 207
Willet Museum 206
William I 130, 183
William II 31, 212, 252
William of Orange 29
William the Silent 176
Willibrord 28
Windmill Museum 306
Wipmolen, windmill 68
Wit, Jacob de 171, 194, 206
Withoos, Matthias 169
Witjes 171
Witsen, N. 147
Witt, Johan de 31
Witte, Emmanuel de 133, 159
Wittel, Caspar Adriaensz van 169
Wittenburg Island 272
Wolvenstraat 186, 188
Writsaert 194
Wynants, Jan 90
Wyngaerde, Antonie van den 34

◆ Z ◆

Zaandam 306
Zaandijk 306
Zaanhof 257
Zaanse Schans 306
Zandhoek 259
Zandvoort 305
Zeedijk 34, 136
Zijl, Lambertus 133
Zocher, Jan David 133, 233, 295
Zuiderkerk 79, 156
Zuiderzee 164, 172, 204
Zuiderzee Museum 307
Zutphen, Jan van 266
Zuylen, Belle van 309
Zuylen castle 309

◆ **CANALS** ◆

Blauwburgwal 166
Bloemgracht 245, 247
Brouwersgracht 175, 236, 240, 292
Damrak 131, 140
Funenkade 273
Geldersekade 35, 152, 153
Grimburgwal 142
Groenburgwal 160
Haarlem canal 252
Herengracht 36, 163, 166, 170, 171, 179, 186, 187, 188, 194, 195,198, 199, 203, 206, 292
Keizersgracht 36, 67, 170, 173, 174, 179, 183, 184, 188, 194, 196, 202
Kloveniersburgwal 151
Krombommsloot 77, 155
Lauriergracht 248
Leidsegracht 36, 162, 163, 170, 193, 194, 195, 197
Leliegracht 172
Lijnbaansgracht 240
Lindengracht 238, 239, 242
Motorwal 262
Nieuwe Vaart 265, 272
Oude Schans 35, 155
Oudezijds Achterburgwal 142, 150
Oudezijds Kolk 138
Oudezijds Voorburgwal 136, 142
Palmgracht 240
Prinsengracht 36, 170, 172, 175, 184, 186, 188, 202, 205, 232, 248, 292
Reguliersgracht 67, 202, 203
Rozengracht 247, 279
Schippersgracht 66
Singel 25, 35, 162, 164, 186, 286, 292
Singelgracht 236, 274
Waals Eilandsgracht 67, 154

◆ **RELIGIOUS BUILDINGS** ◆

Agnieten Kapel (St Agnes Chapel) 142, 143
Amstelkerk (Amstel Church) 204
Armenian Church 155
De Duif 205
Krijtberg Church 78
Luthersekerk (Lutheran Church) 187, 292
Mozes en Aaronkerk (Moses and Aaron Church) 78, 158
Nieuwekerk 34, 78, 128, 130, 131, 135, 136
Noorderkerk 78, 124, 176, 178, 236, 239
Oosterkerk 272
Oude Luthersekerk 121
Oudekerk 28, 34, 120, 131, 134, 136
Portuguese Synagogue 79, 158
Posthoornskerk 251
Sint Nicolaas Kerk (Saint Nicholas Church) 79, 136 137
Synagogue of the German Jews 158
Vondelkerk 79, 233
Walenkerk 145
Westerkerk 79, 179, 182
Zuiderkerk 79, 156

◆ **LEISURE AND THE ARTS** ◆

Albert Cuypstraat market 277, 300
Artis zoo 232, 268
Bolhoed restaurant 178
Botanical Gardens 264, 265
Brouwhuis Maximiliaan café 151
Chris café 296
Concertgebouw 80, 184, 211, 216, 295, 298
Dam 128
Dantzig café 50, 297
De Drie Fleschjes café 50, 130, 296
De Gijs café 242
De Jaren café 50, 160, 293, 297
De Kapershoek café 296
De Spaanse Gevel café 165
De Twee Zwaantjes café 178
De Vergulde Gaper café 178
Dulac café 297
Felix Meritis Theater 184, 216
Flower market 187
Hajenius, tobacco shop 141, 301
Health food market 292
Hooft, shop 196, 197
Hoppe café 122, 296
In de Wildeman café 297
Jacob Hooy, herbalist 52, 151
Jan Beekhuizen, pewter shop 52
Jansen, P. J., hairdresser 53
Jordaan, festival 246
Keijzer, shop 178
Kort café 204
Leidseplein 298
Luxembourg café 122, 297
Metz, department store 196, 197
Muziektheater 48, 160, 298
Noordermarkt 238
Papeneiland café 50, 186, 296
Pompadour, patisserie 188
Rembrandtplein 208
Roux café 145
Schiller café 208
Schinkel café 232
Shaffy Theater 184
Spui 122, 186
Square Theater 205
"Stopera" 33, 160
Stamp market 127
T' Smalle café 237
Theater of the Scientific and Cultural Academy 184
Thijssen café 239
Tuschinski cinema 82, 208, 301
Vondelpark 37, 210, 213, 232, 295
Wallen café 292
Waterlooplein, flea market 300
Welling café 232
Wijnand Fockink café 297
Wijs en Zonen, tea merchants 53
Wildschut café 215

◆ **HOUSES AND WAREHOUSES** ◆

Anne Frank's House 178, 180
Archangel warehouse 193
Bartolotti House 170, 171, 292
Begijnhof 73, 122, 123, 294
Bergen warehouse 175
Berlage's Exchange 81, 133
Binnenhof 303
De Belmonte House 206
De Drie Hendricken 246
De Gooyer windmill 69, 273
De Utrecht apartment block 82
De Zaaier building 174
Deaconesses' almshouse 205
Descartes' House 179
Dutch East India Company House 72, 146
Dutch Riding School 295
Entrepotdok 268, 269
Eykebom warehouse 197
Golden Bend 198
Groenland warehouse 77, 175
Hoop warehouse 178
House of Heads 73, 118, 173
House of Hope 182
House of the Itinerant Poor 178
House of the Rising Sun 170
House on the Three Canals 72, 142
Jacob's Ladder mansion 74
Leopard House 170
Liefde warehouse 178
Lock House 156
Moederhuis (Mothers' House) 267
Montelbaanstoren 155
Mothers' House 266
Munttoren 121, 186, 187
Museums' House 214
Narrow House 74
Nicolaas Tulp's House 182
Ons Huis 247
Oranje-Nassau Barracks 273
patrician houses 171
pawnbroker's 144
Prinsenhof 144
Rasphuis 121
Royal Palace 126, 128, 130
Scheepvaarthuis 84
"Ship" building 84, 256
Swan House 165
Tolhuis 262
Trippenhuis 74, 151, 212
Van Brienen House 170
Vergulde Pot warehouse 121
West warehouse 86

◆ MUSEUMS ◆

Allard Pierson Museum 141
Amstelkring Museum 137
Anne Frank's House 178, 180
Bible Museum 194
Cat Museum 200
Central Museum 309
De Cruquius Museum 305
Frans-Hals Museum 304
Goethe Institute 200
Heineken Brewery 276
Heineken Museum 276
Historical Museum 123, 124
Institute of Contemporary Art 234
Jewish History Museum 159
Kromhout shipbuilding museum 269
Maritime Museum (Scheepvaart Museum) 76, 149, 269
Multatuli Museum 166
Museum Het Catharijneconvent 309
Museum of Dutch Trade Unions (A.N.D.B.) 266
Museum of the Zuiderzee 307
Rembrandthuis (Rembrandt Museum) 156
Rijksmuseum 55, 56, 80, 138, 172, 178, 210, 211, 212, 292
Rotterdam Museum 303
Royal Tropical Institute 274
Stedelijk Museum (Municipal Museum) 211, 214
Teyler Museum 304
Theater Institute 170, 171
Tropenmuseum 274
University Museum 309
Van Gogh Museum 214
Van Loon Garden 202, 203
Van Loon Museum 202
Werkspoor Museum 272
Willet Garden 207
Willet Museum 206
Windmill Museum 306
Zaanse Schans 306

◆ PAINTERS ◆

Aertsz, Pieter 125, 134
Anthonisz, Cornelis 34, 169
Appel, Karel 93, 144, 145, 230
Backhuysen, Ludolf 88, 149, 260
Beijer, Jan de 164
Berckheyde, Gerrit Adriaensz. 90, 198
Berckheyde, Job 132, 133
Bol, Ferdinand 178, 202
Bonnard, Pierre 215
Braque, Georges 229
Breitner, George 88, 127, 170, 248, 258
Canaletto 169
Cézanne, Paul 215
Chagall, Marc 215
Constant 231
Corneille 231
Deventer, Jacob van 35
Dhanani, Christine 202
Doesburg, Theo van 228
Doomer, Lambert 88
Dou, Gerard 199
Dubuffet, Jean 215, 230
Fouquet, Pierre 121, 144, 239
Funke, Lotte 122
Gauguin, Paul 214, 227
Gogh, Vincent van 214, 226
Hals, Frans 203, 224 304
Hekking, Willem 124
Helst, Bartolomeus van der 224, 261
Heijden, Jan van der 134,171,193, 194, 215
Hilverdink, Johannes 205, 213
Hooch, Pieter de 225, 304
Jacob van 222, 304
Kandinsky, Wassily 215
Keyser, Thomas de 224
Klee, Paul 215
Klein, Yves 215
Kooning, Willem De 229
Lairesse, Gerard de 49, 172, 179
Lastman, Pieter 124
Lelie, Adriaan de 178, 199
Leyden, Lucas Van 220
Leyster, Judith 203
Malevich, Kasimir 215, 229
Manet, Edouard 214
Metsu, Gabriel 96
Molenaer, Jan Miense 203
Mondriaan, Piet 57, 215, 228, 309
Monet, Claude 95, 215
Moucheron 172
Neer, Aert van der 221
Nieulandt, Adriaen van 90
Ostade, Adriaen Van 125
Ouwater, Isaak 54, 152
Picasso, Pablo 215, 230
Pissarro, Camille 91
Poussin, Nicolas 172
Premerl, Zelijko 175
Rembrandt 156, 167, 179, 182, 183, 198, 200, 206, 207, 212, 218, 248
Ruisdael, Jacob van 222, 304
Ruysdael, Salomon van 221
Saenredam, Pieter 129, 304
Schuylenburg, H.V. 148
Storck, Abraham 93, 167
Titian 172
Toulouse-Lautrec, Henri de 214
Vermeer, Johannes 49, 225, 304
Vroom, Hendrick Cornelis 146
Wit, Jacob de 171, 194, 206
Withoos, Matthias 169
Wittel, Gaspar van 169
Witte, Emmanuel de 133, 159
Wynants, Jan 90
Wyngaerde, Antonie van den 34

AMSTERDAM

1:30.000 (1cm = 300m)